C0-DKP-066

THE ANARCHY

WAR AND STATUS
IN 12TH-CENTURY LANDSCAPES OF
CONFLICT

EXETER STUDIES IN MEDIEVAL EUROPE

History, Society and the Arts

SERIES EDITORS
Simon Barton, Oliver Creighton,
Anthony Musson and Yolanda Plumley

The Anarchy

War and Status in 12th-Century Landscapes of Conflict

Oliver H. Creighton and Duncan W. Wright

with contributions by Michael Fradley and Steven Trick

LIVERPOOL UNIVERSITY PRESS

First published 2016 by
Liverpool University Press
4 Cambridge Street
Liverpool
L69 7ZU

Copyright © 2016 Liverpool University Press

The right of Oliver H. Creighton, Duncan W. Wright, Michael Fradley and Steven Trick to be identified as the authors of this work has been asserted by them in accordance with the Copyright, Designs and Patents Act 1988.

All rights reserved. No part of this book may be reproduced, stored in a retrieval system, or transmitted, in any form or by any means, electronic, mechanical, photocopying, recording, or otherwise, without the prior written permission of the publisher.

British Library Cataloguing-in-Publication data

A British Library CIP record is available

ISBN 978-1-78138-242-4 cased
ISBN 978-1-78694-185-5 softback

Typeset by Carnegie Book Production, Lancaster
Printed and bound in Poland by BooksFactory.co.uk

Contents

Acknowledgements   vii

List of Figures   ix

List of Colour Plates   xiii

Chapter 1   Introduction   1

Chapter 2   Historical Outline and the Geography of 'Anarchy'   13

Chapter 3   Waging War: Fields of Conflict and Siege Warfare   34

Chapter 4   Architecture and Authority: Castles   80

Chapter 5   Material Culture: From Arts to Coins   119

Chapter 6   Performing Violence: Arms, Armour and Military
             Apparel   154

Chapter 7   Faith and Fortification: The Church   185

Chapter 8   Town, Village and Country   219

Chapter 9   Anarchy on the Fen Edge: Case Study of the
             Isle of Ely   251

Chapter 10   The Twelfth-Century Civil War in Context:
             Assessment and Reassessment   279

Appendix   Key Sites to Visit   290

Bibliography   295

Index   333

Acknowledgements

This volume is the principal output from a research grant from the Leverhulme Trust: *Anarchy? War and Status in Twelfth-Century Landscapes of Conflict* (RPG-2012-734). Oliver Creighton was the Principal Investigator; the award employed Duncan Wright as the Project Officer for the duration of the project and Michael Fradley and Steven Trick as Post-Doctoral Research Assistants, for expertise with GIS, archaeological survey and fieldwork, geophysics and map work. Another volume comprising a series of site reports detailing the archaeological fieldwork and supporting desk-based research undertaken during the project will be published separately as *Castles, Siegeworks and Settlements: Surveying the Archaeology of the Twelfth Century* (Archaeopress, forthcoming).

We would especially like to thank the many landowners who permitted fieldwork on their property and English Heritage for providing Scheduled Monument Consent where required; Will Fletcher of English Heritage and Martin Papworth of the National Trust are acknowledged in particular. Sarah Hamilton, Catherine Clarke and Robert Higham are thanked for serving as Steering Committee advisors on the project and the Portable Antiquities Scheme provided information and support as a project partner. John Blair and Aleks McClain provided specific advice on churches; Steven Ashley, Robert Webley, Michael Lewis and Steve Tucker on portable antiquities; Maureen Mellor and Paul Blinkhorn on pottery; Martin Allen and Richard Kelleher on coinage; and Robert Woosnam-Savage, Tobias Capwell and Ralph Moffat on arms and armour. We thank Julian Munby for providing information on Oxford, Liz Shepherd Popescu on Norwich and Simon Roffey on Winchester. Other general advice or support was provided by Katharine Keats-Rohan, Robert Liddiard and Neil Christie. Ellie March kindly helped compile the GIS database of charters. We would also like to acknowledge Philip Davies's Gatehouse website (www.gatehouse-gazetteer.info) which has been invaluable in researching several sites and in compiling maps.

Seán Goddard and John Davey (University of Exeter) are gratefully acknowledged for producing many of the maps, and Richard Parker for the reconstruction art. Credits and sources for all illustrations are included in the relevant captions. Hugh Thomas is warmly thanked for providing a database of conflict events upon which the project has drawn. We would also like to thank the following for kindly providing images, or for granting copyright to enable their publication: Steven Ashley, James Bond, David and Kerry Donaldson (Archaeological Surveys), English Heritage, Exeter Archaeology, Drew Shotliff (Albion Archaeology), London and Middlesex Archaeological Society, and Leicestershire Archaeological and Historical Society.

This book is dedicated to Suzie.

List of Figures

Fig. 1.1:   The world of the *Gesta Stephani*.   5

Fig. 1.2:   'Rescue' excavation of a small twelfth-century siege
             castle by Exeter Archaeology in 1993.   9

Fig. 1.3:   The earthworks of a campaign castle at Burwell.   10

Fig. 2.1:   Itineraries of key figures in the civil war by period.   22

Fig. 3.1:   Conflict locations, 1135–53.   35

Fig. 3.2:   King Stephen's campaign in south-west England
             in 1136.   41

Fig. 3.3:   Reconstructions of the two main pitched battles of
             the civil war.   44

Fig. 3.4:   A traction trebuchet.   51

Fig. 3.5:   Distribution map of siege castles built or likely to
             have been built 1135–54.   54

Fig. 3.6:   Plans of siege castles built or likely to have been built
             1135–54.   55

Fig. 3.7:   Corfe Castle, Dorset, and the siege work of
             'the Rings'.   59

Fig. 3.8:   The town and castle of Wallingford.   63

Fig. 3.9:   Wallingford in the Anarchy.   66

Fig. 3.10:   Archaeology of the Wallingford bridgehead area.   70

Fig. 3.11:   Anarchy in Wallingford: reconstruction.   71

Fig. 4.1:   Abinger, Surrey.   89

Fig. 4.2:   Ingarsby, Leicestershire.   93

Fig. 4.3: The Roman amphitheatre at Silchester.   95

Fig. 4.4: Plans of castle sites at Trowbridge and Goltho.   96

Fig. 4.5: Plan of South Mimms, Middlesex.   101

Fig. 4.6: Plans of masonry towers.   103

Fig. 4.7: Photographs of twelfth-century towers.   107

Fig. 4.8: The demilitarised zone in north Leicestershire.   113

Fig. 5.1: Selection of finds from South Mimms Castle.   120

Fig. 5.2: Faversham Abbey: reconstruction.   132

Fig. 5.3: Mints issuing coins of King Stephen.   140

Fig. 5.4: Mints issuing 'local coinage'.   144

Fig. 5.5: Hoards of the late eleventh and twelfth century.   147

Fig. 6.1: Illustrative examples of swords dating from around
               the twelfth century held in museum collections.   158

Fig. 6.2: Sculptured decoration from around the south
               doorway of St Nicholas church, Barfreston.   161

Fig. 6.3: Mid-twelfth-century scabbard chape from London.   166

Fig. 6.4: Archaeological finds of twelfth-century weaponry
               from archaeological sites.   170

Fig 6.5:   Twelfth-/early thirteenth-century copper alloy horse
               harness pendants.   178

Fig. 7.1: Fortified ecclesiastical sites and damage to monastic
               property, *c.* 1135–53.   186

Fig. 7.2: Aerial view of Southwell Minster.   193

Fig. 7.3: Plan and photograph of St Mary's, Cuckney.   195

Fig. 7.4: Comparative plans of monasteries established in the
               mid-twelfth century.   198

Fig. 7.5: Comparative plans of monastic sites fortified in the
               civil war.   206

Fig. 7.6: Comparative plans of bishops' palaces fortified in the
               civil war.   210

Fig. 7.7: Excavated and consolidated remains of the solar
               tower of the bishop's palace at Witney, Oxfordshire.   212

Fig. 8.1: Winchester in the mid-twelfth century. 222

Fig. 8.2: Saffron Walden: topography. 230

Fig. 8.3: Mountsorrel: aerial view of the castle overlooking the town. 231

Fig. 8.4: Plans of defended villages and castles. 237

Fig. 8.5: Wellow: map of the defended village. 239

Fig. 8.6: Devastation of the landscape during the civil war. 244

Fig. 9.1: Map of the Isle of Ely. 253

Fig 9.2: Ely Cathedral. 254

Fig 9.3: Burwell Castle under archaeological survey in 2014. 265

Fig 9.4: Geophysics at Burwell Castle. 266

Fig 9.5: Comparative plans of castle sites at Burwell, Caxton, Rampton and Swavesey. 270

Fig 9.6: Reconstruction of Burwell Castle under construction in 1143–44. 271

List of Colour Plates

Plate 1: Geophysical survey at Corfe Castle, Dorset.

Plates 2 and 3: Charters issued by King Stephen, the Empress Matilda and Henry of Anjou, 1135–54.

Plate 4: Viewsheds from Stephanic siege castles.

Plate 5: Excavation of an Anarchy-period castle in Luton.

Plate 6: Distribution of early castles.

Plate 7: Plans of castles adapted from prehistoric hillforts.

Plate 8: Examples of mid-twelfth-century metalwork and other artefacts.

Plate 9: Distribution of beakheads in England.

Plate 10: Distribution of finds of Stephen's type 1, 2, 6 and 7.

Plate 11: Distribution of finds of irregular coinage from Stephen's reign.

Plate 12: Official coinage of Stephen's reign.

Plate 13: Wall paintings from the church of St Michael and All Angels, Copford, Essex.

Plate 14: Temple Pyx.

Plate 15: The tympanum of Fordington church.

Plate 16: Twelfth-century churches at Barfreston and Kempley.

Plate 17: Wolvesey Palace, Winchester, showing the large rectangular keep-like structure.

Plate 18: Beaudesert: LiDAR survey of the castle.

Plate 19: Earthwork plan and interpretation of the earthworks at Wood Walton.

Chapter 1

Introduction

THE WAR AND VIOLENCE of human conflict, whether in the past or present, disturb, fascinate and remain enduringly popular topics of academic research. While the focus of this volume is an infamously destructive conflict which took place in twelfth-century England, during the reign of King Stephen, the approach that it develops – wherein the psychological and symbolic aspects of warfare and its impacts on society are not divorced from the conventional military history of events on the ground – is more universally applicable. War was, and is, a cultural and social as well as a military phenomenon, and to study it in its totality it is essential to take account of the multiple arenas within which it was played out. The place of war is not necessarily the battlefield; equally, landscapes are more than just the setting for violence. The materialisation of warfare and militarised societies can comprise fortifications and other sites as well as artefacts and other forms of material culture and human remains. The impacts of conflict are always felt on social structures and human settlements across both the long and short term. Accordingly, this volume is intended as more than just an exploration of a particular conflict, but as a more detailed analysis of the interplay between war, society, material culture and landscape.

The troubled reign of Stephen, King of England (1135–54) has long held particular fascination for scholars of Anglo-Norman history.[1] Stephen's protracted struggle with a rival claimant to the throne, the Empress Matilda, and her Angevin supporters saw England plunged into political turmoil, rebellion and bitter conflict for almost two decades. Contemporary writers reported with horror the activities of predatory lords responsible for a plague of castle building, damage to church property and devastation of the landscape, and since the late nineteenth century the conflict has been styled as 'the Anarchy'

– although this term is now contentious. That the word 'anarchy' has since often been capitalised in the epithet 'the Anarchy,'[2] puts it in a very select group of historical events including 'the Conquest,' 'the Reformation' and 'the Dissolution,' and has done much to elevate the period to prominence in the public consciousness.

While in an English context the phrase 'the civil war' is synonymous with the clash between Charles I and Parliament in the mid-seventeenth century, 'the Anarchy' was in effect England's first civil war, lasting twice as long, seeing England split down the middle for an extended period and encompassing bitter struggles across the Channel in Normandy and on and across the borders with Scotland and Wales. These tumultuous events have been studied intensively by medieval historians, who have analysed chroniclers' accounts and unpicked charters to present different perspectives on the nature of kingship and royal government and on King Stephen's character. Other studies have examined Stephen's reign from a longer-term perspective and in relation to developments in Continental Europe. Stephen's reign has become closely associated with weak government – a view accentuated by the fact that it was bookended by those of two celebrated monarchs: the respected and long-reigning Henry I (1100–35), renowned for his development of administrative kingship;[3] and Stephen's successor, Henry II (1154–89), synonymous with reconstruction, judicial reform and for bringing into being an Angevin dominion.[4] In the popular imagination, King Stephen has a prominent place among the dubious pantheon of 'weak kings' of England that starts with Æthelred 'the Unready' before the Norman Conquest and continues after his reign with John and Edward II. To the north of England, meanwhile, Stephen's reign coincided with a period of energetic state building by King David I of Scots (reigned 1124–53).[5] In Scotland, the period saw a 'Davidian revolution' that involved fundamental changes to military organisation and the appearance of a European-style monarchy.[6] Another reason for public and scholarly interest in the period is the prominent and proactive role of women in the civil war of Stephen's reign: not only the Empress Matilda – the only female claimant to the English throne in the entire medieval period – but also Stephen's queen, also called Matilda, who campaigned energetically on her husband's behalf during his imprisonment midway through the conflict.

Although the historiography of Stephen's reign and the twelfth-century civil war is substantial, our current understanding of this period is almost entirely based on documentary sources. While Stephen is one of medieval England's most written-about kings, our appreciation of the material evidence of the conflict that dominated his reign and its impact on life and landscape remain woefully underdeveloped. Our project and this book are an attempt to redress this imbalance. The overarching aim here is to collate, present and interrogate a diverse body of archaeological, architectural and other material evidence in order to contribute to ongoing debates – in particular that about whether England witnessed 'anarchy' in the mid-twelfth century – but also to reveal some new directions for our understanding of the civil war and for conflict landscapes more generally. As such, this study focuses not so much on twelfth-century politics and personalities or on the much-debated causes of the war, but on the effects and physical impacts of conflict and on the importance of place and landscape in understanding how, where and why it was conducted (Plate 1).

While the essential pattern is that medieval England saw less internal disorder than great parts of Continental Europe, it is nonetheless important to remember that this was not medieval England's only civil war. The years 1173–74 saw an armed revolt threaten the strong government of Henry II, while the end of John's reign and the start of the minority of Henry III again saw levels of rebellion approach civil war proportions. So too did the baronial uprising of 1264–67 against Henry III and another of 1321–22 against Edward II, while the Wars of the Roses dominated the mid- to late fifteenth century. The length and severity of the civil war of Stephen's reign, combined with the way the military landscape was dominated by castle warfare and the fact that the period witnessed some hugely important changes in the structure and outlook of elite society, ensure, however, that 'the Anarchy' has by far the greatest potential for archaeological and landscape study.

One of the main themes in military history is to explain why one side won and the other lost, but this approach is largely redundant for the conflict of Stephen's reign, which ended in deadlock. This is perhaps one reason why the war has been somewhat marginalised in studies of medieval conflict, alongside the fact that it featured few set-piece battles. Indeed, the volume of literature on the archaeology of the twelfth-century civil war pales into insignificance beside that on the mid-seventeenth-century English Civil War, whose battlefields and fortifications have long received detailed scrutiny.[7]

Writing the Civil War: Historiography

A deeply ingrained doom-laden view of Stephen's reign is of 'nineteen long winters' when, according to the Peterborough Chronicle, 'Christ and his Saints slept,' but this oft-quoted description needs to be understood in context. In particular, it is not quite clear whether the description captures the situation across England or rather a set of circumstances specific to the area in which the chronicler was based (see also pg. 214).[8] Anyone addressing the reign of King Stephen immediately confronts a mountain of historiography including monumental biographies, syntheses and critical editions of source material authored and edited by some towering figures of medieval history. From the very beginning, it is crucial to underline that the view of the period as 'the Anarchy' was not current among contemporaries but one that crystallised more than 700 years later. The association between Stephen's reign and the word 'anarchy' was established by the influential Oxford historian William Stubbs in the 1870s in the first volume of his *Constitutional History of England*, specifically in the sense of 'feudal anarchy' which he saw as a phenomenon witnessed in Continental Europe but never before seen in England.[9] In the 1890s, the image of the period as 'the Anarchy' was cemented by Horace Round in his biography of the quintessential robber baron of the period, Geoffrey de Mandeville, Earl of Essex, with its subtitle *A Study of the Anarchy*.[10]

In terms of the available documentary sources for the study of Stephen's reign, we have no manorial or household accounts, nor detailed tax records, while collections of letters are few. Rather, chronicles and charters are the foundation stones of the period's history. Two important developments in the second part of the twentieth century have transformed the evidence base available to us. First, the missing end portion of by far the most important chronicle of Stephen's reign, the *Gesta Stephani* (*The Deeds of Stephen*), known as the Valenciennes text, was rediscovered and a complete version published in 1955 to provide a continuous history for most of the period.[11] The *Gesta Stephani* provides what is for a twelfth-century source an unusually full and vivid account of Stephen's reign, although one of its shortcomings is a strongly south-western bias in its coverage, which relates to its much-discussed authorship.[12] Figure 1.1 depicts England through the prism of the *Gesta Stephani*. All places named within the text are mapped, highlighting both the prominence within the text of the castles and fortified towns that dominated the military landscape and the status of the Thames Valley and north Wessex regions as the cradle of the conflict in the eyes of the chronicler.

That the two foremost Anglo-Norman historians, William of Malmesbury (d. 1143),[13] and Orderic Vitalis (d. 1142),[14] did not live through the whole of Stephen's reign means that coverage of the latter

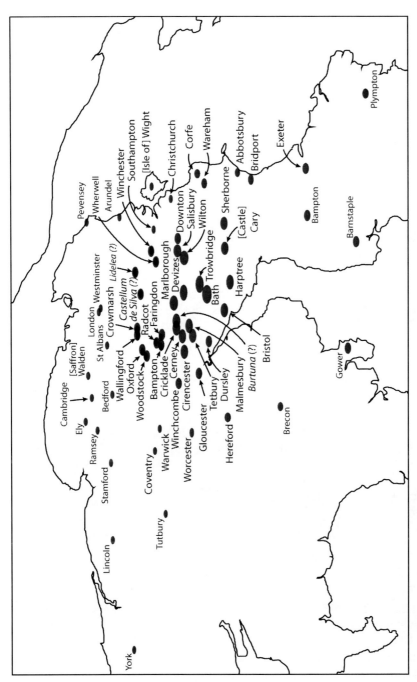

Fig. 1.1: The world of the *Gesta Stephani*, showing all the places in England and Wales mentioned in its text, from the south-western perspective of its likely author (excluding the names of shires and places identified only through personal names). Source: *Gesta Stephani*, Potter and Davis 1976. Map work by Steven Trick and Oliver Creighton.

part of the civil war is sparser than for the early years, especially concerning events in Normandy, for which Orderic is the prime source. The contemporary John of Worcester (d. 1140) similarly covers only the early part of Stephen's reign.[15] The other major chronicler covering the period from a contemporary point of view, although more sparsely than the aforementioned sources, is Henry of Huntingdon.[16] John of Hexham,[17] Robert of Torigni[18] and William of Newburgh[19] are other essential sources for the period, although they wrote a little after the events in question.

The second key development in modern historical study was the publication in 1968 of a monumental collection of over 1,000 charters of Stephen's reign, *Regesta Regum Anglo-Normannorum 1066–1154, Volume III*.[20] The research value of this collection is especially great as it includes not only the charters of Stephen and his queen, but also those of his rivals – the Empress Matilda, her husband, Geoffrey, Count of Anjou and their son, Henry of Anjou (later Henry II). Maps showing the distribution of places where these charters were issued (Plate 2) and the institutions and individuals they were issued to (Plate 3) provide one window into the geography of the conflict. The maps highlight some important aspects of patronage strategies and the reach of royal authority, and display especially well the royalist and Angevin spheres of influence. The number of charters issued at sieges is also striking. That said, the vagaries of documentary loss and survival, and the fact that many charters were issued in batches at particular locations are all factors that distort the distribution.[21]

Financial records for Stephen's reign are lacking, and the extent to which royal accounting procedures continued through the turmoil of the civil war is itself the subject of debate.[22] Richard fitzNigel, treasurer of Henry II and later Bishop of London, wrote in his famous treatise *Dialogus de Scaccario* (*Dialogue Concerning the Exchequer*) that upon the new king's accession, Bishop Nigel of Ely, Henry I's former treasurer, was summoned for his knowledge of the Exchequer, 'that had been almost entirely lost during the many years of civil war,'[23] although the author was magnifying the achievements of Bishop Nigel, his father. The surviving exchequer pipe rolls of Henry II's reign, which summarise accounts payable and receivable, have been analysed for what they tell us retrospectively about the circumstances of Stephen's reign, and a particularly vigorous debate has focused on the distribution and meaning of 'waste' in their text – does it reflect the devastation of the landscape during the conflict, or does it instead have some other explanation?[24]

Histories of Stephen's reign have built upon these foundations. R.H.C. Davis wrote a seminal political narrative,[25] and David Crouch an influential revisionist study that reconsidered the extent of political breakdown in the period.[26] Other important scholarly works have taken a thematic approach to Stephen's reign. We are well supplied with assessments of the civil war's causes, conduct and consequences, and studies of its impact upon different regions and nations, such as Normandy and Wales, on the Church, the aristocracy and coinage.[27] Latterly, Edmund King has produced a monumental biography of Stephen,[28] and Carl Watkins a concise modern guide to his reign.[29] This body of work casts different shades of light on Stephen's personality and character. Behind the image of the 'weak' king of popular renown, Stephen was dogged, energetic, religious and a good soldier but fatally undermined by a lack of political shrewdness. The Empress has her own biography, by Marjorie Chibnall,[30] that presents a rounded account of Matilda's very considerable achievements in the context of her own time, supplanting the negative received wisdom around her supposed arrogance and her ultimate failure to gain the throne.

A prominent recent research theme has been the debate among historians over whether the period should continue to be labelled 'the Anarchy,' with all the connotations this phrase brings. Some have suggested that this epithet should be jettisoned entirely – a view exemplified by David Crouch.[31] Scholars have debated not only the extent and severity of the disturbances of Stephen's reign and unpicked the meaning of the word 'anarchy' – which summons up different images and associations for different people, although strictly speaking, the meaning is an absence of government. Jim Bradbury writes in his popular military history *Stephen and Matilda: The Civil War of 1139–53* that 'There was no anarchy in The Anarchy.'[32] The pendulum of interpretation can also swing backwards, however: another perspective is that historians are seen to have overcorrected and sanitised Stephen's reign; to Hugh Thomas, analysis of the military landscape and the distribution of acts of violence during the period reaffirms 'a traditionally bleak picture of the period of the civil war.'[33] Despite these different points of view, it is quite clear that the disturbances of the twelfth century saw no fundamental overturning of the social hierarchy. Our own volume engages with the debate over the existence or otherwise of anarchy in the twelfth century, and other questions, by adding a fresh body of evidence into the mix: namely the material evidence provided by archaeology and the landscape itself.

Scope and Approach

In terms of the archaeological record, it is no overstatement to style the twelfth century as a forgotten century. It is sandwiched uncomfortably between the Norman Conquest, whose impact on society, landscape, architecture and material culture continues to be very thoroughly debated, and the thirteenth century, which, in so many senses, saw the high medieval period proper really get going, with dramatic population growth and a major expansion of agricultural activity and the rise of many more urban centres.

While many 'Anarchy-period' sites (the term is loaded and problematic) have been excavated and findings published (but not always), the archaeology is fragmented and dispersed, and a framework within which to interpret this body of material has been totally lacking. This volume is a first step towards filling that gap.[34] The events of the civil war are also examined with reference to the preceding and following periods and with glimpses into Scotland, and across the Channel into France and beyond, in order to assess the extent to which the conflict was typical or exceptional in the wider European context. The view of warfare is more social in its approach than is usual for studies of the period, with an emphasis on how archaeology can help us engage with the psychology of conflict and the environments it took place within and impacted upon.

The evidence is reviewed on a wide variety of scales – from individual portable artefacts such as arrowheads, coins and dress accessories, through to buildings and complexes including castles and siege works, fortified monasteries and bishops' palaces, and conflict landscapes viewed locally, regionally and nationally. Besides these categories of archaeological evidence, historical data are also mapped at different levels of spatial resolution, to explore, for example, geographies of royal power (and resistance) in the form of royal itineraries, and to assess the distribution and landscape context of attested battles, raids and episodes of devastation. In amassing, presenting and interrogating a much broader range of evidence than is usual for studies of the period, the aim is partly to present new perspectives on the question of whether England witnessed 'anarchy' in the twelfth century, but also to understand the period's conflict landscapes within a broader archaeological and historical context.

It should be stressed that while serious historical scholarship on the twelfth-century civil war is long-established, medieval archaeology is a far younger discipline. While historians are now more guarded in their

Fig. 1.2: A 'rescue' excavation of a small twelfth-century siege castle in Exeter by Exeter Archaeology in 1993. The ringwork seems to have been built for King Stephen in support of his siege of Exeter Castle in 1136.
Source: photograph © Exeter Archaeology.

characterisation of the civil war of Stephen's reign as 'the Anarchy,' archaeologists in general have continued to use the term relatively freely and often uncritically. Part of the great potential of an archaeological approach to 'the Anarchy' is that new evidence is appearing at a rapid rate, especially through metal-detecting finds and developer-funded archaeology. A particularly clear case in point is the constantly enlarging data set of coins from Stephen's reign, including non-official issues. Being historical sources in their own right as well as artefacts, the period's coins can offer new information about the unique social and political environment created by the war, for instance about control over the mints by the king and his rivals. In terms of evidence from archaeological excavations, a rich body of fresh data is now available due to the explosion of developer-funded excavation since the 1990s, especially in urban areas. At its best, development-led excavation in historic towns has uncovered traces of 'lost' siege castles, with evidence for their construction and sometimes sizable assemblages of finds and environmental material. A good example of a development-led investigation of

Fig. 1.3: The earthworks of a campaign castle at Burwell, built to subdue Geoffrey de Mandeville's fenland revolt of 1143–44. The castle was left unfinished and its earthworks overlie an earlier site or settlement. Source: © Crown copyright English Heritage.

a twelfth-century military site is the excavation in the early 1990s of a Stephanic siege castle at Exeter, Devon, in advance of development of a reservoir site (Fig. 1.2). Many other relevant sites are preserved as earthworks, as is the case with Stephen's campaign castle at Burwell, Cambridgeshire (Fig. 1.3; for full discussion, see pgs 265–71), although not all sites are as well preserved. The evidence base comes with its own set of challenges, however, and one in particular casts a long shadow over any archaeological perspective on Stephen's reign: dating. It can be immensely difficult to date archaeological materials to a specific historical period as brief as a 19-year conflict, and consequently this is a study that necessarily explores the civil war within the context of the archaeology of the twelfth century more generally.

In terms of this book's structure, Chapter 2 presents a chronological outline of the civil war, which provides essential background for the thematically structured text that follows. Conflict archaeology is a growing area of research, but the military landscapes of the twelfth-century civil war have generally escaped close study, partly because of the relatively small number of large-scale pitched battles that took place. Thus, Chapter 3 explores the landscape context of warfare in the twelfth century – an era in which set-piece battles were rare and siege warfare the default mode of conflict. A case study of the town of Wallingford in South Oxfordshire, which was contested more vigorously and often than any other place, brings into sharp focus how archaeology can illuminate the psychological as well as symbolic dimensions of conflict and its material traces.

Fortifications are naturally the most prominent sources of archaeological evidence, and while overviews of the castles of the period have been published,[35] an overall archaeological survey is lacking. This is presented in Chapter 4. The material culture of the twelfth century is particularly poorly understood, and artefacts dating to the period *c.* 1050–1200 are perhaps surprisingly limited compared to the late Saxon period before it and the high medieval centuries that followed. The analysis of twelfth-century material culture contained in Chapter 5 covers pottery, seals, sculpture, coins and hoards, and highlights more than any other section of the book how the archaeological data set is expanding dramatically year by year to add diverse insights. Chapter 6 turns to a more specific category of material culture evidence in the form of arms and armour, including swords, arrowheads and other weapons, and asks whether the civil war saw a departure from existing ways of performing conflict and inflicting violence.

Chapter 7 turns to the impact of the civil war on the Church as an institution and on individual church buildings, exploring both the militarisation of religious structures that caused such consternation among contemporary writers, and the great boost to patronage and monastic foundation that, intriguingly, occurred during the conflict. Urban and rural landscapes are the focus of Chapter 8, which presents the evidence for the planning and reorientation of towns and villages, and discusses the elevated presence of lordship in the countryside. Chapter 9 has a different scope in that it focuses on one specific landscape, the Isle of Ely, one of the most hotly contested zones during the civil war. It presents a case study of conflict and castle building on and around the fens against the background of a cultural landscape synonymous with rebellion.

The ultimate objective of an archaeological approach to 'the Anarchy' must be that this body of evidence not only augments but also potentially challenges historical narratives, thereby questioning the 'real' impact of

Stephen's troubled reign on society, settlement, Church and landscape. The conclusion, Chapter 10, provides a self-contained essay that reflects on this central issue, while acknowledging the challenges of studying a narrow historical period through the medium of archaeology.

Notes

1 For histories of Stephen's reign and biographies of the king, see below, notes 25–29.

2 A very early instance is Round 1888, 112: 'the terrible devastation of the wars of the Anarchy.'

3 For biographies of Henry I, see Hollister 2001; Green 2006.

4 For the standard biography of Henry II, see Warren 1973.

5 For major studies of David I, see Barrow 1985; Oram 2008.

6 Barrow 1985, 5. See also Stringer 1997.

7 See, for example, Foard 2012.

8 Home 2015, 84–90.

9 Stubbs 1874, 353; for the intellectual context of this work, see Crouch 2000, 3–5.

10 Round 1892. For the phrase 'The Anarchy of Stephen's reign', see Davis 1903.

11 For the purposes of this text, the more recent 1976 edition is used: *Gesta Stephani*, ed. and trans. Potter and Davis 1976. Other smaller *lacunae* remain in *Gesta Stephani*; for discussion, see King 2006, 196–7.

12 See, for example, Davis 1962.

13 William of Malmesbury, *Historia Novella*, ed. King, trans. Potter 1998.

14 *The Ecclesiastical History of Orderic Vitalis*, ed. and trans. Chibnall 1969–90.

15 *The Chronicle of John of Worcester, Volume III*, ed. and trans. McGurk 1998.

16 Henry Archdeacon of Huntingdon, *Historia Anglorum*, ed. and trans. Greenway 1996.

17 John of Hexham in Symeon of

Durham, *Symeonis monachi opera omnia*, ed. Arnold 2012, Vol. II.

18 *Chronicles of the Reigns of Stephen, Henry II and Richard I. Vol. IV, The Chronicle of Robert of Torigni*, ed. Howlett 1889.

19 William of Newburgh, *The History of English Affairs* ed. and trans. Walsh and Kennedy 1998; 2007.

20 Cronne and Davis 1968.

21 See Bates 1997.

22 Amt 1993, 120–1.

23 Richard fitzNigel, *Dialogus de Scaccario* I, viii, ed. and trans. Amt, 2007, 76–7, xiv. See also Kealey 1974, 214; Green 1990, 12; King 2007, 44.

24 White 1985; Amt 1991.

25 Davis 1967.

26 Crouch 2000. For another re-evaluation, see Stringer 1993.

27 Cronne 1970; Matthew 2002. For important collections of essays on Stephen's reign, see King 1994; Dalton and White 2008.

28 King 2010.

29 Watkins 2015.

30 Chibnall 1991. See also Chibnall 2006. On Matilda as one of English history's 'she-wolves,' see also Castor 2010, 39–126.

31 Crouch 2000, 1.

32 Bradbury 1996, 193.

33 Thomas 2008, 158.

34 A second volume resulting from the project (Wright and Creighton, forthcoming) presents full reports on archaeological fieldwork carried out at 12 sites across England.

35 See, for example, Coulson 1994b.

Chapter 2

Historical Outline and the Geography of 'Anarchy'

ALTHOUGH THE PRINCIPAL FOCUS of this book is on England in the middle decades of the twelfth century, it is instructive to first provide a sketch of life in town and country between the Norman Conquest and the year of King Stephen's accession in 1135. What was the overall shape of English society, how was the landscape organised and what were the main processes of social, economic and political change then in train? The second part of this chapter provides a year-by-year chronology of Stephen's reign (1135–54) as essential background for the thematic chapters that follow.

Anglo-Norman England before 1135

While the Battle of Hastings in 1066 was a shattering military defeat for the English and cataclysmic for the native aristocracy, the predominant view among archaeologists is that in the aftermath of the Norman Conquest life for the overwhelming majority of the population carried on pretty much as before. That the face on silver pennies changed while the monetary system remained essentially untouched is something of a metaphor for understanding the impact of the Conquest at the grass roots – this was an elite takeover that saw business as usual for the English economy and little or no immediate change to the essential rhythms of everyday life, at least for most.[1] Indeed, the key categories of material evidence speak of continuity rather than change: burial practice, pottery and building techniques show little or no sign of any hiatus or radical difference either side of 1066, and archaeologists usually adopt the label 'Saxo-Norman' for items of material culture and sculpture that could equally be attributed a pre- or post-Conquest date.

The very small number of Norman-French place names in the English landscape highlight that this was an aristocratic conquest rather than a mass folk movement – most namings, such as Montacute, Somerset ('pointed hill') and Belvoir, Leicestershire ('beautiful view') marked new Norman *capita* (estate centres).[2]

Military devastation was localised rather than general, principally affecting the zone of south-east England that was in the path of the advancing Norman army in 1066, and later those regions where rebellions were vigorously stamped out, including northern Yorkshire and the Isle of Ely. Overall, we see little physical evidence of any rupture in society. Instead, many of the processes of landscape change already in train continued and in many cases accelerated into the post-Conquest period, including the formation of nucleated villages in England's 'central province' (the belt of 'champion' landscape running across England from Somerset to East Yorkshire), the emergence of prominent lordly residences and the widespread construction and reconstruction of parish churches. If the impact of the Norman Conquest on the English landscape had a hallmark it was the monumental programme of building in stone that followed closely in its wake: Eric Fernie writes in *The Architecture of Norman England* (2002) that the century after *c.* 1050 saw more building stone used in England than was extracted in France during the three centuries of church building after the same date, and perhaps more than went into the Great Pyramids.[3]

Historians of the Anglo-Norman period have been fond of using models of colonialism and imperialism as analogies to understand the effects of the Norman Conquest on England and the incorporation of its lands – and later parts of Wales and Ireland – into a Norman (and later Angevin or Plantagenet) 'empire.'[4] Models of rapid cultural transformation by conquest are now gradually giving way to different perspectives on the Norman impact, however.[5] Theories of modernisation and development as colonial policy have an important role to play if we are to escape the image of a monolithic Norman regime synonymous with oppression and subjection. In short, we need to see the developments of the late eleventh and early twelfth century as part and parcel of longer-term historical processes. It is therefore essential to consider the Norman Conquest's more indirect and longer-term impacts on life and landscape as a result of more gradual change under a regime that was itself evolving.

By the 1130s the population of England had increased steadily from the level at Domesday (1086), which is best estimated at around 2.2–2.5 million.[6] The most populous areas were the eastern parts of

East Anglia, parts of Kent and Sussex, and a belt of districts running diagonally from the Humber Estuary in the north-east to Somerset in the south-west. Perhaps 10–15% of the population lived in towns. Domesday Book records over 100 boroughs, with London at the apex of a well-integrated urban hierarchy and gradually supplanting Winchester, the principal seat of the pre-Conquest kings of Wessex, as the capital city of kingship. Bristol, Lincoln, Norwich and York were the other major regional centres on the next rung down the urban hierarchy, with a network of shire towns such as Oxford and Northampton and other commercial centres beneath them.

The link between town and Crown was strong and enduring and was strengthened further by the Norman Conquest, which increased the status of towns as strategic centres of royal government and authority.[7] In most shires the principal urban settlement was an old Anglo-Saxon or Anglo-Scandinavian *burh*, or fortified centre, upon which a Norman urban castle had been superimposed, often entailing the clearance of housing.[8] These urban castles were the seats of the sheriffs (or 'shire-reeves') responsible for collecting taxes, while in a rigorously controlled monetary system mints were also based in boroughs. In centres such as Lincoln and Norwich the planning of new cathedral precincts occurred more or less in parallel with urban castle building, while new Benedictine monasteries were characteristic Norman additions, as at Chester and Wallingford. The scale of investment in stone architecture in both ecclesiastical and secular spheres was a hallmark of Norman influence. While the late eleventh and early twelfth century thus saw the nature of royal and ecclesiastical power in the major towns transformed, and their visibility heightened, the aristocracy as a whole had far less presence in these environments than before. With castles becoming the principal focus of defensive and elite investment, few towns and cities saw serious work on the walled circuits that later came to represent the collective efforts and identities of communities.[9]

The precincts of castles, palaces, monasteries and cathedrals could take up huge swathes of intramural space, and urban growth in the late eleventh and early twelfth century was characteristically focused on suburbs. Some industries, such as pottery manufacturing, effectively disappeared from towns in the same period, relocating to the countryside.[10] The short-term destruction wrought by urban castle building was balanced by a positive stimulus to urban growth in other ways, in particular through the growth of ports on the south coast that benefitted from enhanced cross-Channel links, and through the plantation of 'French boroughs' – mercantile colonies, usually close to Norman power centres – in select places such as Hereford, Norwich and Nottingham.[11] Outside the major towns, the growth of boroughs and markets at centres of lordship was the key driver of post-Conquest commercial expansion. 'New towns,' some founded on greenfield sites and others by recasting or adding to pre-existing rural settlements, were established in large numbers by lay and ecclesiastical lords as well as by kings, and were a major factor in the extension of market networks into the countryside. Places such as Alnwick (Northumberland), Arundel (West Sussex), Barnard Castle (County Durham), Launceston (Cornwall) and Richmond (North Yorkshire), all established in close association with Norman *capita*, crept up the ladder of urban success, nurtured by the interests of magnates, to become regionally important commercial settlements as well as administrative *foci*. In Wales, newly established seigneurial boroughs, built as colonising ventures to consolidate lordships centred on castles, constituted the first real urban settlements.[12] The defences of these places typically took the form of embanked and ditched appendages to castles as opposed to truly communal fortifications.

This period of consolidation and settlement sat firmly in the middle of what is often termed the 'Medieval Warm Period' (also known as the Little Climatic Optimum or Medieval Warm Epoch), which extended approximately between the tenth and the thirteenth century. In northern Europe it signalled a climate generally warmer than today, although the epoch had its own climatic complexity and periods of turbulence, meaning that the term 'Medieval Warm Period' should be used with caution.[13] The rural landscape was filling up. Steady demographic growth was underlain by the increasing productivity of arable agriculture and the expansion of the cultivated zone in what is sometimes styled the 'drive to the margins.'[14] The pattern varied intricately between regions; for instance, wetland areas were drained and enclosed in some zones, while in others the cultivated zone crept up onto the uplands.

The most profound transformations to the landscape in the late eleventh and early twelfth century impacted upon the urban scene. Change in the countryside can seem low-key in comparison and significant episodes of development, such as village creation and planning, are notoriously hard to date accurately. The Norman Conquest did see the devastation of rebellious districts, most notably parts of Yorkshire in the wake of the 1069–70 rebellion, although the consequences on the ground are much debated, particularly concerning whether or not the period that followed saw the mass creation of planned villages to resettle the zone.[15] The expansion of Norman control into northern England, which comprised a patchwork of independently minded regions only loosely tied to the south, was a piecemeal and protracted process that continued into the twelfth century, reinforced by religious foundations.[16]

The rural world was marked by intricate regional variation – in terms of agrarian regimes and building styles, and in settlement patterns that saw some areas typified by villages but dispersed landscapes of farmsteads and hamlets characterising others.[17] In different contexts, the late eleventh and early twelfth century saw the expansion and restructuring of existing villages, the growth of secondary 'daughter' settlements and the colonisation of new land through 'assarting' (clearing woodland for agriculture). Energetic debate among archaeologists and landscape historians has focused on the date and circumstances that gave rise to village nucleation and cooperative farming in England's 'central province,' although it seems clear that neither was there was one single 'village moment' nor any monocausal explanation for the phenomenon. Rather, nucleation occurred up to and including the twelfth century, potentially reflecting the involvement of communities as well as the agency of secular and religious landlords.

One major difference between the rural landscape at the time of Domesday Book and the period of Stephen's accession to the throne, easily overlooked, is that slavery and slaves, who had made up a significant minority of the population, had disappeared. The *quid pro quo* was that burdens on the peasant classes substantially increased across the same period. While we should be careful not to caricature the effects of the Conquest on the countryside through the 'Norman yoke' school of thinking, there is no disguising the fact that the post-Conquest world saw an increasingly pressurised peasantry as estate management strategies were refined and introduced to new areas. Newly established lords tightened their grip on rural populations by extracting greater dues in labour service, which must be the major reason why the value of so many Domesday manors increased between 1066 and 1086. Another way in which lords squeezed their estates for profit, especially characteristic of the twelfth century, was by 'farming out' areas of the demesne (the area of a manor directly exploited by a lord) in return for cash payments, rather than managing it directly.[18]

The ethnic mix of England's population was also changing. While the 'Norman' colonisation was an elite takeover rather than a mass folk movement, it had introduced a heterogeneous mix of people that included Bretons, Flemings and Poitevins as well as Normans. Assimilation of these groups with the Anglo-Saxon population was a complex and two-way process; the Normans were gradually anglicised but various aspects of Anglo-Saxon culture were Normanised, so that ethnic distinctions became fluid.[19] That the process of acculturation was well entrenched by the mid-twelfth century is nicely illustrated by the fact that several of the key chroniclers of the period had mixed English and Norman ancestry, including Orderic Vitalis and Henry of Huntingdon. William the Conqueror's plantation of a small population of Jews from Rouen to London brought another element to England's ethnic mix and signalled the start of a close relationship between the English Crown and Jewish financiers.[20]

The Norman Conquest also opened the way for a host of innovations in the area of religious life. The influx of bishops and senior churchmen of Continental origin initially shocked the established Church in England, although new religious attitudes and influences had a much longer-term and more gradual impact on society and the landscape. Existing cathedrals and monasteries were, without exception, rebuilt in the Romanesque style, usually soon after the Conquest, under new bishops and abbots, while others were resited to more convenient (and fortified) locations, as with the transfer of the see of Dorchester-upon-Thames to Lincoln, and that of Selsey to Chichester in the 1070s. The process of Normanising England's major churches ran far beyond the immediate post-Conquest decades; work on Exeter Cathedral only began in 1114, for example. Reorganisation and rationalisation of the dioceses had particularly profound implications for the cities of Chichester, Lincoln, Norwich and Salisbury (Old Sarum), where new cathedrals were built and precincts around them planned. These grand designs, in which different topographic elements formed part of a coherent Norman 'package' imposed upon the cityscape, could see the urban fabric completely remodelled – no more so than at Winchester, where the old Anglo-Saxon church and palace were swept away and supplanted by a new royal and ecclesiastical complex. The upsurge in building projects, sometimes spanning several decades, and the growth of the labour and procurement networks that sustained them, surely also stimulated the economy.[21]

The greatest change in the religious sphere, however, was the revitalisation of monastic life. On the eve of the Conquest, England had perhaps 1,000 monks and nuns.[22] This 'monastic landscape' was fairly swiftly transformed by a proliferation of new religious houses, many of them 'alien' houses dependent on larger establishments.[23] The waves of foundations did not come straight away but followed as part and parcel of Norman consolidation and settlement. The secular elite – the king, and especially the nobility – were the key agents of change, establishing monastic houses for reasons of piety (and as family mausolea) but also to mark power bases and sometimes to help establish territorial control, especially on the borders. The higher-profile new establishments of the 1060s–90s were mainly Benedictine foundations within towns. The Black Monks' hegemony was soon broken, however, first in the final decades of the eleventh century by Cluniac reform, which advocated a return to a purer form of monasticism but whose English houses typically complemented the *capita* of Norman lords, and from *c.* 1100 by the Augustinians, whose activities were more closely engaged with the laity. The early decades of the twelfth century saw monasticism entering its most profound period of growth and change in England and on the Continent, and by the late 1120s the Cistercian order, with its back-to-basics ethos and reforming zeal, had established a foothold in England and was starting to rock the monastic world.[24]

The Civil War: A Chronology

A chronological narrative of Stephen's reign is essential background for the largely thematically based chapters that follow. While many accounts of the period have been drawn to particular events that are identified as somehow pivotal, the chronology presented below attempts a balanced perspective by devoting a single paragraph to each year of Stephen's reign, prefaced by a summary of the conflict's causes and protagonists. Figures 2.1a–b complement the chronology with mapped itineraries for the movements of King Stephen, the Empress Matilda and her son Henry of Anjou around Britain (and indicating periods of time spent in Continental Europe) between 1135–54. This provides a starting point for understanding the geography of the civil war. It is crucial to emphasise from the start that while many of Stephen's movements around his kingdom reflect the progress of military campaigns, itineration was always critical to medieval kingship and governance.[25] Thus, the itineraries of Henry I and II show that these kings spent a very large amount of their time in England in an area defined by a line drawn south-west from London to Portchester on the south coast, then north-west up to Salisbury, Gloucester and Worcester, then east across to Northampton and down again to London – a 'royal enclave' around Wessex and the Thames Valley established in the late Saxon period.[26] Even a superficial glance at Stephen's itinerary highlights that his movements were by and large limited to a similar area, which marked the main contested zone of the civil war. The struggle for England was a struggle for a swathe of landscape with a long-established heritage of kingship.

Causes and protagonists

The succession crisis that precipitated the civil war developed because of the 'White Ship disaster' of 25 November 1120. This saw King Henry I's only legitimate son, the 17-year-old prince William Adelin, drown when the vessel carrying him foundered on a rock *en route* from Barfleur in Normandy to England. While Henry had a large number of illegitimate children, including his favourite, Robert (later to become Earl of Gloucester), his only other legitimate offspring was Matilda, born 1102 to the king's first wife, also called Matilda. Although Henry married for a second time, to Adeliza of Louvain, in the hope of producing a male heir, the marriage was barren. Henry's daughter Matilda is often styled 'the Empress' during the civil war because of her first marriage, in 1114, to the newly crowned Holy Roman Emperor, Henry V. She spent her married life in Germany and northern Italy, but was widowed, childless, in 1125. A second marriage, to Geoffrey Plantagenet (later Count of Anjou) in 1128, produced the first of three sons, Henry (later Henry II, hereafter Henry of Anjou), in March 1133.[27]

Stephen of Blois was Henry I's nephew; his mother was Adela, daughter of William the Conqueror and his father Stephen, Count of Blois and Chartres.[28] Born around 1092 – the precise date is uncertain – it is important to remember that Stephen was the third of four sons who survived to adulthood (another, Odo, died young): the first, William, was defective in some way; the second, Theobald, became Count of Champagne; Stephen's younger brother, Henry ('of Blois') was sent away to become a monk at Cluny and rose to become Bishop of Winchester. Stephen gained early experience of military command in campaigns on the borders of Anjou and Normandy and, as a favourite of Henry I's court, rose to become an influential and wealthy magnate, holding extensive estates on both sides of the Channel. Stephen's marriage to Matilda, daughter of the Count of Boulogne, around 1125, produced five children: Eustace, William, Baldwin, Matilda and Mary.[29] Stephen's oath of allegiance at Henry I's court in January 1127 to recognise the Empress Matilda as heir to the throne, sworn along with other barons, was to dog his career and reputation.

Outbreak (1135–38)

In the words of R.H.C. Davis, waiting for Henry I to die must have been like waiting for a nuclear bomb to go off.[30] The old king died at Lyons-la-Forêt, in Upper Normandy, on 1 December 1135, after eating a dish of lampreys against the advice of his doctor. William Clito, the only legitimate son of Robert Curthose, Duke of Normandy (and elder brother of Henry I) had died in 1128, which removed one possible claimant to the English throne, but the succession was horribly muddled. With lightning-quick reactions, Stephen capitalised on the confusion after Henry's death to cross the Channel from the county of Boulogne to Dover and seize control of the twin centres of English royal power: first London, where the citizens accepted him as king, and then Winchester and the royal treasury. Stephen's brother, Henry of Blois, Bishop of Winchester, was instrumental in orchestrating this success and in securing the critical support of Roger, Bishop of Salisbury, who, as Henry I's justiciar, had been 'not merely powerful in the Church but also second to the king in the kingdom.'[31] Then in his early forties, Stephen was crowned at Westminster Abbey by the Archbishop of Canterbury on 22 December, less than three weeks after Henry's death. In contrast, Matilda had entered Normandy but was unable to make progress beyond Falaise and retreated to her castle of Argentan. Localised violence that had broken out in both Normandy and England upon news of Henry's death quickly blew over and was probably a matter of settling scores rather than coordinated revolt or insurrection. On the borderlands with Wales, however, raids and ambushes – amounting to a sustained campaign of asymmetric warfare – dominated the early years of Stephen's reign.

After attending Henry I's funeral at Reading Abbey on 4 January 1136, Stephen's position was bolstered by the Normandy magnates' acceptance of him as ruler, after first favouring his brother Theobald, and by the pope's confirmation of his position. However, 'it was not long before there was much discord throughout England and Normandy, and the bonds of peace were torn apart.'[32] The first threat came from the north, from King David I of Scots, the maternal uncle of the Empress Matilda and a 'legend in his own lifetime.'[33] David crossed the border to take Carlisle and a number of important border castles, although his motives were partly opportunistic, pursuing Scots territorial claims to these areas as much as advancing the Angevin cause. Stephen's reaction was again speedy, and he arrived in Durham on 5 February to negotiate a settlement that granted David's son, Henry, the Earldom of Huntingdon and other properties in return for the Scots' partial withdrawal. A second major campaign in the summer of 1136 saw Stephen move to the south-west of England, where he first put down a revolt by Robert of Bampton and then a more serious insurrection led

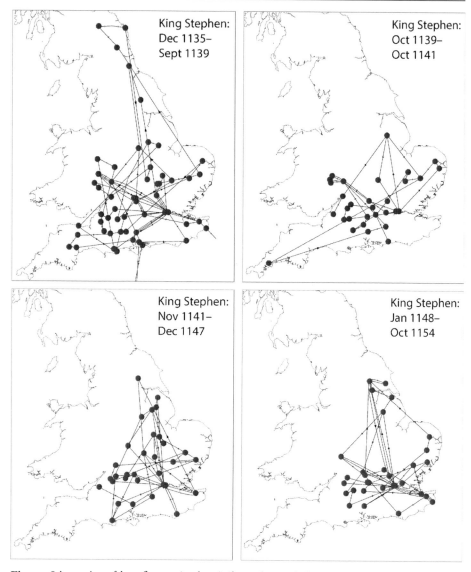

Fig 2.1: Itineraries of key figures in the civil war by period:
a, above King Stephen; **b, opposite** the Empress Matilda and Henry of Anjou.
Compiled from Cronne and Davis 1968. Map work by Steven Trick.

by Baldwin de Redvers, who had seized the royal castle of Exeter. The king led a prolonged, expensive and very public siege that was ended by negotiation when Baldwin's men were permitted to withdraw in good order, under terms that chroniclers considered overly generous.

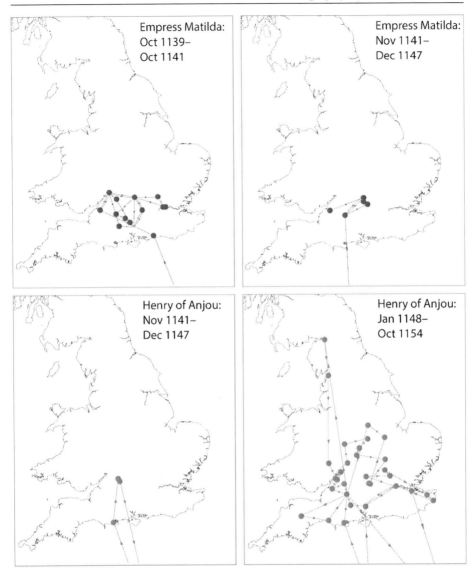

Empress Matilda: Oct 1139– Oct 1141

Empress Matilda: Nov 1141– Dec 1147

Henry of Anjou: Nov 1141– Dec 1147

Henry of Anjou: Jan 1148– Oct 1154

From mid-March to late November **1137**, Stephen was engaged in Normandy during his only visit to the duchy as king.[34] A successful diplomatic offensive in which Stephen's son Eustace was recognised by King Louis VI of France was followed by a failed military offensive, as fallings-out between Norman and Flemish contingents wrecked the projected campaign against Geoffrey of Anjou. Stephen returned to England to find 'the kingdom in turmoil … a hotbed of appalling cruelty and bloody treason,' and was informed of a secret plot 'to kill all the Normans on a fixed day and hand over the government of the kingdom to the Scots.'[35] In December Stephen was engaged in a siege of Bedford Castle, held by the rebellious Miles de Beauchamp, from which he then moved north to meet a renewed Scots threat, which had been temporarily held back by a truce brokered by Thurstan, Archbishop of York.

Stephen arrived in the north of England early in February **1138**, where he 'invaded, burned and laid waste the southern areas of King David's kingdom.'[36] A tactical withdrawal by the Scots ensured that there could be no outright victory, but both sides of the border were devastated. For the remainder of his reign Stephen never ventured further north than York. The second half of the year saw rebellions springing up in the south and west of England, including major outbreaks centred on Bristol, Castle Cary and Dunster (both Somerset), Hereford and Shrewsbury (Shropshire) – some ostensibly in the Angevin cause but others the result of private grievances – which the king met, one by one. This established a geostrategic pattern that was to characterise Stephen's reign: the king campaigned energetically from place to place but was never able to stamp out spreading bouts of insurrection entirely. With the king thus fully occupied, it devolved to the northern barons and the leadership of Thurstan of York to confront the Scots and their Galwegian allies in open battle, inflicting a decisive defeat at the Battle of the Standard (or Northallerton) on 22 August. This did little to change the strategic situation in the north, however. Scots forces remained in possession of large tracts of northern England following the Peace of Durham, established the following year, including Carlisle and its important and lucrative silver mine. The situation on the opposite side of the Channel had deteriorated in Stephen's absence, meanwhile, the Normans 'tearing each other to pieces in their native land.'[37] Finally, a major political swing had been signalled earlier, in the spring of 1138, by the shifting allegiance of Matilda's half-brother, Robert, Earl of Gloucester, at that point based in Normandy, who renounced his homage to Stephen and emerged as a key Angevin figurehead and commander.

Matilda's landing to the Battle of Lincoln (1139–41)

Although the previous four years had been dominated by successive revolts and invasions, **1139** is generally recognised as marking the commencement of the civil war proper. It marked an important turning point in Stephen's reign. The event in June that has come to be known as 'the arrest of the bishops' saw Stephen orchestrate the downfall of three major figures closely associated with the court of Henry I and confiscate their castles. In 'an extraordinarily scandalous and quite unprecedented affair,'[38] the king had arrested at court in Oxford, Roger, Bishop of Salisbury and his nephew Alexander 'the Magnificent,' Bishop of Lincoln, while Nigel, Bishop of Ely, escaped to Devizes Castle in Wiltshire. Stephen's immediate gain of some important strongholds was more than offset by the serious damage the event did to his relationship with the Church. By the end of the year the Angevin cause was given fresh impetus by the arrival in England of the Empress Matilda and her brother, Robert of Gloucester, on 30 September. Continuing the pattern of the previous year, the king had been mobile around central-southern England, putting down rebellions through siege warfare. He immediately confronted Matilda at Arundel, where she was pinned down in the castle of the dowager queen Adeliza of Louvain (the second wife of Henry I) and her new husband, William d'Aubigny, while Earl Robert moved to Bristol. Stephen permitted the Empress to join her brother in Bristol, 'either because he trusted treacherous advice, or because he thought the castle [Arundel] impregnable.'[39] Stephen continued on the offensive, campaigning energetically and with temporary success around the West Country and the Thames Valley, where Wallingford Castle became a major focus of attention, having declared for the Empress under its castellan Brian fitz Count, another favourite of Henry I.

The early part of 1140 saw Stephen campaign to suppress uprisings centred on Ely, led by Bishop Nigel, and Cornwall, led by Reginald, an illegitimate son of Henry I, and William fitz Richard, one of Cornwall's foremost magnates. In the summer the king took Bungay Castle in Suffolk, and made peace with Hugh Bigod, Earl of Norfolk, who was also in revolt. On the wider stage the king remained unable to bring Robert of Gloucester to battle. Angevin military efforts were at this point mainly focused on targets around their chief West Country bases of Bristol and Gloucester, and the area around this zone rapidly became the cradle of the conflict: Hereford was assaulted by Miles of Gloucester and Geoffrey Talbot, while Earl Robert attacked Bath and, in a longer-range foray, Nottingham.

Early in 1141 Stephen was at Lincoln besieging the castle, which had been taken by rebels loyal to Ranulf, Earl of Chester and William de Roumare, Earl of Lincoln. It was outside the ancient Roman city walls that the king was captured in a climactic battle on 2 February. Earl Ranulf had escaped and sought military support from his father-in-law,

Robert of Gloucester, and the combined Angevin force had advanced with a strong Welsh contingent to crush Stephen's demoralised force. The captive king was transported first to Gloucester and then to Bristol, but in the power vacuum the Empress was slow to react: it was a month before her supporters met the legate at Wherwell, near Winchester, when Henry of Blois accepted her as 'lady of the English,' and late June before she entered London. The Empress was rapidly sent packing by the Londoners, who massed and confronted her 'like thronging swarms from beehives,'[40] alarmed at her demands and conscious that Stephen's queen had assembled an army in Kent. The Empress fled to Oxford as a temporary base and then to Winchester, where a complex siege involving many major magnates lasted from late July through to mid-September, and ended in Angevin flight ('the Rout of Winchester'). Robert, Earl of Gloucester, was captured while Matilda escaped northward via Ludgershall Castle in Wiltshire. After prolonged negotiation the two prisoners – Earl Robert and King Stephen – were released 'on terms of equal exchange' in November,[41] although the conflict was no closer to resolution.

Angevin reverse (1142–47)

In the spring of 1142 Stephen was in York. On his return south he 'was kept at Northampton by an illness so dangerous that in nearly the whole of England he was proclaimed as dead.'[42] Recovery saw the king reabsorbed into a familiar pattern of campaigning. From this period into the later 1140s, the conflict settled down into a deadlock without the decisive engagement, death or peace settlement that could end the war. After besieging the Angevin-held port and castle at Wareham on the south coast, Stephen campaigned through Gloucestershire and Oxfordshire before pinning the Empress down in Oxford Castle, from which she escaped dramatically and famously across the frozen River Thames in one of the civil war's most famous and enduring images.

The Battle of Wilton was the principal military event of 1143. The exact date is disputed, but it occurred in July or earlier. More of a fighting withdrawal rather than a full clash of arms, this confused engagement occurred when Stephen's campaign army was assailed by the Earl of Gloucester's men and he narrowly escaped capture for a second time due to a rearguard action fought by his doughty steward William Martel. The king's arrest of Geoffrey de Mandeville, Earl of Essex –'the most perfect and typical presentment of the feudal and anarchic spirit that stamps the reign of Stephen'[43] – at court in St Albans in September precipitated a hugely destructive revolt which dominated the latter part of the year. Upon release, and having relinquished his strategically important castles, the earl flew into rebellion, leading a bitter guerrilla campaign from isolated bases on the fens (see Chapter 9).

The fenland rebellion ended suddenly with the death of Geoffrey de Mandeville in the late summer of 1144. Stephen had been present in the region conducting a campaign of containment for the first part of the year, but had moved to Lincoln by the spring to conduct another siege, and thence to meet threats in the Cotswolds. On the wider canvas, the most important event of 1144–45 was the loss of Normandy following a whirlwind offensive by Geoffrey of Anjou, who was recognised as Duke of Normandy by King Louis VII of France and established the city of Rouen as his capital.

For the early part of 1145, Stephen was engaged in campaigning against Hugh Bigod in the only significant military operations in East Anglia during the conflict. Later in the year the king and a force of Londoners conducted a successful siege of Robert of Gloucester's castle at Faringdon, which had been held as a counterpoint to nearby royalist Oxford. Against the huge setback of the loss of Normandy, this represented a major military success and helped to re-establish Stephen's grip on the Thames Valley: 'at last the king's fortunes began to change for the better and took an upward turn.'[44]

In the wake of Stephen's military successes of the previous year, the political landscape was shaken in 1146 by the temporary defection of the previous arch-rebel Ranulf, Earl of Chester to Stephen's cause. The earl demonstrated his new-found loyalty by assisting Stephen in sieges at Bedford and Wallingford, but the situation was soon reversed following his arrest at court, supposedly for treasonable behaviour, and any benefits Stephen reaped through gaining control of the earl's possessions, including Lincoln Castle, were soon negated by Ranulf's actions upon his release. 'Exceeding fierce and full of wrath,' Earl Ranulf proceeded 'everywhere to rage cruelly with plunder and arson, violence and the sword.'[45]

Little is known about Stephen's movements in 1147, although he was present at Coventry and Pevensey campaigning to contain the fallout of the Earl of Chester's rebellion. In mid-May a Crusader fleet gathered at Dartmouth to attack Lisbon in an early action of the Second Crusade. The year also saw the first intervention in the civil war of Matilda's son, Henry of Anjou. At the head of a small force, the 14-year-old boy crossed the Channel to assist his Angevin allies and capitalise on the chaos. He led a very limited spring campaign in north Wiltshire but the operation was not a success and Henry was back in Normandy before the end of May, having, bizarrely, managed to beg money from Stephen to pay his troops off and end this little venture. The death of Robert of Gloucester on 31 October nevertheless ensured that Henry would be the flag-bearer of the Angevin cause. Stephen's knighting of his son Eustace in the same year signalled that the prince would similarly play a more prominent part in events, his early successes in battle winning 'admiration from men hardened to warfare.'[46]

Henry of Anjou's status as the Angevins' new hope was cemented by his mother's departure to Normandy early in **1148**, never to return (she died in 1167 and was buried in Rouen). Despite the Empress's withdrawal, however, Stephen's position was still far from secure. With the civil war in Normandy now over, the duchy was a secure base and centre for organising operations against England, and the main Angevin sympathisers among the English nobility remained in place. Further afield, the Second Crusade saw the participation of various magnates, including Waleran de Meulan and William de Warenne, and their withdrawal probably contributed to the lull in the fighting in England.

Endgame (1149–54)

From **1149** onwards, Henry of Anjou became more active in the Angevin cause, taking a military leadership role. By now on the cusp of adulthood, he returned to England in the spring and travelled to Carlisle to forge an alliance with the Scots and Angevin-sympathising earls. Here, King David I of Scots, 'with the respect due to a king, ungrudgingly bestowed on him the splendid emblems of a knight's dignity and promised him very ready aid in vanquishing his enemies.'[47] Emboldened, Henry led a large Anglo-Scottish force to York but withdrew in the face of a powerful counter-offensive by Stephen. Henry retreated to the Angevin power base of south-west England, where he campaigned with his earls in Dorset, Devon and Wiltshire. Having failed to break the stalemate, and confronted by Stephen's bitter policy of ravaging the agricultural base around Angevin strongholds, he soon hightailed back Normandy.

With Henry of Anjou re-gathering his energies and building military support on the opposite side of the Channel, **1150** presented an opportunity for Stephen to move decisively against his enemies in England. Yet, intriguingly, this year appears one of military inactivity, with only one significant siege (that of Worcester) recorded. The early 1150s were instead a period of consolidation and stand-off – a 'magnates' peace'[48] during which an exhausted nobility had too much to lose to upset the delicate balance of power.

The political landscape was shaken through the unexpected death of Geoffrey, Count of Anjou on 7 September 1151, at the age of 39. Henry's plans for another invasion of England were initially disrupted as he travelled to Anjou to take up his inheritance, although in the longer term his position was hugely strengthened by this enlarged power base and 'after preparations on a very great scale' he 'resolved to return to England to overthrow King Stephen.'[49]

With the threat from Normandy looming, Stephen's cause was weakened by the death of his queen and occasional military commander, Matilda, in May 1152. Over in Normandy, the same month saw the marriage of Henry of Anjou to Eleanor of Aquitaine, the recently divorced wife of King Louis VII of France, which gave him effective control of a large and wealthy swathe of south-west France. The summer saw a struggle in Normandy between Duke Henry and Stephen's eldest son Eustace, who was fighting a proxy war on behalf of King Louis, although Henry's position in the duchy proved unassailable.

With Normandy secure, Henry of Anjou's invasion of England in January 1153 rapidly moved the conflict into its endgame. Sailing from Barfleur with a small but effective force said to comprise 140 knights and 3,000 infantry,[50] he landed at Wareham. The campaign that followed, sometimes known as the 'Henrician War,'[51] saw the Duke campaigning widely and successfully, first in the south-west and then the Midlands. By the middle of June he had 'brought almost half England over to his side,'[52] before weighing into the long-standing siege of Wallingford. The sudden death of Eustace in August 1153 paved the way for a negotiated peace (Stephen's second son, William, was never a serious contender for the throne). It was war-weariness and wavering support from the barons rather than outright military victory that dragged the conflict to its close. A truce brokered by the bishops laid the foundations for the 'Treaty' of Winchester (or, alternatively, of Wallingford or Westminster) – 'a dawn of peace at the end of a night of misery.'[53] The peace settlement had three essential elements: Stephen would recognise Henry as heir to the throne but would rule until his death; all castles built during the war were to be demolished; and confiscated properties would be restored to those who had held them in Henry I's reign or their heirs. The peace agreement was mutually beneficial to the protagonists so that ultimately the conflict produced few 'losers' in the conventional sense; most of the major Stephanic sympathisers retained their positions and their lands. Yet Stephen had not been decisively defeated by Henry; in a sense, the king 'won the war but lost the peace.'[54] For Henry of Anjou, the time that elapsed between the treaty and Stephen's death the following year provided a cooling-off period for consultation and preparation for kingship.[55]

In 1154, in the wake of the peace treaty, Stephen travelled widely, 'traversing the provinces of England with regal pride ... as though he had just obtained the throne.'[56] Even with the succession resolved, some fighting continued, with Stephen leading a northern campaign in the late summer that included a siege of Drax Castle in Yorkshire. The king, then in his early sixties, died of a sudden abdominal illness at Dover on 25 October; he was buried at the monastery he had founded at Faversham. Henry II and Queen Eleanor were crowned on 19 December and the new king rapidly set about enforcing the demilitarisation of the landscape, ordering 'new castles which had certainly not stood in the days of his grandfather to be demolished' and issuing 'an edict that those who had flocked to England from foreign nations ... should be sent back to their native regions.'[57]

Civil war?

While a major thrust of historical research on Stephen's reign has been to rethink the extent to which the period amounted to 'anarchy,' there are also good reasons to question whether the conflict constituted a 'civil war' as it is usually styled. The period saw invasions by foreign armies, principally the Scots in the lead-up to the Battle of the Standard (1138), although the landings of the Empress Matilda (1139) and Henry of Anjou (1147, 1149 and 1153) were also, in a sense, incursions by external (Angevin) forces. In the medieval world there was arguably a fuzzy distinction between fully fledged civil war – with the implication of widespread and persistent conflict involving all layers of society – and smaller-scale rebellions pursued by elite factions and their direct supporters to settle personal, local and regional grievances. In some senses the conflict of Stephen's reign was not so much a struggle between two clear-cut opposing sides but rather amounted to a myriad of separate but interconnected revolts and private wars. Nor was the struggle purely about the succession to the English throne: for David I and the Scots, it was about pursuing legitimate territorial claims and empire building; for the Welsh, it was about control of the borderlands and revenge.

Another reason why this was not purely an English, or British, civil war is that at its root lay a deep-seated enmity between Norman and Angevin. Control over the duchy of Normandy was central to the struggle: Stephen's brief and ineffective nine-month foray in 1137 was matched by the effectiveness with which Matilda, Count Geoffrey and Henry of Anjou used Normandy as a base to secure their positions, although among the chronicle sources only Orderic Vitalis provides fulsome coverage of events in the duchy. Many magnates in the conflict also had a cross-Channel perspective. Especially relevant in this context are the powerful and colourful Beaumont twins – Waleran de Meulan and Robert of Leicester – who played such an active role in the politics of the civil war and who held estates and had urban and commercial interests, including in the lucrative wine and cloth industries, either side of the Channel.[58] The large scale of Stephen's employment of foreign (mainly Flemish) mercenaries, in Normandy as well as England, is another reason why this was not a purely civil conflict.

If the above historical account is dominated by the activities of King Stephen and his principal rivals, some important changes to Anglo-Norman elite society provide further essential context for understanding the conflict. Stephen's reign was a period of social mobility and reshuffling among the elite. The most notable development was a multiplication of earls: between 1138 and 1141, 23 new earls were created, by both the king and the Empress Matilda.[59] R.H.C. Davis established that these titles were not empty honours but carried with them significant governmental and military responsibilities and were central to a wider administrative shake-up.[60]

The elevation of so many earls also meant the breakdown of the system of sheriffs, who in the earlier Norman period had been powerful figures of high status whose authority had replaced both the humbler late Saxon sheriffs and the all-powerful late Saxon earls. Sheriffs are poorly documented in Stephen's reign and it is only in the south and south-east, and at the very end of his reign, that they can be securely identified.[61] It is clear, nonetheless, that the period saw earls and other key magnates take charge of or supplant sheriffs, who had previously acted as the king's representatives; in some cases the king actively encouraged or permitted this, although elsewhere he was unable to prevent it happening.[62] A very clear case of the latter is the sudden rise of Baldwin de Redvers, Lord of Plympton at the expense of the hereditary sheriffs of Devon; in 1136 he seized Exeter Castle with the ambition of securing the castellanship of the royal castle and the shrievalty of Devon, and was created first Earl of Devon by the Empress in 1141.[63] While major magnates were players in a struggle on the national and indeed international stage, these changes percolated through the hierarchy of the elite so that aristocratic and knightly identity too were negotiated and expressed in more visible ways.[64] These developments provide the sociopolitical context for understanding some of the significant changes in architecture and material culture that we see during the period.

Summary

At the moment of Stephen's accession to the throne in 1135, the longer-term impacts of the Norman Conquest on England's society and landscape were still being played out. Ethnicity and identity in the period were fluid, however, and mid-twelfth-century England was a developing Anglo-Norman state rather that a subjugated dominion. While 'the Anarchy' of Stephen's reign is frequently styled as a civil war, the conflict was unusually complex and protracted, and involved more than two opposing sides. The period witnessed persistent asymmetric warfare on the borderlands of Wales, a succession of major incursions from Scotland and a sequence of Angevin invasions from across the Channel, while the struggle for control of Normandy dominated the wider strategic landscape. The most characteristic feature of conflict during the period was, however, an unprecedented succession of vicious internal rebellions, led by disloyal, disenfranchised or marginalised magnates and underlain by regional grievances. The implications of this were a battered, militarised landscape and a disturbed economy. The following chapters explore the archaeologies of this warfare and detail its consequences on the ground.

Notes

1 For overviews, see Rowley 1997, chs 1–3; Dyer and Hadley 2016.

2 Cameron 1961, 87–94.

3 Fernie 2002, 19.

4 See for example, Le Patourel 1976.

5 West 1999.

6 Dyer 2002, 95.

7 For an overview of urban topography and the Norman Conquest, see Palliser et al. 2000, esp. 160, 173–4.

8 On urban castles generally, see Creighton 2015b, 133–51.

9 On urban defences in the Norman period, see Creighton and Higham 2005, 65–75.

10 For pottery and the Norman Conquest, see Jervis 2014, 86–98.

11 For case studies of the Norman transformation of urban centres, see Lilley 1999.

12 See Lilley 2000.

13 Hughes and Diaz 1994.

14 For a classic account, see Postan 1972, ch. 2.

15 Palliser 1993.

16 For an overview of the Normans in the north, see Kapelle 1979. See also Green 1997, 122–4.

17 For regional variation in medieval England, see Rippon 2008.

18 On the archaeology of rural settlements and the Norman Conquest, see Creighton and Rippon 2016.

19 See Hadley 2011.

20 For an overview, see Abulafia 2011.

21 For an overview of Norman stone building projects, see Fernie 2002, ch. 2.

22 Aston 2000, 73.

23 For an overview, see Burton 1994.

24 Burton and Kerr 2011.

25 Christelow 1996, 187.

26 Keefe 1990, 180.

27 The definitive biography of Matilda is Chibnall 1991.

28 For Stephen's family, see LoPrete 2007.

29 For Stephen's career before 1135, see King 2000.

30 Davis 1967, 12.

31 William of Newburgh, *The History of English Affairs* I, 6, 3, Walsh and Kennedy 1988, 56–7.

32 *The Chronicle of John of Worcester* III, McGurk 1998, 216–17.

33 Barrow 1985, 5.

34 On the detail of Stephen's itinerary in Normandy, see Helmerichs 1993.

35 *The Ecclesiastical History of Orderic Vitalis* XIII, 32, Chibnall 1978, Vol. VI, 494–5.

36 Henry, Archdeacon of Huntingdon, *Historia Anglorum* X, 6, Greenway 1996, 710–11.

37 *The Ecclesiastical History of Orderic Vitalis* XIII, 38, Chibnall 1978, Vol. VI, 524–5.

38 Henry, Archdeacon of Huntingdon, *Historia Anglorum* X, 10, Greenway 1996, 718–19.

39 Henry, Archdeacon of Huntingdon, *Historia Anglorum* X, 11, Greenway 1996, 722–3.

40 *Gesta Stephani* I, 62, Potter and Davis 1976, 124–5.

41 William of Malmesbury, *Historia Novella* III, 66, King and Potter 1998, 118–19.

42 William of Malmesbury, *Historia Novella* III, 73, King and Potter 1998, 122–3.

43 Round 1892, v.

44 Henry, Archdeacon of Huntingdon, *Historia Anglorum* X, 23, Greenway 1996, 746–7.

45 *Gesta Stephani* II, 104, Potter and Davis 1976, 198–8.

46 *Gesta Stephani* II, 109, Potter and Davis 1976, 208–9.

47 *Gesta Stephani* II, 113, Potter and Davis 1976, 216–17.

48 Davis 1967, ch. 10.

49 *Gesta Stephani* II, 116, Potter and Davis 1976, 224–5.

50 William of Newburgh, *The History of English Affairs* I, 29, 2, Walsh and Kennedy 1988, 122–3.

51 Bradbury 1996, ch. 7.

52 *Gesta Stephani* II, 120, Potter and Davis 1976, 236–7.

53 Henry, Archdeacon of Huntingdon, *Historia Anglorum* X, 37, Greenway 1996, 770–1.

54 Bradbury 1998, 115.

55 Warren 1973, 54.

56 William of Newburgh, *The History of English Affairs* I, 32, 1, Walsh and Kennedy 1988, 130–1.

57 William of Newburgh, *The History of English Affairs* II, 1, 2–3, Walsh and Kennedy 2007, 14–15.

58 Crouch 1986.

59 Crouch 1992, 63–4; Green 1997, 298–305.

60 Davis 1967, 129–44.

61 Green 1990, 12–13.

62 Green 1990, 12–13.

63 Higham and Henderson 2011, 140–1.

64 Crouch 1992, 223.

Chapter 3

Waging War: Fields of Conflict and Siege Warfare

T HE DISTRIBUTION of the different types of documented conflict events recorded in England and Wales between 1135 and 1153 is mapped in Figures 3.1a–c. These make clear both the large number and wide variety of military clashes during the conflict. Despite its duration, pitched battles were singularly rare and sieges dominated the military landscape in a conflict that was tightly focused in distinct regions. This chapter explores the landscape context of military engagement. It combines analysis of the documentary sources with scrutiny of the places of battle and the material traces of warfare to reconstruct the conduct of conflict and reveal something of its underestimated psychological and symbolic aspects (the arms and armour of the military forces of the period are examined separately in Chapter 6). Following an overview of the settings of conflict and an assessment of the two most significant battlefields (the Battle of the Standard or Northallerton, 1138, and the Battle of Lincoln, 1141), the chapter goes on to explore siege warfare in particular detail. It concludes with a case study of Wallingford, Oxfordshire, one of the most bitterly contested sites of the conflict.

Landscapes of War: Settings and Contexts

Attitudes to the conduct of medieval warfare were inextricably fused to religious belief.[1] The momentum to regulate warfare in north-west Europe in the eleventh and early twelfth centuries amounted to what some scholars have styled a 'peace movement.'[2] By the first quarter of

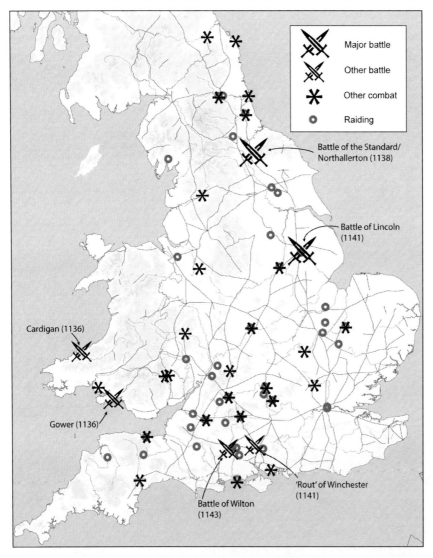

Fig 3.1: Documented conflict locations, 1135–53: **(a)** battles and other military engagements; **(b)** *page 36* depopulations, raids and devastation events; **(c)** *page 37* sieges and castle seizures. Reconstructed from a database of twelfth-century chronicles.

the twelfth century, the First Crusade had done much to rehabilitate the social validity of the *bellatores* in the eyes of the Church, but for ecclesiastical traditionalists, much acquainted with classical precedents of military discipline and service to the state, contemporary knighthood

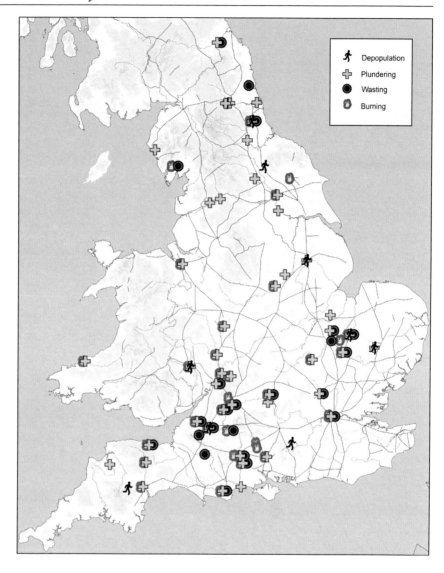

had become the antithesis of its divinely ordained function and the Church acted to regulate the excesses of conflict.[3] The Church deemed that the appropriate role of the *bellatores* was not restricted to the defence of Christendom's frontiers against external enemies, but extended to the protection of the poor and helpless and, above all, the Church.[4] The repression of pillage and exactions, respect for the Church's possessions and the establishment of protocols for truces all featured in new attitudes to warfare linked to an emerging chivalric culture. It is important to

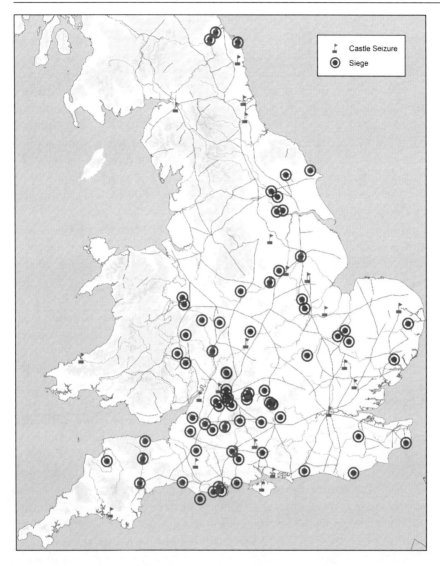

relate the conflict events of 'the Anarchy' to this wider context: to what extent were these codes of martial behaviour adhered to?

Overall, the mechanics of how war was conducted in Stephen's reign were essentially the same as under the other Anglo-Norman kings, even if the strategic context was transformed by the sheer proliferation of conflict events.[5] Chroniclers recoiled with horror at the devastating effects of wasting by field armies, although the targeting of an enemy's estates, especially during sieges, was a normal by-product of Anglo-Norman warfare rather than a phenomenon peculiar to the Stephanic conflict. Despite the bitterness and duration of the civil war, it is also important to remember that campaigning was mainly seasonal and that truces were often observed during religious festivals.[6]

The civil war's geopolitics were complex and fluid, so that the strategic map resembled a fluctuating mosaic of competing interests rather than a clear-cut pattern with distinct borders between factions. That said, the nationwide distribution of recorded conflict events relates quite strongly to a distinct Angevin heartland in central-southern England, forming an approximately diamond-shaped zone between the Isle of Purbeck in the south, Bristol in the west, Worcester in the north and Wallingford in the east. Many important sieges and clashes occurred on the northern and eastern fringes of this zone, although conflict was also distributed across the interior, as both royal and Angevin armies campaigned along east–west routes, especially within the Thames Valley. This pattern is critically important for understanding the severity and persistence of the civil war: while some of the other hotspots of the conflict were in regions with an established rebel heritage, such as Yorkshire and the Isle of Ely (which had resisted William the Conqueror in 1069–70 and 1070–71, respectively), the real fault line of the conflict ran through the traditional heartland of English kingship in Wessex. Outside this zone, documented conflict is far more sparsely distributed, if with significant scatterings in the east in parts of Cambridgeshire and Lincolnshire, in the north in Yorkshire and Northumbria, and in the south-west in Devon. While south-west England cannot be styled as a borderland, a coalition of influential families in the counties of Devon, Dorset, Cornwall and Somerset ensured that this region was a bedrock of support for the Empress in which familial ties, especially from those strongly linked to Brittany, moulded allegiance.[7] The areas without significant concentrations of conflict events, which were most obviously bypassed by the civil war, were the extreme south-east of England, East Anglia and the area west of the Pennines.

The Anglo-Welsh and Anglo-Scottish border regions, which formed the most intensively contested conflict landscapes across the medieval period more generally, had sharply different experiences during the conflict. In the north, invasion and occupation by the forces of King David of Scots took great swathes of land away from English royal control. To see this as a cross-border incursion is misleading, however: the affected area of 'northern England' was no such thing from a Scots' perspective, as their king had long-standing claims to northern

Northumbria and Cumbria. In the context of twelfth-century English political geography, the north can be regarded as a 'semi-autonomous appendage loosely tied to the remote Westminster-based core.'[8] This was a contested and fluctuating buffer zone rather than an established linear frontier.[9] By the end of the period, King David had created an 'English empire' that he and his successor Malcolm IV held until 1157.[10] The concentration of conflict events in this region is focused upon the eastern end of the border, reflecting the relative ease of access between England and Scotland at this point. This part of the border zone was characterised by powerful but under-garrisoned castles such as Norham and Wark (both Northumbria) which consistently failed to halt incursions.[11]

On the border with Wales, meanwhile, Stephen's reign saw major baronial families take opposing sides and form power bases in their castles and castelries – most prominently the Mortimers of Wigmore and the de Sais of Clun for the king and the Fitzalans of Oswestry for the Angevins, alongside a ratcheting up of hostilities by the Welsh involving raids and ambushes.[12] As the civil war progressed, direct action by Stephen against the marches became problematic because of the swathe of the West Country under Angevin control.

In stark contrast to the intense military action on England's terrestrial borders, naval conflict was unusual. Armies moved primarily by road; the Anglo-Norman military system made no evident use of inland waterways for transport: rivers were seen as obstacles rather than highways.[13] A successful integrated operation led by Stephen's queen, Matilda, against Dover in 1138 saw a fleet from Boulogne deployed on the seaward side and an army on the landward side to blockade a rebel force,[14] while amphibious warfare was a feature of the campaigns on the Cambridgeshire fens (see Chapter 9). Overall, however, naval operations were limited in effectiveness and the king seems to have been unable to prevent the Angevins using the port of Wareham, Dorset, as their key point of communication with northern France. Stephen also had a strategic interest in maintaining good maritime links with the Continent via the ports of south-east England. Particularly significant in this context is a newly discovered writ of King Stephen issued *c.* 1140 that notifies his enfeoffment of the mercenary commander William of Ypres with estates including the port of Orford on the Suffolk coast, highlighting the importance of secure access to the Anglo-Flemish maritime route to channel in mercenaries and trade.[15]

Battles and Battlefields

The image of medieval warfare provided by the Battle of Hastings, the most celebrated armed clash of the Norman period, is misleading. This was an atypical encounter in terms of scale, ferocity and decisiveness. Siege warfare was the default means of waging war in the eleventh and twelfth centuries, while ambushes, raids and other low-intensity martial events were far more common than major battles, which noble commanders often deliberately avoided (see below). This might prompt us to reflect on the extent to which 'battlefield archaeology,' focused on the sites of major clashes of arms, can represent the true nature of medieval conflict. Stephen's reign featured only two set-piece battles: the Battle of the Standard (or Northallerton) (22 August 1138) and Lincoln (2 February 1141). Two other major actions (Winchester, 1141, and Wilton, 1143) saw routs rather than both sides electing to fight in the open (see pgs 26, 221–3). Most other major military operations tended to comprise sequences of sieges and episodes of landscape wasting without large-scale battles. A prime case in point is Stephen's south-western campaign of 1136 (reconstructed in Figure 3.2), in which the royal army moved in linear fashion from location to location in order to extinguish discrete areas of rebellion centred on castles.[16]

We have only fleeting references to two battles in Wales which marked a departure from the usual pattern of asymmetric warfare: a clash in the Gower in January 1136, which may actually have been a large-scale Welsh ambush, killed 516 men (although it is unclear which side won); and in October of the same year a battle at Cardigan saw an Anglo-Flemish force defeated with many deaths, although the castle there did not fall.[17] Despite 19 years of conflict, it is salutary to note that the total number of pitched battles in England that took place across the whole of the twelfth century is actually lower than the number for either the eleventh or the thirteenth century.[18] However, this mode of fighting, in which sieges and low-intensity warfare predominated, did not necessarily mean light casualties. We of course have no accurate figures for numbers of casualties in twelfth-century warfare, but the experience of the English Civil War of the mid-seventeenth century is instructive. Even in this conflict of big battles, only 15% of the total 'battle' casualties occurred in major actions, as compared to 24% in sieges, while 47% were suffered in minor skirmishes; however, the vast majority of military deaths were attributed to non-combat circumstances, especially outbreaks of disease during sieges.[19]

'Rational' military behaviour does not always explain the location of conflict landscapes; in the Early Middle Ages favoured sites for battles were specific topographical locations that were readily identifiable and easily located.[20] Conflict landscapes of the Anglo-Norman world were not without symbolism of their own. In Stephen's reign a very high proportion of military actions were directed at people rather than places, so that a military strategy apparently aimed at securing territory was instead intended to attack a rival's landed assets and demonstrate his inability to fulfil the obligations of lordship. Capturing rather than killing noble opponents was often the aim in twelfth-century warfare.

Fig. 3.2: King Stephen's south-west campaign of 1136. Reconstructed from twelfth-century chronicles. Map work by Oliver Creighton and Robert Higham.

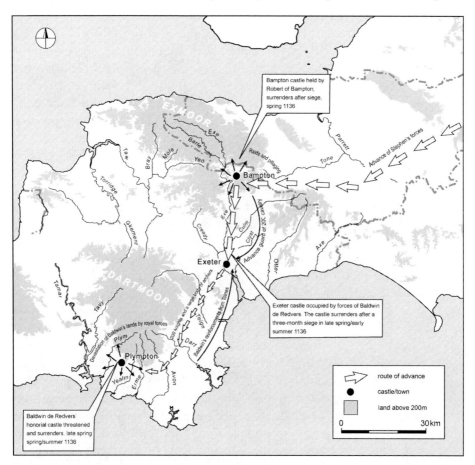

Often, too much was at stake for the nobility to risk all in a major clash of arms: open battle was the last resort rather than the first instinct of baronial commanders. Stephen's failure to bring Robert of Gloucester to battle in his south-western campaign early in 1140 and his inability to confront Henry of Anjou near York in the summer of 1149 are further cases in point. Stephen's successor, Henry II, has also been characterised as 'a specialist in battles which did not take place.'[21] No fighting occurred at Breteuil in 1173, despite Henry's army being drawn up opposite the French, while peace was brokered at Châteauroux in 1187 by the bishops with the two armies again arrayed for battle.[22] An extreme case is the Battle of the Two Kings (Brémule) fought between Henry I of England and Charles VI ('the Fat') of France in Normandy in 1119.[23] Orderic Vitalis reports that of the 900 knights engaged at Brémule, only three were killed; this was partly because of their armour ('They were all clad in mail'), but more important was the fact that combatants 'spared each other on both sides out of fear of God and fellowship in arms; they were more concerned to capture than to kill the fugitives. As Christian soldiers they did not thirst for the blood of their brothers.'[24] In the following century, during the Second Barons' War a 'newly discovered' eyewitness account of the Battle of Evesham in 1264 reveals how the future Edward I handpicked a 'death squad' of 12 men-at-arms to kill Simon de Montfort.[25] This calculating approach to de Montfort's slaughter might also explain the landscape setting of the battle, with the Montfortians deliberately isolated and encircled on top of a hill to prevent escape and to ensure their annihilation. This contrasts sharply with how noble adversaries were targeted for capture rather than slaughter during the Anarchy.

Direct military attacks on the king were actually exceptionally rare in Anglo-Norman warfare. In the context of baronial rebellions, most actions were fought in the absence of the king, rebels being reluctant or fearful of confronting 'the Lord's anointed' on the field of conflict.[26] The civil war of 'the Anarchy' was as much characterised by the deliberate avoidance of battle as large-scale clashes of arms. Twice in 1153, during the closing stages of the conflict, large royal and Angevin armies faced off across rivers but backed down: at Malmesbury, Wiltshire, where the forces were arrayed either side of the swollen Avon;[27] and at Wallingford, Oxfordshire, where negotiations across the Thames concluded the lengthy but indecisive siege and brought the war to a close (see also pg. 73).[28] River locations were not only chosen as places of potential conflict, they were also favoured landscapes for peace making. During 1138, in the events leading up to the Battle of the Standard, a delegation of English lords met King David I of Scots on the banks of the River Tees in an effort to stop his invasion.[29] As traditional environments for conflict resolution, rivers not only frequently delineated territorial boundaries, but also offered a neutral setting for negotiation that minimised the risk of loss of face and life.[30]

The Battle of the Standard (1138) and the Battle of Lincoln (1141)

Reconstructions of the two main pitched battles of Stephen's reign, at Northallerton and Lincoln, are offered in Figures 3.3a–b. It is worth reflecting, however, that such conventional mapped representations of battlefields give an aloof and divorced perspective.[31] Neatly plotted dispositions of troops obscure the harsh contemporary reality of frenzied engagements that descended into individual battles for survival. Few combatants on the ground likely appreciated the strategic importance of topography in the manner of military historians: any combatant's radius of visibility was limited and commanders will not have had a full overview. Contemporary sources make clear that there was a dense early morning fog that would have obscured the terrain altogether at the Battle of the Standard. We can also easily neglect the importance of the hullabaloo – or soundscape – of war, which in a twelfth-century context is captured by chroniclers' references to war cries and blaring trumpets that identified friend from foe, rallied forces and boosted morale.[32]

The pitched clashes at Northallerton and Lincoln occurred in very specific circumstances and, as noted above, are not actually very representative of conflict in the civil war more generally. In fact, the Battle of the Standard was not strictly part of the 'civil war' at all, as it witnessed the defeat of an invading force, while the Battle of Lincoln was effectively the by-product of a siege. The outcome of neither battle did much to alter the overall trajectory of the conflict: despite crushing defeat for King David at Northallerton, the Scots remained in possession of Cumberland and Northumberland, while Stephen's defeat and capture at Lincoln in 1141 had little impact on the outcome of the war, being reversed later that year by the capture of Earl Robert of Gloucester at Winchester and the exchange of the two leaders. The general vicinities in which the two battles took place are well known, although pinning down their precise locations relies heavily on the interpretation of historic landscape evidence. Neither site has seen a detailed archaeological survey although the Battle of the Standard has by far the highest potential for future work: the battlefield

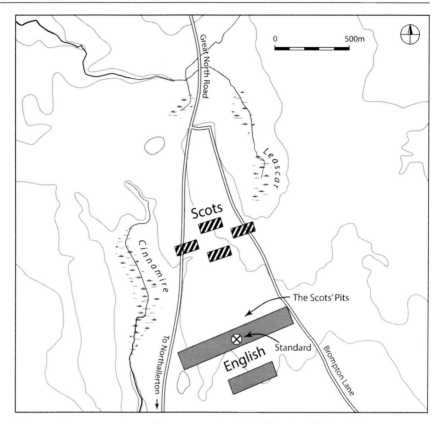

Fig. 3.3: Reconstructions of the two main pitched battles of the civil war:
(**a**) *above* Battle of the Standard (1138); and (**b**) *opposite* Battle of Lincoln (1141).
Drawing by Seán Goddard, incorporating information from Foard and Morris
2012; Jones et al. 2003.

is unobscured by later development (unlike Lincoln); the far larger
number of combatants involved will have led to greater artefact loss;
and the opposing forces had contrasting tactics and, to some extent,
apparel, which will have left distinctive archaeological signatures and
inflicted particular forms of trauma on victims (see also pgs 160–2).

The main events of the Battle of the Standard are reconstructed
largely from accounts by Abbot Aelred of Rievaulx and Henry of
Huntingdon, both of whom detail pre-battle speeches that provide vivid
insights into the psychology of the English forces and the moral and
religious justifications for an action against a foe viewed as marauding
barbarians.[33] English deployment determined the location of the action
although the force then remained static and the Scots' initiative instead

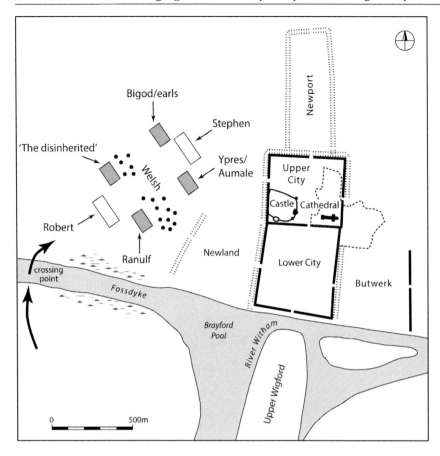

dictated the flow of the action (Fig. 3.3a). The English army, large by Anglo-Norman standards but outnumbered, was composed of county levies and urban militias, stiffened by household knights sent by Stephen and others supplied by nobles from the Midlands and the north of England. It deployed on the plain north of Northallerton to block the Scots' southern advance down the Great North Road. The English knights fought dismounted, intermingled with the infantry in a great mass around their standard – a ship's mast mounted on a wagon, displaying saints' banners and topped with a pyx holding the consecrated host, constituting a spiritual weapon as well as a rallying point.[34] The Scots deployed with King David in the rear, a mounted force under his son Henry on the right, and much larger forces of Galwegians and men of Lothian in the left and centre, although their exact disposition is less clear.

The action had two distinct phases. The unarmoured Galwegians demanded their right to lead the first charge, which disintegrated into chaos under volleys of English arrows, leaving two of their leaders dead. A second but smaller-scale Scots attack by mounted knights under Henry met with greater success, breaking through the line on the English flank before being repulsed. Collapse and withdrawal of the Scots army soon followed. Many modern accounts of the Battle of the Standard stress the decisive effect of English archery on the battlefield long before the Hundred Years' War.[35] We should also take into account, however, how Anglo-Norman propagandists magnified the extent of the Scottish defeat and overemphasised the Galwegians' culpability in it.[36] Historic landscape analysis has a critical role in clarifying our understanding of the action. The site of a mass grave ('Scots Pits') survived as an earthwork until the nineteenth century and can be located precisely from place name and historic map evidence; this is likely to be close to the point where the Galwegian charge met the English line, placing the core of the battlefield a little further south than usually thought.[37] Reconstruction of the surrounding environment based on field names shows how the English occupied an area of open field flanked by slightly lower-lying marshy areas that would have funnelled in the initial attack and might have limited the effectiveness of Henry's flanking charge.

Accurate reconstruction of the historic landscape is equally critical in understanding Stephen's defeat at Lincoln by a larger Angevin force commanded by the Earls of Chester and Gloucester and supported by a contingent of Welsh infantry (Fig. 3.3b). The documentary sources are explicit that Stephen left his siege of Lincoln Castle and the high ground around the city to meet the advancing Angevins, who had scattered a royalist holding force and forded the Foss Dyke; thus, the action is usually placed immediately west of the city.[38] An important factor not taken into consideration in traditional reconstructions of the battlefield is that the western suburb of Newland was probably in existence by the mid-twelfth century, which would place the action a little further west or, more likely, north.[39] William of Malmesbury's account recalls that Stephen's knights 'first attempted that prelude to the fight which is called jousting, for in this they were accomplished'[40] before the Angevins rode down and scattered them, fighting with swords rather than lances.[41] The sieges of Ludlow in 1139 and Winchester in 1141 also featured such war games outside city walls (see pg. 181). An area recorded from the thirteenth century as 'Battle Place' (also 'Trial Piece') lay immediately west of Lincoln Castle and the city, outside the walls on the likely site of the battlefield; it is interpreted as the traditional site of trial by battle, being attached to the castle and near the county gallows.[42] Could this tournament venue have been transformed into a battlefield proper? After a second charge by the opposite wing of the royalist force had met with greater success but was sent fleeing, the core of the action focused on an Angevin assault upon the mass of dismounted knights and infantry around Stephen. As noted above, the default position on the twelfth-century battlefield was to capture rather than kill noble opponents, and Stephen was eventually taken prisoner after a spirited struggle. By contrast, retribution against the historic city was vicious: the victors sacked Lincoln 'like barbarians' and 'slaughtered like cattle all the rest of the citizens they could find or capture,' while hundreds more drowned escaping the carnage.[43]

Siege Warfare

Landscapes of siege warfare merit particularly close scrutiny as this mode of warfare dominated the conflict and aspects of its landscape context can be reconstructed through physical evidence in the form of siege castles.[44] The mid-twelfth century saw the largest spike in recorded incidences of siege warfare in England across the entire medieval period.[45] Across the Anarchy period, 1135–53, documentary sources record 105 separate sieges involving 75 sites, with a long list of places including Lincoln, Malmesbury, Wallingford and Worcester besieged on multiple occasions. The distinction between sieges and lower-intensity attacks or raids is a fine one, however, and the terminology used by chroniclers to describe these events is often problematic and inconsistent.

The total number of sieges must have been larger still as some doubtless went unrecorded or are concealed in generic references to campaigning in particular regions – for example Stephen's foray into the Scottish Lowlands in 1138 and his south-western campaign of 1140 – while other undocumented sieges are evidenced by the earthworks of siege castles, as with sites such as Beacon Hill, Pickering in North Yorkshire and East Chelborough in Dorset (see below). Again, however, there is a blurred distinction between siege warfare proper and stand-offs between rival lords whose interests were represented by castles built in close proximity and held against each other in conditions of mutual hostility if not open conflict.[46] A good example is the Devon parish of Winkleigh, where the separate earthworks of two earth and timber castles (Croft Castle and Court Castle) lie in the same village yet within separate manors, and are usually ascribed an Anarchy-period date.[47]

The vast majority of documented sieges (78%) targeted castles; others involved fortified towns (18%) or churches pressed into military use (4%). This broad pattern conceals considerable complexity, however: in some instances, castle and town were held together as an integrated unit, as at Bristol (1138) and Wallingford (1139–40, 1146 and 1152–53). More commonly, however, urban castles or palaces resisted independent of the cities within which they lay, as at Exeter (1136), Lincoln (1141), Winchester (1141) and Oxford (1142). Another consideration is that some besieged sites which chroniclers styled as 'castles' equated to garrisoned towns rather than implying that new castles had been built, as at Wilton (1143) and Cricklade (1144) for example (see also pgs 226–7).

Siege engines and technologies

Typical Anarchy-period sieges were drawn-out affairs in whose outcome the morale of one side or the other usually proved a more decisive factor than the success of an armed storming. The conventions of twelfth-century siege warfare arguably represent a conscious attempt by the knightly and noble classes to moderate the full violence of warfare and thus minimise its impact on their own sort, although the peasantry remained vulnerable to a martial culture quite happy to ravage territories and execute non-noble prisoners.[48] An interesting measure of how far contemporary armies could ravage is Symeon of Durham's account of Henry I's siege of Pont Audemer, Normandy, in 1123, and how the king's troops devastated the lands surrounding the castle in a circle 20 miles across, perhaps implying that the whole honour was targeted.[49] The logistical needs of even small medieval armies could be immense: a Norman warhorse required 12 pounds of grain (oats or good barley) and 13 pounds of hay per day, not to mention great volumes of fresh straw and clean water.[50] Sieges were protracted, which also meant that armies had to forage progressively further from their bases to source supplies.

Only exceptionally were attacks as direct as that on Winchcombe, Gloucestershire, in 1144: here, Stephen ordered that his men 'make ready with all speed for the storming of the castle, that some should advance shooting clouds of arrows, others should crawl up the mound and everyone else should rush rapidly round the fortifications and throw in anything that came to hand.'[51] This sounds like medieval 'shock and awe' – a show of force to put psychological pressure on the defending garrison. Even so, it is instructive that the castle was still given up by agreement rather than falling to the assault.

Siege engines were mainly used by Stephen's forces – not only because he was the aggressor in the majority of cases, but because of his access to skilled engineers. Engineers and materials could be critical in the success of sieges but were clearly costly; strikingly, the *Gesta Stephani* claims that the three-month siege of Exeter cost King Stephen almost 15,000 marks,[52] although this insight is exceptional. That the logistical networks needed to support major sieges in the twelfth century could span entire regions is indicated by pipe roll evidence for the reign of Henry II: at the 1173 siege of Leicester the king called on 115 carpenters from Leicestershire and Warwickshire and 24 from Staffordshire, equipment for siege machines from Northamptonshire and other core materials, including arrows, spades and pickaxes from Gloucestershire and Worcestershire.[53]

Events in the Latin East show that techniques of siege warfare could evolve rapidly during intense periods of conflict, but the conflict of Stephen's reign provides no evidence for changes in tactics. Twelfth-century siege warfare drew on Roman models: at the siege of Montreuil-en-Bellay in 1147, Geoffrey of Anjou consulted Book IV of Vegetius's *Epitoma rei militaris* and produced an incendiary bomb that could be hurled at beams that the defenders had used to repair their fortress.[54] While Vegetius contained no specific information on such devices, it was important to rulers to demonstrate cognisance of ancient traditions. Stephen used smoke and fire to suppress the defenders of Shrewsbury in 1138,[55] and in the same year his siege engine at Castle Cary, Somerset, 'scattered fire and showers of stones among the besieged,'[56] but most direct assaults employed far simpler tactics. Scaling ladders were employed at Bath (1138), Devizes (1140) and Malmesbury (1153).[57] The Scots made some use of engines against borderland castles such as at Wark, Northumberland (1138), although with limited effectiveness, suggesting inexperience in the Anglo-Norman style of siege warfare.[58] There are no references to siege towers (or 'belfries') in the conflict in England, although the technique was in contemporary use in Normandy.[59] Henry I employed a belfry to attack Pont Audemer Castle in 1123; it was tall enough to overlook the castle ramparts by 20 feet, enabling archers and crossbowmen to pour fire on the defenders.[60] Chroniclers' generic descriptions of 'engines' (*machinas*) often make it difficult to tell what these devices were used for. An un-named engine 'rising high in the air' at Stephen's siege of Exeter Castle in 1136 may have been used for observation rather than assault, and was probably immobile.[61]

Mining was used only exceptionally in the eleventh and twelfth century; it was deployed by William the Conqueror against the walls of Exeter in 1068,[62] and in the 1136 siege of Exeter Castle, King Stephen summoned skilled miners to undermine the wall.[63] Mining was most suited to attacks on masonry fortifications without water defences, which might also explain the reference to a work constructed against Lincoln by Stephen in 1144: nearly 80 workmen were buried alive while building an earthwork (*munitionem*) against the castle.[64] The capability of twelfth-century mining techniques is demonstrated by an archaeological discovery of the 1930s at Bungay Castle, Suffolk: an unfinished mining gallery, *c.* 8m long and with two smaller lateral galleries, had been driven at an angle through the foundations of the keep; this was identified by the excavator as part of the documented siege of 1174.[65] Henry of Huntingdon describes a dramatic event at the siege of Ludlow, Shropshire, in 1139, when Prince Henry, the son of King David of Scots, who was accompanying the English king on military operations, 'was pulled off his horse by an iron hook [*unco ferreo*]' but rescued by Stephen before he could be taken captive.[66] This seems to have been a 'crow' – a kind of giant fishing rod wielded from the wall-head.[67]

Chroniclers are inconsistent in their usage of terminology for bombarding siege engines; the Latin term *petraria* ('stone-thrower') is sometimes used, but exactly which technologies were employed is the subject of debate in the absence of archaeological support.[68] Crucially, the notion that the technology of the torsion-powered late Roman *onager* remained in use into the Middle Ages, as perpetuated in much academic as well as popular literature on medieval siege warfare, appears to be no more than a myth.[69] Instead, the characteristic siege artillery of the mid-twelfth century was the 'traction trebuchet': a rotating beam engine powered by a human team who pulled down on one side of the beam to hurl a stone projectile using a sling connected to the other (Fig. 3.4). In England, the counterweight trebuchet was seemingly not deployed until the second decade of the thirteenth century, when it was used to besiege castles including Dover and Berkhamsted, Hertfordshire (in 1216), where earthwork platforms for these machines (or conceivably others used in its defence) still survive around the site's perimeter.[70]

Experimental reconstructions allow us to gauge something of the effectiveness of traction trebuchets. Rocks weighing an average of 2.5kg

Fig. 3.4: Traction trebuchet, as depicted on a bas relief in the church of Saint-Nazaire and Saint-Celse, Carcassonne, France. Photograph by Oliver Creighton.

can be consistently hurled 100m with a high level of accuracy; smaller projectiles have been recorded achieving ranges up to 137m.[71] The relatively modest crew required (as few as 12 pullers) and the relative simplicity of the machine (with no more than two dozen structural components and no single part too heavy for a single person to lift) highlights the suitability of these devices for rapid relocation from one site to another. That said, the traction trebuchet would have had limited effectiveness against well-built stone curtain walls, especially given the parabolic arc along which stones were hurled. Its primary use would have been to hurl projectiles into the interior of fortifications rather than to try to batter down perimeter defences, and the psychological impact of such missiles may have been just as important as any physical damage inflicted.

Landscapes of Siege Warfare: Siege Castles

Siege castles are an especially characteristic but frequently misunderstood facet of Anglo-Norman conflict. These sites are sometimes styled in the literature on siege warfare as 'counter-castles'; the word 'siege-work' is also occasionally used but best avoided, as it has connotations of post-medieval artillery fortifications built as platforms for bombardment, and can also describe mines and siege lines constructed to protect attacking forces. In the modern vocabulary, siege castles are best equated with the word 'fieldwork.'[72] They were recognised as a distinct category of site by a major early pioneer of castle studies, Ella Armitage, who distinguished between works placed immediately outside defences for the purpose of bombardment and the siege castle proper, whose 'purpose was not for actual attack, but to watch the besieged fort and prevent supplies from being carried in.'[73] Most Anglo-Norman siege castles were of this latter type – self-contained strongpoints, usually of earth and timber, erected to blockade and support attacks on enemy fortifications. Of those siege castles where we have clear evidence of their physical form, it is apparent that most were built as small ringworks – a form whose advantage over the motte in terms of construction time was critically important in siege warfare.[74] Through the thirteenth and fourteenth century the increasing power and range of siege artillery ensured that new techniques of direct assault on castles and towns were in the ascendency, and siege castles disappear from the records. Equivalent fortifications built in the age of gunpowder artillery were of very different form; in the Hundred Years' War, the English bastilles built during the siege of Orléans in 1428–29 formed a complex of linked strongpoints around the city, some of them able to contain 350–400 men.[75]

While twelfth-century chroniclers usually identified a siege castle with the word *castellum*, these sites do not conform to castles as conventionally understood. Most were built on land to which their builders had no tenurial rights and they were never intended as permanent residences.[76] Their lack of longevity and construction technologies should not lull us into characterising siege castles as somehow primitive martial features, however. Careful scrutiny of their uses and landscape settings shows that they also had psychological value. The following account considers first the employment of siege castles by earlier Anglo-Norman kings before turning to their use in Stephen's reign.

Siege castles in the late eleventh and early twelfth century
In the decades before and after the Norman Conquest, Duke William's campaigns in Normandy and on its frontiers often entailed the construction of siege castles. The fortification he built to blockade Arques, Pas-de-Calais, in 1053 was strong enough to resist a vigorous attack by King Henry I of France, for example, while William's protracted and ultimately unsuccessful siege of Sainte Suzanne, Mayenne, in 1083–85 reused an extant Gallo-Roman or perhaps prehistoric site as a fortified campaign base.[77] The earliest known deployment of siege castles in England was by William II against Rochester, in 1088, when two such

strongpoints were built, both now lost.[78] Better documented is Rufus's construction of a siege castle against Bamburgh Castle, the stronghold of the rebellious Earl of Northumbria, Robert de Mowbray, in 1095.[79] The Anglo-Saxon Chronicle makes quite clear that the king resorted to this tactic upon realising that he could not capture the castle by other means.[80] William Rufus built his siege castle, named Malveisin ('Bad Neighbour'), 'in front' of Bamburgh; it was clearly within shouting distance of its prey, since rival forces exchanged insults.[81] When the king had moved on to Wales to put down another disturbance, the siege castle's garrison spotted the earl's move towards Tynemouth and orchestrated an action in which Robert was wounded and captured; he was then taken back to Bamburgh, where he was displayed and threatened with having his eyes put out unless the castle was given up, which promptly happened.[82]

Henry I also employed siege castles in England, most prominently at Arundel, West Sussex, in 1102,[83] but more frequently to quell rebellions in Normandy. It was the besieged rather than the besiegers who named the two counter-castles he built against Gasny at some point between 1116 and 1118; they mocked the location of one (*Malassis*, 'Ill-placed') and the appearance of the other (*Tulla Leporus*, 'Hare's Form').[84] Another, erected outside Old Rouen, was named *Mate-putain* ('Whore-humbler') out of contempt for Countess Hawise, who had been instrumental in the rebellion.[85] Actions around siege castles could be complex and bloody: in the Brémule campaign of 1119, Henry I built a blockading work against the castle of Évreux and left it under his star commander, Ralph the Red of Pont-Echanfray; it was attacked by Amaury de Montfort's relieving force and bitterly contested in a struggle that claimed many lives over several days.[86] Likewise, Henry's blockading castle at Vatteville, built in 1123–24, was the focus of a counter-attack by rebels who were eventually brought to battle upon returning from their raid.[87]

Siege castles in the Anarchy: archaeology and landscape evidence
If the tactical employment of siege castles in Stephen's reign followed a pattern that was already established, the extent of their usage was unprecedented:[88] at least 17 examples are recorded in documentary sources and others are suggested by field evidence (Fig. 3.5). Earthwork plans of a sample of the better preserved sites are presented in Figure 3.6. Even so, such evidence must still underestimate the actual number of siege castles constructed in the period, especially given the thoroughness of their subsequent slighting. In several cases, chroniclers specify that sieges were long and arduous but do not relate

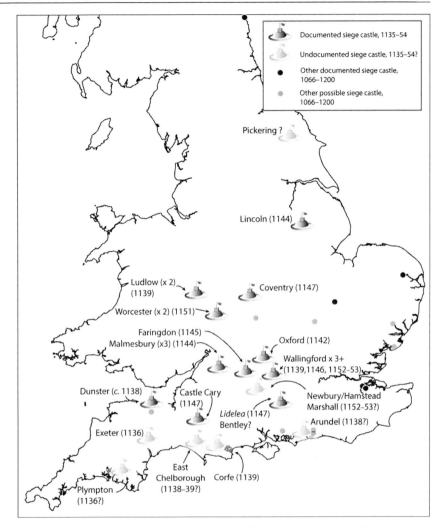

Fig. 3.5: Distribution of siege castles built or likely to have been built 1135–54, plus others of the late eleventh and twelfth century. Reconstructed from a database of twelfth-century chronicles and other sources. Map work by Steven Trick and Oliver Creighton.

that siege castles were built when they probably were, their use being almost *de rigueur* in this protracted mode of cat-and-mouse warfare. Earthworks at Corfe in Dorset ('the Rings') and Exeter in Devon ('Danes Castle') are clear examples of undocumented siege castles that are almost certainly related to documented twelfth-century sieges (see below); siege castles could well have been employed also at the

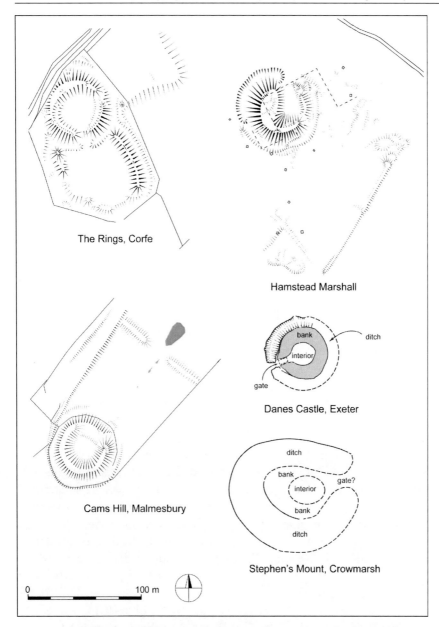

The Rings, Corfe

Hamstead Marshall

bank
ditch
interior
gate

Danes Castle, Exeter

Cams Hill, Malmesbury

ditch
bank
gate?
interior
bank
ditch

Stephen's Mount, Crowmarsh

0   100 m

Fig. 3.6: Plans of siege castles built or likely to have been built 1135–54.
Source: plan of Danes Castle based on Higham and Henderson 2011;
Crowmarsh Castle based on Laban 2013; other plans are original surveys.
Drawings by Michael Fradley, Mike Rouillard and Oliver Creighton.

sieges of Bedford (1138 and 1153), Ludlow (1139), Pevensey (1147), Trowbridge (1139), Stamford (1153) and Tutbury (1153). Other sieges were unrecorded, as is probably the case with the event that led to the construction of the ringwork known as 'the Beacon' adjacent to Pickering Castle, North Yorkshire.[89] One of the closely juxtaposed mottes at East Chelborough, Dorset, is another prime candidate for an undocumented Stephanic siege castle; the place's geostrategic context in the civil war points to a putative construction date of 1138–39.[90] Siege castles also continued to be used in Normandy through the period: at Count Geoffrey of Anjou's siege of Montreuil-Bellay from 1149–51, for example, several were built to surround the place and protect his forces.[91]

Following the Anarchy, siege castles were not abandoned entirely as a tool of warfare in Henry II's reign. In 1174, a royalist force built a siege work to contain Earl David's garrison in Huntingdon Castle; archaeological investigation of the site has shown it to have been a timber-revetted motte established on a low natural mound occupied first by a Roman villa and then an Anglo-Saxon church.[92] Siege castles did not feature in the Anglo-Norman conquest of Ireland in the late twelfth century, however, when Hiberno-Norse fortified centres such as Dublin, Waterford and Wexford were taken into Anglo-Norman control without attested set-piece sieges.

The landscape contexts of siege castles and the limited missile range of contemporary traction trebuchets confirm that they were not intended as platforms for direct bombardment. They were typically constructed beyond bow range (*c.* 180–270m from their target), but in Normandy and England could alternatively be located several kilometres distant, in which case they were clearly intended to blockade.[93] The strategy of building siege castles ensured that a large army or a leader was not immobilised and pinned down to a specific objective, which was important in a dynamic conflict environment when threats developed rapidly in different locations. A siege castle allowed a modest force to contain an enemy stronghold, avoiding the risk of mass casualties or catastrophic failure through direct assault. It deterred armed forays and denied foraging parties free access to the hinterland, while also blocking movements by relieving forces. Attacks on siege castles were not usually sallies by besieged garrisons but counterstrokes by relieving forces, often from unexpected directions.

While siege castles are the primary archaeological trace of Anarchy-period sieges, interpretation of the evidence is challenging, not least given the pitfalls of correlating chroniclers' accounts with physical remains in the field. Being temporary sites, and often slighted (deliberately destroyed) after use, few siege castles survive as well-preserved field monuments. Remains are mainly small, eroded and unimpressive. They can, however, have multiphase histories: the key example of Danes Castle, Exeter (discussed below) has been interpreted variously as a Norman motte or outwork of the city's royal castle, but also as a prehistoric ritual enclosure, a Roman amphitheatre and a late medieval theatre; it was probably left unfinished and was used much later as an animal pound in the early modern period, and perhaps as a gun emplacement in the English Civil War.[94] The few archaeological excavations of siege castles have yielded few artefacts and poor dating evidence, and the fact that these were purely military installations without manorial functions means that the internal buildings typically found in twelfth-century castles – halls, chapels and service buildings, for example – are entirely absent; indeed, several were left unfinished. Two archaeological excavations of sites built for King Stephen are crucial to our understanding of the construction and appearance of Anarchy-period siege castles and are considered in turn: Danes Castle, Exeter, which was excavated in 1992–93, having been buried beneath a reservoir since the mid-nineteenth century, and Stephen's Mount, Crowmarsh, Berkshire, which was evaluated in 2011 during a trial excavation prior to site redevelopment for housing.

The Danes Castle excavations give us the best insight into a siege castle of the period, almost certainly dating to Stephen's siege of Exeter Castle (Rougemont Castle) in 1136, although it is puzzlingly not mentioned in the otherwise full account of the encounter in the *Gesta Stephani*.[95] The site (Fig. 3.6; see also Figs 1.2 and 3.2) comprises a powerfully defended but compact circular ringwork, *c.* 55m across including its ditched and embanked defences and with an interior area only *c.* 17m across. The defensive ditch was 7–8m wide and 3.8m deep and the rampart, of dump construction, up to 11m across and perhaps originally 4m high. The powerful defences were superimposed upon ridge and furrow of a field system containing some early twelfth-century pottery. That Stephen chose to build his siege castle in this extramural location – overlooking Rougemont Castle from a prominent open position on the opposite site of the valley – is striking as the king had control of the city, and suggests a public act of defiance in the face of rebellion as well as blockading the rebel-held castle. The site's archaeology is remarkably simple, the interior bereft of any signs of occupation and sterile in terms of artefacts despite near-total excavation. The only sign of pretension was evidence for a timber-built gate tower, its post-holes dug but never filled with timbers, confirming that the site was unfinished. At Cam's Hill, near Malmesbury, another ringwork probably built as an Anarchy-period siege castle (probably in 1144), geophysical survey shows similar furnishing of its entrance with a tower gateway.[96]

Crowmarsh Castle, near Wallingford, was subject to less comprehensive excavation than Danes Castle, but 13 evaluation trenches, combined with a large-scale stripping, mapping and recording exercise, revealed an ovoid enclosure of similar form but slightly larger proportions (Fig. 3.6). Surrounded by a ditch *c.* 25m wide and surviving to a depth of *c.* 2–3m (although the upper levels had been truncated), the work enclosed an internal area *c.* 35m across, dumped chalk blocks indicating that some form of embanked internal structure was present before a large-scale episode of slighting.[97] The site produced one of the more important Anarchy-period assemblages of pottery (832 sherds, 13.07kg) in England, remarkable not only for its homogeneity, which enables the fortification to be ascribed a mid-twelfth-century date with near total certainty, but also for the light it casts on everyday life in this short-lived site (the construction date and context of the site are discussed below in the case study of Wallingford). The extremely high proportion of jugs and pitchers (26% of the total sherd count) suggests a style of consumption more akin to a high-status manorial site than a garrison's bolthole, and despite its royal connections the ceramic products were overwhelmingly locally sourced, with outliers coming from no further than east Wiltshire. An assemblage of charred plant remains indicated the presence of free-threshing wheats that had been cultivated to mill for flour, and barley destined for brewing; the small finds included a high proportion of high-status and military items, including horse fittings, knives and plain dress ornaments.

Excavation on other mid-twelfth-century siege castle sites has been rather less informative. Investigation of a small motte-and-bailey siege castle at Bentley, Hampshire, built 300m from the much larger ringwork and bailey known as Barley Pound, serves to highlight many of these issues. Trial trenches revealed no evidence whatsoever of internal buildings or of a motte-top superstructure. While the motte ditch was quite substantial, V-shaped in profile, 6–7m wide and up to 2.8m deep, its bailey was defined only by a low bank, originally no more than 1m wide and revetted with a rough chalk wall, and the motte itself would have stood only *c.* 1.2m above ground level.[98] These 'defences' were hastily built and temporary, the bailey perhaps demarcating an area where horses were tethered or troops encamped.

Fig. 3.7: Aerial view of Corfe Castle, Dorset, and the siege work of 'the Rings' towards the top of the photograph. Source: © English Heritage.

In terms of surviving field monuments, as opposed to excavated evidence, the best-preserved siege castle that can firmly be dated to the civil war is the earthwork known as 'the Rings' at Corfe, Dorset (Figs 3.6 and 3.7), set on a low ridge 300m distant from the imposing royal castle occupied by Baldwin de Redvers in 1139 and blockaded by Stephen in a long but unsuccessful siege.[99] The powerful ringwork and bailey defences are clearly integrated and the scale of the work is little different from that of a permanent lordly earth-and-timber castle, although reworking during the English Civil War of the 1640s is apparent in the form of an internal step within the ringwork (the site is labelled 'Cromwell's Battery' on the nineteenth-century tithe map). Geophysical survey also indicates anomalies within the bailey interior that point to later reuse rather than twelfth-century occupation.[100] The site's remarkable level of preservation, immediately below and in full view of the royal castle, is an anomaly and might even point to a conscious desire to preserve or even curate the site in the later medieval period, which is at odds with the usual pattern of slighting and erasing monuments associated with political disorder.

An earthwork within parkland at Hamstead Marshall, near Newbury, Berkshire, is another informative site as it seems to represent a partly completed siege castle of the period (Fig. 3.6); from this we can learn about construction methods. A marking-out ditch defined the circular perimeter of the castle earthwork, which was created by transporting spoil up an earthwork ramp on the north side of the site.[101] The monument is one of three castle earthworks within the parish, lying 800m east of two adjacent motte-and-bailey castles, one of which seems to have succeeded the other.[102] The most likely context for the siege castle is King Stephen's 1152–53 siege of the 'lost' castle of Newbury, which he took by assault.[103] Archaeological excavation in the area of Newbury Wharf, where 'Newbury' Castle was traditionally thought to lie, has identified no evidence of a fortification here,[104] and an alternative explanation is that the 'lost' castle is more convincingly associated with the remains in Hamstead Marshall Park.[105]

Another likely site of one or more 'lost' siege castles is Oxford, where Matilda held out in the castle for three months in 1142 before making her dramatic escape across the frozen Thames. During the siege Stephen probably used the royal palace later known as Beaumont Palace, outside the North Gate, as his base, and while the site was not fortified it would have possessed a wall and substantial gate.[106] Immediately outside the castle's northern ditched defences, and therefore between it and Beaumont Palace, lay two prominent mounds known as Mount Pellam and Jews' Mount, identified in the mid-sixteenth century as siege works of the period.[107] They are depicted (but unnamed) on Aggas's map of 1578 and on maps of the seventeenth and eighteenth century, but were later built over and lost.[108] They were close together and might equate to a ringwork/motte and a bailey rather than two separate siege castles. Other candidates for Stephanic siege castles are more problematic. Outside Arundel there are several sites that, while usually dated to the siege of 1102 during the revolt against Henry I, may have been used by Stephen to besiege Matilda in 1139.[109] The form of King Stephen's siege work built against the Earl of Gloucester's new castle at Faringdon, Oxfordshire, in 1145 remains a mystery. Here the king's men 'surrounded themselves with a rampart and stockade' (*uallo et propugnaculis caute circumcingerent*), apparently to protect themselves from a sudden counter-attack, prior to bombarding and then assaulting the earl's stronghold, although the castle was given up in a shady deal and not taken by force.[110] Extensive geophysical survey around the site of Faringdon Clump, traditionally held to be the site of the earl's castle, reveals nothing identifiable as a siege castle, however. Also completely unidentified are the locations of the forts Stephen had built against Ludlow in 1139 'in two places … garrisoned with strong military forces.'[111]

Where chroniclers supply details about the location of siege castles it is usually in relation to the visual relationships between these sites and their targets, rather than specifying the positions they were built in. The *Gesta Stephani* describes several siege castles as being built 'in front' of their prey, as at Coventry, Warwickshire,[112] Castle Cary, Somerset,[113] and 'Lidelea' (location uncertain, but perhaps Barley Pound, Hampshire; see pg. 58)[114] (all in 1147), and Wallingford, Oxfordshire (1152);[115] that at Dunster, Somerset (1139), was 'before the very eyes of the enemy.'[116] In 1152 the Angevin cause was weakened by the fact that many of their castles had royal siege works 'within sight' of them.[117] The importance of this visual link between besiegers and besieged could be magnified further by the shock tactic of hanging, or threatening to hang, captives in garrisons' view, as occurred at Bampton, Devon (1136) and Devizes, Wiltshire (1139 and 1140). An unusually detailed and vivid description of King Stephen's 1152 siege of 'Newbury' Castle in the poem *Histoire de Guillaume le Maréchal* details how the young William Marshal, then a royal hostage, was threatened first with hanging in front of his father's castle and then with being slung into it with a siege engine.[118]

Visual relationships between siege works and their target castles are represented in Plate 4. This depicts 'viewsheds,' or areas which were intervisible with the sites. If part of the purpose of siege castles was to signal the imperilment of garrisons or urban populations, they would have served also to boost the spirits and security of besieging forces, providing protection and a focal point of activity in otherwise drawn-out and morale-sapping encounters. The display of banners was an essential part of eleventh- and twelfth-century warfare, being symbolic of lordly authority as well as territorial control; they were flown over captured castles and towns and are prominent in pictorial sources,[119] and it is natural to imagine that they would have bedecked siege castles too.

An important dimension of medieval conflict, often underes-timated, is the use of violence as a 'communicative strategy' that built and affirmed the identities of groups as they conducted and presented themselves for war.[120] In many senses, siege castles were the materialisation of exactly this. They were an extension of the powerful military aura or charisma exerted by Anglo-Norman kings. The very presence of a king could be decisive in a period when rebels very rarely confronted a royal lord 'hallowed by unction.'[121] Sieges and siege castle building could be spectacles that put magnates' allegiance on public display: thus Stephen personally conducted the 1136 siege of Exeter Castle 'before the eyes of all the barons.'[122] The archaeological evidence shows that even the larger siege castles (very few of which had baileys) could only have accommodated forces of scores rather than hundreds of men, meaning that large portions of besieging armies must have camped outside them. Some of the more important royal siege castles were even interim venues for the court. That the royal administration continued uninterrupted when the king was present at sieges is indicated by the fact that charters were issued *in obsidione* ('at the siege'), as at Exeter and Wallingford.[123] Siege castles allowed royal government the appearance of operating 'normally' in the face of rebellion. In such cases, siege castles might have accommodated the royal household or provided security for the treasury.

A further reason, easily overlooked, for the predominance of this mode of protracted siege warfare is that it provided opportunities for negotiation between attacking and defending forces. Anglo-Norman siege warfare could put attackers and defenders within sight, and sometimes earshot, of one another over many weeks, months or even years; and, as we have seen, siege castles presented opportunities for demonstrating resolve, for displaying and threatening hostages, and served as platforms for parley. Siege castles, like other castles, were therefore instrumental in the evolving 'customs of war' of the Anglo-Norman period,[124] and it may not be stretching the point to suggest that in some contexts they may have actually heightened the prospects of conflict being resolved without mass bloodshed.

Case Study: Wallingford under Siege

As a bedrock of Angevin support in a strategically important but exposed location, Wallingford in south Oxfordshire (historically part of north Berkshire) was contested militarily more often and more vigorously than any other place in the civil war, but never changed hands.[125] The castle and, by extension, the fortified town (Fig. 3.8) were subjected to three sieges: in 1139–40 (first siege by King Stephen),

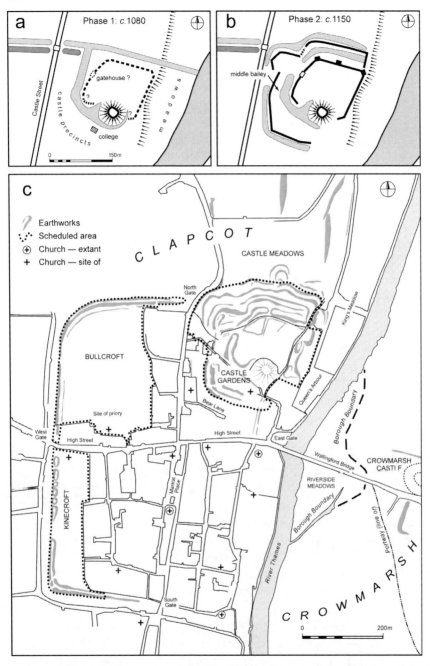

Fig. 3.8: The town and castle of Wallingford: **(top)** development of the castle, *c.* 1066–1150; **(bottom)** topography of the town showing key sites. Drawing by Mike Rouillard and Oliver Creighton, depicting results of the Wallingford *Burh* to Borough Research Project.

1146 (second siege by Stephen and Ranulf, Earl of Chester) and 1152–53 (third siege by Stephen and counter-siege by Henry of Anjou). It is not entirely clear whether we should think of these episodes as separate military actions, however, and on the ground the experience must have been one of a state of more or less perpetual siege over 14 years.

Given the vivid documentation of the sieges, most notably in the *Gesta Stephani* but with other chroniclers providing supplementary detail, and the fact that the town has been the focus of a major archaeological project,[126] Wallingford provides us with an especially informative case study of the strategies, tactics and realities of twelfth-century warfare.[127] Although Wallingford is not registered or recognised as a battlefield, the events that took place in the environs of the town arguably better represent the characteristic mode of twelfth-century warfare than pitched battles, which were atypical of the period. Multiple siege castles were built or rebuilt in all three campaigns. Their deployment and use highlights many key aspects of Anglo-Norman siege castle strategy, although it can be challenging to relate fleeting documentary references to actual locations on the ground. Depending on how the primary sources are interpreted, as many as six separate siege castles, or as few as two, may have been built in the immediate hinterland of the town over the course of the three sieges.[128]

The principal factor explaining the unusual number and intensity of sieges at Wallingford was its status as the Angevins' 'flagship castle,' being continuously occupied by the Empress's supporters through the conflict.[129] Significantly, the town lay not in a heartland of Angevin-controlled territory but on its eastern fringes, at the tip of a salient projecting into royalist lands (Fig. 3.9: top left). In the geostrategic context of the civil war, it stood at the extremity of a disputed zone incorporating a great swathe of Oxfordshire and Berkshire, stretching westward into north Wiltshire and south Gloucestershire. Wallingford effectively became a border town and took on immense symbolic importance for the Angevin cause out of all proportion to its raw military value. The town occupied a strategic location whose value had been recognised much earlier, in the late ninth century, when a vast rectangular *burh* or fortified enclosure had been constructed on the terrace above a ford across the Thames, on the frontier between Wessex and Mercia; its impressive defences comprised a massive rampart rising *c.* 12m above its ditch, an intramural ditch marking the rear of the military zone and fortified gateways, at least two of them adjoining stone church towers.[130]

Wallingford also marked a crossroads of communication routes, overlooking an all-weather ford over the Thames (near the site of the bridge) before the river ran south to cut through the Chiltern Hills via the 'Goring Gap'; it thus commanded routes heading north and west and was important for the control of the entire upper Thames region. It was at Wallingford that Duke William's army had crossed the Thames *en route* to London in 1066, before implanting a royal castle in the *burh*, and William of Poitiers makes clear that it was here that negotiations were held with English leaders prior to the surrender at Berkhamsted.[131] An earlier tradition of Julius Caesar leading his army across Wallingford's ford in 54 BC is also mentioned by King Alfred in his translation of Orosius.[132] Such high-status heritage can only have magnified the importance to King Stephen of taking the rebel castle and town back into his royal control.

1139: first siege (Fig. 3.9: top right)

The Angevin figurehead in Wallingford was the castle's constable, Brian fitz Count, an illegitimate son of the Count of Brittany nurtured at the court of Henry I, who declared for the Empress in the autumn of 1139. He remained an arch-loyalist and held the castle through the first two sieges, before retiring to Reading Abbey as a monk, ill or infirm, *c.* 1148.[133] Brian may have been one of the independently minded barons who minted their own coinage, possibly in Wallingford Castle itself, although this theory rests on an interpretation of a single coin of uncertain provenance.[134] Neutralising Wallingford was a priority for Stephen and in autumn 1139 he advanced on it from the direction of Arundel, where he had besieged the Empress. According to the *Gesta Stephani,* Wallingford Castle, already 'impregnable,' had been strengthened, provisioned with several years' supplies and garrisoned with 'a very strong force of invincible warriors' that threatened Stephen's forces with sorties.[135] Intriguingly, archaeological excavation confirms that a major upgrade of the castle's defences took place in the mid-twelfth century, at which point the middle bailey was laid out or strengthened, although dating evidence is inevitably not precise enough to tie this to a specific phase of the civil war or its immediate aftermath.[136] The Thames, now a canalised and tamed version of its twelfth-century form, when it was two or three times wider, formed a natural moat to the east, and water flowed around complex moated defences embracing the inner bailey, middle bailey and town ditch. In the eyes of chroniclers, the castle and town were indivisible. While the castle was the centrepiece of the Angevin stronghold, the *burh*'s

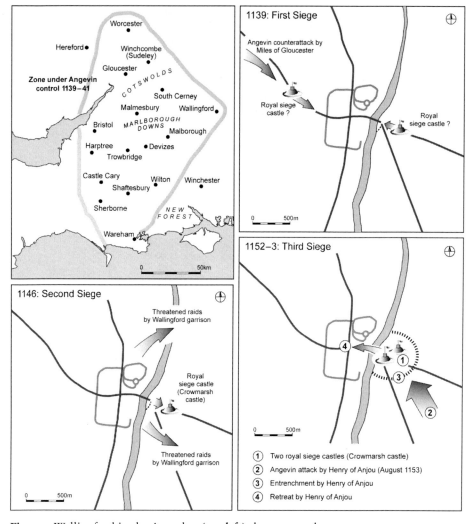

Fig. 3.9: Wallingford in the Anarchy: **(top left)** the contested zone of southern England in the first phase of the civil war (*c.* 1139–41) (based on Bradbury 1998); **(top right, bottom right and bottom left)** schematic maps locating key events and possible locations for siege castles and other works during the three sieges. Drawing by Mike Rouillard.

ancient circuit provided effective outworks to the west and south, and the town itself functioned as a support system for it. *The History of the Church of Abingdon* records that during the war a force of the castle's knights had taken possession of two holdings of houses that were a gift to the abbey from Roger, priest of Wallingford, and that other property had been destroyed.[137] Actual levels of destruction and dislocation must have been much higher, although the war would also have presented commercial opportunities as Wallingford swarmed with people – combatants, reinforcements and refugees from the devastated hinterland.

Faced with such an intimidating fortress, on the advice of his barons Stephen elected to build two siege castles, which were put up 'hastily' and garrisoned, freeing the king to campaign westward into Wiltshire.[138] The erection of siege castles was a less risky strategy than direct assault and ensured that large forces did not become bogged down. In the king's absence, however, the Angevin leader Miles of Gloucester carried out a surprise night attack, killing some of the king's men, wounding others and taking prisoners before returning west. The levelling to the ground of one of Stephen's works – apparently later, in 1140 – is recorded by William of Malmesbury.[139] This is one of a number of examples of a chronicler highlighting when and sometimes how siege castles were slighted: their construction was an aberration and their eradication from the landscape signalled that law and order were restored.

The chroniclers provide no indication of exactly where Stephen built his two siege castles, although one probably lay outside the north or west gate, because the *Gesta Stephani* specifies that the royal army faced the danger of being caught between Wallingford's garrison and other Angevin forces, which were operating out of a West Country heartland. The reason for building two siege castles must have been to blockade the town from different directions, and so the positioning of another to the east, on the opposite (east) bank of the Thames, seems most likely. It is here, in Crowmarsh Gifford, that the noted siege castle ('Stephen's Mount,' or Crowmarsh Castle) was later occupied (see below). The work may well have been built during the first siege episode, developing into an almost 'traditional' siege castle site that was periodically reactivated. The *Gesta Stephani* supplies one other important detail: in the eyes of the chronicler, the royalists were defeated because one of Stephen's castles had desecrated a church: 'from a house of religion and prayer, he allowed a castle to be made, and a home of blood and war to be raised up.'[140] St Peter's, standing on a low mound at Wallingford's east gate is one candidate for the church cited in this description,[141] although it is surely too close to the town walls to have been effective as a siege castle. Instead, the church of St Mary Magdalene, just east of the aforementioned Crowmarsh

Castle on the opposite side of the Thames and containing eleventh/
twelfth-century fabric, seems to have been the church affected. Given
its physical separation from the siege work, however, converting a
church into a castle probably meant garrisoning the only stone-built
structure in the vicinity, rather than transforming it into something
physically resembling a fortress.

1146: second siege (Fig. 3.9: bottom left)

It was to Wallingford (via Abingdon) that the Empress fled in the
winter of 1142 after her famed escape from a besieged Oxford Castle
across the frozen Thames.[142] Her rapid movement thereafter to Angevin
strongholds further west probably belies the town's vulnerability at this
stage of the conflict. It was not, however, until 1146 that Wallingford
was besieged once again and another siege castle 'built.' Chroniclers did
not distinguish between new creations or adaptations of older works,
although the castle of 1146 probably fell into the latter category. Henry
of Huntingdon reported King Stephen's 'impregnable' siege castle
'positioned against Wallingford';[143] the chronicler of the *Gesta Stephani*
described this 'work of wondrous toil and skill' as being built 'within
sight' of the town.[144] This was clearly the site known as Stephen's Mount
in Crowmarsh, on the east bank of the Thames. Early Ordnance Survey
maps show that the site was apparently destroyed by an iron foundry
and agricultural engineering works, but its truncated below-ground
remains were revealed by archaeological evaluation in 2011 (as outlined
above, pg. 58).[145] It was positioned to command the critically important
place where two roads met at the east end of Wallingford Bridge – the
principal road heading east from the town towards Crowmarsh, and
the ancient route known as the 'Portway,' heading south-east towards
Reading. The present terminus of the bridge (which was present as a
timber construction by this period: see below) lies *c.* 120m to the west
of the siege castle, so egress from it could be commanded by archers
positioned on the site's battlements.

The siege castle's ostensible purpose was to check the raids of
Wallingford's garrison into the countryside, which was plundered by
both sides in the 1140s. *The History of the Church of Abingdon* records
that troops from the castle had pillaged the abbey's vill at Culham,
which lay some 11km to the north-west, even though the garrison had
received protection money to prevent raids on the abbey's lands.[146]
Crowmarsh Castle's menacing position provided a deterrent against
chevauchées, but it had propaganda value too. Its construction was
a conspicuous joint venture by Stephen and Ranulf, Earl of Chester,

who had very recently come over to the royalist cause and was present at the siege with a powerful military force including 300 'stout-hearted cavalry.'[147] Cavalry played little part in siege warfare under the Anglo-Norman kings,[148] making their presence here unusual. Whether the earl's mounted knights were deployed to move against Angevin raiding parties or constituted a mere show of force is difficult to say; what seems certain is that the king had the earl where he wanted him, distant from his own power base in the north-west and close to the heartland of royalist support, with Ranulf's new-found loyalty on full display to Angevins and the king's men alike. A royal charter was issued to St Peter's Hospital, York, 'at the siege' (*in obsidione*) of Wallingford, its list of witnesses showing that the earl was present alongside Richard de Lucy and Baldwin fitz Gilbert.[149]

While this episode is enshrined in documents as a 'siege,' it did not involve any direct military action against the castle or town. Unlike the siege castles of 1139, which were provided with small garrisons while the main army campaigned elsewhere, Crowmarsh Castle was clearly the headquarters for a field army arrayed around it for some time. To Wallingford's townsfolk, the siege castle was a conspicuous reminder of intimidation and imperilment, proclaiming that the royalist cause was in the ascendency; to the king's men, it was a tangible emblem of royal presence amidst political turbulence and a rallying point. Quite how long the siege lasted is unclear; chroniclers do not record the destruction of this work – as was often the case – suggesting that it may have remained semi-active, with a long unofficial truce representing a further lull in the conflict.

1152–53: third siege and counter-siege (Fig. 3.9: bottom right)
Through the late 1140s until 1152, Wallingford's garrison remained a thorn in the royalists' side, menacing castles in the wider region. In 1147 a company of Brian fitz Count took by trickery the 'castellum de Lidelea', probably identifiable as Barley Pound in Hampshire, only for the king to retake it.[150] In 1152 a foray destroyed royal castles at Reading and Brightwell, Oxfordshire.[151] Stephen was on the offensive in 1152 and his final attempt to wrest Wallingford Castle from the Angevins precipitated the most complex and protracted siege of the town. Brian fitz Count had died around c. 1150, having retired to Reading Abbey as a monk, although the fortress of Wallingford continued to be held stubbornly by its Breton constable William Boterel.[152]

The king's ascendancy at this point ensured that his forces were swelled by a contingent of Londoners and soldiers provided by the

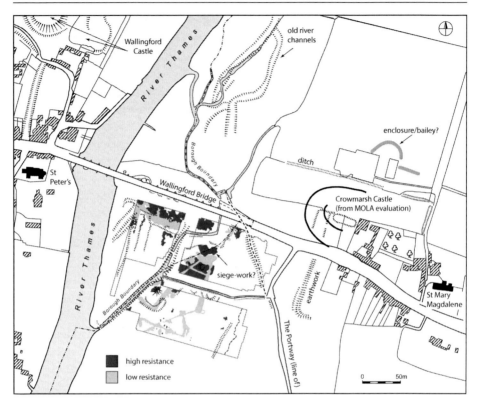

Fig. 3.10: Archaeology of the Wallingford bridgehead area, showing earthworks, key sites and geophysical anomalies. Drawing by Mike Rouillard, depicting results of the Wallingford *Burh* to Borough Research Project.

barons. Despite a clear position of strength, Stephen repeated the earlier policy of blockading Wallingford with siege castles. 'Hastily built,' according to the *Gesta Stephani*, the two castles were constructed 'in front of the castle'; the king also succeeded in taking the bridge that was 'the master-key not only of the town but of the castle on that side.'[153] This is the first time the bridge is formally recorded, and its capture resulted in the driving back of a sally led by the Earl of Hereford, killing and capturing men in the process. The strategically vital bridge was secured by strengthening existing siege works and possibly building others. Gervase of Canterbury recounts that Stephen built a 'timber tower with fortifications' on the bridge, although this may have been one of the two siege castles.[154] Henry of Huntingdon mentions only one siege castle, built 'at the entrance to the bridge ... which prevented

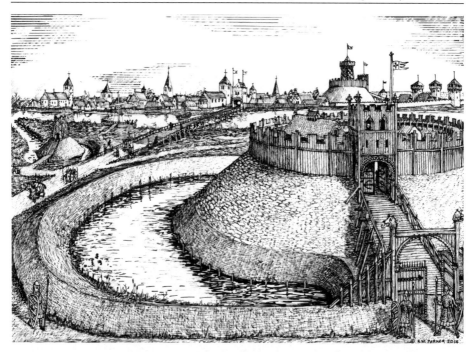

Fig. 3.11: Anarchy in Wallingford. Reconstruction of the bridgehead area *c.* 1152, looking west across the Thames towards the town. Crowmarsh Castle is on the right and there is a second royal siege work at the end of the bridge to the left. Drawing by Richard Parker.

those trapped inside from having food taken in and from free passage.'[155] It seems clear that the reactivated royal siege castle of Crowmarsh was complemented by at least one further work, and geophysical survey may indicate the location of such a fortification on the south side of the bridge (Fig. 3.10). This might be a compact ringwork or motte, with an adjoining enclosure stretching away to the south, although episodes of reuse and later disturbance make interpretation hazardous.[156] Importantly, the river crossing at this time comprised a bridge adjacent to a ford, meaning that a wider area of the opposite (east) bank of the Thames had to be controlled to blockade the town. Conceivably the experience of the 1146 siege demonstrated that Crowmarsh Castle was too distant from the bridgehead to control it effectively. Whatever the precise form and positioning of his siege castles, Stephen's strategy worked well, hemming in the garrison, which sent an appeal for relief to Henry of Anjou in order to avoid having to surrender. A reconstruction of the bridgehead area at this point is offered in Figure 3.11.

Duke Henry weighed into the siege late in the summer of 1153, energised by his success in taking castles and towns including Bedford, Malmesbury, Tutbury and Stamford. The *Gesta Stephani* chronicler's description of Henry's first action, attempting to storm Stephen's castle at Crowmarsh, is by some measure the most vivid account of siege castle warfare in the entire period:

> and coming to Crowmarsh, a castle rising on a very high mound in front of Wallingford with only the river in between, he [Henry of Anjou] ordered his troops to attack it with great vigour on every side. When, behold, the king's men, who on hearing of the duke's arrival had withdrawn to places where they could not be seen, though a few put up a show of resistance in the outer parts of the castle, burst out in small parties from different hiding places and made a gallant charge on those who had already climbed the mound and entered the outer part of the castle, and capturing some and killing others they compelled by their valour the whole body to give way.[157]

While the 'mound' that Duke Henry's soldiers had climbed sounds deceptively like a motte, chroniclers deployed the word *aggere* as a generic term for 'earthwork' or 'rampart.' In this case the fortification was clearly a ringwork castle, as archaeology has demonstrated, like most other siege works of the period. The excavated traces of Crowmarsh Castle show no traces of a bailey, however, prompting the question of what the 'outer parts of the castle' comprised. The likely answer is provided by a geophysical survey of the recreation ground to the north, which shows a large D-shaped anomaly that could be part of the 'lost' bailey enclosure. The enclosure, identified by magnetometer survey, measures approximately 30m in diameter and apparently extends to the south in the direction of the excavated castle, in an area now occupied by a sports pavilion (Fig. 3.10).

Duke Henry responded to his failure to take Crowmarsh Castle by digging in. In the words of Henry of Huntingdon, 'he surrounded the king's castle and his own army with a great rampart [*uallo maximo*], so that his own forces had egress only by way of the castle of Wallingford, while the besieged had no way of escape at all.'[158] Henry's entrenchment is not styled as a castle in the same way as other siege works and its purpose seems to have been to stop his own battered forces deserting as much as to surround Stephen's siege castle. Archaeological survey and excavation in the area have provided no secure evidence of the work, which was presumably a rampart and ditch enclosing part of the bridgehead. This siege within a siege was broken when King Stephen, accompanied by Eustace, re-entered the conflict with a large army, forcing Henry to dismantle his encampment and withdraw under pressure to the west bank of the Thames.

The landscape setting for this critical phase of the civil war is instructive: the rival armies were arrayed on opposite banks of the Thames, crossed by a single fortified bridge. Direct assault via Wallingford Bridge was too risky for both sides. The visibility of these vast armies across the riverside meadows provided an incentive to seek a negotiated end to hostilities, the barons keen to shirk a climactic clash of arms.[159] Clerics were instrumental in the peace talks but King Stephen and Duke Henry also negotiated in person across a stream outside the town.[160] An initial truce lasted five days, during which the king agreed to 'raze to the ground the castle that was the seed-bed of war [i.e. Crowmarsh Castle].'[161] That this was the same place used to negotiate the English surrender in 1066 (see above) highlights Wallingford's enduring importance as a venue for conflict resolution. Robert of Torigni provides the further intriguing details that the king was permitted to remove 80 of his soldiers and that 20 more had been captured 'in a wooden tower,' although Duke Henry had also beheaded 60 royal archers.[162] These figures might indicate the sizes of garrisons assigned to siege castles, while the beheading sounds like a public spectacle – executing low-grade combatants detested by the baronage for their ability to maim and kill aristocratic opponents indiscriminately. Ransomable knights were presumably afforded more humane treatment. Wallingford was also indeed unique as the only town or castle to offer hostages, as well as homages of allegiance, to Stephen as conditions of the peace negotiations.[163]

Archaeology reveals the thoroughness of Crowmarsh Castle's slighting. Its wide ditch was backfilled with redeposited alluvium and chalk blocks from the defences, as well as burned daub (presumably from buildings), charcoal and occupational debris.[164] Although physical traces of the siege castles were eradicated, memory of the town's martial history was preserved in other ways. The townsfolk's endurance and loyalty to the Angevin cause were reflected in Henry II's unusually generous charter of liberties in 1155.[165] Wallingford stood at the very heart of what has been styled the 'royal-administrative enclave' of the Norman and Angevin kings,[166] and control over the town had great symbolic value. Henry kept the honour and its castle in his hands throughout his reign, while Angevin favour was also manifested in the endowment of Wallingford's two suburban hospitals: St John the

Baptist, founded outside the south gate in the 1150s, and the leper hospital of St Mary Magdalene near the east end of the bridge in Crowmarsh, which is first recorded *c*. 1142.[167]

In conclusion, while Wallingford was at the sharp end of the conflict and on a war footing for many years, actual fighting here was episodic. The royalist attack on the bridge in 1152 was the closest any of the sieges came to a direct assault. Although this was the civil war's most besieged castle, in 1152–53, as in 1146 and 1139, there is no record of any attempt to storm it. Nor is there any indication that siege engines were used (partly as the width of the river made bombardment impossible given the range of contemporary siege artillery), and references to casualties are few. Indeed, apart from the king's attack on the bridge, all other chroniclers' references to bloodshed during the three sieges occur during assaults on besieging troops made by relief forces rather than during attacks on the castle itself. Instead, the siege castles here, as elsewhere, were primarily employed in chess-like power plays and shows of posturing, force and resolve. The 'action' of 1146 in particular has something of the flavour of a mock siege and, even in the climactic third siege, sporadic outbursts of killing and atrocity were punctuated by long truces. This stand-offish mode of warfare minimised risk for noble military commanders (other than to those living in the surrounding districts, of course) but maximised possibilities for negotiation. Rather than pointing to a collapse of the rules of war, all these features of Wallingford's civil war experience reveal how a code of martial conduct was fully in operation.

Summary

The civil war of Stephen's reign saw no radical departure in the ways of waging war. Many of the characteristic features of conflict – such as the employment of mercenaries, the avoidance of pitched battle, devastation of landscapes and the predominance of siege warfare – were not aberrations but part and parcel of the already existing pattern of Anglo-Norman warfare. The Anarchy saw the siege castle cemented as an essential part of the repertoire of Anglo-Norman conflict, mixing psychological and martial functions and favoured by rulers in an era when siege warfare was static and protracted while leaders needed to be mobile. While the chroniclers reveal many aspects of this mode of conflict, it is crucial to highlight how archaeology can and will contribute much to understanding the place, context and logistics of these siege landscapes.

Notes

1 Strickland 1996b, 56, 73.
2 Contamine 1984, 270–5.
3 Morris 1978, 87–96.
4 Strickland 1996b, 55–6.
5 Morillo 1994, 4.
6 For example, see William of Malmesbury's *Historia Novella* on the campaigns of 1142: 'The arrival of Lent enjoined upon all a truce from war' (III, 71, King and Potter 1998, 122–3); and 'because the holy season urged rest if only for a little while, they thought they should refrain from war' (III, 78, King and Potter 1998, 132–3).
7 Green 1997.
8 Stringer 1997, 42–3.
9 Barrow 1994.
10 Blanchard 2002, 23.
11 Foard and Morris 2012, 38; Strickland 1989, 179–80.
12 For overview, see Crouch 1994; Lieberman 2010, 75–7, 119–20, 251.
13 Morillo 1994, 119.
14 *The Ecclesiastical History of Orderic Vitalis* XIII, v. 112, Chibnall 1978, Vol. VI, 520–1.
15 Nieus 2015.
16 On this campaign generally, see Higham and Henderson 2011, 140–1, 147–9.
17 Crouch 1994, 269–70; Bradbury 1996, 32.
18 Foard and Morris 2012, 38, Fig. 3.1.
19 Carlton 1992, 206–11.
20 Cathers 2002; Williams 2015.
21 Prestwich 1996, 314–15.
22 Prestwich 1996, 315; Hosler 2007, 145–6.
23 On the battle generally, see Strickland 2011.
24 *The Ecclesiastical History of Orderic Vitalis* XII, iv. 361, Chibnall 1978, Vol. VI, 240–1.
25 De Laborderie et al. 2000, 403–4, 411.

26 Strickland 1994, 66.
27 *Gesta Stephani* II, 119, Potter and Davis 1976, 232–3.
28 *Gesta Stephani* II, 120, Potter and Davis 1976, 238–9.
29 John of Hexham in Symeon of Durham, *Symeonis monachi opera omnia*, Arnold 2012, Vol. II, 293.
30 Dalton 2005, 13–18.
31 See Carman and Carman 2012, 98.
32 See, for example, *Gesta Stephani* I, 9, 50, II, 72, Potter and Davis 1976, 16–17, 50, 104–5, 142–3.
33 For accounts of the battle, see Beeler 1966, 88–92; Bradbury 1996, 33–6; Strickland and Hardy 2011, 75–6. On the campaign generally, see Strickland 1989. On English portrayals of the Scots as barbarians, see Bliese 1988; Gillingham 1992.
34 Strickland 1996b, 65–6; Jones, R.W. 2010, 151–3.
35 See in particular Strickland and Hardy 2011, 75–6.
36 Toolis 2004.
37 Bodies on medieval battlefields were usually buried where they fell. See Foard and Morris 2012, 59–61. Other reconstructions put the English deployment north of Scots Pits Lane (e.g. Beeler 1966, map 6).
38 For key reconstructions of the action, see Beeler 1966, 108–19; Bradbury 1996, 90–8.
39 Jones et al. 2003, 228–30.
40 William of Malmesbury, *Historia Novella* III, 43, King and Potter 1998, 85.
41 See also Barber and Barker 1989, 18–19.
42 Jones et al. 2003, 220, 300, 304, Fig. 9.59.
43 *The Ecclesiastical History of Orderic Vitalis* XIII. 44, Chibnall 1978, Vol. VI, 546–7.

44 For a chronological outline of siege warfare in Stephen's reign, see Purton 2010, 265–79.

45 Foard and Morris 2012, 55, Fig. 3.13.

46 For examples of 'paired' castles, see Creighton 2005b, 54–64 and below pgs 47–8.

47 Higham 1982, 105; 1988, 144.

48 Strickland 1996b. See also Speight 2000.

49 Symeon of Durham, *Symeonis monachi opera omnia*, Arnold 2012, Vol. II, 274. See also Crouch 1986, 18 n.75.

50 Bachrach 1985, 15.

51 *Gesta Stephani* II, 89, Potter and Davis 1976, 174–5.

52 *Gesta Stephani* I, 18, Potter and Davis 1976, 38–9.

53 Latimer 2015, 176.

54 Rogers 1992, 238–9.

55 *The Chronicle of John of Worcester* III, McGurk 1998, 250–1.

56 *Gesta Stephani* I, 31, Potter and Davis 1976, 66–7.

57 *Gesta Stephani* I, 28, 31, 50, II, 118, Potter and Davis 1976, 58–9, 68–9, 104–5, 230–1.

58 Purton 2010, 267–8.

59 Le Maho 2000, 186–7. See also Higham and Barker 1992, 361–2.

60 Symeon of Durham, *Symeonis monachi opera omnia*, Arnold 2012, Vol. II, 274. See also Crouch 1986, 19.

61 *Gesta Stephani* I, 16, Potter and Davis 1976, 34–5.

62 Higham 2013, 117.

63 *Gesta Stephani* I, 17, Potter and Davis 1976, 34–5.

64 Henry, Archdeacon of Huntingdon, *Historia Anglorum* X, 22, Greenway 1996, 744–5. Stephen's *munitionem* has normally been interpreted as a siege castle (see, for example, Renn 1968, 227). The identification of a square earthwork outside the west gate, now lost, is unconvincing (Hill 1948, 180), but the deaths of so many men in such a manner sounds very much like it was caused by the collapse of a siege mine rather than the ditch of a siege castle, although the siege could still have entailed the construction of one or more siege castles.

65 Braun 1934, 113, 118.

66 Henry, Archdeacon of Huntingdon, *Historia Anglorum* X, 10, Greenway 1996, 718–19. An alternative interpretation is that this event occurred during some form of tournament organised by Stephen's forces. See King 2010, 106–7. See also pg. 181.

67 Bradbury 1992, 85.

68 See Purton 2010, 379–88.

69 Purton 2006.

70 For arguments for and against a 'hybrid' trebuchet, in which a counterweight added to rather than replaced the human 'pullers,' see Purton 2010, 380–2.

71 Tarver 1995.

72 Coulson 1994b, 70.

73 Armitage 1912, 85.

74 King 1966, 100.

75 Jones 1999, 172.

76 Creighton 2005b, 57, 90, 92.

77 Strickland 2001; Purton 2009, 160–3; Hicks 2013, 145–56. The Sainte Suzanne site survives as an earthwork known as Le Camp de Beugy/des Anglais, *c.* 800m from the castle. Comprising two adjoining embanked enclosures covering more than 2 hectares, it is quite unlike the ringworks or mottes more usually built and may have functioned as an encampment for a much larger field force than was usually accommodated within siege castles.

78 King 1983, 237. The belief that a siege motte was built against Norwich in 1074 (Renn 1959, 11) seems mistaken. There is no reference to such a work in the chronicles, although the siege (more appropriately dated to 1175) lasted three months, which would have been long

enough for the construction of a counter-castle. See Shepherd-Popescu 2009, 289–90.

79 For the campaign of 1095, see Beeler 1966, 67–70; Barlow 1983, 346–56.

80 Swanton 2000, 231.

81 *The Ecclesiastical History of Orderic Vitalis* VIII, iii, 408–9, Chibnall 1973, Vol. IV, 280–3. See also Higham and Barker 1992, 125; Strickland 1994, 57.

82 Barlow 1983, 354–5. The site of the counter-castle at Bamburgh is lost. It is conceivable that the place name 'Maison Head,' recorded on late nineteenth-century OS maps at NU17813467 remembers the fortification, although this site is *c.* 650m from Bamburgh Castle. Topographically, the most likely location is on rising ground immediately south-west of the castle and *c.* 250m from it, at NU18113496.

83 Hollister 2001, 158.

84 *The Ecclesiastical History of Orderic Vitalis* XII, iv, 311, Chibnall 1978, Vol. VI, 186–7. See also Hollister 2001, 246.

85 *The Ecclesiastical History of Orderic Vitalis* XII, iv, 395, Chibnall 1978, Vol. VI, 280–1.

86 *The Ecclesiastical History of Orderic Vitalis* XII, iv, 354, Chibnall 1978, Vol. VI, 230–1; Strickland 1996b, 163; Hollister 2001, 260. Other siege castles of this period were built at Tinchebrai (*The Ecclesiastical History of Orderic Vitalis* XI, iv, 224, Chibnall 1978, Vol. VI, 84–5) and Brionne, where two were constructed (*The Ecclesiastical History of Orderic Vitalis* XII, iv, 462, Chibnall 1978, Vol. VI, 354–5).

87 *The Ecclesiastical History of Orderic Vitalis* XII, 39, Chibnall 1978, Vol. VI, 346–57. See also Crouch 1986, 20–2.

88 For an overview of siege castles in the civil war, see Speight 2000.

89 The only known attack on Pickering Castle was in John's reign, when siege castles had fallen out of favour and fashion. See King 1983, 523.

90 Lewis 1989.

91 Bradbury 1990, 31.

92 Wilson and Hurst 1968, 17.

93 Renn 1959 110–11; Le Maho 2000, 181–6.

94 Higham and Henderson 2011, 128, 138.

95 Higham and Henderson 2011.

96 Wright et al. 2015a, 109–12.

97 Laban 2011; 2013.

98 Stamper 1984.

99 *Gesta Stephani* I, 39, Potter and Davis 1976, 84–5. *The History of the King's Works* sees the Rings as 'the only surviving fortification which can be identified as the work of Stephen.' See Colvin et al. 1963, 42.

100 See Wright et al. 2015b, 313–15.

101 Bonney and Dunn 1989, 178. For a new archaeological survey, including geophysics, see Wright et al. 2015, 315–18.

102 Myers 1932; Renn 1959, 111.

103 Henry, Archdeacon of Huntingdon, *Historia Anglorum* X, 32, Greenway 1996, 758–9.

104 Vince et al. 1997. For the problematic documentary evidence for a castle at Newbury, see Astill 1978, 51, 56.

105 Higgott 1998.

106 Dodd 2003, 59.

107 Clark 1889, 215–16, 267–8.

108 Dodd 2003, 48, 50, Fig. 4.2. We are grateful to Julian Munby for pointing out the existence of the mounts on Loggan's map of 1675 and Taylor's map of 1751.

109 Purton 1998.

110 *Gesta Stephani* II, 94, Potter and Davis 1976, 182–3. See also Speight 2000, 271–2.

111 *The Chronicle of John of Worcester* III, McGurk 1998, 267.

112 *Gesta Stephani* II, 104, Potter and Davis 1976, 198–9.

113 *Gesta Stephani* II, 110, Potter and Davis 1976, 212–13.
114 *Gesta Stephani* II, 109, Potter and Davis 1976, 210–11.
115 *Gesta Stephani* II, 117, Potter and Davis 1976, 226–7.
116 *Gesta Stephani* I, 37, Potter and Davis 1976, 82–3.
117 *Gesta Stephani* II, 117, Potter and Davis 1976, 228–9.
118 Crouch 1990, 16–18.
119 Jones, R. 2010, 48–9.
120 Williams 2015, 336–7.
121 Strickland 1994, 57.
122 *Gesta Stephani* I, 17, Potter and Davis 1976, 38–9.
123 Cronne and Davis 1968. See for example nos 11, 232, 961 and 992 concerning Wallingford.
124 Strickland 2001.
125 For an overview, see Keats-Rohan 2015a. Malmesbury, Wiltshire, was also besieged three times (in 1139, 1144 and 1152), although these were less bloody and intense events (see pg. 47).
126 Christie and Creighton 2013.
127 The following discussion draws and enlarges upon an account provided in Christie and Creighton 2013, 202–8. For other discussions of the military actions that took place around the town, see also Slade 1960; Spurrell 1995; Hosler 2007, 135–8; Speight 2000, 272–3; Purton 2010, 263–78.
128 King 1983, 13.
129 Bradbury 1996, 161.
130 Christie and Creighton 2013, 394–6.
131 Keats-Rohan 2012, 172–3.
132 Christie and Creighton 2013, 47, 70.
133 Keats-Rohan 2015b, 56.
134 The evidence is problematic: a unique coin of Stephen's reign has the obverse reading '+B.R:C.I.T.B.R.', which has been attributed to *Br(ienus) C(om)it(is) Bri(ttanie) F(ilius)*: 'Brian, son of the Count of Brittany'. The reverse reading,

'+BRIIT.P.ON.TO:,' is thought to refer to the moneyer Brihtwi, and to locate the mint 'at Tor' ('at the tower'), presumably in Wallingford Castle. See Boon 1988, 29–32. See also Blackburn 1994, 167, 189. An alternative reading is that the coin was minted for Baldwin de Redvers, possibly at Dunster, Somerset. See North 1963, 159.
135 *Gesta Stephani* I, 42, Potter and Davis, 1976, 92–3.
136 Christie and Creighton 2013, 217; Keats-Rohan 2015b, 41.
137 *Historia Ecclesie Abbendonensis* II, 276, 277, ed. and trans. Hudson 2002, 289–90.
138 *Gesta Stephani* I, 42–3, Potter and Davis 1976, 90–5.
139 William of Malmesbury, *Historia Novella* II, 37, King and Potter 1998, 72–3.
140 *Gesta Stephani* I, 43, Potter and Davis 1976, 94–5.
141 Renn 1968, 33.
142 *Gesta Stephani* II, 72, Potter and Davis 1976, 142–3.
143 Henry, Archdeacon of Huntingdon, *Historia Anglorum* X, 24, Greenway 1996, 749.
144 *Gesta Stephani* II, 94, Potter and Davis 1976, 184–5.
145 Laban 2011; 2013.
146 *Historia Ecclesie Abbendonensis* II, 276, 277, Hudson 2002, 314–17.
147 *Gesta Stephani* II, 94, Potter and Davis 1976, 184–5.
148 Morillo 1994, 160–1, 191.
149 Cronne and Davis 1968, no. 992. Other royal charters issued *in obsidione* ('at the siege') at Wallingford were to Abingdon (either 1139, 1146 or 1152–3), Colchester St John's (1153) and Woburn Abbey (1140–3). See Cronne and Davis 1968, nos 11, 232 and 961.
150 *Gesta Stephani* II, 109, Potter and Davis 1976, 208–9. For a possible identification of the site as Barley Pound, Hampshire, see King 1983, 195.

151 *Chronicles of the Reigns of Stephen, Henry II and Richard I*, Howlett 1889, 174. See also Spurrell 1995, 261–2 on the distinct possibility that Robert of Torigni mistakenly identified a small royal castle at Cholsey, 3km south-west of Wallingford, as 'Reading.'

152 Keats-Rohan 2015a, 134; 2015b, 56; Crouch 2000, 262.

153 *Gesta Stephani* II, 117, Potter and Davis 1976, 226–7.

154 Gervase of Canterbury, Stubbs, Vol. I, 1879, 153.

155 Henry, Archdeacon of Huntingdon, *Historia Anglorum* X, 33, Greenway 1996, 88–9.

156 Christie and Creighton 2013, 23–6.

157 *Gesta Stephani* II, 120, Potter and Davis 1976, 236–7.

158 Henry, Archdeacon of Huntingdon, *Historia Anglorum*, X, 34, Greenway 1996, 766–7.

159 White 1990, 3, 5, 7–8.

160 Henry, Archdeacon of Huntingdon, *Historia Anglorum* X, 34, Greenway 1996, 767.

161 *Gesta Stephani* II, 120, Potter and Davis 1976, 238–9.

162 *Chronicles of the Reigns of Stephen, Henry II and Richard I*, Howlett 1889, 173–4.

163 King 2010, 287, 331.

164 Laban 2013, 195–6. The ditch fills contained distinct first and second phases, the latter defined by darker material, hinting at more than one episode of slighting. The first phase of slighting might conceivably relate to the aftermath of the siege of 1139–40, or 1146, or the two phases might alternatively reflect successive slighting of different elements of the siege castle in 1153.

165 Dewey and Dewey 2005.

166 Keefe 1990, 182–3.

167 Christie and Creighton 2013, 288–91.

Chapter 4

Architecture and Authority: Castles

C ASTLES WERE FIRMLY CENTRE STAGE in the civil war's military and political landscape – they were invariably the focal points of events in a conflict in which control of castles equated to control over territory. Chroniclers' accounts have long dominated our understanding of castle construction and use during the period. As symbols of tyranny, disorder and oppression, castles – especially those newly built or strengthened – were a cause of consternation for ecclesiastical writers, who singled them out as the cause rather than just a symptom of the disorder. The question of these so-called 'adulterine' (*adulterina*) castles – usually interpreted as 'unlicensed' – has cast a shadow over how we have interpreted the physical remains of twelfth-century castles and deflected from our understanding of the totality of castle-building practices and contexts. While brief overviews of the 'castles of the Anarchy' have already been published,[1] this chapter will provide a platform for a more systematic survey of the evidence that can enable us to confront the familiar caricature of the Anarchy-period castle as a simple, warlike and transient feature of the English landscape. Drawing upon an upsurge of archaeological evidence alongside the documentary sources, it starts with an account of the castles of Stephen's reign from the perspective of chroniclers, before exploring and analysing as far as is possible the forms, function distribution, relationships and chronology of these sites, in order to assess the extent to which the landscape was militarised.

Reassessing the 'Castles of the Anarchy'

Numerous historical and archaeological studies perpetuate the notion that the castles of Stephen's reign were mostly short-term and martial in nature. For Frank Stenton, writing in his classic and influential 1932 study *The First Century of English Feudalism*, 'castles of the Anarchy were rarely, if ever, castles of stone'; instead, conditions of feudal anarchy saw the proliferation of temporary and underdeveloped earth and timber fortresses built on defensive sites.[2]

A revisionist view is that the late 1130s and 1140s actually saw greater variation in construction forms and in the social context of castle building than previous decades. Indeed, all of Stenton's points require rethinking: the twelfth century saw several masonry great towers built for magnates, especially those rising rapidly in the social order,[3] while archaeological excavation has transformed our understanding of earth and timber castles so that these no longer need to be viewed as humble, inferior and impermanent compared to their more glamorous stone-built counterparts.[4] The discussion in Chapter 3 has already underlined how even the most warlike castles of the period had other functions: thus, siege castles had psychological and symbolic purposes and were built to pursue a mode of warfare that was heavily codified. Despite the prominence of castle warfare in sources such as the *Gesta Stephani*, castles were not necessarily weapons that were actually used. A revisionist view of Stephen's reign sees many of the magnates as 'reluctant anarchists.'[5] According to this view, castles could be used to further a policy of 'armed neutrality,'[6] and not necessarily as fighting machines. In the rural world, most twelfth-century castles were centres from which lords exacted taxes from the peasantry and icons of seigneurial authority as much as medieval equivalents to the twentieth-century pillbox.

Traditional explanations attribute an explosion of castle building in Stephen's reign to a slackening of centralised royal authority during a civil war when private defence was becoming increasingly necessary to protect elite individuals and their property, although these conditions did not apply equally to all areas. Of equal if not greater importance in explaining the phenomenon are notable social changes that saw elite identity transformed during the period. These processes created unusual potential for castle building: the multiplication of earls and earldoms gave magnates not only the resources necessary for prodigious castle building and the territories within which to enact these policies, but opposition between rivals created a hotbed of competitive emulation in which private fortification flourished and percolated down the hierarchy of the elite. Castle building became closely linked to power projection, and it was very often one component within wider strategies through which seigneurial authority was negotiated and stamped onto the landscape, for example through ecclesiastical patronage and settlement planning. These dramatic developments in 'private' fortification were strikingly matched by a grinding halt in royal castle building amidst financial pressure and disruption caused by the king's movements to subdue revolts. Not one of the king's numerous campaign castles, siege works or fortifications on ecclesiastical sites (discussed in Chapters 3 and 7) endured to see investment beyond the short term, and other initiatives were left unrealised, as with the intention to build a castle at Beverley, East Yorkshire, in 1149.[7]

It is tempting but wrong to lump 'the castles of the Anarchy' together as a single species of fortification; the term can be misleading in that it conflates fortifications that were founded during the period with those pre-established sites that were occupied and developed during it. Many castles great and small were inhabited through Stephen's reign but were not necessarily founded or strengthened during the disturbances. It is important to remember that a great many nationally significant fortresses – indeed, most of them – have no evidence whatsoever of building works during the conflict. A valuable paper by Charles Coulson established some essential ground rules by dividing the castles of the period into three categories: first, castles already established and active, some of which were refurbished during the civil war; a second, much smaller, number of sites founded as part of the development of lordship; and, third, a plethora of siege works and campaign castles.[8] To this framework we can add forms of fortification that stretch the definition of 'castle' in the strictest sense and were more *ad hoc* in nature. These include the fortified churches and monasteries to be discussed in Chapter 7, as well as improvised fortifications such as that raised on Wallingford Bridge in 1152–53 (above, pg. 70). Crucially, these last two categories of site differ from the others in that the castle builder did not necessarily *hold* the land upon which the fortification was raised, although a degree of prior territorial *control* is implicit.

'Adulterine' castles

Our view of the fortifications of Stephen's reign has long been coloured by the infamous 'adulterine castles' of the period. Medieval use of this problematic term is not confined to the mid-twelfth century, although this is often thought to be the case. It seems to have been used first by Orderic Vitalis or Abbot Suger of Saint-Denis in reference to events in Normandy in the final decades of the eleventh century, while the 1217 reissue of Magna Carta later stated that *castella adulterina* built in the Barons' War should be destroyed.[9] Although it is Henry II who is most closely associated with the destruction of 'adulterine' castles in the wake of the peace treaty of 1153 (the archaeological and historical evidence are discussed later: see pgs 111–15), it is important to note that King Stephen too saw fit to demilitarise the landscape in certain contexts, as on his return eastward after his Cornish campaign of 1140, when he 'demolished a great many *adulterina castella*.'[10]

It is unfortunate that the term 'adulterine castle' is invariably equated with 'unlicensed castle,' as it presupposes that all other castles were somehow licensed. The issue of 'licensing' castle building has a long and complex historiography: when was castle building legitimate and illegitimate; who had the authority to build; and when and why did castle building occur outside accepted parameters have all been heavily debated. To summarise the situation in England in the late eleventh and twelfth century: before the reign of John (1199–1216) there were no licences as such for castle building, and their emergence thereafter is linked to important changes in royal record-keeping, although in some exceptional cases earlier charters could convey their spirit. A well-known example is Henry I's confirmation in January 1127 of custody of Rochester Castle, Kent, to the Archbishop of Canterbury and his successors, along with permission to build there a *municionem* ('fortification') or *turris* ('tower').[11] There is, however, no evidence that the Anglo-Norman kings consistently gave their explicit authority in written form for the construction of 'private' castles, although this term is itself troublesome, for in a sense all castles were private, including those of kings, dukes and counts, while their functions could be at least partly public.

Rather than any formal Anglo-Norman system for licensing castles, a tradition of royal (and, in Normandy, ducal) control inherited from eleventh-century customs ensured that their construction was condoned when it was in the king's (or duke's) interest, and that these fortifications could be taken over if and when circumstances changed.[12] It is instructive to bear in mind that even in the later Middle Ages, when the king issued 'licences to crenellate,' that by no means all the builders of new castles were licensed and that, conversely, not all licences – which also had important honorific purposes, signalling royal favour – resulted in the erection of defensible structures.[13]

The 'adulterine castle' of the mid-twelfth century was not a strictly and legally defined entity but rather a catchword used by clerical writers horrified at the construction of these troublesome fortifications, and so it is wrong to think of 'adulterine' and 'unlicensed' as synonyms here.[14] More appropriate alternatives might be 'counterfeit,' 'spurious,'[15] or 'misbegotten' and 'improper.'[16] 'Bad castle' is the simplest shorthand.

Chroniclers and Castles

The problematic issue of adulterine castles aside, chroniclers' descriptions of castles in the civil war are a rich source of evidence, furnishing plentiful reports of castle building and vivid accounts of the role of the castle in war. From the archaeological point of view, relating these reports to evidence and events on the ground can be challenging, given that testimonies can seem maddeningly vague and inconsistent, the physical realities of castles blurred by literary convention. We should, however, bear in mind how twelfth-century chronicles represented literature in a broad sense rather than history in a narrow sense, so that what we might criticise as distortion, omission and simplification are actually characteristics of the intended product – an elegant account with a specific audience or patron in mind.

Many aspects of castles that are hugely important to archaeological and historical study were irrelevant or unknown to twelfth-century chroniclers. Details of castles' physical appearance, their scale or the technologies used in their construction are sparse. If castles are described as strong it is often due to the qualities of their settings or garrisons, the nature of the defences themselves usually obscure. For example, the *Gesta Stephani* styles numerous sites held against King Stephen as 'impregnable' (*inexpugnabili*), part of a standardised way of describing castles that magnifies his achievements.[17]

The 'towers of hewn limestone' at Exeter Castle, besieged by Stephen in 1136, were clearly reused Roman features.[18] Only infrequently do chroniclers otherwise indicate that fortifications were of masonry, although the castle at Carisbrooke, on the Isle of Wight, where Baldwin de Redvers fled in 1136, was 'very finely built of stone.'[19] Archaeology shows that the first Norman castle at Carisbrooke comprised a rectangular enclosure that was then transformed into a powerful motte and bailey, perhaps shortly after 1100, when Richard de Redvers was granted the Isle of Wight, with a stone curtain wall and shell keep replacing a short-lived timber phase, while stone buildings including a chapel and domestic structures were also in place in the twelfth century.[20] The castle at Ely built by Bishop Nigel early on in the civil war was apparently of 'stone and cement.'[21] This similarly represented a refurbishment of an earlier motte and bailey, built by William I *c.* 1070, rather than a new work, although the site, known as Cherry Hill, on the south-west side of the cathedral park shows no evidence of stonework, and it is not inconceivable that the stone structure in question was an early version of the bishop's palace.[22] At Wallingford, archaeological investigation of the middle bailey in 1972 showed that this enclosure was built in the middle years of the twelfth century, very likely as an Anarchy-period upgrade, and defended by a box rampart fronted with a stone wall, and that earlier domestic occupation was levelled to make way for it (see also pg. 65).[23] It is likewise in the late 1130s and 1140s that Bristol Castle seems to have been transformed structurally through massive rebuilding in masonry, including the addition of a monumental keep said to be built or faced with stone imported from Caen by Robert, Earl of Gloucester, when Bristol served as the Angevins' capital.[24]

Chroniclers also emphasise how castles drew their strength from their physical positioning in the landscape as much as from their defences. The *Gesta Stephani*'s memorable description of Stephen's failed attack on Bristol in 1138 – a high peninsula surrounded by the confluence of two deep tidal rivers – is a prime example.[25] The landscape itself could be encastellated: according to William of Malmesbury, in 1142 Robert of Gloucester subdued the Isle of Portland, which had been 'turned into a castle' (*quam incastellauerant*).[26] Similarly, on the Isle of Ely, impenetrable marshes and a fortification at the head of the causeway ensured the whole island was made into an 'impregnable castle' in 1139–40, in the eyes of the chronicler of the *Gesta Stephani* (*inexpugnatum efficit castellum*).[27] This illustrates the crucial point that the distinction between 'real' castles and other militarised sites was far less clear or important to contemporary chroniclers than in modern historical and archaeological scholarship. The word *castellum* in particular could be applied very flexibly: in the *Gesta Stephani*, for instance, it is used over 250 times, employed to describe a wide range of fortifications – old and new, great and small, ranging from siege castles to great centres of lordship, and including defended towns and militarised churches and other landscape features.

It is also often unclear from chroniclers' accounts whether any given account of a castle being 'built' (*firmare*) implies that the site was constructed *de novo* as opposed to an existing fortification being refurbished, reactivated or simply provisioned, garrisoned and readied for war. Another possibility is that non-defended seats of lordship were being given a defensive makeover – a sequence sometimes revealed through archaeological excavation (see below, pg. 97). The castle that the Empress had fortified at Radcot, Oxfordshire, in 1142 seems not to have been a new fortification but had been built earlier in the twelfth century by Hugh of Buckland; excavation and geophysical survey have revealed its square tower, although a substantial dump of ashlar blocks around its base, haphazardly arranged and mortared *in situ*, may suggest *ad hoc* strengthening, after the manner of Mount House, Witney (also Oxfordshire) (see pgs 211–12).[28] Similar is the case of the castle at Castle Cary, Somerset, twice besieged by King Stephen (in 1138 and 1148) and often identified as a mid-twelfth-century foundation; excavation reveals, however, that the keep was built earlier in the twelfth century, and shows how the site was slighted and demilitarised soon after the civil war.[29]

'Lost' castles of the period – those named and referred to by chroniclers but which cannot be confidently connected to any known physical remains – present a particularly intractable problem. Indeed, the proportion of documented castles that have vanished entirely is higher than for any other period of medieval history.[30] It is the political context within which castles were built or rebuilt that is of primary interest to the chroniclers, as opposed to the precise places they were constructed, and writers sometimes referred to castles by 'pet names' rather than neatly geo-referencing them to known locations.[31] In other cases, archaeological searches for vanished 'castles' might be entirely in vain, as writers were using the word *castellum* much more generically, to describe a town or monastery, for example, that became militarily important. Three such sites illustrate the issue. The castle of 'Galchlin/ Galclint' is documented in 1140–41, when taken by Alan of Brittany, who gave it up to Ranulf, Earl of Chester; several sites have been suggested, among the more plausible that it was part of Lincoln Castle, or that it equates to Giddersdale, East Yorkshire or, more likely, Belvoir, Leicestershire.[32] Two sites taken by King Stephen in 1147, the 'Castle of the Wood,' which was stormed, and 'Lidelea,' which surrendered, are similarly unlocated, and while the *Gesta Stephani* mentions the two together this is no sure-fire indicator that they were near each other.[33] The former is most likely to be equated with a fortification of Silchester's long-abandoned Roman amphitheatre, although locations at Woodchester, Gloucestershire, and Woodgarston, Hampshire have also been put forward on the basis of place name evidence;[34] the latter may well be Barley Pound, Hampshire, which is associated with nearby siege works.[35]

It can also be difficult to judge whether accounts of the proliferation of castle building report a truly nationwide phenomenon or rather extrapolate local circumstances to a wider canvas. Most striking and oft-quoted are the words of the Anglo-Saxon Chronicle (E version) on 1137: 'for every powerful man built his castles and held them against him [King Stephen] and they filled the country full of castles. They oppressed the wretched people of the country with castle-building. When the castles were built, they filled them with devils and wicked men.'[36] There is good reason to think that the sporadic and dispersed nature of the conflict, as discussed in Chapter 3, points towards more regionally specific activity. Robert of Torigni's figure of more than 1,115 castles overthrown or destroyed in 1153 as a product of the peace is also frequently cited as evidence of the scale of private castle building,[37] but is best seen as 'castro-phobic fantasy.'[38] It is odd that the figure is so specific – especially as the author was based in France, at the monastery of Le Bec; presumably, the appearance of stated accuracy lent his account authority and weight. This number cannot, of course, be taken literally; its purpose was to stress the magnitude of Henry II's achievement in demilitarising the landscape so thoroughly and cleansing it of private castles and potential threats. In contrast to Robert of Torigni's astronomical figure, and notwithstanding the caveats discussed above, the best estimates of the number of documented 'new' castles of the period 1135–53 stand at around 27 sites, in addition to at least another 17 attested siege castles (see Chapter 3), out of a total of around 110 castles mentioned for the first time.[39]

However one sees the proliferation or otherwise of castles during Stephen's reign, one thing seems indisputable: castle building shifted down the social scale, albeit temporarily, to a level lower than had applied previously, so that the mid-twelfth century marked the high watermark of private fortification in England. Unlike in Ireland and Scotland, where late medieval tower houses proliferated to make these among Europe's most heavily castellated regions, in England private fortification never again reached anything like the levels witnessed during the twelfth-century civil war.

Excavating 'the Anarchy':
Archaeological Evidence for Castles

What, then, can be traced archaeologically of these castles and their fortifications? First, we need to stress that the physical remains of many are ephemeral and problematic. As many documented castles raised *de novo* in the civil war were used for relatively short periods of time and a high proportion were subsequently slighted, their traces disappeared early from townscapes and landscapes. Our understanding of the physical forms of 'castles of the Anarchy' is also inevitably biased towards the defences of these sites. We have a far poorer understanding of their internal arrangements and structures, which can only rarely be glimpsed in the archaeological record. The sort of high-quality secular building project that could be realised within the defences of a castle by a major magnate during the period is demonstrated by the example of Leicester Castle's great hall, whose early structure has been revealed by close archaeological analysis during renovation work. Attributable to *c.* 1150 on the basis of dendrochronological (tree-ring) dating and therefore clearly built for Robert de Beaumont, Earl of Leicester, the hall was something of a stylistic leader, comprising a magnificent clerestoried structure decorated with Romanesque-style semi-circular arches.[40]

In contrast, the earthworks of many twelfth-century earth and timber castles are mainly unimpressive grassed-over vestiges – 'green ghosts of the Anarchy,' in the words of Brian Hope-Taylor, the first archaeologist to systematically excavate one of these challenging sites, at Abinger, Surrey, in the late 1940s.[41] The small motte and bailey at Abinger has – unfortunately – become a type site for our understanding of Anarchy-period castles.[42] Hope-Taylor employed considerable methodological ingenuity for his time to strip and systematically excavate the motte top and reveal the 'ghosts' of rotted timbers that were identifiable as discolourations in the sandy surface. The flat summit was crowned with a square timber tower, 3.66m across, that was interpreted as standing on stilts (i.e. without a lower storey) within a palisade (Fig. 4.1: top). The excavator saw this as 'an observation point, a sniping point, and also a last place of refuge.'[43] The reconstruction of this watchtower-like phase (Fig. 4.1: bottom) has proven hugely influential in our understanding of timber castles generally, and castles of the Anarchy in particular, as somehow temporary, expedient and simple.[44] There are good reasons, however, why this reconstruction provides a skewed idea of the appearance of timber castles of the period.

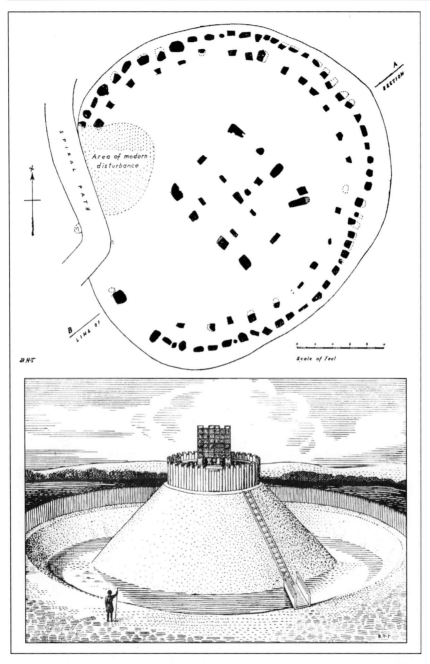

Fig. 4.1: Abinger, Surrey: **(top)** plan of excavations;
(bottom) reconstruction. Source: Hope-Taylor 1950.

First, the castle at Abinger was not in fact first built in the Anarchy.[45] Rather, the motte was raised *c.* 1100, the mid-twelfth-century phases representing a rebuild. Traces of an earlier motte-top tower were also mapped, showing that this was of a similar plan to its successor, but on a different orientation.[46] The 'castle of the Anarchy' therefore looked very similar to the castle of the immediate post-Conquest period, while the pottery assemblage for the twelfth-century phase shows little supporting evidence for the site being only temporarily occupied.[47] Second, the influential reconstruction of Anarchy-period Abinger is deceptive, as it includes only the motte, which was but one component in a larger complex. Traces of a likely bailey have been removed by landscaping and the motte stands adjacent to the medieval parish church, indicating that it was the focus of a lordly power centre rather than an isolated strongpoint. Indeed, John Blair has provided a tenurial context for the first castle on the site, showing that the motte was the *caput* of a small lordship created through subinfeudation by the end of the eleventh century.[48] Third, there is good reason to think that the structural details of the tower may not be correct. More recent excavations of timber castles in Britain and Europe provide a corrective to the notion that the 'typical' earth and timber castle comprised a motte with a simple timber tower perched on top. Instead, we now recognise that these sites could be impressive, permanent and well-defended, redolent with symbolism in the same way as their masonry counterparts.[49] Hope-Taylor's reconstruction of the tower at Abinger as a stilted structure leant heavily on pictorial and sculptural evidence – in particular, the Bayeux Tapestry and a Romanesque capital from Westminster – while the fact that the motte top was heavily truncated meant that the extant remains are misleading, with wall-lines potentially lost.[50]

Elsewhere, excavation in advance of development has occasionally discovered 'lost' Anarchy-period castles almost by accident, a clear example being the motte and bailey beneath Castle Street, Luton, Bedfordshire, whose massive defensive ditch was detected through construction work in 1963 and excavated more extensively prior to redevelopment in 2004–05 (Plate 5).[51] A small private castle rather than a siege work, this was a transient feature of the landscape, probably built *c.* 1139 for the foreign mercenary Robert de Waudari, who received the manor of Luton from King Stephen, but demolished after quite a brief period of activity. The archaeology of the site throws up familiar challenges. Excavation provides good insight into the plan and strength of the defences. The castle took up an area of about a hectare and was defined by a V-shaped ditch 4.5m wide and 2.3m deep, but nothing is known about internal structures and the site offered a paucity of finds.[52] While most accounts of the castles of the period have focused on the structural evidence, finds assemblages reveal other sorts of angles and perspectives on everyday life within these sites. In terms of the artefacts recovered from excavations, items of military apparel might catch the eye (see Chapter 5), but among the more characteristic items of metalwork from twelfth-century castles are copper alloy binding strips, often gilt, which probably adorned boxes or caskets containing items of portable wealth or religious significance; mounts and hasps that were fixed to movable items of furniture such as chests, or to doors; and padlocks and keys.[53]

Time and again archaeologists have pigeonholed undocumented earth and timber castles, especially those in isolated or especially defensible positions, into 'Anarchy' contexts without sufficient caution. Numerous undocumented mottes or ringworks are listed in inventories of medieval fortifications as likely 'adulterine' castles with little or no direct evidence, when a context in the earlier period of Anglo-Norman colonisation might be more appropriate. Each case is unique and only minutely detailed analysis of what is known about the likely tenurial context in the late eleventh and early twelfth century can help place sites into one context or another. Other mottes or ringworks unknown to history could relate to later periods of disturbance, such as in the reigns of Henry II or John, or reflect the development of lordship in a given locality. County-based studies of castles bring this issue into focus, undocumented earth and timber castles invariably making up a large proportion of the total number of known castles. In Norfolk, for example, sites such as Raveningham and Quidenham, both mottes without baileys in 'military' positions, have sometimes been ascribed Anarchy-period dates, despite the documented struggle between the Bigod and Albini families in the 1170s offering an equally plausible context for their construction.[54] In Devon, the similarly undocumented sites of Durpley, Shebbear and Woodford, Milton Damarel, lay respectively on the fringes of the mid-twelfth-century holdings of the royalist supporter Henry Tracy of Barnstaple and the Angevin-sympathising Baldwin de Redvers of Plympton, which provides a possible context for their construction, although post-Conquest dates cannot be ruled out.[55]

A further issue that has confused the interpretation of the period's castles is the misidentification of other landscape features as 'adulterine' mottes. Often, it seems, designating a site as an Anarchy-period castle is more interesting and glamorous than finding a more mundane explanation, leading to some fanciful but often enduring interpretations. Early identifications, including by the Ordnance Survey, have tended to stick when other origins now seem much more likely. The fact that medieval castle-builders were also capable of reusing pre-existing features such as prehistoric, Roman or early medieval barrows (especially the latter, given their often large size), moot mounds and gallows/execution mounds further complicates the issue. Hill-top beacons, natural knolls and medieval moated sites and mill mounds have all erroneously been identified as Anarchy-period castle earthworks, while post-medieval archaeology was quite poorly developed when early surveyors examined many 'mottes' that are more likely to be features such prospect mounds and ice houses. The context of such earthworks within or adjacent to designed landscapes is often key in recognising them as later features, although post-medieval constructions themselves may represent acts of reuse. One illustrative example is the mount known as 'Monks Grave' near the deserted medieval village of Ingarsby, Leicestershire, which has traditionally been seen as an 'adulterine' motte, being identified as such by the great landscape historian W.G. Hoskins in the 1950s (Fig. 4.2).[56] The monument, however, stands just outside a landscape of formal garden earthworks around Ingarsby Old Hall, over which it commands excellent views, suggesting that it might instead be a prospect mound.[57] Leicestershire is typical of English counties in preserving a large number of other undocumented earthworks whose status as early castles is disputed: examples at Gumley, Scraptoft and Shackerstone might alternatively be prospect mounds and those at Garthorpe and Launde might be mill mounds, while a larger mound at Melton Mowbray seems to be a genuine motte reused as the base for a mill.[58]

Individual sites present individual puzzles that excavation is not guaranteed to solve, especially given the difficulties of dating material culture to a period as discrete as a 19-year civil war (see Chapter 5). But while some supposedly Stephanic castles have been struck from the list, others have been added (see below). Indeed, dating the construction of 'genuine' mottes or ringworks on evidence derived from excavation – typically in the form of pottery – is rarely, if ever, precise enough to pin activity down to even a particular decade. In any case, excavation of numerous early castles has revealed long-term sequences of occupation whereby the appearances and defences of lordly sites evolved across and beyond the Saxo-Norman divide, so that identifying the 'origin point' of a castle is not straightforward.

In answer to the inevitable question of how many new castles were built in Stephen's reign?, therefore, the only legitimate answer is: not

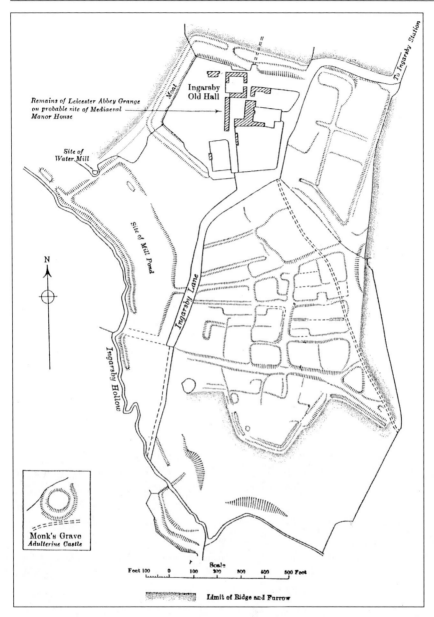

Remains of Leicester Abbey Grange
on probable site of Mediaeval
Manor House

Ingarsby
Old Hall

Site of
Water Mill

Site of Mill Pond

N

Ingarsby Lane

Ingarsby Hollow

To Ingarsby Station

Monk's Grave
Adulterine Castle

Feet 100   0   100   200   300   400   500 Feet
Scale

Limit of Ridge and Furrow

Fig. 4.2: The deserted village earthworks of Ingarsby,
showing the alleged earthwork of an Anarchy-period motte
in the bottom left-hand corner. Source: Hoskins 1956.

as many as once thought, and certainly not the 1,000+ figure claimed by one twelfth-century source (Robert of Torigni; see above, pg. 87). It is simply impossible to create a total distribution map of 'castles of the Anarchy,' and any attempt to do so would be misleading. Accordingly, Plate 6 maps all known and possible 'early' (pre-1200) castles, but is an illustration that should be viewed in the knowledge that not all examples would have been active across the period. This provides the broader context for understanding the castle sites discussed below, where excavation, survey and documentary study confirm construction in the period *c.* 1135–54. The evidence base for 'Anarchy-period' castles is reviewed in terms of three important themes: reuse of earlier sites, small towers set within mottes, and great free-standing towers or donjons of the period.

Reuse of earlier sites

Perhaps the most remarkable known example of an earlier site transformed into an Anarchy-period fortification is that of Silchester, Hampshire, where a crumbling, abandoned amphitheatre on the edge of the former Roman town was repurposed as a huge ringwork castle (Fig. 4.3).[59] Excavation has shown that the amphitheatre was modified in three main ways. First, a series of pits and trenches demonstrates that a timber gateway was built in the southern entrance, the Roman walls to either side revetted to form a refurbished entrance passage. Second, a massive palisade was built around the arena bank, as indicated by a trench cut into it. Third, within the arena itself, a post-built single-aisled timber hall-like building, *c.* 11–12m long and 8.5m wide, was built on the west edge of the Roman surface, close to the wall where the ground rises up slightly, and traces of a second structure lay nearby. Pottery aside, there were few medieval finds and occupation seems to have been brief; the site's drainage problems imply an unattractive location. The dating of these refurbishments seems clear: structurally, all these elements can be regarded as contemporary and stratified material from the hall and southern entrance belongs to the second half of the twelfth century, suggesting reoccupation by the 1150s.[60] One tantalising possibility is that this is the otherwise lost 'Castle of the Wood' (*Castellum de Silva*) recorded in the *Gesta Stephani* in 1147 (see above).

Repton, Derbyshire, has a prominent place in British medieval archaeology because of the famous excavations that took place there from the mid-1970s, revealing the winter quarters of a Viking army of the 870s that incorporated an important Mercian church into the

Fig. 4.3: The Roman amphitheatre at Silchester,
repurposed as an Anarchy-period ringwork.
Photograph by Oliver Creighton.

defences of a D-shaped enclosure built against the River Trent. Less well known is that the site saw military reactivation through the imposition of a twelfth-century castle – a phase unknown before the excavations and entirely undocumented; the 4m ditch around the motte was initially thought to be a Viking-age slipway into the River Trent.[61] Built on the point of the bluff, almost certainly by the earls of Chester, the motte-and-bailey castle overlooked fords both up- and downstream. Its construction disrupted the north-east corner of the cemetery, removing earlier burials, although the castle was short-lived and built over by the new Augustinian priory established on the instructions of Countess Matilda, widow of Earl Ranulf of Chester (who died in 1153).[62]

These two cases, a Viking-age fortification and Roman amphitheatre adapted as Anarchy-period castles, speak of pragmatism but also, perhaps, of harnessing the power of past power centres. They are also exceptional, since a more common sequence seems to have been the transformation of Anglo-Saxon manorial sites into earth and timber castles. Two clear archaeological case studies, Trowbridge in Wiltshire

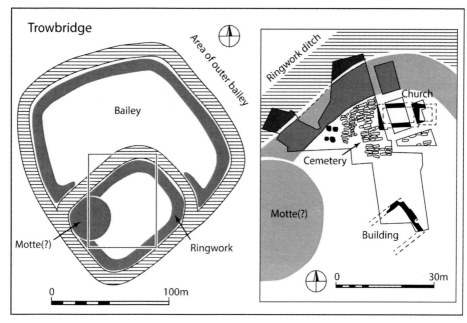

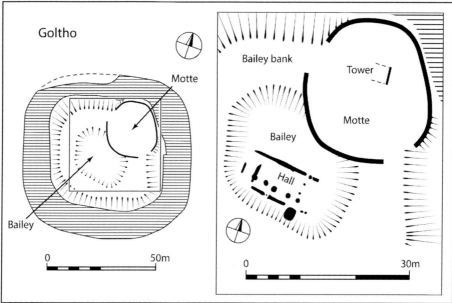

Fig. 4.4: Plans of castle sites at Trowbridge and Goltho.
Drawing by Seán Goddard, based on Graham and
Davies 1993; Beresford 1987.

and Goltho in Lincolnshire, highlight how reuse could work, although the phenomenon is likely to have been far more widespread.

At Trowbridge (Fig. 4.4: top), rescue excavation has provided a clear idea of the layout and strength of the Anarchy-period castle's defences but revealed little of its interior. Built on a ridge overlooking the River Biss, the castle comprised sub-rectangular inner and outer baileys and occupied 2.5 hectares. While no trace of a motte was revealed, historic map evidence suggests the presence of one in the corner of the inner bailey. Excavated sections across the defences emphasise their scale and strength: the inner bailey was defended by a V-shaped moat 10m wide and 4.50m deep and a clay rampart also 10m across, while the outer bailey's ditch was 11m wide, 5m deep, flat-bottomed and probably water-filled.[63] The ramparts of both inner and outer baileys bore signs of backing by massive timber structures, as indicated by postholes up to 1m across, and the outer bailey had some form of retaining wall. The only element of the castle interior that we can reconstruct in any fashion is the inner bailey, where an earlier stone-built church with a tiny cemetery was retained and embraced within the new ramparts, accompanied to the south by a large rectangular building, which may have been the hall.

Trowbridge Castle already existed in 1139, when it was in the hands of Humphrey de Bohun and besieged, unsuccessfully, by King Stephen.[64] While it is not entirely certain whether the defences represent a single phase of construction or the enlargement of an existing twelfth-century castle, the archaeological and morphological evidence are most consistent with the view of the outer bailey as a secondary expansion to a pre-existing ringwork, into which was superimposed a motte (in exactly the same manner as Goltho).[65] The site also supplies definitive archaeological evidence for the clearance of earlier settlement to make way for Anarchy-period defences: timber buildings associated with a Saxo-Norman manorial site were systematically levelled and the land surface sealed with a thick band of clay on which the outer bailey bank was built.[66] The settlement was displaced to the north, in the area where the later town grew up, with a street pattern fossilising the layout of the castle's defences.

The site of 'Goltho' (Fig. 4.4: bottom), where a castle/manor house and adjacent deserted village on the Lincolnshire claylands have both been excavated (although published separately),[67] has exceptional importance as a case study of a small seigneurial castle of the mid-twelfth century within its rural context. But it comes with considerable issues of interpretation – not least of which being that a reappraisal of the evidence suggests that the site was not Goltho at all but medieval Bullington, while the dating of the castle/manor site is almost certainly wrong, so that the phasing needs to be shifted forwards in time.[68] The excavator's published sequence sees a small motte, which succeeded a series of ringwork enclosures containing a hall and other buildings, erected after the Norman Conquest, but the revised dating of the site recommends that the motte and bailey instead first date to the mid-twelfth century, when the manor was united under the Kyme family.

This revised sequence has major implications for how we understand the impact of lordship on this otherwise unremarkable little parish. While the Norman Conquest saw the seat of lordship fundamentally unchanged (although the ringwork was rebuilt on a larger ground plan), the Anarchy saw a transformation in the image of seigneurial authority. Converted into a more compact and heavily defended site, with a far smaller and much more cramped interior than any of the earlier phases, the complex also had a more elevated and imposing appearance than before. The new motte was studded with stones to create what looked like a crude ersatz shell keep, and the entrance to the site faced away from the village rather than into it, as before.[69] The same period saw the village reordered with a regular planned extension, a deer park established in a corner of the parish and a small priory built just within sight of the castle and intervisible with Lincoln Cathedral.[70]

Both Trowbridge and Goltho emphasise how over the *longue durée* of settlement history, Anarchy-period castles often represent but one phase in the increasing visibility of lordship rather than a sudden moment of seigneurial imposition. A less thoroughly excavated but potentially comparable site is the motte and bailey of Middleton, Norfolk, where investigations show underlying late Saxon occupation within an earlier rectangular enclosure, and the castle shows clear evidence of twelfth-century occupation.[71] That investigations at Mount Bures, Essex, have identified a late Saxon building next to the suspected Stephanic motte and its adjacent church presents another potential example of a church/manor complex given a fortified upgrade in the civil war.[72] The two Cambridgeshire sites of Burwell and Wood Walton are further likely candidates, to be discussed in full in the case study of the fens offered in Chapter 9.

An alternative but also quite widespread strategy of castle building adopted by local lords in the mid-twelfth century was the reoccupation of prehistoric fortifications. This sequence is exemplified by the important but little-known site of Castle Combe, Wiltshire (Plate

7: top). A series of earthwork defences cut transversely across an Iron
Age promontory fort divided this vast site into four or five enclosures,
the innermost featuring the base of a keep known from early investigations.[73] Geophysical surveys reveal surviving buildings in all but the
outer bailey, which was open.[74] The site is usually dated *c.* 1140 and
associated with the Angevin-sympathising Dunstanville family, who
consolidated the Castle Combe barony in the mid-twelfth century. It
occupied a strategic location at the heart of a region heavily contested
during the conflict.[75] A mint in fact operated from Castle Combe in the
1140s, which was exceptional as the place was not a borough; as such,
the site seems the very embodiment of one of the castles in which, in the
words of William of Newburgh, tyrants minted their own coinage (see
pg. 137). On a smaller scale is the site of Hailes, Gloucestershire (Plate 7:
bottom), where Ralph of Worcester seems to have redeveloped an Iron
Age promontory fort ('Hailes camp') high on the western slopes of the
limestone Cotswold escarpment into a small earth and timber castle,
and also built a church in the valley bottom to create a short-lived
power base.[76] The triangular hillfort's defences were remodelled and
a circular platform *c.* 25m across and isolated within its own separate
enclosure was superimposed into its south-west corner, reusing the
remaining enclosure as a huge pre-positioned bailey. A comparable
site is Richmont, at East Harptree, on the Mendip plateau in Somerset,
another triangular promontory fort, which was held by William de
Harptree in 1138.[77]

The large multivallate hillfort of Castle Hill, Almondbury, that
overlooks Huddersfield, West Yorkshire, is another clear example. First
documented as the 'castellum de Almanberia' in a charter of 1142–54,
when granted to Henry de Lacy by King Stephen,[78] the site was
adapted during the civil war as a fortified outpost comprising a motte
with two baileys inserted into the oval hillfort. Excavation on the site
shows how large-scale modifications saw a great shale bank thrown up
over the prehistoric inner rampart to form the outer perimeter of the
castle, while the transverse bank of the original promontory fort was
reconstructed and its ditch recut to isolate what became the inner from
the outer bailey, and a motte was thrown up at the southern point of
the site.[79] The de Lacys followed a similar strategy on other estates:
a second castle mentioned in the same charter, Barwick upon Elmet,
West Yorkshire, took a very similar form, with a motte inserted into
a large hillfort that was subdivided into separate units. Excavation at
Desborough Castle, High Wycombe, Buckinghamshire, suggests that
the defences of a hillfort were recut in the mid-twelfth century to

form an outer bailey for a contemporary ringwork,[80] while at Merdon, Hampshire, another ringwork, somewhat oddly placed in the middle of an Iron Age hillfort, is usually attributed to Henry of Blois.[81] Other potential parallels are Hembury Castle and Loddiswell (both in Devon), where small timber castles were superimposed within large hillforts, although the potential date ranges for their construction span the period between the Norman Conquest and the mid-twelfth century.[82]

All these examples of hillforts adapted as castles feature multiple baileys, the prehistoric defences usually forming one vast outer enclosure. The possible uses to which these spaces were put include corralling stock but also as places of refuge and settlement for surrounding civilian populations.

'Enmotted' towers

A key case study of a timber castle built and occupied during the civil war is South Mimms, Hertfordshire (formerly Middlesex), which was excavated in the 1960s (Fig. 4.5). Almost certainly constructed for Geoffrey de Mandeville, Earl of Essex, the castle was built at some point between 1135 and the earl's rebellion of 1143–44, which culminated in his death after a fatal injury incurred while besieging Burwell Castle, Cambridgeshire (see pgs 265–71).[83] The very short period of time for which the site was intensively occupied means that the finds assemblage is of exceptional importance for our understanding of mid-twelfth century ceramics in the region (see pg. 120). Even within a period characterised by a wide variety of castle-building projects and technologies, the appearance of South Mimms stands out as unusual. The castle's focal point was a timber tower set within and partly covered by a contemporary motte, which was cut through to provide a walkway to the tower. This shows how the appearance of earthworks can disguise individuality in the design of sites easily labelled as, for example, 'motte and baileys,' which could have been strikingly different in appearance. Built on flint foundations, the tower had a rectangular ground plan measuring 9.6m x 8.4m, and there is evidence that its walls sloped in towards the top. Constructed of pegged-together timbers, the spaces filled with mortar or daub, it would have had much the same appearance as a church belfry. A floor level was provided at the same height as the motte summit, with upper storeys presumably reached by ladder.[84] While the site is easily dismissed as a temporary installation, in its local context the castle presented a multi-tiered spectacle, with its tower, at over 15m tall,

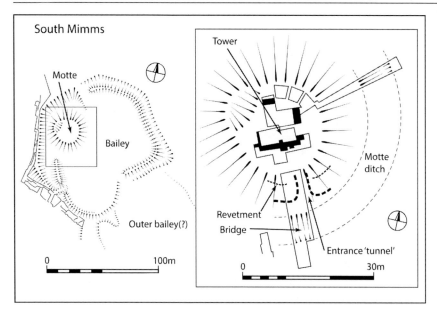

Fig. 4.5: Plan of South Mimms, Middlesex.
Drawing by Seán Goddard, based on Kent et al. 2013.

rising above a palisade surrounding the motte (and hiding the interior from view); the ensemble was approached first via a timber bridge, then through a passageway with a gate at its inner end, before the tower could be accessed.

The tower at South Mimms cannot have been the principal lived-in structure, which must have lain within the bailey, although the focus of the excavations on the motte – characteristic of castle archaeology at this time – means that we have little insight into how this space was used (although part of its bank sealed an earlier structure of some sort), and indeed aerial photographs suggest that the castle may have been planned with a second (outer) bailey.[85] In terms of function, Geoffrey de Mandeville's diminutive castle seems most likely to have served as a hunting lodge, lying on the edge of grounds that were to become Enfield Chase – which is another reason why we can question its styling as a 'castle of the Anarchy.' Small finds from the excavation of South Mimms support this interpretation: hunting arrowheads feature prominently in the assemblage, an inscription on one tile appears to represent a hunting dog and a piece of red deer skull whose antler is pierced with a nail is suggestive of a hunting trophy or else some sort of ostentatious, perhaps ceremonial, headgear.[86]

The castle site at Middleton Stoney, Oxfordshire, was seen as an adulterine motte before archaeological investigation revealed a longer and more complex sequence of occupation. The appearance of a motte is illusory (Figs 4.6 and 4.7d); instead, the mound comprised a mass of rubble from an earlier structure piled around a substantial new rectangular tower. We know little about the plan or appearance of the building as only one corner was excavated, although it seems to have been square, possibly with an open central area, had a latrine shaft and walls over 3m thick, and was accessed via an external stone stair. The structure is attributed to *c.* 1130–50, when the manor was in the hands of Richard de Camville, one of King Stephen's closest advisors; and although archaeological dating cannot confirm whether it was built before or during the civil war, the fact that Richard rose dramatically in the ranks as a result of Stephen's favour suggests that we can be confident in attributing the building to the Anarchy.[87] Deposits from a latrine shaft confirm the privileged and varied diet of the castle's inhabitants, who enjoyed fruit and grapes from a garden or orchard but also ate figs, which may have been imported.[88] At Ascot D'Oilly, Ascot-under-Wychwood, Oxfordshire, excavation similarly showed the 'motte' to consist of a mass of clay piled around a stone tower while it was being constructed.[89] A simple square structure *c.* 10m across with plastered internal walls, the tower had a latrine chute and seems to have been accessed via an external ladder or timber stair, the mortared base of which survived. Historical sources suggest that it was put up by the d'Oilly family *c.* 1129–50 and abandoned *c.* 1170–80.

The classic archaeological example of a mid-twelfth-century tower encased within a mound is, however, that at Farnham, Surrey, excavated by Michael Thompson in 1958.[90] The rectangular tower, some 14m across and with a central well shaft, was encased within a conical mound of marl. Identified as one of the castles built for Henry of Blois in 1138 but slighted in 1155, this structure was superseded by the shell keep around the mound that stands today. An alternative interpretation is that the tower could be part of a phase of the earlier twelfth century, perhaps for Bishop Giffard, and that the motte alone was the work of Henry of Blois, in which case the Winchester annalist's reference to the castle being 'built' in 1138 would indicate an earlier country house being given a makeover.[91] Regardless of the precise sequence of building, the appearance of the site – as a tower encased within a motte (i.e. 'enmotted') – would have been the same for much of the civil war.

In England, the phenomenon of enmotted towers seems to be predominantly twelfth-century in date; this type of construction

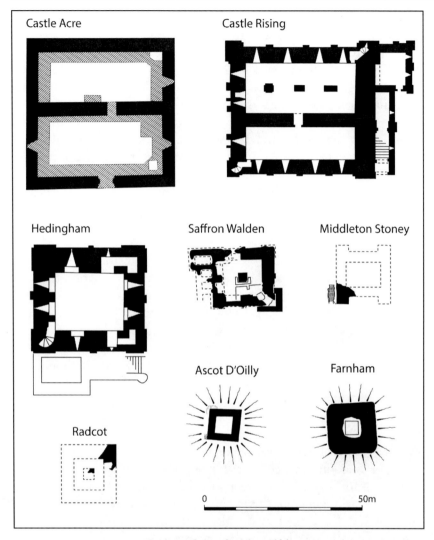

Fig. 4.6: Plans of mid-twelfth-century masonry towers.
Drawing by Seán Goddard and Oliver Creighton.

appears not to characterise castles of the Norman Conquest period, and the key later example of Lydford, Devon, which dates to the mid-thirteenth century, is a rebuild of an earlier structure rather than a *de novo* creation.[92] Other less clearly datable excavated examples of square towers within mottes are Great Somerford, Wiltshire,[93] and Groby, Leicestershire.[94] A fundamental question is why this method of castle building that surrounded a masonry tower with an earthwork was favoured. On the one hand, an earthwork abutment around a tower gave it added stability and strengthened it against attack (especially mining), but probably of greater importance was the image redolent with lordly associations that it projected – that of a tower apparently surmounting a motte. For newly important families wanting to stamp their mark on the countryside rapidly, this type of construction possessed advantages, as it removed the need to dig deep foundation trenches for the tower, and a newly constructed motte would need to settle for a considerable time before bearing the weight of a major masonry structure. An 'enmotted' tower also gave the impression of a well-established structure, perhaps amounting to a feigned sense of antiquity, which might be appropriate for *arriviste* seigneurial families.

Great towers

Stephen's reign marks an important moment in the history and evolution of the great tower in that it saw a grand type of construction that had previously been limited to royal castle-building projects imitated by magnates (Figs 4.6 and 4.7). Early waves of royal works in the late eleventh and early twelfth century, including the great towers at the Tower of London, Colchester and Rochester, and latterly Carlisle and Wareham, had already made their mark on urban centres, although the 1130s marked a lull in new works before the symbolism of the Norman great tower was seized upon and re-energised by the richest barons.[95]

In the absence of pipe rolls for Stephen's reign, we know little about whether royal castles were refurbished when they were put on a war footing. Roger of Wendover's *Flores Historiarum* does state that the Tower of London, centred on the great palace-donjon, which had by then stood for more than 60 years, was strengthened by its custodian, Geoffrey de Mandeville; this seems to have occurred at some point before it was threatened by Londoners in the summer of 1141.[96] We have no indication of the form these works took, however, and there is no hard archaeological evidence for improvements to the site's defences between *c.* 1100 and the 1190s.[97] At this early stage of its development, the White Tower was accompanied by at least one bailey,[98] and it is tempting to think that de Mandeville's efforts focused on these outer defences rather than the great donjon itself. The Tower may not have been the only fortification in this part of London: the first charter between the Empress Matilda and Geoffrey de Mandeville, usually dated to midsummer 1141, granted the earl hereditary custody of 'the Tower of London with the little castle which was Ravenger's' (*cum parvo castello quod fuit Ravengeri*).[99] That the other charters of the same period do not name Ravenger's castle but refer to the Tower of London and the castle 'beneath it/that belongs to it,' makes it more likely that the donjon was being differentiated from the enclosure(s) within which it lay rather than indicating that 'Ravenger's castle' was a separate fortification.[100] Ravenger, recorded in Domesday Book as a former Essex landholder, might have been an earlier Norman constable whose name became attached to the enclosure or perhaps to a tower on its perimeter.

The small number of newly built great towers of the mid-twelfth century were as multifunctional as other earlier examples – blending the needs of defence, residence and ceremony – and it would be unwise to downplay their military roles.[101] The key sites of Castle Hedingham, Essex, known from its superb upstanding remains (Figs 4.6 and 4.7b), and Castle Acre, Norfolk, whose development has been revealed by large-scale excavation campaigns (Figs 4.6 and 4.7c), are both worth examining in detail. It is important to underline that both of these classic case studies of Anarchy-period great towers were erected in regions that saw little or no actual military action in the civil war, lying as they do in what were strongly royalist areas.

Construction of the impressive ashlar donjon at Castle Hedingham in Essex can be pinned down closely to the mid-twelfth century. It was almost certainly built from *c.* 1142 to mark the elevation of Aubrey de Vere III to the earldom of Oxford by King Stephen.[102] From the exterior, the structure appears to comprise three storeys over a basement, but the upper windows were originally 'dummy' features that stood just above the level of a pyramidal roof. With their striking zig-zag decoration, these were the most ostentatious windows in the structure – for looking *at* rather than looking out of. Within the donjon, the uppermost level comprised a large reception hall, clearly 'public' in nature as it was overlooked by a well-lit surrounding mural gallery; below this lay a first-floor lower hall, entered through an ornate Romanesque door, with a plain basement below. Provision for accommodation is strikingly lacking, pointing to the building's primarily ceremonial purpose – for receiving, and variously impressing and intimidating, the earl's visitors, who were channelled through the structure via carefully positioned stairs and access arrangements intended to maximise the grand building's impact on the senses. The Albinis' squat but imposing tower of *c.* 1140 at Castle Rising, Norfolk (Figs 4.6 and 4.7a), is another with grand access arrangements; it was built in conjunction with impressive ringwork defences and a contemporary replanning of the settlement, although

Fig. 4.7: Views of mid-twelfth-century towers: **(a)** *opposite top* Castle Rising; **(b)** *opposite* Castle Hedingham; **(c)** *above top* Castle Acre (excavated remains); **(d)** *above* Middleton Stoney (tower contained within motte-like earthwork). Photographs by Oliver Creighton.

the structure itself remained unfinished and was completed only in the mid-thirteenth century.[103]

Important though this reinterpretation is, we have probably focused too much on the detail of such great buildings and downplayed the fact that they were single elements within much larger – and often powerfully defended – complexes. For example, the donjon at Castle Hedingham was centrally positioned within an older ringwork connected to a vast adjoining bailey.[104] It was within these spaces that the majority of those entering the castle would have conducted their business; few people would have gained any experience of what the donjon looked like inside, despite its visibility, which must only have enhanced its mystique. Although parkland at Castle Hedingham is not documented until the thirteenth century, there is a strong suspicion that the complex of the mid-twelfth century was accompanied by two parks – a detached 'great park' for hunting and income, and a 'little park' that enveloped and provided a backcloth for the residence.[105] Aubrey de Vere's social elevation as first Earl of Oxford was further displayed by his endowment of the nearby Benedictine priory of St Mary, St James and the Holy Cross for nuns; he founded it at some point before 1191 with his wife, Lucy, who became its first prioress.[106] He also funded rebuilding of the parish church, and the village plan strongly suggests that this too was recast.[107]

The de Warennes' great stronghold of Castle Acre, Norfolk (Figs 4.6 and 4.7c), whose evolution is well known through extensive and ambitious archaeological excavation in the 1970s and early '80s, is the key case study of the transformation of an already established masonry castle during Stephen's reign.[108] Period I (1070s) comprised a two-storey stone-built structure – styled by the excavators as a 'country house' — surrounded by a modest bank and ditch; it was preceded by a substantial timber building which was probably an Anglo-Saxon manor house. Period II (c. 1135–50) saw an initiative to transform this 'country house' into a great tower or donjon, which was left unfinished. Initially planned as a two-cell structure divided by a spine wall, on the footprint of the earlier building, the great tower was ultimately built with a ground plan only half this size (Period III), and after c. 1200 the focus of occupation had shifted to the lower ward. Crucially, the dating evidence for the conversion of the 'country house' into a great tower is clear: nine coins dating to c. the 1140s (principally of Stephen's type 1) were found in the Period II make-up of the southern half of the tower.[109]

The de Warennes' building project of the mid-twelfth century began by gutting the earlier structure of all internal features and timberwork. The ground floor was raised by approximately 1m and the doorway and windows at this level were blocked, in one case with mortared rubble extruding through the opening 'like toothpaste.'[110] Access must have been intended at first-floor level. The thickness of the walls was doubled and the perimeter defences were rebuilt in massive form, with the surrounding bank elevated over 5m above the land surface and crowned with a curtain wall.[111] Further excavations on the gatehouses confirmed that these too had seen extensive building work, with new timber bridges added and, in the case of the east gate, the addition of a stone causeway with a removable bridge section.[112] The excavators were certain that the same period saw the defences of the lower ward strengthened, although direct dating evidence is lacking.[113] A further possibility is that the defensive enclosure around the attached settlement was built or at least renewed in this period; excavations have shown that the castle was surrounded by a busy settlement landscape in the eleventh and twelfth century and that the ditch surrounding it was 17m across.[114]

Archaeologists have tended to portray changes to castles during Stephen's reign in terms of a narrative of defensive 'improvement.' To Castle Acre's excavators, its transformation shows that 'defence became of paramount importance,' with life in the upper ward 'considerably less comfortable' than before.[115] Yet we should not neglect glimpses of finer living: architectural stonework includes rich decorated pieces, and the animal bone assemblage too speaks of high-quality living, for example, the percentage of fallow deer bones remaining constant through all three phases and thus confirming a stable animal population for hunting.[116]

Another corrective to the idea that the 1140s represented a time when castle lords hunkered down in ever-strengthened fortresses is provided by reassessment of Castle Acre's landscape context.[117] To the south of the castle, a diversion of the Roman route known as the 'Peddars Way' seems to have been an initiative of the Norman period intended to create a manipulated route of approach that showcased an 'impressive tableau' of priory, castle and planned town to visitors.[118] Whether this 'landscape of lordship' was an initiative of the late eleventh or twelfth century is not absolutely clear, but circumstantial evidence favours the latter, as the Cluniac priory immediately west of the castle was only completed and dedicated in the mid-1140s and the visual impression of this ensemble will have made more sense with a towering donjon as its focal point.[119] That the stretch of curtain wall immediately in front (to the south) of the donjon was reduced to half of its original height[120] perhaps also shows the importance of opening up a clear vista of the new construction. In a wider regional context that also saw de Warenne's rivals the de Veres and D'Albinis engaged in grand castle building, these changes to Castle Acre's architecture and landscape may speak more of baronial one-upmanship than outright militarism.

At Saffron Walden, Essex, only the lower levels of the twelfth-century flint-built keep or donjon survive (Fig. 4.6), although archaeological excavation in the 1970s, combined with a structural survey and antiquarian sketches, allow much of its form to be reconstructed and its context to be understood.[121] A square structure, c. 20m across with massive clasping buttresses on three corners and a forebuilding adjoining the fourth, the donjon comprised at least three storeys, the lowermost being a basement provided with arched recesses for secure storage, above which was a large undivided hall-like space with high windows perhaps denoting a gallery. Excavations demonstrate that the donjon was raised in a single building operation contemporary with two ditched enclosures around it and a mound piled around its base.[122] This initiative can be assigned to the early to middle part of the twelfth century, although it is impossible to verify with archaeological dating evidence alone whether this was enacted by Geoffrey de Mandeville, as is usually supposed. The castle is first documented in 1141, when Geoffrey was given permission to move Newport's market into the castle that he later surrendered to King Stephen in 1143, although the tenurial history does not rule out the possibility that the castle was built by another owner or tenant of the manor after c. 1103–05.[123] A structure marking Geoffrey's elevation to the earldom of Essex in 1140 is nonetheless the likeliest scenario, and excavation within the adjacent town confirms the contemporary planning of a fortified settlement here (see pg. 226).

Shell keeps had emerged as an alternative to the square or rectangular great tower by the 1130s and the mid-twelfth century saw several significant works.[124] Most notably, Lincoln Castle uniquely preserves two towers both dating to the middle years of the twelfth century: the shell keep known as the 'Lucy Tower' on the principal south-west motte and the smaller rectangular 'Observatory Tower' (heavily rebuilt) on the smaller south-east motte. There is a general consensus that this unusual duplication of towers and mottes reflects the division of lordship between the constable and sheriff, although interpretations of the dating of the towers differ, partly depending upon a reading of a charter of King Stephen in which Earl Ranulf was permitted to fortify one tower within the castle and retain another which his mother,

Countess Lucy, had built or strengthened.[125] Only the Observatory Tower has seen archaeological investigation. This suggests that the structure was built in the mid-twelfth century and extended down into the core of the motte after the manner of Farnham.[126]

In terms of other excavated evidence for shell keeps of the period, Castle Neroche, Somerset, saw a brief but intense mid-twelfth-century phase of reactivation during the civil war that included the construction of a miniature shell keep and bailey on top of the motte, whose ditch was recut, although the earlier bailey seems to have been abandoned.[127] This makeover turned the castle into a far tighter and more elevated defensive nucleus, although the site was abandoned later in the twelfth century and eventually given over to rabbit farming. Not all masonry castles of the period feature towers, however. Excavations at Deddington Castle, Oxfordshire, revealed how a mid-twelfth-century phase attributed to William de Chesney, King Stephen's military commander of Oxford and its region, included an approximately diamond-shaped masonry enclosure.[128] Defined by a 2m-thick mortared wall, and with an entrance way consisting of a simple gap (the gatehouse came later), this enclosure partly perpetuated the line of an old inner bailey but also cut through the old motte, which became disused.

Deliberate Destruction: Castle Slighting

We should remember that while the Anarchy of Stephen's reign is renowned as a time of unparalleled and rapid castle building, the period and its immediate aftermath saw energetic efforts to demilitarise the landscape. Numerous fortifications were slighted, not only in the early years of Henry II's reign, but also in the final year of King Stephen's, after the peace settlement. In the words of William of Newburgh, the threat of illicit castles 'melted away like wax in the presence or fire' in 1153.[129] The Treaty of Winchester can best be regarded as an element of a peace *process* rather than a peace treaty *per se*,[130] and the destruction of castles provided evidence that this process was in train. The provisions of the 1153 settlement made clear that it was castles built after the death of Henry I that should be removed from the landscape and several chroniclers are very specific about the matter.[131] The *Gesta Stephani* states baldly that 'the new castles' should be demolished.[132] Henry of Huntingdon affords more detail in reporting Henry of Anjou's displeasure early in 1154 that 'the castles which had been built for evil purposes all over the land since King Henry's death were not being demolished, as had been settled between them [between King Stephen and Henry of Anjou] and confirmed in their permanent treaty of peace.'[133] John of Hexham's account is the most detailed and may capture the wording of the edict sent to all provinces that 'fortifications built by individuals on their own possessions after the death of King Henry' should be destroyed.[134] Of the key sources, only the *Liber Eliensis* refers specifically to Henry II pulling down illicit 'adulterine' castles after the peace settlement,[135] while Gervase of Canterbury reports that the new king caused 'very nasty little fortlets' (*munitiunculas pessimas*) to vanish from the landscape.[136]

The most famous instance of landscape demilitarisation during the period is, however, the pact or *conventio* between Ranulf, Earl of Chester, and Robert, Earl of Leicester, dating to some point between 1149 and 1153 and demonstrating how control of castle building had, in this area at least, become a magnate's prerogative.[137] Bearing some resemblance to contemporary Continental castle pacts, the *conventio* details links between a series of fortifications, including Mountsorrel, Leicestershire, that defined a region within which no new castles were to be built, while Earl Robert's castle at Ravenstone, where both earls had small estates, should be demolished unless Ranulf permitted it to remain. A moated site with adjacent fish ponds marks the only known lordship site in the Ravenstone parish,[138] and unless this represents a deactivated castle transformed into a manorial site, the fortification is lost. The large tract of the East Midlands covered by the treaty, marking an arc north of Leicester where the two earls' estates were intermixed, is mapped in Figure 4.8.[139] It is striking how the Earl of Chester's tenurial relationship with Leicester was played out not only through treatment of castles on their estates, but also through protocols of access to different elements of Mountsorrel Castle and its settlement: Ranulf and his *familia* were granted access to the Earl of Leicester's 'borough and baileys' (*burgo et baliis*) but Ranulf alone should be received into the 'capital castle' (*in dominico castro*) subject to the Earl of Leicester making him an oath of fidelity.[140]

While the symbolism of castle building is now a well-researched theme, the symbolism of castle destruction has received far less attention. In the English Civil War of the mid-seventeenth century the reasons for the widespread slighting of castles and manor houses extended far beyond the need to deny them to the enemy; they were also demolished, often systematically and with careful organisation, for profit and for the personal gain of commanders.[141] In the context of the mid-twelfth century, slighting was a much more severe sanction than castle confiscation; as well as removing a military strongpoint, it

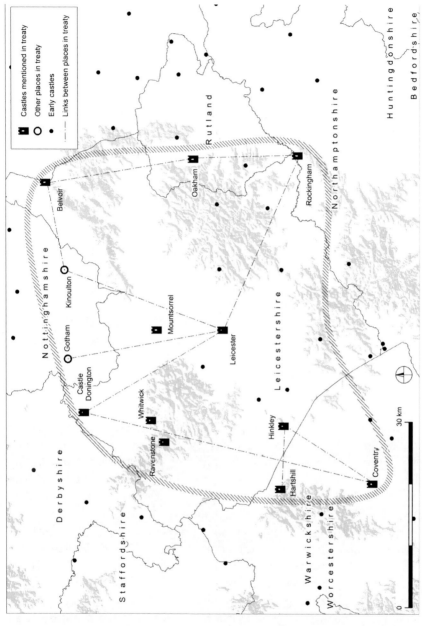

Fig. 4.8:
Reconstruction
of the
demilitarised
zone of the
East Midlands
covered by
the *conventio*
between the
earls of Chester
and Leicester,
c. 1149–53.
Map work by
Steven Trick.

symbolised nothing less than the emasculation of a lord, eradicating an ancestral seat for future generations of a noble dynasty.

As written sources are almost totally silent on the actual nature of slighting in the twelfth century, archaeology has an important contribution to make. The destruction of a castle could be a very public statement that peace had returned, although evidence of slighting is often overlooked by archaeologists, whose interests are more drawn to the functional lifetime of the sites they investigate. In the absence of excavation, evidence for the deliberate and targeted slighting of a motte or ringwork can look very much like the erosive and destructive processess that act upon all earthwork sites in their post-abandonment phases. One likely diagnostic trace of slighting, however, is the tearing out of a chunk of a motte to target the foundations of an internal tower – as is the case with the site at Groby, Leicestershire, dismantled on the orders of Henry II in 1174.[142] The foundations of a slighted twelfth-century keep or donjon at Wareham, Dorset, square in plan and with polychrome masonry forming eye-catching horizontal bands, were explored archaeologically in the 1950s.[143] The castle survived into the reign of John but the donjon seems to have been slighted before this, probably following the Treaty of Winchester; it was demolished thoroughly, the walls dismantled to just above the level to which the structure was sunk into the ground and its floor littered with charred oak timbers.[144]

Demolition of other sites extended far beyond a tokenistic burning of buildings or timber superstructures to include the levelling or reduction of defensive earthworks by spreading these into ditches. The nature of the ditch fill of the mid-twelfth-century castle at Luton, Bedfordshire, indicates a massive and rapid accumulation of chalk and other materials that points towards a sudden episode of slighting, for example,[145] while archaeology shows how the royal siege castle at Crowmarsh was levelled to the ground in 1153.[146] At Therfield, Hertfordshire, the vertical timbers that revetted the bailey bank were deliberated removed rather than left to rot *in situ*, and the character of the ditch fills confirmed slighting of the unfinished motte and bailey.[147]

The picture afforded by archaeology is a varied one, although there is enough evidence to show that there was no blanket slighting of all castles built during the war. Where defences were decommissioned, manorial occupation typically continued on and around their sites, while the foundation of a church or monastery on or near a slighted castle site was another means of highlighting its demilitarisation, as occurred at Repton, Derbyshire (see pg. 194). Excavation shows that

Trowbridge Castle, Wiltshire, was not in fact downgraded into a manorial site until late in the twelfth century or early in the thirteenth, when the de Bohun family, who had held the castle for the Empress, lost the honour of Trowbridge; the defences were levelled and spread, to form a level platform encompassed by the moat.[148] The circumstances of individual families seem to have dictated the fate of their castles, with some favourites of Stephen retaining their properties. The castle of the de Camville family at Middleton Stoney, Oxfordshire, is a case in point. Richard de Camville was one of Stephen's closest advisors, frequently witnessing his documents, although following the accession of Henry II he made himself useful to the new king, serving as Sheriff of Berkshire in 1156–57 and accounting for revenues from the Oxfordshire forests.[149] Accordingly, the little stone castle on Richard's chief manor of Middleton Stoney remained intact in the wake of the Treaty of Winchester, was passed to his son after his death in southern Italy and was only abandoned following slighting ordered by King John in 1216.[150] This saw the tower demolished and the castle's ditches backfilled, although high-status occupation continued in the form of a manor house built within the former bailey.

Summary

The considerable challenges of identifying and dating castle sites built and strengthened during the civil war mean that the total picture of fortification in the period will always remain somewhat murky, irrespective of how much new archaeological evidence comes to light. That Stephen's reign saw a marked increase in the density of castles is beyond doubt, although this was probably more intensive in contested regions rather than being a genuinely nationwide phenomenon, and it is likely to have involved scores rather than hundreds of 'new' sites. Overall, archaeology highlights individuality in twelfth-century timber castle design, which went far beyond the 'motte and bailey' or 'ringwork' labels. 'Enmotted' towers were a hallmark of the period, as was the reactivation and remodelling of Iron Age hillforts as castles and the construction of great masonry donjons, which evolved from being a royal to a magnate prerogative during the civil war. The essential motif of castle design, adopted broadly across the spectrum of construction, was the physical elevation of a central structure. The proportion of unfinished and lost sites is also far higher than for other periods, due partly to the thoroughness of slighting, which had strong symbolic undertones as well as a practical military purpose.

Notes

1 See in particular Renn 1968, 46–53; Coulson 1994b; Speight 2000.

2 Stenton 1932, 201–2.

3 Dixon 2008.

4 Higham and Barker 1992.

5 Hollister 1993.

6 Dalton 1992.

7 John of Hexham in Symeon of Durham, *Symeonis monachi opera omnia*, Arnold 2012, Vol. II, 323. See also Colvin et al. 1963, Vol. I, 40–2; Dalton 1994, 175.

8 Coulson 1994b, 67.

9 Coulson 1994b, 75–6.

10 *Gesta Stephani* I, 49, Potter and Davis 1976, 104–5. This is the only point at which the text contains the phrase 'adulterine castle.'

11 Johnson and Cronne 1956, no. 1475, 203.

12 Pounds 1990, 27–32; Higham and Barker 1992, 126–7.

13 Coulson 1993; 1994a.

14 Coulson 1993, 3; 1994a, 99; 2003, 129–30.

15 Hamilton Thompson 1912.

16 Coulson 2003, 129.

17 Among the more important castles described as having 'impregnable' fortifications are Exeter (1136), Devizes, Trowbridge, Malmesbury, Wallingford (1139), Oxford (1142) and Winchcombe (1142–5). See *Gesta Stephani*, Potter and Davis 1976.

18 *Gesta Stephani* I, 16, Potter and Davis 1976, 32–3.

19 *Gesta Stephani* I, 21, Potter and Davis 1976, 44–5.

20 Young 2000, 194–5.

21 *Liber Eliensis* III, 62, trans. Fairweather 2005, 389.

22 Pugh 1953, 28–9; Davison 1967.

23 Christie and Creighton 2013, 193–4, 217.

24 Patterson 1991, 172–3. On the archaeology, see Good 1996, although much on the excavations remains unpublished.

25 *Gesta Stephani* I, 27, Potter and Davis 1976, 56–9.

26 William of Malmesbury, *Historia Novella* III, 78, King and Potter 1998, 130–1.

27 *Gesta Stephani* I, 47, Potter and Davis 1976, 98–9.

28 *Gesta Stephani* II, 69, Potter and Davis 1976, 138–9. See also Wessex Archaeology 2009, 23–5, 45–6.

29 Prior 2007, 77–82.

30 King 1983, xxxi.

31 Higham and Barker 1992, 125.

32 King 1980b.

33 *Gesta Stephani* II, 109, Potter and Davis 1976, 208–9.

34 Davis 1962, 220, 228 n.10; King 1983, 560; Fulford 1985, 72–7.

35 Stamper 1984. An alternative location, based on the place-name, is Tytherley (Davis 1962, 213, 229 n.11).

36 *Anglo-Saxon Chronicle*, ed. Whitelock 1961, 199.

37 Robert of Torigni wrote: *ut everterentur; quorum multitudo ad xj. c. et xv. summam.* See *Chronicles of the Reigns of Stephen, Henry II and Richard I*, Howlett 1889, 177. Not all versions of the manuscript have the same figure, however: one has 126 (Coulson 1994b, 69, n 5).

38 Coulson 2003, 119.

39 King 1983, xxxi–xxxii.

40 Alcock and Buckley 1987.

41 Hope-Taylor 1956, 249.

42 Hope-Taylor 1950; 1956.

43 Hope-Taylor 1950, 32.

44 See Higham and Barker 1992, 201, 273, 293–6.

45 For the incorrect view that this castle was erected during the civil war, see, for example, Pounds 1990, 12.

46 Hope-Taylor 1950, 29–30.

47 In the motte ditch, 'Mid-twelfth-century pottery formed a quantitatively and stratigraphically superior group' (Hope-Taylor 1950, 24, see also 33–8).

48 Blair 1981.

49 Higham and Barker 1992, 244–325.

50 Higham and Barker 1992, 152–8, 293–6. On the rationale for the reconstruction, see Hope-Taylor 1950, 32–3; 1956, 242–3.

51 Coles 2004; Abrams and Shotliff 2010.

52 Abrams and Shotliff 2010.

53 Ashley 2015, 282–4.

54 Liddiard 2000, 101–4.

55 Higham 1982, 105.

56 Hoskins 1956, 47, Fig. 5. See also Creighton, 2000, 29.

57 Everson and Brown 2010, 56.

58 Creighton 1997, 27–9.

59 Fulford 1989.

60 Fulford 1989, 59–65; 175–6, 193–5. See also Fulford 1985, 73–5, 77–8.

61 Biddle and Kjølbye-Biddle 1992, 37–8; Stroud 1999, 11–12.

62 Biddle and Kjølbye-Biddle 1992, 37–8.

63 Graham and Davies 1993, 58–60.

64 *Gesta Stephani* I, 43, 45, Potter and Davis 1976, 92–3, 96–7.

65 Graham and Davies 1993, 148; Creighton 2000, 107.

66 Graham and Davies 1993, 61–2.

67 Beresford 1975; 1987.

68 Everson 1988; 1990. For a summary see Creighton 2005b, 21–7. For the rural context, see also Bassett 1985.

69 Beresford 1987, 103.

70 Creighton 2005b, 25–6. See also Creighton and Rippon 2016.

71 Ashwin 2001, 653–6.

72 Lewis and Ranson 2011, 46.

73 Creighton 2000, 114.

74 Sabin and Donaldson 2007.

75 Scrope 1852, 18–23.

76 Wright and Fradley 2013.

77 Brown 2008.

78 Cronne and Davis 1968, no. 430.

79 Manby 1968.

80 Collard 1988.

81 Cole 1994. Documentary and place name evidence points to a defended pre-Conquest manorial residence on the site. See Hughes 1989, 31–2.

82 Higham 1982, 108, 111; 1988, 144–5.

83 Kent et al. 2013.

84 Kent et al. 2013, 20, 30–2.

85 Kent et al. 2013, 11.

86 Kent et al. 2013, 10, 61, 63–4, 73–5.

87 Rahtz and Rowley 1984, 156–7. See also Rowley 1972, 123–4.

88 Rahtz and Rowley 1984, 61, 151–2.

89 Jope and Threlfall 1959. See also Bond 2001, 48–50.

90 Thompson 1960; 1967.

91 Riall 2003.

92 Saunders 1980. For examples, see Kenyon 1990, 40–4.

93 Goddard 1930.

94 Wessex Archaeology 2011.

95 Dixon 2008.

96 Impey 2008, 5, 142.

97 Keevil 2004, 8.

98 Impey 2008, 19–22, 142.

99 Cronne and Davis 1968, no. 274. See also Round 1892, 328.

100 Parnell 1993, 17; Impey 2008, 21. For the alternative view that Ravenger's castle was a discrete early Norman castle, see Colvin et al. 1963, 707.

101 Hulme 2007–8.

102 Dixon and Marshall 2003; Dixon 2008, 267. See also Liddiard 2005b, 39–40.

103 Morley and Gurney 1997, 133–5. See also Dixon 2008, 255–6.

104 See Brown 1989, 77–9.

105 Liddiard 2005b, 40; Liddiard and Wells 2008, 90–1.

106 Page and Round 1907, 22–3.

107 Brown 1989, 78.

108 Coad and Streeten 1982; Coad 1983; Coad et al. 1987, 256–8. See also Dixon 2008, 267.

109 Coad and Streeten 1982, 166, 192, 268–72. Although it should be noted that, architecturally, some of the features would be more appropriately ascribed an earlier twelfth-century date.

110 Coad and Streeten 1982, 167, 169.

111 Coad and Streeten 1982, 164–71, 193–4.

112 Coad et al. 1987, 275, 282, 285.

113 Coad et al. 1987, 270, 284.

114 Leah 1993, 505–6.

115 Coad and Streeten 1982, 179.

116 Coad et al. 1987, 194, 256–7, 282.

117 Liddiard 2000, 44–74, 134–9; 2005b, 46–51.

118 Liddiard 2005b, 48.

119 Liddiard 2005a, 139; 2005b, 49.

120 Coad and Streeten 1982, 168–9.

121 Bassett 1982, 48–61.

122 Bassett 1982, 16, 22; Ennis 2011b. See also Lewis and Ranson 2013, 17–18.

123 Bassett 1982, 15–18.

124 Higham 2015, 19.

125 Thompson 2004, 27–8; Marshall 2004b, 61–3; Higham 2015.

126 Reynolds 1975.

127 Davison 1972, 26.

128 Ivens 1983; 1984, 111–12.

129 William of Newburgh, *The History of English Affairs* I, 32, 1, Walsh and Kennedy 1988, 130–1.

130 Holt 1994, 293–5. On the peace settlement generally, see Garnett 2007, 262–326.

131 King 2010, 290.

132 *Gesta Stephani* II, 120, Potter and Davis 1976, 240–1.

133 Henry, Archdeacon of Huntingdon, *Historia Anglorum* X, 38, Greenway 1996, 772–3.

134 John of Hexham in Symeon of Durham, *Symeonis monachi opera omnia*, Arnold 2012, Vol. II, 331; translation in King 2010, 290.

135 *Liber Eliensis* III, 62, Fairweather 2005, 460.

136 Gervase of Canterbury, Stubbs, Vol. I, 1879, 160. See also Coulson 1994b, 69; 2003, 141.

137 Coulson 1995; 2003, 211–12.

138 Renn 1968, 290; King 1983, 256.

139 For other (cruder) depictions of the demilitarised zone, see Renn 1968, 53; Pounds 1990, 8.

140 Coulson 1995, 66–7. See also King 1980a, 2, 6–7.

141 See Rakoczy 2008.

142 Creighton 1997, 22.

143 Renn 1960.

144 Renn 1960, 56, 59–60, 68.

145 Abrams and Shotliff 2010, 392.

146 Laban 2013.

147 Biddle 1964, 60, 62.

148 Graham and Davies 1993, 149.

149 Amt 1993, 60.

150 Rahtz and Rowley 1984, 12, 61, 157.

Chapter 5

Material Culture:
From Arts to Coins

MATERIAL CULTURE – the physical evidence of artefacts and architecture – is of course core to archaeological discourse but has played a very marginal role in previous discussion of 'the Anarchy.' While the period's coinage has been the subject of several important studies and is the focus of its own specific debates and literature, a great volume of other evidence – including pottery and other artefacts recovered from archaeological excavations, single finds of artefacts (especially through metal-detecting), architectural sculpture, building remains and environmental evidence – has been badly overlooked. This body of information, which is growing all the time as new discoveries come to light, has much potential to illuminate aspects of everyday life, including at a level below the social elite, but making sense of it comes with a set of challenges – not least the ever-present issue of dating materials precisely to the period in question.

It is important to underline from the outset that it is simply not possible to identify 'the Anarchy' as a clear event horizon with most of the evidence explored in this chapter. An obvious exception is the coinage, which represents an exceptional category of material as coins are simultaneously historical sources and everyday items of material culture. If we were to reimagine the mid-twelfth century as a hypothetical prehistoric research context, stripped of all our knowledge and preconceptions of the period based on its documents, it is highly unlikely that archaeologists would identify the 'signature' of any great rupture in society or crisis in the landscape. Indeed, the same is broadly true of the Norman Conquest, with key categories of evidence such as pottery showing imperceptible change and the

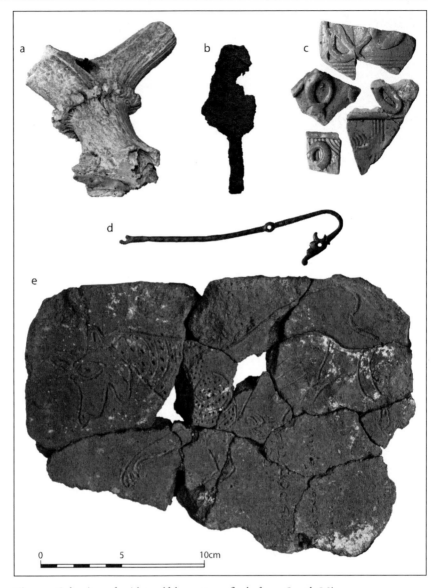

Fig. 5.1: Selection of mid-twelfth-century finds from South Mimms
Castle, Middlesex. **(a)** red deer antler and skull fragment with
drilled hole and iron fastening; **(b)** arrowhead; **(c)** assemblage of
Stamford-type ware; **(d)** copper alloy binding strip; **(e)** ceramic tile
with grafitto. Source: reproduced with the permission of the Museum
of London. Photographs by Oliver Creighton.

archaeology instead pointing towards life carrying on pretty much as before for the vast majority of people, although a clear horizon of coin hoards deposited in the 1060s and 1070s provides one likely indicator of disruption – at least in some regions (see pg. 149).[1] For the most part, changes in the material evidence occurred over much longer timescales, although political and concomitant economic turmoil could act to variously accelerate and amplify or hold back longer-term processes that were already in train.

New information about twelfth-century portable material culture is being revealed especially through metal-detected finds reported through the Portable Antiquities Scheme.[2] The data set is growing yearly (a sample of artefacts is presented in Plate 8), although the dating of such items is sometimes problematic. A great body of other information remains hidden away in the catalogues and appendices of excavation reports; especially significant assemblages come from sites constructed and then dismantled within the period of the civil war, such as South Mimms, Middlesex (Fig. 5.1).[3] Much more may be revealed by systematic revisiting of old published sites and finds of medieval date. This chapter explores the material culture of the mid-twelfth century in three parts: the first examines the period's pottery and the changing pottery industry; the second focuses on items that can in one way or another be regarded as late Romanesque art, including seals, sculpture and funerary monuments; and the third provides a synthesis of coin types, use and mints during Stephen's reign.

Pottery

Pottery is of course one of the medieval archaeologist's prime sources of evidence. Sherds are more or less ubiquitous on most excavated post-Conquest sites and occur frequently in the plough soil. The standard ceramic product of the twelfth century was the cooking pot, the other most commonly occurring vessels being jars and jugs. Other products might be restricted to high-status contexts: for example, in the royal castle of Ludgershall, Wiltshire, early to mid-twelfth-century dripping pans were placed next to the fire to catch the juices running off joints of meat; they were only used once, presumably for special feasts.[4] Where decoration occurred on pots, it typically took the form of incised linear marks, combing, stamping or rouletting; the most elaborate vessels could feature zoomorphic handles or spouts, although pottery vessels of the period can only rarely be regarded as exercises in Romanesque art. Ceramic products could be used for a wider range of functions beyond cooking and dining, including storage and lighting (lamps), in industry (crucibles) and as building materials (floor and roof tiles).[5]

In the early years of the development of medieval archaeology, excavators sometimes targeted documented or suspected Anarchy-period sites to obtain closely datable ceramic material. At Ascot D'Oilly, Oxfordshire, for example, Martyn Jope excavated a motte because the documentary evidence suggested a short-lived site built and demolished in the twelfth century.[6] Such an approach has its problems, however, as it is easy to assume that excavated material is twelfth-century in date when it might equally derive from unanticipated earlier or later phases. A very clear example is the site of Faringdon Castle, Oxfordshire, where E.T. Leeds, who excavated here in the 1930s, attributed the ceramics he recovered to the period 1144–45, when this 'adulterine' castle is documented as having being built by the Earl of Gloucester.[7] In light of all we know about pottery of the period, however, the material cannot be this early; instead, the assemblage, which includes decorated wares, dates primarily to the thirteenth century and must derive from some phase of post-Anarchy activity.[8] That said, where we can be confident about the dating of archaeological layers on sites occupied through the twelfth century, the range and quality of pottery sometimes show clear evidence of change either side of the civil war period. In the case of the Anarchy-period castle at Trowbridge, Wiltshire, late twelfth-century deposits contain a completely different range of fabrics from more distant sources than before.[9] Intriguingly, other sites have produced significant quantities of Roman material. Excavation of the siege castle at Bentley, Hampshire, produced 4.7kg of pottery, of which 4.6kg comprised residual Roman material along with roofing tiles and glass. It is not clear whether this was derived from an underlying building or from a known villa site to the north.[10] At South Mimms, Hertfordshire, meanwhile, the base of the timber tower yielded quantities of reused Roman brick and tile.[11] These examples throw up fascinating possibilities of the conscious reuse of Roman sites and/or material culture, utilised both as a convenient source of building material as well as for the potentially powerful associations in the minds of twelfth-century castle builders.

Besides the evidence from high-status sites such as these, pottery evidence can provide a possible route into assessing the impact of the civil war on everyday life, and trade and industry more generally, and it seems only natural to ask whether pottery and the networks through which these products were supplied show evidence of direct or indirect change.

Presumably, the turmoil of the Anarchy would have seen disruption to centres of pottery manufacture and supply networks in affected areas. Do we see evidence of developments, new production centres emerging and others in decline, that can be attributed to the disturbances? Did the political allegiances of certain regions have any bearing on where ceramic products were sourced from? These are questions that few ceramicists have grappled with, due in no small part to the difficulty of dating assemblages precisely to the period in question, and we should be cautious in assuming that major historical events and processes can be discernible in the pottery evidence. The complexity of these issues is highlighted by new perspectives on the impact of the Norman Conquest on pottery. While the event is naturally seen as a traumatic episode that transformed English society, developments in ceramics relate to changing cooking practices and the construction of new identities in very intricate ways, and while the Conquest was one factor in the processes of change, it was not the sole driver.[12]

Even if our evidence base makes it difficult to give direct answers to these intriguing questions, what is crystal clear is that the mid-twelfth century saw radical changes in pottery production and the pottery market. Understanding pottery production and supply in the period is especially difficult, as developments were neither consistent across England nor evolutionary in nature. Indeed, in many parts of the country, the quality of ceramic products actually declined over the course of the twelfth century and in some areas then improved again towards the end of the period. These factors mean that dating supposed twelfth-century phases of archaeological sites on the basis of pottery alone is fraught with problems. Furthermore, we should remember that great swathes of medieval rural England, including the extreme south-west and north-east, and large parts of Wales, were effectively aceramic well into the twelfth century. Even in the case of the largest and most thoroughly excavated sites of the period, such as Wolvesey Palace, Winchester, phasing must be based on structural relationships, cross-related to documentary evidence, rather than on the pottery.[13] Yet amidst the mosaic of local and regional patterns in the rapidly changing twelfth-century pottery industry, three broad trends are clear.

A first important factor was the post-Conquest decline of the major late Saxon wheel-thrown pottery industries supplying kiln-fired wares across much of eastern and north-eastern England. Several such industries were based in towns, especially in the Midlands and the east of England, including those producing Thetford ware, St Neots ware and Stamford ware (see Fig. 5.1c), and their shutting down in the eleventh and twelfth centuries, albeit over subtly different timescales, marked a major watershed in the pottery industry. This broad picture conceals intricate regional variations. For example, examination of the important archaeological discovery of a kiln manufacturing Stamford-style wares in Pontefract, West Yorkshire, produced evidence via scientific dating that it was last fired in the early eleventh century, although high-quality developed Stamford ware was in use well into the late twelfth century elsewhere.[14]

A second broad trend recognised is the emergence in the late eleventh and twelfth century of a plethora of much smaller-scale rural industries producing cruder handmade wares (many of them shell-tempered), cooking pots tending to be squatter and broader than before. These products were often fired in clamp kilns and supplied markets that were far more localised than those of the late Saxon pottery production centres.[15] Potting became overwhelmingly a rural industry, conducted by groups of peasant potters, perhaps on a seasonal basis, so that a major urban centre such as London was supplied by a network of production sites in the surrounding countryside. This trend was the starting point for the very high level of regional diversity that was to be so characteristic of later medieval pottery, although the areas over which products were distributed do not neatly map regional cultural groupings.[16] Illustrative examples of such products include the Shelly ware industries of Buckinghamshire, Bedfordshire and Northamptonshire, and the Hertfordshire Greyware industries.

Against this general picture of change, albeit with subtle regional variations, it is clear that in most areas the pottery industry was settling down towards the end of the twelfth century, certainly by the middle of the thirteenth century. By this time, a third major trend had seen some of the rural production centres grow to pre-eminence, producing mainly kiln-fired, wheel-thrown and glazed pottery, including jugs. It is also from the middle of the twelfth century that we see the popularisation of tripod pitchers – jug-like decanters for wine or ale, resting on three small feet to enable pouring, that speak of display at the table.[17] Another departure was the production of ceramic building materials for the first time since the Roman period: in London, ceramic roof tiles appear in the archaeological record just before the mid-twelfth century, and floor tiles come a little later.[18] An unusual and crude example, depicting what seems to be a hunting dog, was excavated at Geoffrey de Mandeville's castle at South Mimms, Middlesex (Fig. 5.1e)

These high medieval pottery industries tended to serve larger areas than previously, with potters specialising, centralising and working in larger groups. The growth of the marketing network is usually invoked as the principal explanation for this transformation of the industry, with potters more receptive to new ideas and the technologies of the wheel and permanent kiln.[19] The trend is charted particularly well in archaeological evidence from London, where the changeover from handmade to wheel-thrown and glazed wares occurred broadly in the period *c.* 1140–90, perhaps during a couple of decades within this date range, immigrant potters playing a critical role in the process.[20] One of our foremost case studies of such a production site is Pound Lane, Canterbury, Kent, where in 1986 archaeologists excavated a kiln operated by a Continental potter around the middle of the twelfth century to produce glazed, decorated and wheel-thrown wares.[21] Comparable developments tended to be a little later and slower in other parts of southern England, and in areas of the south-west much handmade pottery continued to be produced through the medieval period. Again, each region has its own sequence.

By and large, these trends occurred irrespective of the disturbances of King Stephen's reign: the decline of the late Saxon industries was in train long before, and the twelfth-century move towards rural industries and localised networks pursued a piecemeal evolution rather than being a sudden response to any given factor. It is also important to stress that in the mid-twelfth century the hinterlands supplied by pottery production centres were sufficiently localised that military and political events probably had little impact upon them, although future studies may reveal localised responses by the pottery industry to the disturbances of the period in the hotly disputed heartlands of the civil war – particularly the Cotswolds and Thames Valley. It is in the emergence of the new industries later in the twelfth century that we are more likely to detect the impact of the civil war, albeit indirectly, in the sense that their growth occurred in the context of the commercialisation and market growth that followed the Anarchy.

Late Romanesque Art and Portable Material Culture

The disruptions of the civil war in England need to be seen within the wider context of a Western Europe that in the twelfth century witnessed not only strong economic growth but also great cultural and intellectual achievement. Charles Homer Haskins's *The Renaissance of the Twelfth Century* (1927) made a powerful case for the period as a vibrant and formative moment in European cultural development, although historians and art historians have since debated the appropriateness of the label 'renaissance.'[22] The intellectual landscape of the twelfth century transformed amidst a revival of science and philosophy, the translation and re-emergence of classical literature and the development of new intellectual centres, while in art historical terms the period witnessed the culmination of Romanesque art and the genesis of the Gothic.

There is actually remarkably little evidence that the civil war held back cultural achievement in England and good reason to think, perversely, that the chaotic political landscape was actually a stimulus to patronage and experimentation in the arts. In several different spheres 'Romanesque art blossomed into maturity' during Stephen's reign.[23] The illustrated books of the mid-twelfth century, including the world-famous Winchester Bible, are the most prominent manifestation of this, but other artistic achievements are found in the evidence of stone sculpture and seals and, to a lesser extent, carved ivory items, textiles and stained glass.[24]

Much debate on artistic achievement in twelfth-century England has focused on the cultural networks and affinities of the hugely powerful figure of Henry of Blois, Bishop of Winchester. Educated at Cluny and widely travelled, Bishop Henry has long been recognised as a cosmopolitan patron and early antiquarian; for a period during the civil war he issued his own coinage, depicting his crowned bust with a sceptre.[25] At Glastonbury Abbey, fragments of blue lias carving from the cloister built under the patronage of Henry of Blois, who was abbot between 1126–71, are 'amongst the finest examples of Romanesque sculpture produced in England.'[26] Polished in appearance, precise in detail and crisp in execution, decoration on the fragments includes foliage, animal figures and berry clusters, and shows sufficient similarity to carvings from Wolvesey Palace, Winchester, to suggest that the same sculptors were at work.[27] Such coherence of form and style underlines Henry's ability to control production at his workshops to develop a bespoke brand of Romanesque architecture.

According to John of Salisbury, Henry of Blois purchased ancient statues from Rome and had them transported to Winchester in the 1140s, although his taste for the classical world has probably been overstated, and his gifts to religious institutions included items from a very wide range of cultural contexts.[28] Defining features of Bishop Henry's building projects were the pioneering use of Purbeck marble – later to become a hallmark of Gothic architecture – and imported Tournai marble, including the font in the nave of Winchester Cathedral.[29] A more general reflection of the interest in the past shown by the twelfth-century aristocracy is the fashion of reusing ancient engraved gemstones, often of classical origin and sourced from Italy and the Levant, as counterseals, with the legend engraved on a metal rim that was sometimes attached to a finger-ring.[30] Henry of Blois was an early user of one of these gem counterseals, underlining his reputation as a man of taste and cultural influence.

Patronage at the highest social level accounts for the luxurious illustrated bibles and psalters manufactured during Stephen's reign, when English book production was more prolific and illumination more original than in contemporary France.[31] Especially innovative was the 'damp fold' technique (whereby the thinness of clothing on figures highlighted the human form) adopted by the celebrated Master Hugo, who operated out of the abbey at Bury St Edmunds during the second quarter of the twelfth century and adopted Byzantine conventions in a rich body of work that also extended to bronze casting and stone sculpture.[32] An archaeological angle on the art of the twelfth-century book, easily overlooked, is provided by finds of copper alloy book clasps, which could feature ornate openwork ornament (Plate 8b).[33] Twelfth-century stray finds of book clasps are not as uncommon as might be imagined: the parish of West Acre, Norfolk, for example, has produced two, one with ornate quatrefoil decoration and an animal head terminal, and the other inlaid with red enamel.[34]

Fine metalwork of the twelfth century presents considerable problems of interpretation as high-quality items were peripatetic and it is often uncertain whether individual *objets d'art* were manufactured in England or on the Continent. Among the more important items in museum collections are bronze objects from ecclesiastical contexts such as crucifix figures, doorknockers and candlesticks, both gilded and ungilded.[35] In terms of more everyday metalwork, a major issue is that dress accessories attributed to the Anglo-Norman period survive in tiny numbers compared to both the late Anglo-Saxon period before it and the thirteenth century after. Items such as brooches and finger-rings are particularly uncommon in the archaeological record between the late eleventh century and the first half of the twelfth. The distinct impression is that the display of portable wealth at a level below the social elite was relatively limited in the post-Conquest period.[36] Nor do twelfth-century hoards tend to contain other gold or silver items or other valuable objects, unlike some deposited during and after the Norman Conquest.[37]

Excluding military items such as scabbard chapes and harness pendants, which are discussed in Chapter 6, the main surviving dress accessories of the period are copper alloy items such as buckles (Plates 8c–d), strap fittings and strap ends and, more rarely, decorated pins (for fixing hair or headwear).[38] Finger-rings (e.g. Plate 8f) were either plain hoops or decorated with incised lines and crosses, sometimes in panels; some were oversized, to fit on the thumb. Gaming pieces of bone or ivory and gilt strips (e.g. Fig. 5.1d) whose function is open to debate, but which could often derive from boxes or caskets, are other luxury items found in archaeological contexts. Mounts come in a wide variety of shapes and sizes; the most elaborate could be enamelled and might also have adorned caskets or even reliquary boxes (Plate 8g). Exotic creatures such as lions, wyverns and griffins feature heavily on dress accessories, sometimes in pairs, and with an emphasis on heads and mouths; other reoccurring designs depict *fleurs-de-lis* and hunting scenes.

A particularly exotic form of twelfth-century copper alloy buckle has been recognised in eastern England that features lion-like beasts with gaping mouths through which the strap passed; some had deep-set eye sockets that held glass pellets (Plate 8c), and such items may have had some special status.[39] Representations of mythical creatures on portable metalwork often show a taste for the fantastic and even the humorous, with fashions for armorial display contributing to the rich mix. It is mainly through zoomorphic decoration that stray finds are datable to the period, however. In stratified assemblages of medieval portable objects from London it is striking how only a tiny fraction show any oblique reference to mainstream artistic styles.[40] Many plain examples of dress accessories could equally have been manufactured in the twelfth century but are not recognised as such. Archaeological evidence of other items of clothing in the period is miniscule, although it is interesting that in London the fashion for shoes with long curling toes can be dated quite closely to the second quarter of the twelfth century, showing how its citizens emulated conspicuous and showy court styles.[41]

Sculpture

Architectural sculpture provides us with a window into patronage across a slightly wider social spectrum than illustrated books and fine metalwork. The political circumstances of the civil war gave local lords a myriad motives to invest in architectural sculpture in parish churches – it proclaimed seigneurial power to populations and announced competition to rivals, expressed piety, and materialised affiliations and engagement with elite social networks. The principal architectural features within parish churches singled out for particular investment and ostentation were south doors and chancel arches, while many twelfth-century fonts survive. Pinning down given examples of sculpture to the decades around Stephen's reign is challenging but not impossible. The date '*c.* 1150' is often assigned arbitrarily to a given phase of church building, but there is little hope of dating more accurately the structural fabric (such as rubble-built walls) that, of course, comprised the majority of building work in the period.

Increased elaboration with floral and multi-ordered geometric motifs and figural sculpture are hallmark devices of the period, as is the blending of military and seigneurial imagery with biblical themes and, in some areas, the rebooting of Anglo-Saxon iconography. In Gloucestershire, for example, magnificent Romanesque sculpture on the doorways of St Swithin's in Quenington and All Hallows, South Cerney, can be dated on the basis of historical as well as stylistic reasons quite closely to post-1137 and before *c.* 1160; scenes of the Harrowing of Hell, representing conflict resolved in the favour of humankind, must have had resonances for contemporary audiences as well as showing how networks of architectural patronage were blossoming.[42] Such motifs and themes gave English Romanesque sculpture of the mid-twelfth century a distinctive character that does not neatly link up with developments on the Continent.[43] An especially ambitious depiction of the Harrowing of Hell of the same period is found on a band-like limestone frieze on the west façade of Lincoln Cathedral. Dated to the bishopric of Alexander the Magnificent (1123–48) it is usually attributed to the early 1140s and is distinctive in depicting John the Baptist behind Christ, who is releasing souls from the mouth of hell while standing on the devil.[44] In the mid-twelfth century, architectural sculptural representations of this sort were far more than decorative collections of biblical figures – they were also theological tools. While depictions of the Harrowing of Hell are found earlier and later, their meanings would have had special resonance given the turbulence and destruction of the civil war.

The clearest example of an architectural form that can be dated with relative precision to the period around the civil war is the 'beakhead' – an architectural embellishment taking the form of a real or imaginary creature whose jaw or 'beak' appears to grip the moulding on which it is set.[45] The beakhead seems to have originated in western France, where human heads were also used, and subsequently introduced to Anjou, Normandy and England, where forms tend to be more savage and grotesque. While a handful of examples are known in Ireland, they are virtually absent in Scotland and Wales. Crucially, English beakheads can be ascribed a relatively tight date range, the style demonstrably percolating down from the highest rungs of the social ladder to local lords during the decades of Stephen's reign. The earliest examples were in buildings for patrons at the summit of the social spectrum: Sarum Cathedral, rebuilt by Bishop Roger of Salisbury in the late 1120s and 1130s,[46] and the cloisters of Reading Abbey, founded by Henry I in 1121, although some time clearly elapsed before work on the cloisters commenced.[47] A form of proto-beakhead ornament is also found at Norwich Castle, established by William Rufus but completed by Henry I, exemplified by the richly decorated doorway into the donjon that carried messages psychologically preparing visitors about to enter the complex's inner sanctum.[48] Beakheads were employed in particular on doors and thresholds, almost universally in churches and occasionally monasteries: in the Thames Valley they are often found on continuous orders, extending from the apex of the arch to ground level, to dramatic effect.[49] The meaning of beakheads was complex and multilayered, although most scholars see them as nightmarish reminders of sin and vice, from which churches provided sanctuary. They clearly suited the mid-twelfth-century *zeitgeist*, being at once forms of expression for an upwardly mobile local seigneury in a period when lords were indulging in monastic foundation as never before, and perhaps reflections of the horror of civil conflict. They were not used much later than *c.* 1160.[50]

The distribution of beakheads across England is uneven; it has long been recognised that there are two distinct concentrations, focused around Oxfordshire and Yorkshire.[51] Plate 9 maps an expanded data set of 166 certain and possible examples that enlarges upon but does not contradict this basic pattern. Overall, beakhead distribution provides the closest approximation to an index of church building work during the decades around the civil war that we can obtain, although blank areas on the map do not imply that no church building occurred – it is rather that we do not have the means to date it easily. The distribution highlights how Gloucestershire, the Thames Valley and parts of Yorkshire were centres of local investment in churches and sculpture, with concentrations suggesting familial networks of patronage or regional patterns of emulation, although deep local studies are needed to fill in the detail. The message a local lord sent out through investment in lavish sculpture was especially profound where the parish church stood adjacent to his *caput*. Churches featuring beakhead sculpture at Aughton, East Yorkshire, English Bicknor, Gloucestershire and Earls

Barton, Northamptonshire, follow this pattern and in some cases stood within the outer defences of castles. The exemplar is, however, Kilpeck, Herefordshire, where the famous church of St Mary lies in the outer earthworks of a castle and forms part of a Norman unit of settlement comprising *caput*, priory and small borough; the sculpture is usually ascribed to the lord of the castle, Hugh de Kilpeck, and dated to the 1130s or early 1140s.[52] A more unusual case of 'twinned' castle and church is Silchester, Hampshire, where the earliest phase of St Mary the Virgin dates to *c.* 1120–50 and is likely to have been built in tandem with the refurbishment of the adjacent former Roman amphitheatre as an Anarchy-period ringwork. The church was unusual in having a Norman north doorway, linking it to the site of lordship.[53]

Funerary monuments provide another potential area of closely datable evidence for twelfth-century sculpture. The tombs of especially high-status individuals could take the form of effigies by the mid-twelfth century, although we should be cautious in using these as direct sources of evidence for personal appearance as they idealised individuals and followed convention. There are other reasons why we should not take effigies at face value: while the tomb of Robert Curthose (d. 1134), eldest son of William the Conqueror, in Gloucester Cathedral might be thought to depict the appearance of a mid-twelfth-century knight, it dates to *c.* 1250, more than a century after his death.[54] Other effigies attributed to prominent figures of the civil war are likewise much later, including the military example associated with Geoffrey de Mandeville in Temple Church, London, and that attributed to Robert of Gloucester, in simple drapery, in St James' Priory, Bristol.

We have very little evidence for the tombs of most of the key players in mid-twelfth-century history. The funerary monuments of King Stephen and Henry I were both destroyed.[55] There was no traditional location for the burial of Norman kings, who were generally interred within monastic houses they had favoured or founded. There was therefore nothing 'unusual' about the location of King Stephen's burial, outside London, in the priory he had founded at Faversham, Kent, in 1147; indeed, it mirrored the burial of his predecessor Henry I at his Cluniac priory of Reading.[56] An honorific church offered an appropriate setting not only for an ostentatious tomb but also for the personalised prayers that would be offered by the religious community long after the king's death. Given its scale, St Saviour's Priory in Faversham was clearly intended as a mausoleum of the royal house of Blois (Fig. 5.2). Archaeological investigation in 1965–66 revealed the position and size of Stephen's tomb, if few of its architectural qualities.

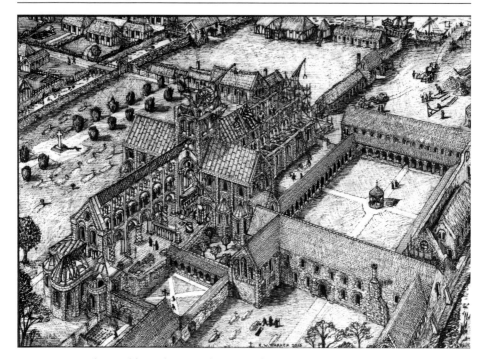

Fig. 5.2: Faversham Abbey, showing the site under construction with King Stephen, Queen Matilda and Eustace interred in the royal vault. Reconstruction drawing by Richard Parker.

The tombs were intended as the focal point within the original plan of the church, which was later modified. Stephen's tomb lay within a royal chapel that also contained the tombs of his queen, Matilda, and son, Eustace; the chapel was a large rectangular structure at the east end of the church, 29m east–west x 8m north–south, and flanked by aisles that formed a continuous ambulatory.[57] Excavations revealed a pair of deep rectangular pits, originally stone-lined and a little over 2m square, and interpreted as royal burial vaults. Both were backfilled with rubble following the building's demolition c. 1540 and sadly no traces of bones or coffins survived.[58] Indeed, the vaults had been destroyed so thoroughly that the only clues to the appearance of the tombs were fragments of finely carved Romanesque stonework, including a ragstone column base with 'fine scallop decoration of Burgundian type' painted red and gold, and traces of coloured plaster.[59]

Other insights into royal attitudes to burial and commemoration come from archaeological investigation of Holy Trinity Priory, Aldgate, in the City of London. Two of Stephen's children, Baldwin and Matilda, were buried here shortly before 1147–48, when the cartulary records that the king gave the priory 100 shillings of land in 'Brackyng,' Hertfordshire, for the repose of the souls of his children who lay in the church.[60] The cartulary also records that Baldwin was interred to the north of the altar and Matilda to the south. Archaeological investigation shows that both tombs were indeed grandly set in spaces between columns of the presbytery arcade, and it is not inconceivable that Stephen himself originally intended to be buried between them.[61]

In terms of the burial practices of the vast majority of the population, the archaeological record provides no evidence whatsoever of changes during the civil war period. Skeletal analyses have the potential to reveal horizons of stress within populations although, as yet, there is no evidence for this in the mid-twelfth century. Most graves of the period were unmarked, or marked only temporarily, although in some parts of the country grave slabs were a fashionable means of commemoration among parish elites. Often incorporating simple cross-type designs, both vertical and horizontal grave slabs of the twelfth century are mainly found *ex situ*, such as in church porches, yet have received far less scholarly attention than later effigies and brasses or earlier Anglo-Saxon funerary sculpture. The evidence can nonetheless play a role in illuminating how local elites made their mark and negotiated their identities.[62] For example, detailed study of cross slabs in the North Riding of Yorkshire shows how the trajectory of commemorative patronage steadily accelerated through the mid- to late twelfth century into the thirteenth century, with several examples displaying symbols of lordship such as swords and hunting items as secondary emblems.[63]

Seals

Sigillography (the study of seals) offers us a very different perspective on twelfth-century attitudes to material culture. Seals used to authenticate documents can be considered forms of material culture in their own right, both their impressions in sealing wax – a blend of beeswax and resin – and surviving examples. Unlike most of the other forms of material culture considered in this chapter, many seals are both closely dateable and associated with known individuals, making them invaluable for understanding diverse aspects of elite culture in the twelfth century, from the king and the higher nobility through to bishops and lesser aristocrats. As small-scale personalised expressions of Romanesque art, seals of the period can also illustrate changes in costume, appearance and military apparel as well as providing intriguing insights into the construction and expression of elite identities.

As the official seals of monarchs, medieval 'great seals' remained essentially unchanged in terms of their pattern and appearance. From the reign of William II, the characteristic great seal depicted the monarch enthroned on the front (the majesty side) and mounted on a horse on the back (the equestrian side), in a format that both captured and proclaimed the 'aura of kingship.'[64] The political upheavals of the Anarchy had some very direct consequences for royal seals, and King Stephen used two consecutively, although opinions differ on their precise date ranges. Stephen's first great seal was commissioned immediately upon his coronation, manufactured in London, and in use from February 1136 until either June 1139 (the 'arrest of the bishops') or his capture at the Battle of Lincoln in February 1141, although most commentators favour the first of these theories.[65]

The differences between Stephen's two seals are for the most part minor: the first shows a more ornamented throne on its majesty side and the king armed with a sword rather than a lance with a banner emblazoned with a cross on its equestrian side; the second seal is slightly larger and has a square rather than rounded capital 'E' in the surrounding text.[66] It has also been argued that the second seal's slightly cruder design may be symptomatic of disruption to royal administration, although this seems far-fetched in light of what we know about the survival and flourishing of the arts in the period.[67] In 1902 St John Hope reported to the Society of Antiquaries of London the apparently startling discovery of a third seal of Stephen, appended to a charter of confirmation to the church of St Andrew at Rochester, which he interpreted as for use when the king was in Normandy.[68] The seal has since been recognised as a forgery and other examples identified.[69] This need not be taken as indicative of governmental instability during the period, however, as forged seals from the reigns of other medieval monarchs are well documented. The proportion of forgeries in Stephen's reign does not stand out as unusual.[70] Stephen was not alone or unusual in having two seals: his successor, Henry II, used at least two (styled the 'first' and 'second'), which followed the same convention of equestrian and majesty sides, although the reason for the replacement of one by the other is obscure.[71]

The twelfth century is clearly an important moment in the development of private seals in England, as it is in north-west Europe more generally.[72] Metal-detected finds of lead seal matrices (e.g. Plate 8a) are adding constantly to the data set. The first half of the century in particular saw aristocrats experimenting with seals not only as a means of proving the veracity of documents in an increasingly legalistic and bureaucratic culture, but also a means of image-making. Emulation of sealing practices within the social elite was rapid, the use of personal seals percolating down the ranks of the lower nobility in the middle of the twelfth century, to the point that even wealthy townsmen were using them by the first years of the thirteenth century.[73] An instructive piece of anecdotal evidence comes from the case of one Gilbert de Balliol, owner of three knight's fees in Sussex in the first years of Henry II's reign. In a dispute with the Abbot of Battle over land rights, Gilbert complained about the *sigillorum* (seals) of his predecessors, although the king's chief justiciar, Richard de Lucy, rebuked the country knight, who had a seal of his own, because 'it was not usual in former times for any petty knight (*militulum*) to have a seal' and that these were 'appropriate for kings and great men only.'[74]

Up to the early twelfth century, seal matrices were predominantly of bone or ivory, but their widespread manufacture out of metal thereafter created opportunities for artistic expression through deeper and smoother forms with more three-dimensional emphasis.[75] Size mattered: personal seals of the twelfth century are quite large (a typical seal was *c.* 70–80mm across) compared to their later successors, using a large amount of valuable wax, which was a statement in itself, although members of the higher nobility also sometimes used small gem seals, as counterseals or for private correspondence.[76]

The notion of private seals as status symbols is reflected well in their evolving iconography. The classic equestrian figure on a circular seal was almost universally adopted in the late twelfth century as the definitive icon of the warrior-aristocrat, aping the reverse of royal seals.[77] The seals used by the twelfth-century earls of Chester provide vivid insight into how evolving seal iconography and sealing practices mirrored changes in aristocratic identity.[78] The large seal of Ranulf II, in use 1129–53, depicted the earl on horseback armed with a sword but without a shield, helmet or mail hauberk (he instead wore a tunic); by contrast, the first seal of Earl Hugh, made for him in his minority and in use 1153/57–81, displays more elaborate military iconography, with the earl sporting a long mail surcoat, helmet, shield and a lance complete with banner.[79] Both Ranulf and Hugh similarly used small gem counterseals, highlighting the sophistication and flashiness of their chanceries. While most depictions of individuals on seals were unsurprisingly generic, the seal of Henry of Blois is an unusual case of a potentially individualised design. His heavy build and long, flowing beard are likely indicative of Henry's actual appearance.[80] Personal seals of the mid-twelfth century also provide some of our earliest evidence of embryonic forms of heraldry, predating the earliest rolls of arms of the thirteenth century.[81] The second seal of Waleran, Count of Meulan and Earl of Worcester, dating to *c.* 1139, depicted a 'chequy' device on his shield, surcoat, saddlecloth and gonfanon, and members of his kin group adopted similar devices, which may have been intended to emphasise their line of descent from Charlemagne.[82] Likewise, the seal of Gilbert de Clare, Earl of Hertford (*c.* 1146) shows the family's three chevrons.[83]

We should not overlook the fact that noblewomen possessed seals of their own, some from an early date; once again, it is demonstrably in the mid-twelfth century that the practice spread.[84] The seals of noblewomen tended to be pointed, oval and deployed a fairly standardised repertoire of symbols – most typically a standing female figure holding a lily, *fleur-de-lis* or bird of prey (or a combination thereof). This need not be taken as evidence for the suppression of female individuality, as these seals equally show experimentation with female imagery and identity at a time when gender roles were being negotiated.[85] The Empress Matilda's seal was small and without a counter-seal, which may be indicative of German tradition, reflecting her marriage to the German Emperor.[86] It depicts her enthroned, dressed in a long robe with long sleeves, holding a long sceptre and wearing a three-pointed crown, thus stating her legitimacy.[87] It reads 'S + MATHILDIS DEI GRATIA ROMANORUM REGINE': 'Matilda by the grace of God Queen of the Romans.'[88]

Coinage in Context

Numismatic evidence – or coinage – represents an exceptionally important element of the archaeological record of the Anarchy. As the foregoing discussion has shown, it is rare that items of material culture can be assigned to a period as specific as a king's reign, but coins provide a prominent exception as most are inherently datable, being precise historical documents as well as archaeological artefacts. The recovery of silver pennies of Stephen's reign during archaeological excavations of sites including the castles of Castle Acre, Norfolk, and Trowbridge, Wiltshire, for example, has been instrumental in pinning down construction phases to the conflict (see Chapter 4).

As well as being instrumental to a functioning economy, medieval coins were a key means of claiming authority, as is evident in designs redolent with the imagery of kingship. Few documents exist relating to the activities of mints and moneyers before the thirteenth century and scholars are largely reliant on the coins themselves as evidence.[89] The data set of coins issued during Stephen's reign is expanding dramatically, more so than any other category of material evidence, especially through metal-detecting finds. New discoveries have unusually high potential to reveal fresh information, including about aspects of the period's complex and turbulent political geography. For example, the metal-detected find of a single coin near Derby in 2013 confirmed the existence of a mint active in the civil war period, in Tutbury, Staffordshire, where the moneyer Walchelin struck coins of an unofficial issue in the 1140s, presumably within or near the castle under the control of Robert de Ferrers, Earl of Derby.[90]

The coins of the Anarchy have long held a particular fascination for historians, archaeologists and numismatists because the period witnessed massive disruption to a previously tightly controlled coinage, the essential elements of which had been in place since the late tenth century. The civil war's impact upon coinage was certainly far greater than that of the Norman Conquest, which had left the monetary system largely untouched.[91] The key developments of Stephen's reign saw an orderly coinage and nationwide network of mints at the point of his accession give way to a loss of royal control over minting in many parts of the country, a drop in the standard of coins and, uniquely, the appearance of a mass of non-official variant types, including those issued by the Empress Matilda and various barons, as well as coins struck from defaced dies. Something of the disorder is captured by William of Newburgh's claim that tyrants minted their own coins like kings,[92] while William of Malmesbury states that the coinage was debased and counterfeiting rife in the face of rampant inflation.[93] A national system of coinage was rapidly re-established following the peace agreement of 1153, with mint control and die supply centralised once again. These circumstances ensure that the coinage of Stephen's reign is probably the most complicated but fascinating in the entire English series,[94] and the body of literature on the topic is substantial.[95]

Different elements of the numismatic evidence afford different but complementary insights into the period's economy and shifting geopolitics: the changing numbers and locations of mints controlled by the king and his rivals; the distributions of different types of coin found individually (single finds) and in buried treasure (hoards); and the physical properties of the coins themselves, including their weight, fineness and designs. This is a powerful body of evidence that can help illuminate the fluctuating spatial extent of both royal control and dissent among Angevin and baronial rivals over time, although interpretation comes with a set of challenges. The study of coins is extremely specialised, and archaeologists have in the past often been guilty of naivety in dealing with coinage, leading to misinterpretation of the evidence.[96] Numismatic studies too are constrained by disciplinary boundaries and can seem overtly specialised.[97] An interdisciplinary approach incorporating the insights of numismatics within the broader sociopolitical context of archaeological and documentary research is therefore of crucial importance when seeking to understand coins and hoarding. Given that the weight of scholarship on the coins of Stephen's reign far outweighs that on any other aspect of the period's archaeology and material culture, the following is a condensed synthesis of the evidence.

Anglo-Norman kings and coinage

As was the case under the other Norman kings, the silver penny was the only denomination issued by the mints in Stephen's reign.[98] In archaeological contexts, these are also sometimes found cut in half (as halfpennies) and in quarters (as farthings), although complete examples are more common. The proportion of fractional denominations in circulation appears to have been appreciably higher than in the preceding period. Whole pennies still constitute the majority of finds (65%), with a far larger proportion of cut halfpennies than usual (28%), the remainder being cut farthings (7%), which seems very likely to be another reflection of the disruption to the monetary system.[99]

King Stephen's official (or 'substantive') issues followed long-established convention in that the obverse side of the coin showed a representation of the king, associated with paraphernalia of kingship such as the crown and sceptre, and a legend indicating his name and title. The reverse depicted a cross and a legend identifying the place the coin was minted and the moneyer who was answerable to the king for the product's weight and fineness. The rival issues of Stephen's reign also tended to follow this pattern, but with designs that were of poorer quality and slightly more experimental (occasionally drawing on heraldic devices) and coins that were sometimes (but not always) lightweight and base. Coins were all struck in designated mints located within boroughs, by moneyers who worked in their own workshops. In Stephen's reign, the busiest mints, such as London, could have ten or more active moneyers, while those in smaller centres typically hosted one or two.[100] Foreign coins entering the country were rigorously excluded from the system and melted down – not one is found in a hoard of Stephen's reign. In the period following the Norman Conquest, most moneyers had Anglo-Saxon names, although by the middle of the twelfth century the proportion was less than half, many now bearing Norman French names.[101]

The iron dies from which coins were struck were engraved and issued centrally, moneyers travelling to London to collect them. The designs were periodically replaced, so that coins form a series of successive 'types' characterised by subtle design variations. The issue of different types generated revenue (as moneyers paid for their dies) and ensured a regular coinage as only one type was supposedly in use at any point in time. Surviving dies of the Anglo-Norman period are exceptionally rare, although a used official reverse die of Stephen was one of four found by metal-detectorists in spoil from London's northern waterfront in 1989–90; it derived from the Northampton mint and seems to have been returned to the London workshop after use.[102] Another surviving die of Stephen, this one an obverse, now in the Museum of London collections, was reputedly recovered from Little Bell Abbey, Moorgate and is unusual for its hexagonal shape.[103]

The changing minting landscape

Stephen's reign was characterised by a dramatic increase in the number of active mints. The preceding period saw few new mints: indeed, with the exception of Rye in East Sussex, none was established south of Yorkshire between the accession of William II in 1087 and the death of Henry I in 1135.[104] The half-century preceding Stephen's accession was characterised by mint closures, most notably during Henry I's infamous assize of moneyers at Christmas 1124–25. The Anglo-Saxon Chronicle and other sources detail how the king, suspecting manipulation of the coinage, had Roger of Salisbury summon the moneyers to Winchester at Christmas and had many of them castrated and their right hands amputated, although some managed to pay fines instead and a number continued in business. In order to re-establish the authenticity of English coinage, the Henry I type 15 was introduced and the number of mints was reduced by more than 50%, to just 23.[105] Stephen reopened many of these mints in the very early years of his reign, and 15 were soon reinstated for production of his new coinage.[106] Political strategy as well as economic policy explains this rapid transformation of the minting landscape in the late 1130s. Minting was a vital means by which Stephen could legitimise his kingship at a time of political uncertainty, and the restoration of minting rights can also be seen as part of a broader series of concessions made by the new king to strengthen his

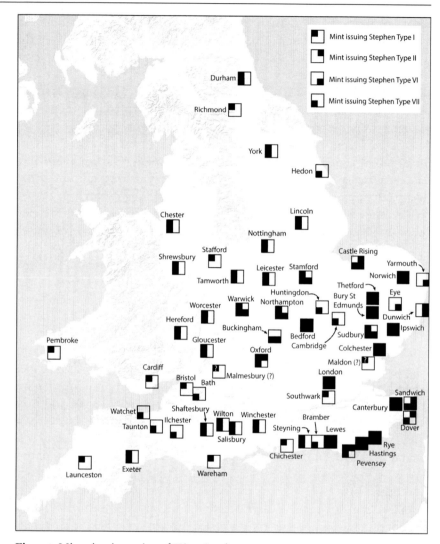

Fig. 5.3: Mints issuing coins of King Stephen.
Source: image based on Blackburn 1994, updated
from Allen 2012a; 2012b.

grip on the throne. Many earls had lost a source of revenue following
the closure of mints in the 1120s, and Stephen hoped to win favour
through their re-establishment.[107]

Coins struck in this expanded minting network early in Stephen's
reign are sometimes known as the 'Watford type' on account of a hoard
containing more than 600 examples deposited there in a ceramic vessel

in the early 1140s and discovered in 1818.[108] In total, Stephen issued four substantive (or 'official') types, confusingly known as BMC (British Museum Catalogue) types 1, 2, 6 and 7, which constitute over 80% of all single coin finds of the period.[109] Following the 'Watford' type 1, type 2 was issued to regularise the coinage by removing non-official types from circulation in areas under the king's control. Type 6 probably represents a recoinage intended to raise revenue, and type 7 was the direct result of the 1153 peace settlement between Stephen and Henry of Anjou.[110] It should be stressed that the issue of successive types during Stephen's reign followed standard practice under the Norman kings, although it is significant that the rate at which new types were issued was far lower than his predecessors, with type 1 circulating for far longer than was customary.[111] The minting network across which these issues were struck is mapped in Figure 5.3, and the known distribution of the coins themselves in Plate 10.

Stephen's official issues

The 'Watford' (or, alternatively, 'cross moline') type 1 (Plate 12a), by far the most common coin of Stephen's reign, depicts the king in profile facing right, wearing a lily crown and diadem and holding a sceptre in his right hand, with a cross moline (i.e. with the arms of the cross forking out at the ends) on the reverse. The date range across which the type 1 was struck is the subject of debate: it was issued from 1135–36, and while it was originally thought to have been replaced by type 2 in 1142, upon Stephen's release from captivity, another view extends it into the mid- or even late 1140s.[112] The network of 44 mints striking type 1 coins was genuinely nationwide, nearly all English shires having a mint, with examples at the extremities of the kingdom at Durham, Pembroke and Launceston, Cornwall. The spatial distribution of single finds of type 1 shows the easterly bias that was typical of coins of the Norman kings more generally, although it may also indicate a circulation network that was being pulled towards the gravitational centre of royal control in the south-east and east of the country through the late 1130s and early 1140s. The bias towards East Anglia apparent in the distribution map probably says as much about the intensity and success of metal-detecting (and the way that finds are reported) as it does about contemporary circulation patterns.[113]

Stephen's type 2 ('cross voided and mullets') (Plate 12b) was minted *c.* 1142/45(?)–50 (interpretations of the duration of its use are dependent upon the dating of type 1). It shows a three-quarter bust of the king, wearing an arched crown with pendants, and a plain cross on the reverse. It was minted in a far more restricted network of centres in the royalist regions of the south and east, the overall number of mints having dropped to less than half. Notable is the large number of mints in secure ports, such as Dover and Sandwich, neither of which struck type 1. Much silver entered England in the form of bullion and foreign coins exchanged for goods.[114] The loss of royal control over the productive silver mines in the north of England must have increased the importance of obtaining imported silver.[115] In north Norfolk a new mint striking type 2 operated in the shadow of William d'Aubigny's new donjon of the early 1140s at Castle Rising, thus showing how royal and baronial economic interests could coincide: the little castle-dependent settlement in which it lay had been planned in gridded form more or less contemporaneously with the castle, although the place was not recognised as a borough until the mid-thirteenth century.[116] The spatial distribution of Stephen's type 2 coins, albeit very sparse given the rarity of the type, is overwhelmingly focused in eastern areas.

The 'cross and piles' type 6 (minted *c.* 1150–53) (Plate 12c) depicts the king's face in profile but here facing to the left, crowned and holding a sceptre; a cross fleury (i.e. with flowers at the ends of the cross arms) is on the reverse. The network of mints producing type 6 was similar to type 2 but slightly enlarged to include boroughs north of the Thames Valley, including Buckingham, Stamford and Northampton, of which the king had regained control. The distribution of single finds is again sparse, if a little less so than type 2, with slightly larger numbers of single finds in Kent and Sussex.

The 'Awbridge' (or, alternatively, 'cross pommée') type 7 (minted *c.* 1153–58) (Plate 12d) shows a three-quarters bust of the king, facing left. It was once again minted across a national network, which was actually slightly larger (44–6 mints) than in the early years of Stephen's reign. Significantly, several mints that had issued coins in the Empress's name were excluded, including Cardiff, Wareham and Bristol, which was pointedly denied a mint while its neighbour Bath saw its mint revived. The extremities of the kingdom were not as well served with mints as earlier in Stephen's reign: Exeter's mint was the furthest west and Wales was without a mint. The reopening of the Durham mint coincided with Stephen's grant of rights to the Weardale silver mine to the bishop.[117] Newly opened (or reopened) mints included the port towns of Bramber, West Sussex, Hedon, East Yorkshire, and Watchet, Somerset. The distribution of type 7 single finds remains biased to the eastern half of England, although it stretches into parts of Lincolnshire and Yorkshire, with small numbers recorded in parts of central and even south-west England, where types 2 and 6 were totally absent. It should be noted that type 7 was issued for around four years after Stephen's death and continued to carry a version of his name (*Stiefne*).[118] It is instructive that a monarch known for weakness (Stephen) issued coins in his name immediately upon his succession, while another synonymous with reform (Henry II) delayed doing so. Henry's recoinage of 1158 (the 'cross-and-crosslets type') saw most of the moneyers replaced and the number of mints drastically reduced, although that of Wallingford, the Angevins' flagship castle and town, was resuscitated in an act of political favour.[119] The trend towards greater centralisation of minting was to continue throughout Henry's reign, thus accentuating how the complex and dispersed minting landscape of Stephen's reign was an anomaly.[120]

The physical properties of individual coins, in terms of their metrology (weight) and fineness (percentage of silver), can also be seen as barometers of twelfth-century England's economic health. That the period saw weights decrease from the roughly 22-grain standard is well established. Weight standards deteriorated through Stephen's type 1 and lower weights are also generally more typical of Angevin and independent issues and Stephen's type 7, although the pattern is complex and variable. Weight standards seem to have held up well in mints under control of the Scots in northern England, probably as they were closer to the important silver mining centres.[121] Perhaps surprisingly, there is less evidence for debasement of the coinage by deteriorating fineness. This is partly due to the very small number of coins of the period that have been subjected to detailed metallurgical analyses and the variability of techniques used, but if any pattern is discernible it is that Angevin issues are sometimes characterised by lower silver content.[122] At any rate, debasement of the coinage appears not to be as endemic as asserted by William of Malmesbury.[123]

Irregular issues

A clear index of the political instability of Stephen's reign is the operation of mints in areas of England outside royal control, which began with the loss of Cumberland and Northumberland to the Scots in 1136 and became widespread across the south-west in the early and mid-1140s (Fig. 5.4 and Plate 11). In the north, copies of Stephen's type 1 were issued from Carlisle and Durham, while King David I of Scots and his son Henry (of Northumbria) issued coins from Bamburgh, Carlisle, Corbridge and Newcastle.[124] A particularly damaging loss

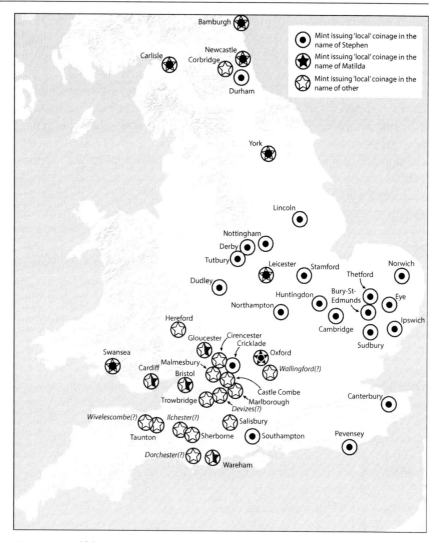

Fig. 5.4: Twelfth-century mints issuing 'local coinage.'
Source: image based on Blackburn 1994, updated from
Allen 2012a; 2012b. Map work by Oliver Creighton.

for the English Crown was the network of small but hugely profitable silver mines in the uplands east of Carlisle that had operated since at least the second quarter of the twelfth century; their exploitation continued under the occupying Scots, and King David made grants out of the revenue of 'his mine of Carlisle.'[125] The mines did not generate revenue for the English Crown again until the reign of Henry II.

For the period following Stephen's capture at the Battle of Lincoln in 1141, the evidence from coinage adds significant detail to the overarching pattern that the west and south-west of England were strongly Angevin while the Midlands were largely characterised by earls acting quasi-autonomously. This changing political landscape was reflected by type 1 variants and coins struck from defaced dies preceding the production of local coinages, although interpretation of mint signatures on coins of irregular issues is often more problematic than for Stephen's official issues.[126] Coins of the period struck from defaced dies are the subject of debate: it is unclear whether this represented symbolic defacement, for instance with a cross, bar or scratching, in some cases superimposed upon the king's image, or rather reflects the cancelling of a die that actually continued in use.[127] Different explanations may fit different examples. In the East Midlands the mints of Derby, Leicester, Lincoln and Leicester struck local variants in the name of Stephen, while a weakening of control over the northern parts of East Anglia is evidenced by similar issues from mints in this region.

In the West Country, the key mints for the production of the Empress Matilda's coinage were Bristol, where Stephen's moneyer Thorketill remained in position, Cardiff, Oxford and Wareham.[128] A great deal of debate has focused on the meaning of the legend 'PERERIC M' on some copies of Stephen's type 1, although the most likely explanation is that the 'M' references Matilda; the coins seem to have been issued for the short period of the Empress's ascendancy in 1141 and some were struck at mints in areas of the country that she never controlled, including Canterbury, Ipswich and London.[129] A later Angevin issue was the 'lion' coinage (so-called on account of the heraldic lion on the obverse) of Robert, Earl of Gloucester and then his son William, Earl of Gloucester, issued from *c.* 1143 and manufactured professionally from stamped rather than engraved dies, which was revealed by the discovery of a hoard at Box, Wiltshire, in 1993–94.[130] Military as well as economic imperatives clearly influenced the locations of the mints producing this coinage: at Castle Combe and Trowbridge, they lay within or near new castles (at the former, a vast reoccupied Iron Age hillfort; at the latter, a thegnly complex converted into a motte and bailey), while those at Salisbury (Old Sarum) and Marlborough were close to established fortresses.[131] These centres complemented the other mints producing the lion coinage in the Angevin 'capital' of Bristol and the key port of Wareham, forming a tight network in what was in effect a small breakaway state. The Angevin-controlled mints were more closely spaced than was typical in royalist-dominated zones of the country, however, and the patterns of circulation of the coins struck within them were similarly more localised. While most medieval minting took place in urban settlements, a number of these centres, including Castle Combe, Sherborne, Trowbridge and Wiveliscombe, were not of borough status and lacked urban privileges until much later.

According to Roger of Howden, Henry of Anjou struck his own coinage (*moneta Ducis*) after his invasion in 1149; a unique coin of Henry found in the Salisbury area and held by the Fitzwilliam collection, styles him as 'future king.'[132] If this design looked to the future, an issue from the Derby and Tutbury mints, which were controlled in the 1140s by Robert de Ferrers, Earl of Derby, rebooted a late Anglo-Saxon motif: the use of four 'martlets' (a heraldic device depicting a bird) in the angles of the reverse cross drew on the well-known Sovereign issue of Edward the Confessor.[133] A good part of the interest of Stephen's coinage lies in these rare irregular issues, although they constitute less than 10% of the surviving coins of the period. Another recently found example is the first known coin of William of Aumale, Earl of York, who is depicted helmeted and armoured, brandishing a sword.[134] The Yorkshire baron Robert de Stuteville similarly translated a seal-like equestrian design to the pennies he had struck at York *c.* 1148–54.[135] Crucially, however, it is not axiomatic that these irregular issues indicate a direct challenge to royal authority. Baronial issues could proclaim neutrality rather than outward hostility. Some issues carried Stephen's name on the obverse and could reflect independence within a locality or shire while recognising the king's ultimate sovereignty. The extent to which they were the product of fractured communications which made access to official dies in London problematic, rather than signifying opposition to royal rule, is also debatable. Equally, the plethora of Angevin types in the 1140s might be taken as evidence of an inability to rigorously control mints as much as testify to the emergence of an independent state.

Hoards and hoarding

Medieval coin hoards were composed of currency withdrawn temporarily from circulation, usually with the aim of later retrieving the contents. While single coin finds mainly represent *accidental* loss, coin hoards are *deliberate* deposits. Even if hoards were accumulated over a period of time, they were sealed or buried at a definable date. Interpretations of dates of deposition can vary, however, and it can be

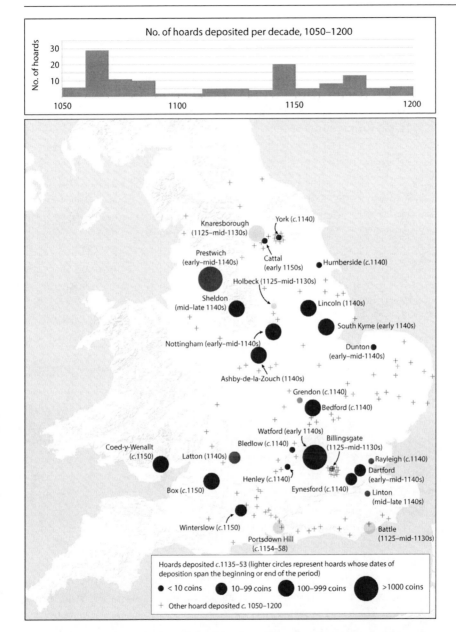

Fig. 5.5: Hoards of the late eleventh and twelfth century: **(top)** graph showing the number of recorded hoards deposited per decade (where the date range spans more than one decade, the middle of the range is taken); **(bottom)** distribution of hoards deposited between *c.* 1050–1200, highlighting those likely to have been deposited during Stephen's reign. Source: based on Allen 2012a. Map work by Oliver Creighton and Duncan Wright.

difficult to assess whether the contents are truly representative of the total coinage in circulation.[136] It can also be hard to differentiate a small hoard from the accidental loss of, say, a purse, while other supposedly 'isolated' single finds may represent content from a disturbed hoard.[137] Coin hoards have a particular significance for our understanding of the civil war of Stephen's reign as they have yielded important evidence of previously unrecognised new issues and issuers, while the chronology of hoarding over time provides a potential index of insecurity. Between 21 and 29 recorded coin hoards are known to have been deposited in Stephen's reign – the figure cannot be definitive as in several cases likely date ranges span either the beginning or end of the period. Particularly large or significant mid-twelfth-century hoards have been recovered from Ashby-de-la-Zouch (Leicestershire), Coed-y-Wenallt (Glamorgan), Box (Wiltshire), Nottingham, Prestwich (Manchester) and Watford (Hertfordshire) (Fig. 5.5: bottom).[138] This marks a very pronounced spike in the chronology of medieval hoard deposition, as discussed below.

The discovery of even modest hoards can shed radically new light on our understanding of coinage and the networks through which it was distributed. The unearthing of the Coed-y-Wenallt hoard, consisting of 102 pennies, by metal-detectorists in 1980 trebled the number of known coins of Matilda and revealed issues by barons not previously known to have struck coins, as well as the existence of a mint at Swansea.[139] That the majority of the coins were struck at Cardiff, and to a lesser extent Bristol, confirms quite how localised circulation patterns were within the Angevin zone of control in the 1140s. The hoard was discovered just north of Twmpath motte in the lordship of Whitchurch, on a hillside overlooking Cardiff.[140] One intriguing possibility is that it represented payment for Welsh mercenaries.

While numismatists have focused largely on the 'primary' contexts of where and when coins in hoards were minted, archaeologists are naturally drawn to the 'tertiary' contexts of hoards – where, how and why they were deposited. That many hoards were discovered in the nineteenth century means that reporting is variable, find spots hazy and there are often questions about completeness (i.e. whether some coins remained undiscovered or were taken and sold on).[141] It also means that thorough contextual archaeological work, which has the potential to reveal associations and illuminate the environments in which hoards were deposited, was not carried out. Only rarely is there any evidence of a containing vessel; for the most part, we can only assume that hoards were deposited in containers made of perishable organic materials, such as leather or cloth bags or wooden boxes, although some mid-twelfth-century examples were deposited in lead containers (Ashby-de-la-Zouch, Leicestershire; Colchester, Essex; and Sheldon, Derbyshire) or ceramic vessels (Linton, Kent; Watford, Hertfordshire).[142]

The question of whether the distribution of hoards in time and space is a reflection of fear and violence during Stephen's reign has been largely overlooked. It seems logical that hoarding can provide a barometer of public fear, on the premise that fewer hoards were deposited during peaceful periods, although some studies have noted a lack of relationship between historically attested disruption and an increase of hoarding.[143] Crucially, we must assume that the vast majority of medieval coin hoards will have been successfully retrieved. The graph of coin hoards by decade (Fig. 5.5: top) therefore reflects rates of non-recovery by owners rather than a straightforward index of how many hoards were being buried.

The correlation between documented periods of warfare and numbers of hoards is still undeniable. While research on prehistoric hoards is dominated by questions of ritual and votive deposition,[144] in this particular medieval context it seems that the death and displacement of hoarders, allied perhaps to higher levels of public fear and uncertainty, accounts for the spike in hoards. The 1140s represent a spike of deposition second only to the period of the Norman Conquest, and a smaller but still significant later peak in the 1170s may well reflect the consequences of the revolt of 1173–74 against Henry II.[145] The number of recorded hoards deposited during Stephen's reign was around two and a half times higher than in that of Henry I, and markedly higher than under Henry II.[146] Where these hoards can be assigned precise dates of deposition, a clustering of hoarding activity in the very early 1140s is also clear, including several very modest deposits of fewer than ten coins, hinting at hoarding by relatively ordinary households. Archaeologists have sometimes been tempted to link individual hoards to peak periods of insecurity, although this can be hazardous. For example, a hoard from spoil from Billingsgate, London, containing coins of the last issue of Henry I's reign and the first of Stephen's has been tentatively attributed to the high watermark of tension in 1141,[147] as has a hoard from Lincoln found in the area of Malandry, a leper hospital south of the city.[148] In both cases, however, earlier date ranges are equally plausible.[149]

The geographical relationship between the locations of hoards deposited during periods of warfare in the late eleventh and twelfth century and zones affected by these conflicts is also marked. A cluster of hoards in Sussex deposited *c.* 1066 points towards deposition and non-recovery around the time of the Battle of Hastings, while another concentration in the York area from the late 1060s is usually associated with the Harrying of the North.[150] Likewise, several significant hoards of the 1170s were deposited in zones of the country directly involved in the 1173–74 revolt (especially East Anglia and the East Midlands) or near routes used by forces.[151] Anarchy-period hoards display a notable geographical bias: the distribution is far more westerly than the 'background noise' of hoards deposited in the late eleventh and twelfth century as a whole (Fig. 5.5: bottom). This again provides broad evidence for a connection between hoarding and war-affected zones, although the geographical pattern is less focused than for hoards of the 1060s or 1170s. One interpretation is that this points to disruption across quite a broad swathe of western Britain in the 1140s, although hoards of the period were by no means wholly absent in the royalist south-east.

Summary

This review of material culture, arts and architecture reveals no evidence whatsoever of any hiatus nor of declining standards during Stephen's reign. Instead the period witnessed achievement and innovation in several different areas. While it is difficult to isolate developments in the 1130s, 1140s and 1150s from longer-term trends, it does seem clear that sculpture in parish churches features particularly high levels of experimentation, while grave slabs were a modish means of commemoration and expressing identity for emerging parish elites. Coinage provides our best means of mapping the fluid geopolitics of the civil war on the ground, and an ever-expanding data set highlights the existence of an Angevin proto-state in south-west England during the 1140s; however, we should be cautious about assuming that all 'rival' issues during the period provide straightforward evidence for opposition to Stephen's rule. Finally, pottery shows a great variety of regional patterns but the trend towards pre-eminent centres towards the end of the twelfth century reflects the post-war boom and growth of the network of markets.

Notes

1　Rowley 1997, 12–13.
2　The Portable Antiquities Scheme, www.finds.org.uk.
3　Renn et al. 2013.
4　Ellis 2000, 183.
5　Moorhouse 1981.
6　Jope and Threlfall 1959. See also Bond 2001, 48.
7　Leeds 1936; 1937.
8　Hurst 1962–3, 141–2.
9　Graham and Davies 1993, 111.
10　Stamper 1984, 87.
11　Kent et al. 2013.
12　Jervis 2014, 86.
13　Biddle 1969; 1986.
14　Cumberpatch and Roberts 2013, 120–1, 141–7.
15　Vince 2005, 232–3.
16　Jope 1963.
17　Hinton 2005, 175–7.
18　Egan 1998, 27–8.
19　Vince 1981, 319–20.
20　Vince and Jenner 1991, 46–7.
21　Cotter 1997.
22　For an overview, see Swanson 1999.
23　Zarnecki et al. 1984, 23.
24　For an important catalogue of Romanesque art in England including mid-twelfth century material in all these categories, see Zarnecki et al. 1984.
25　Archibald 1984, 337, no. 449.
26　Gilchrist and Green 2015, 433.
27　Baxter 2015.
28　For discussion, see West 2007.
29　Kusaba 1993, 71–6.
30　Heslop 1984, 299; Ailes 2008; Henig 2008.
31　Saxl 1954, 17–18.
32　Zarnecki et al. 1984, 84–5.
33　Ashley 2015, 287.
34　Rogerson and Ashley 2013, 565–7.
35　Oddy et al. 1986.
36　Hinton 2005, 171–4. See also Egan 1998, 24.

37　Hinton 2005, 179.
38　Ashley 2015, 287–91.
39　Rogerson and Ashley 2011.
40　Egan 1998, 8.
41　Pritchard 1991, 121.
42　Wood 2014.
43　Saxl 1954.
44　Zarnecki 1970, 1–2, 9–10; Kahn 1992, 72–4; Tamburr 2007, 69–71.
45　Salmon 1946; Henry and Zarnecki 1957–58; Zarnecki et al. 1984, 174.
46　Stalley 1971, 76–9; Zarnecki et al. 1984, 174.
47　Stalley 2012, 126; Baxter and Harrison 2002, 305–7.
48　Heslop 1994, 8, 34–5.
49　Newson 2013.
50　Newson 2013, 85.
51　See Salmon 1946, 349, 352–3; Henry and Zarnecki 1957–58, 20, Fig. 8.
52　King 1995, 89–91. See also Creighton 2005b, 168–71.
53　Fulford 1985, 77–8.
54　Gilchrist 2012, 192.
55　Steane 1999, 14–15.
56　Hallam 1982, 369.
57　Philp 1968, vii.
58　Philp 1965, 23.
59　Philp 1968, 15–17.
60　Schofield and Lea 2005, 14, 86.
61　Schofield and Lea 2005, 86, 96, 144.
62　McClain 2012, 146–56.
63　McClain 2007, 181–6.
64　Harvey and McGuinness 1996, 27.
65　Round 1892, 50–1; Cronne and Davis 1968, xv. For the alternative view, see Steane 1999, 27–8.
66　Cronne and Davis 1968, xv.
67　Steane 1999, 28.
68　St John Hope 1901–03.
69　Cronne and Davis 1968, xvi–xvii.
70　Public Record Office 1968, 29–31.
71　Vincent 2015, 9–11.

72 For an overview, see Bedos-Rezak 2011.

73 Heslop 1984, 298–99; New 2010, 89–90; 2013, 330–2.

74 *Chronicle of Battle Abbey*, Searle 1980, 212–15. See also Public Record Office 1968, 6; Crouch 1992, 138–9, 243.

75 Heslop 1984, 299.

76 Ailes 2008, 9; Henig 2008.

77 Harvey and McGuinness 1996, 43.

78 Heslop 1991.

79 Heslop 1991, 180, 184, 196.

80 Kusaba 1993, 69.

81 Cherry 1997, 125.

82 Crouch 1986, 211–12.

83 Ailes 1990, 6.

84 Harvey and McGuinness 1996, 48; Cherry 1997, 126; Johns 2003, 126; New 2010, 92.

85 Johns 2003, 123–4.

86 Steane 1999, 28.

87 Johns 2003, 126, 204. See for example the Empress's charter to the Cistercian abbey of Bordesley, Worcestershire, datable to *c.* 1141–42, in Borrie 1970.

88 Johns 2003, 204; Garnett 2007, 219.

89 Allen 2012a, 103.

90 Corpus of Early Medieval Coin Finds: EMC 2013.0332. For the suspicion of an earlier mint at Tutbury, see Mack 1966, 69, no. 179.

91 Dolley 1966; Metcalf 1998, 74; Allen 2011, 2; Allen 2014, 104–5.

92 William of Newburgh wrote: 'Numerous castles had been raised in individual areas through the eager action of factions, and in England there were in a sense as many kings, or rather tyrants, as there were lords of castles. Each minted his own coinage, and each like a king had the power to lay down the law for his subjects' (*The History of English Affairs* I, 22, 2, Walsh and Kennedy 1988, 98–9).

93 William of Malmesbury wrote: 'because of counterfeiting there were such problems with the coinage, that on occasion hardly 12 pennies could be accepted out of 10 shillings or more. It was said that the king himself had ordered the weight of pennies to be reduced from what it had been in King Henry's time' (*Historia Novella* II, 37, King and Potter 1998, 74–5).

94 Blackburn 1994, 145.

95 For overviews, see Mack 1966; Cronne 1970, 236–44; Archibald 1991; Blackburn 1994; Boon 1988. For summaries, see Archibald 2003, 79–81; King 2010, 210–15; Allen 2012a, 29–35; Kelleher 2015. For Norman coinage more generally, see Allen 2011; 2012b.

96 See the critique by Casey 1980.

97 Aitchison 1988, 270.

98 Henry I made a brief and unsuccessful experiment with issuing round halfpennies. See Allen 2011, 6.

99 Kelleher 2012, 74.

100 Allen 2012b, 85–106.

101 Stewart 1978, 98–9; Allen 2012a, 15.

102 Archibald et al. 1995, 187–90.

103 Andrew 1937.

104 Allen 2012a, 27.

105 Blackburn 1990, 64; Allen 2012a, 27–9.

106 Allen 2012a, 29.

107 Blackburn 1994, 153; Allen 2011, 16; 2012a, 29.

108 Rashleigh 1849–50. See also Allen 2012a, 464, no. 130.

109 Brooke 1916. Of the seven types originally identified in the British Museum Catalogue, three were later recognised as not being official issues. See also Kelleher 2015, 75.

110 Allen 2012a, 40. See also Blackburn 1994, 151–66.

111 Thirteen types were issued under William I and II and 15 (and an additional short-lived halfpenny type) under Henry I (Allen 2011, 2).

112 See Seaman 1978; Archibald 1991; 2003, 80.

113 Kelleher 2011, 1493.

114 Allen 2012a, 238.
115 Blanchard 2002, 33–4.
116 Morley and Gurney 1997, 1, 144; Liddiard 2000, 44–6, 57–8.
117 Allen 2012a.
118 Allen 2006, 242–6; 2007, 258–9.
119 Christie and Creighton 2013, 359.
120 Crafter 1998; Allen 2006; 2007.
121 Blackburn 1994, 169–73; Allen 2011, 8; Allen 2012a, 263–4.
122 Allen 2011, 9–10; 2012a, 158–9.
123 See above, n.83.
124 Mack 1966, 71, 97–101; Stewart 1971, 191–200; Blackburn 1994, 191–3; Allen 2012a, 29; 2012b, 67–8.
125 Claughton 2003, 146–7; 2011, 62–3.
126 Blackburn 1994, 167; Allen 2012b, 56; 2012b, 33. For examples, see Archibald 1984, nos 437–54.
127 Blackburn 1994, 176–8.
128 Boon 1988, 24–32; Blackburn 1994, 187–8. See also Chibnall 1978, 121–2.
129 Boon 1988, 21; Blackburn 1994, 113–15.
130 Archibald 2001.
131 Archibald 2001, 74–82.
132 Allen 2012a, 34; Fitzwilliam Museum CM.1226–2001. See also Blackburn 1994, 168.
133 Mack 1966, 68; Archibald 1984, 335, no. 438; Blackburn 1994, 181; Allen 2012a, 33.

134 Blackburn 2005.
135 Blackburn 1994, 182–7. The dating offered by Archibald is incorrect (1984, 336, no. 442).
136 Allen 2002, 24.
137 O'Neil 1936, 70; Allen 2012a, 447.
138 Allen 2012a, 462–6. See also Mack 1966, 101–7; Seaman 1978.
139 Boon 1988.
140 RCAHMW 1991, 70.
141 Seaman 1978.
142 Mack 1966.
143 See, for example, Reece 1981, 86–7.
144 See, for example, Bradley 1990.
145 Figures calculated from Allen (2012a), taking the middle date of each hoard's likely date range as the date of deposition.
146 See n.141 on the date ranges of hoards. The figures are: one hoard per 2.12 years under Henry I; one per 0.83 years under Stephen; and one per 1.3 years under Henry II. For alternative figures, based on a smaller dataset that gives a greater differential for deposition rates during Stephen's reign, see Thomas 2008, 142.
147 Stott 1991, 300–2, 317–19.
148 Jones et al. 2003, 165.
149 Allen 2012a, 462–3.
150 Metcalf 1998, 174, 194.
151 Crafter 1998, 52.

Chapter 6

Performing Violence: Arms, Armour and Military Apparel

A S WELL AS equipping men to fight, the military material culture of the knightly classes expressed the corporate identity of their elite group. Blending functionality with ceremonial and symbolic value, distinctive forms of arms and armour proclaimed membership of the warrior classes and demonstrated an individual's access to the resources and networks necessary to purchase or have manufactured expensive and sometimes bespoke items. The mid-twelfth century is a period when the practice and image of knighthood were evolving in important ways bound up with an emerging culture of chivalry. On the battlefield, the mail shirt, helmet, shield and sword will have marked out the owner as a member of a martial elite who should be treated according to the rules of war, while quite different treatment could be expected for those outside chivalric society.[1] This chapter identifies the key characteristics of arms and armour in the twelfth century and evaluates the evidence for change in the period, exploring how this can be linked to the construction and expression of knightly identity.

Combat and Combatants

Chroniclers marvelled at the aesthetic spectacle of large gatherings of armed men, and while they were doing so to make political points about the ability of their rulers and leaders to raise and lead armies, there is no mistaking the powerful visual impression that massed groups of soldiers left on contemporary minds. While armies were small by later medieval standards, so too was the contemporary population and it is instructive to remember that armies will have constituted exceptional gatherings of people for the period that could equate to the population of a medium-sized city.

Knights formed the backbone of twelfth-century armies, although this term is a catch-all for subtly different types of combatant. The author of the *Gesta Stephani* differentiates the elite belted knight from the more basic sort of serving knight, specified with the words 'rustic' or 'common/ordinary' (*rustici* and *gregarii*).[2] These forces did not act alone but were combined with lower-ranking infantry – primarily archers and spearmen, whether of the *fyrd*, paid mercenaries, and occasionally armed peasants. While chroniclers tended to exaggerate the size of military forces, detailed studies of knight service reveal that even major magnates mobilised relatively modest numbers of elite warriors. For example, Miles, Earl of Hereford, was able to draw upon a maximum of 90–95 knights in the period of the civil war, although many of these would have been busy garrisoning his castles.[3]

Civic militias comprised a further distinctive element in armies. Those of York, Beverley and Ripon fought at the Battle of the Standard, and Londoners proved decisive for the royalist cause at several encounters (see pg. 220). The supposed dominance of cavalry on the Anglo-Norman battlefield has probably been overstated. The main set-piece battles of the conflict were marked by knights fighting on foot, while the dominant mode of siege warfare provided few opportunities for mounted men to make any decisive impact in engagements.[4] A particularly distinctive aspect of Anarchy-period warfare was the polyglot and loosely organised nature of armies, with morale presenting a constant problem for commanders. Chapter 3 has shown how siege castles may have served as morale-building focal points during protracted sieges, while in the siege of Wallingford in 1153, Henry of Anjou's 'siege-work' seems to have been intended to stop his own forces deserting as much as to defend against the king's men (see pg. 72). Morale was clearly a major factor in commanders' decisions for knights to fight dismounted. It ensured that they could not flee while also bolstering the spirits of the infantry, who were the largest element within any force but whose cohesion and commitment was usually suspect.[5] In the chronicle sources peasants appear mainly as the victims of the conflict rather than participants in it, although the *Gesta Stephani* recounts that in the wake of the Rout of Winchester (1141), fleeing Angevin knights and magnates were captured and beaten by peasants.[6]

Another very prominent feature of warfare in the Anarchy was the use of mercenaries. Identified by writers with the words *mercennarius* or *stipendiarius*, these soldiers of fortune were employed in great numbers by both sides, and included contingents of Bretons and especially Flemings.[7] Chroniclers were unanimous in vilifying mercenaries, whose activities served to intensify the conflict in their eyes. They were stereotyped for their greed, cruelty and fickleness, and lambasted for their lack of respect for church property. A lack of deep allegiance, combined with the fact that mercenaries lay outside the emerging culture of chivalry, might explain the propensity of these men to ravage landscapes and populations, although we should also be aware of prejudice against 'outsiders' who were unpopular with Anglo-Norman barons. In the absence of pipe rolls, our understanding of how mercenaries were recruited and paid is unclear, although a grey area probably existed between men who served purely for money and others who had some longer-standing social or tenurial relationship with their commanders. The word *tenseria* (or *tenserie*) is sometimes used to describe protection money exacted from populations by military forces. The term had not previously existed in England or Normandy, but instances occur quite broadly across southern England in Stephen's reign; the word has Flemish origins and seems to represent an imported mercenary tax intended to maintain landless garrisons and forces.[8] A further interesting reflection of the Flemish presence in the period's material culture is the appearance of coins with Flemish affinities. Thus some coins found in the Coed-y-Wenallt hoard, discovered near Cardiff in 1980, show an un-English style that lacked the moneyer's name and replaced or interspersed other parts of the legend with ornaments;[9] they may have served a special purpose, such as payment of mercenaries concerned about debasement of the coinage.

Particularly notorious was the mercenary force commanded by the Flemish noble William of Ypres, who had fought with Stephen in Normandy in 1137 and emerged as his most loyal lieutenant, organising his household in the aftermath of the Battle of Lincoln.[10] According to William of Newburgh, the Flemish's support for the king led to their expulsion in 1154 as 'their great numbers were then a burden on England.'[11] William of Ypres nevertheless remained in Kent, where he continued to draw income from his estates until 1157.[12] The use of mercenaries was far from an anomaly, however; they were employed quite widely in earlier and later Anglo-Norman armies and rhetoric against their depredations was a more or less universal feature of medieval war reporting. Mercenaries first appear in England in the late tenth century,[13] while Flemish mercenaries were employed on a particularly large scale in the campaigns of Henry II, as recounted by John of Salisbury.[14] In the reign of John, their use was such that their expulsion was written into Magna Carta.[15] Indeed, it seems to have been in the later twelfth century that the scale of mercenary involvement in warfare transformed and attracted new forms of hostility, as evidenced in the *History of William Marshal*.[16]

The fact that the English throne was contested by a man and a woman has lent an extra level of drama to accounts of the civil war, and we should not neglect the involvement of women in the conflict. Geoffrey of Monmouth's twelfth-century *Historia Regum* was 'peppered with positive images of women in power.'[17] Significantly, it was written in the mid-1130s, when the Angevin cause urgently needed such role models. Matilda was not always considered a key political player: other chroniclers 'effaced Matilda's participation in political friendship entirely and focused instead on the relationships of her half-brother Robert of Gloucester.'[18] There is also the question of whether King Stephen deliberately held back from direct military attacks on Matilda because she was a woman; that he permitted her to withdraw from Arundel in the autumn of 1139 provides a case in point. Anecdotal evidence of female involvement in the conflict shows that siege warfare was not exclusively the domain of men, since Matilda, Countess of Chester and Hawise, Countess of Lincoln played a key role in Earl Ranulf's capture of Lincoln Castle in 1141, acting as decoys and distracting the knight on guard there, as recounted by Orderic Vitalis.[19]

Arms and Armour: Sources of Evidence

Surviving weaponry and military apparel datable with certainty to any part of the twelfth century are exceptionally rare. Consequently, we can only explore the equipment that would have been used in the conflict in quite a general way.[20] The survival of items such as swords and spearheads from the eleventh and twelfth century is poor relative to the pre-Conquest period, and even in the case of well-preserved objects in museum collections (often representing the finer end of the medieval market) it can be very difficult to narrow down date ranges to a particular century, let alone decades within a century, as is the case with swords (Fig. 6.1). Of those major items of twelfth-century military material culture that do survive in museums and private collections there are many more swords than shield bosses and helmets, and mail armour is exceptionally rare.

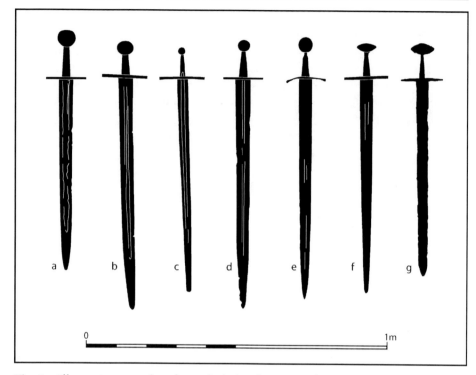

Fig. 6.1: Illustrative examples of swords dating from around the twelfth century held in museum collections. **(a)** St Mungo Museum of Religious Life and Art, Glasgow Museums, A.1987.31, 1100–50; **(b)** Fornham Sword (held at Moyses Hall, Bury St Edmunds), mid-twelfth century; **(c)** Kelvingrove Art Gallery and Museum, Glasgow Museums, A.1965.22, *c.* 1150; **(d)** Royal Armouries, IX.1082, late twelfth century; **(e)** Wallace Collection, A458, twelfth century; **(f)** Wallace Collection, A457, *c.* 980–*c.* 1150; **(g)** Royal Armouries, IX.5610, eleventh to mid-twelfth century. Drawing by Seán Goddard.

Funeral effigies of knights are another invaluable source for understanding medieval arms and armour but these are mainly too late in date to aid our study of Anarchy-period apparel. A military effigy of William Clito, Count of Flanders (d. 1128) dating to *c.* 1170, from his tomb in the abbey of St Bertin at St-Omer is known from antiquarian sketches,[21] but no authentic English example exists for the twelfth century. In England, production of 'mail and surcoat' effigies of reposing figures began *c.* 1240,[22] although occasionally the tombs of important figures of the twelfth century are remembered with later memorials. An example is the painted bog oak effigy of Robert Curthose (d. 1134) in Gloucester Cathedral, which dates to the mid-thirteenth century (pg. 131). Another effigy sometimes identified as that of the civil war's most famous and notorious robber baron, Geoffrey de Mandeville, Earl of Essex (d. 1144), in Temple Church, London, is also later in date, although the earl was buried in the church's porch.[23] While 'furnished' burials are usually thought of as a pagan tradition, the custom of interring high-status individuals with their weaponry was not entirely unknown in the post-Conquest period. At the site of North Elmham, Norfolk, an exceptionally interesting coffined burial excavated in the 1950s was accompanied by the 'ghosts' of a decomposed shield, helmet and sword, the form and context of which suggests a very late eleventh-century date at the earliest.[24] Such evidence is totally exceptional, however, and so it is to pictorial sources – primarily manuscript illustrations – that scholars have turned to assess the military material culture of the period.

We need to be cautious in taking manuscript illustrations and other visual sources as faithful and accurate representations of eleventh- and twelfth-century arms and armour, however. Michael Lewis's assessment of the archaeological authority of the Bayeux Tapestry concludes that depiction of artefacts was 'influenced more by artistic convention than by the contemporary scene.'[25] A common characteristic of twelfth-century representations of soldiers, especially in manuscript illustrations, is that they depict biblical scenes but with characters equipped with contemporary (i.e. twelfth-century) military apparel. A fine example is the depiction of David slaying Goliath in the frontispiece to the first book of Samuel in the Winchester Bible, produced *c.* 1160–80, in which the giant is shown as a Norman knight complete with mailed shirt, leggings, a kite-shaped shield, sword and spear of the period.[26]

Seals, used in ever-greater numbers from the middle decades of the twelfth century, including by knights of middling status, are another valuable source of information, especially as many are closely datable and associated with known individuals. We must also bear in mind that seals were vehicles for the expression and communication of rank, however, so that the depiction of weaponry carried important social messages as well as reflecting trends in apparel. For example, the tendency through the twelfth century for lances topped with flags or gonfanons to give way to swords reflects the fact that lesser knights were using seals rather than actual changes in weaponry.[27] Other rare but important visual evidence for the appearance of twelfth-century knights comes from gaming pieces and sculpture (Fig. 6.2), while we also have a handful of representations on wall paintings that provide striking if heavily stylised images (Plate 13).[28] Another particularly informative visual source falls into none of these categories: the 'Temple Pyx' (Plate 14) is a bronze-gilt ornament (perhaps part of a reliquary) said to have been discovered in Temple Church, London, in the early nineteenth century and dated on stylistic grounds to *c.* 1140–50.[29] Depicting three sleeping knights, the pyx is remarkable in showing three-dimensional details not only of weapons but also clothing: behind large individually decorated kite-shaped shields can be glimpsed long cloth tunics under mail shirts as well as sheathed swords. Another ornamental piece of similar date (apparently wrenched off a larger piece) depicting a single, identical soldier may have come from the same workshop, if not necessarily the same pyx.[30]

To these sources we should add the small but important collection of personal military artefacts recovered from archaeological sites, especially from excavations of castles, towns and high status residences. Such objects are especially informative where they derive from well-stratified and closely datable contexts. It is a mistake to differentiate the martial and symbolic functions of display on the medieval battlefield.[31] Items of military apparel had practical functions but were also instrumental in building and expressing group identity as well as proclaiming an individual's standing. The most common items of twelfth-century military material culture recovered from archaeological contexts are unsurprisingly small portable metal objects such as arrowheads and spurs. Objects derived from battlefield sites of the twelfth century are extremely rare, and even where items such as swords have been recovered from the vicinity of known conflict locations, uncertainties over dating can still make it difficult to ascertain that a piece was used in a particular documented action (see below, pgs 165–6). Numerous portable twelfth-century military artefacts have also been recovered and recorded through metal-detecting. Besides logging numerous ferrous objects such as arrowheads and spurs, the Portable Antiquities Scheme, coordinated through the British Museum, has recorded large numbers of copper alloy items of military apparel including harness pendants and stirrup strip mounts dated to the twelfth century, providing important new evidence for display on the battlefield (see also pgs 178–80).[32]

Another promising but very rare category of archaeological evidence comes in the form of human skeletons from battlefields, trauma providing grim insight into the technologies and capabilities of medieval weapons.[33] Well-analysed assemblages from medieval mass

Fig. 6.2: Sculptured decoration from around the south doorway of St Nicholas church, Barfreston, Kent, depicting **(a)** knights; **(b)** an archer; and **(c)** jousting mounted knights. The carvings date to *c.* 1170. Photographs by Oliver Creighton.

war graves are mainly later in date, however, including particularly important evidence from the battlefields of Towton (North Yorkshire, 1461)[34] and Visby (Sweden, 1361).[35] The most plausible evidence for the skeletal remains of Anarchy-period battle casualties comes from Lincoln. A group of 16 burials (14 males, two females) excavated close to the west gate of Lincoln castle and dated to *c.* 1140 included a double male burial, one of which had clear evidence of traumatic injuries to the skull. A 'gaping wound' from a heavy weapon such as an axe had partly healed, while two other injuries were inflicted peri-mortem (i.e. around the time of death): a penetration from a bodkin-type arrowhead and a massive oval wound that seems to have represented the coup de grace.[36] If the burials can indeed be assigned to the civil war period then the casualty or casualties might well be related to the Battle of Lincoln in 1141, or else the siege that preceded it or the violent sacking of the city that followed, or perhaps to Stephen's later siege of 1144. While the circumstances that caused the injuries must remain unclear, the evidence nonetheless provides a tantalising glimpse of the intensity of contemporary warfare, with the fact that the individual in question had a part-healed wound suggesting that he was not new to the horrors of combat. Elsewhere, the skeletons of five Frankish soldiers killed during the siege of the Crusader castle of Vadum Iacob (Israel) in 1179 give some indication of the effectiveness of twelfth-century arms and armour, albeit in a different cultural context.[37]

The site with the greatest potential for the study of the realities of Anarchy-period combat is the battlefield of the Battle of the Standard (1138), north of Northallerton, North Yorkshire, where mass graves can be pinpointed quite accurately and which are likely to contain the remains of unarmoured Scots or Galwegians cut down by massed archers whose arrows would have inflicted distinctive injuries.[38] The archaeological potential of undisturbed mass graves on twelfth-century battlefields is also indicated at Fornham, Suffolk, where nineteenth-century reports describe the discovery of a large number of skeletons piled tier upon tier in a circle with the heads facing inwards, marking likely casualties of the battle of 1173, where Earl Robert of Leicester's mercenary army was crushed by a royalist force.[39] While arms, armour and dress accessories marked out the status and sometimes ethnicity of different types of combatant, there would be little to differentiate the stripped bodies that littered battlefields in the aftermath of battles, which would have left a very different sort of visual impression on contemporary observers.

While it is clear from these various sources of evidence that fashions of military apparel were changing in profound and intriguing ways during the twelfth century, it is important to remember that not all combatants had access to the latest equipment. Typologies of military apparel can highlight evolutionary change, but combatants below the ranks of the knightly classes probably used archaic weapons. The use of old-fashioned weapons and apparel might also be characteristic of civil wars that broke out in otherwise peaceful periods. It is instructive that the collection of English Civil War arms and armour recovered from

Plate 1: Geophysical survey by the authors of the earthwork known as 'the Rings,' below Corfe Castle, Dorset. The site is a siege castle built against Corfe Castle, almost certainly during a lengthy but unsuccessful siege led by King Stephen. The earthworks comprise a powerfully defended ringwork and bailey which show signs of modification in the seventeenth-century English Civil War. Photograph by Duncan Wright.

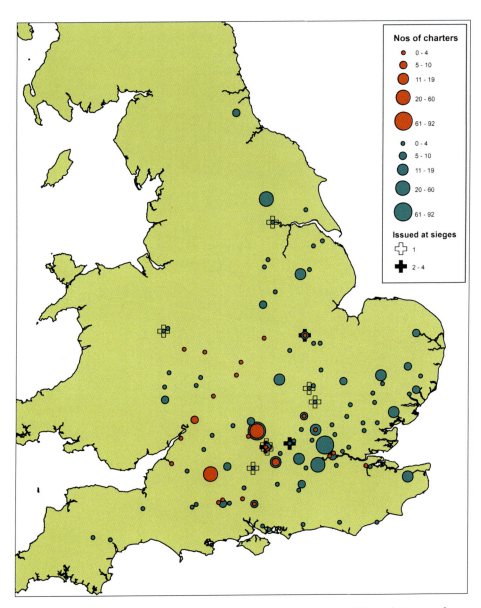

Plates 2 and 3: Charters issued by King Stephen, the Empress Matilda and Henry of Anjou, 1135–54: **(a)** places of issue of charters; **(b)** places charters were issued to. Red symbols identify Stephen's charters and blue symbols those of the Angevins. The size of each symbol is proportionate to the number of charters issued. Compiled from Cronne and Davis 1968. Map work by Steven Trick.

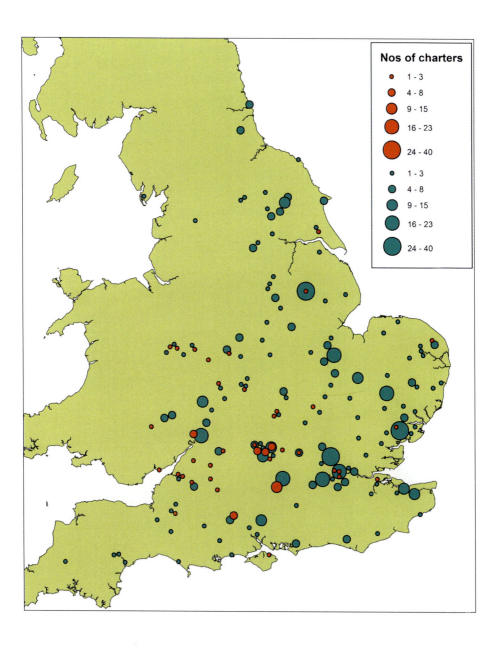

Nos of charters

- 1 - 3
- 4 - 8
- 9 - 15
- 16 - 23
- 24 - 40

- 1 - 3
- 4 - 8
- 9 - 15
- 16 - 23
- 24 - 40

Plate 4: Viewsheds from known or suspected Stephanic siege castles (the lighter area is the zone intervisible with the siege castle): **(top left)** Danes Castle, Exeter; **(top right)** Crowmarsh Castle, near Wallingford; **(bottom left)** 'the Rings,' Corfe; **(bottom right)** Hamstead Marshall. GIS-generated map by Duncan Wright, incorporating LiDAR data supplied by the Environment Agency.

Plate 5: Excavation of an Anarchy-period castle in Luton town centre (work commissioned by Bellway Homes).
Source: © Albion Archaeology.

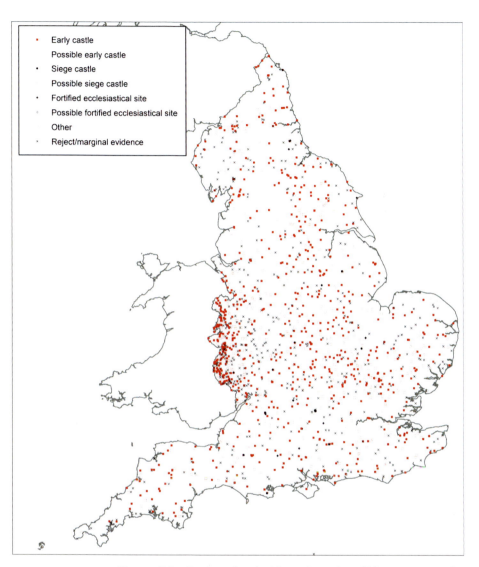

Plate 6: Distribution of early (eleventh- and twelfth-century) castles in England and Wales. Map work by Steven Trick.

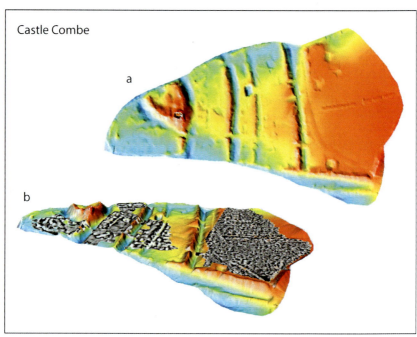

Castle Combe

a

b

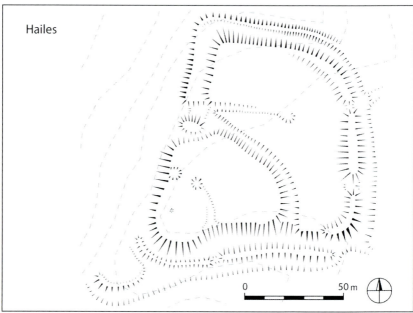

Hailes

0   50 m

Plate 7: Plans of castles adapted from prehistoric hillforts. **(top)** Castle Combe: **(a)** digital terrain model; **(b)** 3D digital terrain model with draped geophysics and vertical exaggeration. **(bottom)** Hailes. Source: Hailes plan © Anarchy? War and Status Project; Castle Combe © Archaeological Surveys.

Plate 8: Examples of mid-twelfth-century metalwork and other artefacts recorded by the Portable Antiquities Scheme. **(a)** seal matrix, SF-8921F3; **(b)** book clasp, NMS-A664F2; **(c)** buckle, NMS-2357E8; **(d)** buckle, SWYOR-9F5465; **(e)** figurine (vessel handle?), DENO-CB2681; **(f)** finger ring, DENO-A0AFF8; **(g)** mount (for a book/reliquary box?), KENT-DFBFBC. Source: images courtesy of the Portable Antiquities Scheme.

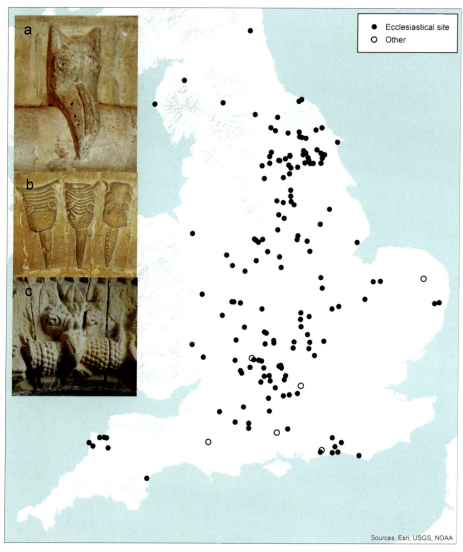

Legend:
● Ecclesiastical site
○ Other

Sources: Esri, USGS, NOAA

Plate 9: Distribution of beakheads in England.
Inset images: (a) Astall, Oxfordshire; (b) Great Rollright, Oxfordshire;
(c) Bishopsteignton, Devon.
Image based on Henry and Zarnecki 1957–58 and Zarnecki et al. 1984,
with additions. Photographs by Oliver Creighton; map work by Steven
Trick.

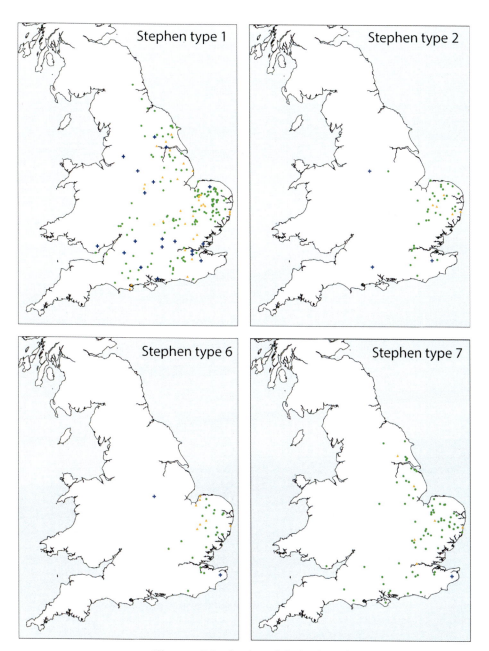

Plate 10: Distribution of finds of Stephen's type 1, 2, 6 and 7. Green circles represent single finds; yellow triangles are finds of 2–10 coins and blue crosses indicate hoards. Data drawn from the Portable Antiquities Scheme and the Corpus of Early Medieval Coin Finds.

Plate 11: Distribution of finds of irregular coinage of Stephen's reign. Green symbols represent royalist issues and variants, and blue symbols Angevin or Scots' issues. Hoards are represented by crosses. Data drawn from the Portable Antiquities Scheme and the Corpus of Early Medieval Coin Finds. Map work by Duncan Wright.

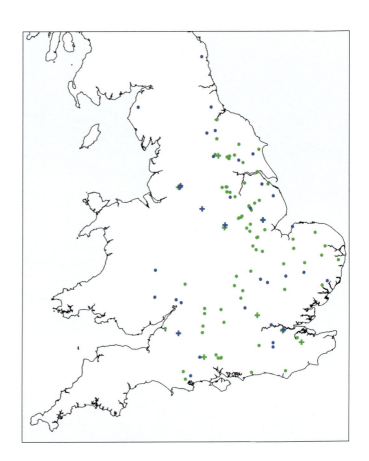

Plate 12: Official coinage of Stephen's reign. Stephen issued four official (or 'substantive') types: type 1 ('a'), minted *c.* 1135/36–1142/45, type 2 ('b') minted *c.* 1142/45–1150, type 6 ('c') minted *c.* 1150–53 and type 7 ('d') minted *c.* 1153–58. The coins once identified as types 3, 4 and 5 are now recognised as not being official issues. a (type 1) SOM-DAA632, minted by Ricard at Shaftesbury; b (type 2) NMS-99A443, minted by Thor, probably at Norwich; c (type 6) NMS-0CDD40, minted by Aedgar at Ipswich; d (type 7) SF-4EFA85, minted by Hacun at Thetford. Images courtesy of the Portable Antiquities Scheme.

Plate 13: Wall paintings from the church of St Michael and All Angels, Copford, Essex, showing two knights. The paintings are situated either side of a window in the north wall of the church and date to *c.* 1130; the knight on the right-hand side was restored in the nineteenth century. Photograph by Oliver Creighton.

Plate 14: The Temple Pyx, northern European, about 1150.
Overall dimensions: 92mm x 73mm x 20mm.
Source: Burrell Collection, Glasgow Museums, 5-6.139.

Plate 15: *opposite* The tympanum of Fordington church, *c.* 1100, depicting St George and soldiers in typical eleventh-/early twelfth-century military apparel. Note the cross-shaped harness pendants on the horse. Photograph by Oliver Creighton.

Plate 16: Twelfth-century churches: **(a)** St Nicholas, Barfreston; **(b)** St Mary, Kempley. Photographs by Oliver Creighton.

Plate 17: Wolvesey Palace, Winchester, showing the large rectangular keep-like structure added to the complex during its extensive redevelopment in the mid-twelfth century by Henry of Blois. Photograph by Oliver Creighton.

Plate 18: Beaudesert: LiDAR survey of the ridgetop castle that contained a market in the mid-twelfth century. The castle is surrounded by the earthworks of medieval ridge and furrow and water management features including fish ponds. © Anarchy? War and Status Project; LiDAR data courtesy of the Environment Agency.

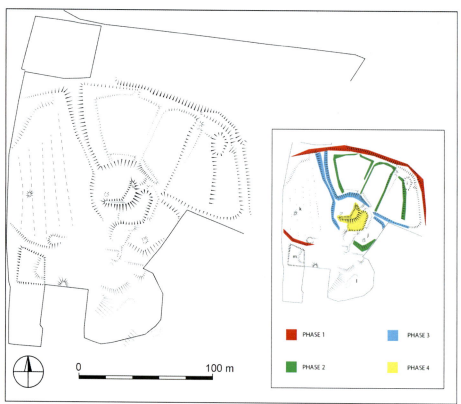

PHASE 1		PHASE 3	
PHASE 2		PHASE 4	

Plate 19: Earthwork plan and interpretation of the earthworks at Wood Walton. Source: © Anarchy? War and Status Project. Map work by Michael Fradley.

excavations at Pontefract Castle, West Yorkshire, representing probably the most important archaeological assemblage of the mid-seventeenth century, was characterised by outdated items, some of them up to 50 years old.[40]

We also have a far poorer understanding of the arms and armour (if any) used by such lower-ranking soldiers. Chroniclers' accounts point out ethnic differences in the composition of twelfth-century armies, which may have been reflected in differences in material culture, as well as distinctive tactics. Large forces of Scots invaded northern England leading up to the Battle of the Standard (1138) and smaller contingents fought with the Angevins at Winchester in 1141, while Welshmen were routed by Stephen's forces in the early stages of the Battle of Lincoln (1141). Large parts of such forces were distinguished by their lack or armour, rendering them 'naked' for battle in the chroniclers' eyes, although the propaganda of Anglo-Norman commentators probably aimed to discredit the military capacity of 'Celtic' forces (see pgs 46, 175). The arms and armour of the omnipresent Flemish mercenaries would probably have been little different to those of 'English' knights, although crossbows were a favoured weapon of these paid professionals (see pg. 156).

Swords, Scabbards and Chapes

As the very embodiment of knightly identity – expressing social status and religious ideals as well as martial prowess – swords were elegant and well-proportioned objects of beauty as well as instruments of death. The sword acted as a ceremonial tool in the ceremony of 'dubbing,' through which an individual made the transition into knighthood; the ritual could also involve bathing and placing gilded spurs on the new knight's heels.[41] Dating any sword with precision to the mid-twelfth century on stylistic grounds is extremely difficult. Even the finest museum pieces are assigned date ranges sometimes spanning more than a century (Fig. 6.1). Medieval swords of any period recovered from well-dated archaeological contexts are again exceptionally rare; component parts such as pommels, grips and scabbard chapes are recorded a little more frequently but are still very uncommon.[42] Some complete post-Conquest swords have been recovered from rivers, such as the Thames, although whether these represent casual loss or ritual deposit is hard to judge.[43]

High levels of cross-fertilisation between different traditions of design mean that there is no simple linear chronology of sword form covering the period of the twelfth-century civil war, although some underlying trends can be detected. The blades of the twelfth century had developed little from late Viking forms; it was in the following century that blades tended to become narrower and more pointed.[44] There is also nothing particularly distinctive about 'English' swords of the period. Sword design followed wider Continental trends and most blades were forged abroad, particularly in Germany. Sword blades of the eleventh and twelfth century were straight, quite broad and double edged, without a ricasso (or unsharpened length of blade below the guard). Lengths vary, but c. 75–85cm was perhaps typical. Children of the elite classes were trained in swordplay from an early age, and the earliest boy's sword in Europe dates to this period (Fig. 6.1g).[45]

As these weapons were primarily for slashing rather than stabbing, their blades were manufactured without a sharply tapering point, and depictions on manuscript illustrations can show an almost blunt appearance. Cross-guards (or quillons, as they became known from the sixteenth century) were mainly simple and straight, or else slightly downturned, while a metal pommel at the end of the grip of wood, bone or horn helped ensure that the weapon was balanced as well as providing a striking weapon of last resort at very close quarters.[46] Characteristic pommels of the twelfth century were brazil nut forms (whose use continued from the previous century) (Figs 6.1f–g) and disk-like types (which seem to have become more popular from c. 1100 onwards) (Figs 6.1a–e).[47] Pommels could display heraldic devices such as lions, although these are usually dated from the last quarter of the twelfth century onwards and are likely associated with the Crusades.[48] Grips would have been manufactured from hardwood, with an outer layer of leather or textile, although these organic materials do not survive. A wide central groove (or fuller) running down each face of the blade served to lighten the weapon without significantly weakening it and also provided a natural position for inlaid decoration or an inscription, typically in alloys such as brass or tin, or occasionally silver. Permutations of blade, pommel and cross-guard type are exceptionally complex. As items of material culture, swords of the period had complex biographies: while blades were manufactured on the Continent, the pommel, hilt and cross-guard were assembled closer to the eventual buyer and user, meaning that these elements show a higher level of individuality, with gilt pommels and examples made of stone not unknown.

While the problems of dating swords to a defined period within a single century have already been discussed, scholars of the medieval sword have identified some possible characteristics of swords manufactured towards the middle to the end of the twelfth century.

The cross-guard was sometimes a little longer and thinner than before, its ends curving down slightly towards the blade, or were 'waisted' and thicker towards the ends (Figs 6.1c and e), while pommel shapes tended to become perhaps a little bulkier.[49] Such fashions seem characteristic of the period around 1150 and immediately after, but before the more radical changes in sword design connected to the introduction of plate armour in the thirteenth century.

The primary function of a scabbard was to protect the blade and, of course, to allow the sword to be carried. The fact that the surface of a scabbard provided a chance for decoration was secondary, but judging from manuscript illustrations these items became more decorative and showy in the twelfth century. Physical evidence is lacking given that these were largely organic items of wood and leather and do not survive, although a remarkable assemblage of knife scabbards recovered from excavations on the Thames waterfront in London shows the range of painted and gilded decoration in use in the mid-twelfth century and the different means of embossing and stamping leather panels.[50] Metal chapes (reinforcements for the scabbard tip) attributed to the twelfth century survive in greater numbers, being used for dagger scabbards as well as sword scabbards. These were usually manufactured of folded copper alloy sheets but occasional iron examples are known. The practical purpose of a chape was to stop the scabbard scuffing, although they were also a focus for display, and it is instructive to remember that they would have been far more visible day-to-day than the blades themselves. Some derive from scabbards for knives rather than swords, especially those with longitudinal folds and pointed tips. Chapes of the period could be ostentatious and elaborate: one copper alloy example from Broughton, Hampshire, seems to show two squirrel-like animals copulating.[51] Another especially fine example of the mid-twelfth century, also of copper alloy, found in Angel Court in the City of London in 1912, depicts a mounted knight wielding a huge battleaxe and carrying a kite-shaped shield on one side and a figure wrestling a beast on the other (Fig. 6.3).[52] A related piece of military apparel of similar material that sometimes survives archaeologically is the mount that fastened the scabbard to the owner's belt, although these were mainly plain and functional.[53]

It is nonetheless hazardous to attribute individual examples of swords or their components to 'Anarchy' contexts, even where they were recovered near known conflict locations. In Cambridgeshire, for example, a 20km stretch of the Great Ouse south of Ely, which was such a hotbed of contestation in the early 1140s (see Chapter 9), has produced

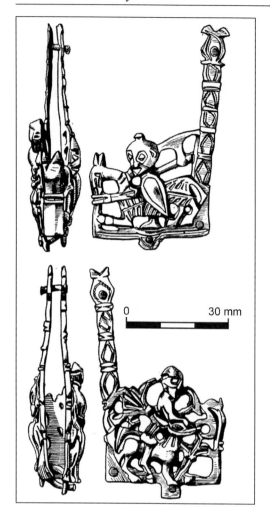

Fig. 6.3: Mid-twelfth-century scabbard chape from London. Source: Spencer 1961, reproduced with the permission of London and Middlesex Archaeological Society.

seven medieval swords, including one of likely late eleventh- or twelfth-century date in the Collection of the Museum of Archaeology and Ethnology, Downing College, Cambridge; a sacrificial context has been suggested,[54] although it could equally be a casual loss. At Wallingford, which was the focus of three separate sieges in Stephen's reign (see pgs 62–74), the Thames River Collection (comprising items recovered during dredging) contains eleventh- or twelfth-century spearheads but the swords and scramasaxes are pre-Conquest and again probably votive deposits.[55] The stretch of the River Witham marking the southern edge of the battlefield of Lincoln (1141) has produced a fine collection of swords, mainly from dredging in the late eighteenth century, now in the City Museum of Lincoln; the assemblage includes at least one Roman and one seventeenth-century weapon, although six others date broadly to the period 1120–1320.[56]

A final consideration is that while weapons of war might seem the very embodiment of functionality, it is striking how items that could be expected to be damaged in use could be expensively and lavishly decorated. Inscriptions embellished many of the finer twelfth-century blades. These rarely named the sword's owner or manufacturer; rather, most were talismanic slogans, invoking divine protection and assistance in battle, proclaiming biblical proverbs and/or dedicating the weapon to the service of God.[57] Other items of material culture with religious meanings that were taken onto the field of battle include holy relics and banners remembering saints, as deployed by the English at the Battle of the Standard (pg. 45), while war cries were another means of invoking 'divine aid' prior to engagement.[58]

An excellent example of a twelfth-century sword with clear Christian associations was found in 1933 in a ditch on the site of the 1173 Battle of Fornham (Fornham St Genevieve, Suffolk) (Fig. 6.1b). On one side the inlaid silver inscription reads 'I– I Nomine Dom ...,' presumably *In Nomine Domini* ('in the name of the lord'); the reverse proclaims '+SCS BENEDICTVS,' the first three letters being an abbreviation of *sanctus*.[59] Another important sword of the same period in the Glasgow Museums collections (Fig. 6.1a), attributed to *c.* 1100–50, has the repeated inscription 'BOAC' alongside circular and other symbols, which is probably an abbreviation for *Beatus Omnipotensque Armatus Christi* ('Blessed and Omnipotent [is] the Warrior of Christ').[60] Other blade inscriptions are obscure or indecipherable, and might not have been intelligible to anybody other than their owners, underlining the immensely personal associations of these weapons.

That swords were seen as quasi-religious implements is neatly indicated in poetic and literary sources, in which writers sometimes imbued weapons with divine powers. Literary sources also remind us that swords were perceived as extensions of their owners' personalities. In the late eleventh- or early twelfth-century French poem *La Chanson de Roland* (*The Song of Roland*), for example, the sword of the hero, Roland, was named Durendal ('enduring') and that of his friend Oliver, Hauteclere ('high and clear'). Roland's sword both embodied its owner and symbolised his past conquests, proving indestructible when he tried to break it against a boulder before dying.[61] How often might the recovery of bent or broken medieval sword blades from archaeological contexts represent similar processes? An intriguing case in point is the inscribed

'Wallingford Sword' dredged from the River Thames,[62] although is hard to judge whether such bent or broken forms resulted from ritual breaking after the deaths of their owners or post-depositional processes.

Bows and Crossbows

Bows and crossbows were common weapons of the civil war, although chroniclers are not usually specific about which was used in any certain context. Massed English archers proved decisive at the Battle of the Standard (1138) and were used to garrison castles and siege works, but they also proved versatile in small units, being deployed as mobile field forces, patrols and as advanced detachments to harass approaching enemies.[63] Exceptionally, King Stephen hired slingers (*funditores*) to assist in the siege of Exeter in 1136.[64] Crossbows were favoured by mercenaries and ideally suited to siege warfare, as they allowed the user to take careful aim with far less movement than required with a conventional bow. Crossbowmen demanded a high price: by the early years of Henry II's reign, when we have reliable information in the pipe rolls on the costs of hiring soldiers, a crossbowman cost 4d a day, which was only half the price of a knight (8d), while a sergeant of the period cost 1d.[65]

The technology of the crossbow was current in the Roman period although the circumstances of its survival or reintroduction into Britain are controversial. In Winchester, it is extremely difficult to tell whether boltheads from ninth- and tenth-century contexts provide evidence for the weapon in late Anglo-Saxon England or are residual Roman objects.[66] Crossbowmen certainly served in Duke William's army at Hastings: *balistantes* are mentioned by William of Poitiers and in Guy of Amiens's poem *Carmen de Hastingae Proelio* (*Song of the Battle of Hastings*).[67] Men styled *arbalistarius* are also recorded holding land in Domesday Book.[68]

In twelfth-century warfare, bows and crossbows had a special sort of status as they held the potential for relatively untrained combatants to kill or disable expensively armoured knightly opponents. The death of Geoffrey de Mandeville days after being struck in the face by an arrow outside Burwell Castle in 1144 is the clearest case in point (see pg. 264). Little more than half a century later, Richard I was killed by a crossbowman who picked him out from the walls of the castle of Châlus, Haute-Vienne, France.[69] Aristocratic fear of this sort of incident – or deterrence of it – might account for 'war crimes' such as the mass beheading of 60 royal archers, perhaps as some sort of spectacle, at the siege of Wallingford Castle in 1153 following the capture of a siege castle (see pg. 73).[70] There are suggestions that crossbow use was in fact deliberately restricted in the eleventh and early twelfth century to avoid use against knightly opposition: Matthew Strickland points out that of the main battles between 1066 and 1144, the crossbow was documented as in use at Hastings (1066) and Alençon (1118) but not Tinchebrai (1106), Brémule (1119), Bourgthéroulde (1124) or Lincoln (1141).[71] There is an argument that the weapon was not depicted in the Bayeux Tapestry as its barbarity would have been inappropriate in a propagandist work, although it has also been taken as evidence that the Tapestry's (English) makers were unfamiliar with the weapon.[72]

Pressure from the social elite might have partly inspired the Church's efforts to ban handheld missile weapons altogether. It is commonly asserted that in an early exercise in arms control, the Second Lateran Council of 1139 banned crossbows from being used against Christians.[73] A close reading of the canon shows that *all* types of bow were prohibited, however.[74] All lines of evidence agree that the ban was ignored totally and utterly, and archers and crossbowmen played a prominent role in the civil war, with arrowheads and crossbow bolts and fittings found fairly widely at castles and other sites of the period.

Turning to the archaeological evidence, crossbow quarrel heads can easily be confused with arrowheads, especially before the thirteenth century; similarly, hunting and military forms of crossbow bolts are difficult to distinguish from one another. More diagnostic evidence for crossbow use comes in the form of surviving crossbow 'nuts' – small perforated circular objects, usually carved from antler, which formed part of the mechanism that held back the bow-string until released by a trigger (or 'sear') (Figs 6.4m–n). Examples from archaeological contexts show that these were manufactured on a lathe; some were decorated with grooves and exhibit signs of wear and weakening where they were used.[75] Archaeological excavations have recovered several examples, mainly from thirteenth-century and later contexts, reflecting the increasing role of the crossbow as the dominant handheld missile weapon from this time.[76] Crucially, however, the earliest post-Conquest crossbow nuts come from mid-twelfth-century contexts.[77] One example was found in the excavation of Goltho Castle, Lincolnshire, in the phase now redated to the mid-twelfth century.[78] Another example of almost identical dimensions was recovered from destruction deposits around the 'keep' at Wareham, Dorset, demolished shortly after 1142.[79] These examples differ from those of the thirteenth century and later in that they lack evidence of an inserted metal wedge – a development

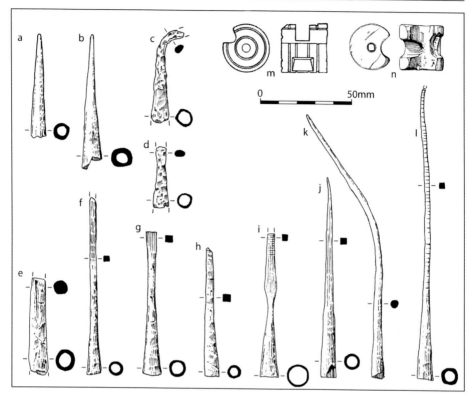

Fig. 6.4: Archaeological finds of twelfth-century weaponry. 'Bodkin'-type arrowheads: **(a–b)** Goltho, Lincolnshire; **(c–d)** Trowbridge, Wiltshire; **(e–h)** Castle Acre, Norfolk; **(i)** Exeter, Devon; **(j)** Winchester, Hampshire; **(k–l)** Goltho, Lincolnshire. Crossbow nuts: **(m)** Goltho, Lincolnshire; and **(n)** Wareham, Dorset. Drawing by Seán Goddard, based on Renn 1960; Goodall 1982; Allan 1984; Beresford 1987; Goodall 1990a; Graham and Davies 1993.

associated with more powerful composite bows that exerted much greater pressure on the string.[80]

Surviving arrowheads, derived from archaeological excavations or stray finds, provide further insight into the changing uses of bows and crossbows. The typology of forms in the Museum of London catalogue of arrowheads, which was for many years the key source of reference,[81] has now been revised by Oliver Jessop to take account of newer archaeological evidence from 23 excavated sites.[82] Twenty-eight generic forms fitting into four broad groups are identified: tanged, multipurpose, military and hunting. Tanged forms were used no later than the tenth century, while hunting arrowheads (with their characteristically large barbs) were developed mainly from the thirteenth century. A wide range of multipurpose arrowheads were in use in the twelfth century, mostly with triangular heads. Of the military forms there is intriguing evidence that bodkin-type arrowheads came into use in the mid-twelfth century. Long and narrow with thin points, the purpose of this weapon was quite specific: these were mail armour-piercing projectiles, although this form is probably under-represented on archaeological sites as corroded examples are almost identical to medieval iron nails.[83]

The purpose of a bodkin-type arrowhead was for the narrow point to enter mail, its gradually broadening profile splitting open the armour so that the projectile could penetrate deeply and lethally.[84] Twelfth-century examples have circular cross-sections in contrast to later forms, which have square or diamond cross-sections (Figs 6.4a–l). These are forerunners to the better known, more fully developed and heavier bodkin-type arrowheads of the Hundred Years' War, although twelfth-century examples could still be *c.* 150mm long. The potential for such projectiles to puncture a twelfth-century hauberk is clear from bodkin-type arrowheads that entered the soft tissue of Frankish soldiers at Vadum Iacob, Israel, during the siege of 1179.[85] At Goltho, Lincolnshire, long narrow bodkin-type points were dated in the report by the site's excavator to the eleventh century but redating places them firmly in the middle of the following century.[86] At Castle Acre, Norfolk, several bodkin-type points are associated with firmly dated mid-twelfth-century contexts.[87] The only potential earlier examples are from Winchester, in deposits dated between the eleventh and twelfth century.[88] A site not considered by Jessop that has produced bodkin-type projectiles is Trowbridge Castle, Wiltshire, where two incomplete examples derive from a deposit behind the mid-twelfth-century outer bailey bank thought to have accumulated shortly after its construction.[89] There is therefore tentative evidence that the bodkin-type projectile was used for the first time on a large scale in England during the mid-twelfth century, reflecting the particular type of warfare of the period and the unusual potential of handheld missile weapons operated by combatants from the lower social classes to maim expensively armoured men.

Other Weapons

While spears must have been the most commonly used weapons in the twelfth century, spearheads evolved least of all the major weapon types, so that differentiating late Anglo-Saxon from Anglo-Norman examples can be extremely difficult. If there is any trend, it is that later forms tend to be more substantial, with larger socket holes.[90] The distinction between spearheads used by infantry and cavalry is also blurred. The Bayeux Tapestry depicts Bishop Odo on horseback wielding a mace – a type of weapon carried by clerics. The earliest surviving mace-heads are of the second half of the twelfth century, of copper alloy or iron, often featuring 'knops' or pyramid-shaped projections. Some mace-heads may be misidentified ecclesiastical staff-fittings, however, and it is not out of the question that select examples had a dual purpose.[91] At the Battle of Lincoln, King Stephen wielded a Norse battleaxe given him by a citizen – an anachronistic weapon for the period that may in some way reflect the place's Viking heritage – with apparently lethal effect before it broke.[92] According to William of Malmesbury, the battle was brought to an end when Stephen was finally felled by a stone wielded or thrown by an anonymous combatant.[93] In this unusual context the use of such an unconventional weapon might have distanced the enormity of physical assault on the king himself.[94] The incident probably shows the *ad hoc* use of an object found to hand rather than paralleling Simon de Montfort's demise outside the gates of Toulouse in 1218, when he was killed instantly when hit on the head with a stone fired by a mangonel purportedly operated by women and children.[95]

We have no surviving siege engine ammunition of the civil war period. The remarkable assemblage of stone projectile balls from excavations in Winchester relates to the siege of the castle by Prince Louis of France in 1216 or its recapture by the English in the following year.[96] That these projectiles were dressed from ashlar blocks, some featuring architectural detail, suggests that most were prepared for use by the garrison. Averaging 7.9kg in weight, but the largest example weighing 22.3kg, they were presumably intended to be fired from the counterweighted trebuchet, introduced into England in the thirteenth century and with a much greater capacity for hurling heavy projectiles (see pg. 50) – marking one significant difference from the technology of siege warfare in the Anarchy.

Armour and Helmets

To understand the armour of the twelfth century we are almost totally reliant on pictorial sources, as the earliest examples of mail in museum collections date to the thirteenth or fourteenth centuries.[97] The term 'mail' is preferable to 'chain mail' or 'ring mail' as it is more authentically medieval.[98] Archaeological finds of entire mailed garments are almost unknown, the most relevant survival (from a much earlier period) being the heavily corroded mail tunic from the Sutton Hoo ship burial. Much smaller mail fragments are, however, occasionally found, including through metal-detecting, although dating is very difficult.[99]

The principal mail item of the twelfth century, as in the eleventh, was the hauberk composed of interlinked iron rings, which could provide excellent protection against sword cuts. It was worn like a long shirt; the 'trousered' mail shown in the Bayeux Tapestry is almost certainly an error as it would make fighting on horseback impossible.[100] The essential technology of mail manufacture shows little evidence of change, other than the rings becoming finer and smaller; a diameter of c. 15mm may have been typical in the twelfth century, as indicated by examples recovered from excavations at the Norman motte-and-bailey castle of Hen Domen, Montgomeryshire.[101] Manufacture of replica items using authentic medieval technologies shows that a single hauberk could take 140 hours to produce – several weeks' work.[102] The physical properties of mail hauberks gave little possibility for display, which is one of the main reasons why early heraldic devices are instead found on other items of apparel, such as shields and pendants. In a remarkable piece of archaeological evidence from a very different cultural context, the distribution of blade injuries on the skeletons of Frankish soldiers killed at the siege of Vadum Iacob, Israel, in 1179 shows how opponents might have specifically targeted areas of the body unprotected by the hauberk during combat.[103]

The twelfth century saw some subtle but important developments in armour as knights endeavoured to better protect themselves. Visual sources show that protection of the extremities became more commonplace from around the middle of the century, with hose-like mail 'chausses,' protecting the legs, and sleeves and mittens covering the arms and hands.[104] Duke William was depicted wearing mail hose in the Bayeux Tapestry (other knights wear criss-cross strappings on their legs), although this practice did not become widespread for a century or more. On the battlefields of the twelfth century only a small proportion of combatants would have been armoured with mail, however, and warhorses were unprotected (see below, pg. 177). In the speech attributed by Henry of Huntingdon to Ralph, Bishop of the Orkneys before the Battle of the Standard, the lack of armour differentiated the two forces, the Scots disparagingly labelled as 'unarmed and naked.'[105]

Helmets
Conical helmets were probably still the most common type in the twelfth century. Manufactured from iron plates either riveted together or attached to an underlying framework, also of iron, the external

appearance was essentially as depicted on the Bayeux Tapestry. A mail coif went under the helmet and also protected the vulnerable area at the back of the neck. A strengthening horizontal 'brow-band' was usual; embellishments could include the sorts of flowing ribbons (*infulae*) occasionally depicted in manuscript illustrations.[106] A helmet with a more rounded top was also in use in the second half of the century judging from manuscript illustrations; it appears to have been an alternative to the conical helmet rather than a development from it.[107] It is this rounded form – sometimes with a brow-band, sometimes without – that is depicted in a leaf intended for the Winchester Bible, dated to *c.* 1150–80.[108] The very rare surviving examples of eleventh- and twelfth-century helmets in museum collections in northern Europe show little standardisation, however, and helmets hammered from single pieces of iron are also known.[109]

In all these types of helmet, the wearer's face was left exposed aside from a 'nasal,' sometimes decorated with horn or inlaid with another metal, which protected the nose.[110] It is not until the last decades of the twelfth century and the first years of the thirteenth that helmets incorporated face guards; an early version comprising a nasal expanded into a cross-piece pierced with ventilation slits is known from the now lost effigy of William Clito, who was killed in 1128, although the effigy was perhaps produced 40 years later.[111] The first firmly dated evidence for the use of the great helm is on the second great seal of Richard I, cut in 1195 and in use by 1198.[112] Lacking visors, helmets of the mid-twelfth century rendered men particularly vulnerable to missile attack, especially from elevated fortifications. Archaeological evidence from the much later battlefield of Visby (1361) shows the enduring susceptibility of armoured men to facial injury: 10% of bodies in the mass grave here had been struck in this area by one or more arrows, showing either that they lacked visors or that their visors had been lifted.[113]

Shields

Anglo-Norman shields were generally kite-shaped with slightly curved tops. Pictorial sources suggest that the curvature at the top became less pronounced through the twelfth century,[114] perhaps to avoid blocking the view of its user. Manufactured of leather over wood with a central iron boss and perhaps iron reinforcement around the edges, shields, or their components, are unsurprisingly rare in archaeological contexts, although an iron shield boss of conical shape was recovered from a twelfth-century recut ditch of the motte-and-bailey castle at Repton, Derbyshire.[115] The fact that kite-shaped shields were held by leather straps actually made the boss functionally redundant, although bosses remained in use and formed the centrepieces of decorative schemes.[116] This is clear on the mid-twelfth-century Temple Pyx (Plate 14), which shows corresponding cross-hatched decoration on the shield and helmet of the central knight. It also shows that Norman shields were not flat but a flattened U-shape in cross-section, to curve around the body and deflect blows and missiles. This concave appearance may have become more pronounced through the twelfth century. Manuscript illustrations and personal seals confirm that shield decoration could take the form of ostentatious geometric designs, including star or ray-like patterns centred on the boss. The heraldic charge known as the 'escarbuncle' – composed of radiating rods around a central ornament – may well derive from such designs. In sharp contrast, Galwegian forces at the Battle of the Standard carried shields of cowhide which, to judge from depictions of early medieval warriors, would have been small, round and probably used more actively in combat, to deflect rather than absorb blows; essentially similar apparel was probably used by Welsh forces such as the contingent at the Battle of Lincoln.[117]

The battlefields of the civil war were probably the first time in England that shields carried heraldic designs, although heraldry is a very specific concept, and its early form in the twelfth century is a difficult and controversial area. Heraldry means the systematic and structured use of motifs, patterns and colours, based around the shield but extending to other elements of apparel, to proclaim lineage and title as well as a means of identifying people in battle. We should be cautious in describing any eye-catching shield design as necessarily heraldic. The vivid designs displayed on Norman shields on the Bayeux Tapestry are not strictly heraldic in nature (though they could be proto-heraldic), as they were not regulated but existed for visual effect. This had changed by the mid-twelfth century: the 1130s were the 'crucial decade' for the adoption of heraldry.[118] Aelred of Rievaulx's account of the Battle of the Standard relates that retreating Scots knights stripped away the banners or insignia that marked them out from the English to blend in with their victors, although these may not have been items of dress apparel but banners.[119] What seems to be the earliest representation of the arms of a noble family appears in a marginal illustration of the Battle of Lincoln in a copy of Henry of Huntingdon's near-contemporary *Historia Anglorum*. It shows a soldier whose shield is emblazoned with the three red chevrons of the Clare family, to which Baldwin fitz Gilbert, who is orating to Stephen's army in the scheme, belonged.[120] This representation also occurs on the family's seals by the 1140s.[121]

Cavalry

Horse trappings had become status symbols long before the Norman Conquest,[122] but by the twelfth century the accoutrements of the equestrian warrior had been taken to a new level. An exceptionally rare object that gives a good impression of a mounted twelfth-century warrior is the Carlton-in-Lindrick knight, a bronze figurine *c.* 5cm tall – probably decoration for a larger item rather than a gaming piece – found by a metal-detectorist in Nottinghamshire in 2004. The knight wears a conical helmet and carries a kite-shaped shield, while his warhorse wears a caparison (or ornate cloth garment), reminding us of another opportunity for display on the battlefield or tournament ground. While it is commonly supposed that the eleventh century first saw the shock tactic of mounted knights using their lances 'couched' (i.e. underarm: see Fig. 6.2c) revolutionise the medieval battlefield, some revisionist military historians now propose that this way of fighting evolved more gradually, although it was certainly established by the mid-twelfth century.[123] Light and heavy horsemen of the twelfth century fought in a variety of ways, striking overarm in the old-fashioned way as well as underarm, and in set-piece battles they mainly fought dismounted. In terms of the material culture of warfare, the couched lance technique might be evidenced by the attachment of pennants or 'gonfanons,' sometimes decorated with tassels, near the ends of lances, which must have also been popularised by tournaments (see below). In the Bayeux Tapestry the possession of a gonfanon seems to have marked out an individual as the leader of a unit (or *conroi*) of mounted men.[124] Lance-heads of the eleventh and twelfth century tend to be either leaf-shaped, with two edges and a sharp point, or long and slender, for piercing mail, while cross-pieces (*lugs*) to prevent the lance penetrating too far into a victim are also known.[125]

We should not think of the 'medieval warhorse' in a monolithic sense, as warfare required horses for different purposes and horse breeding evolved rapidly. By the mid- to late twelfth century a sophisticated network of studs existed, many of them embedded within deer parks. Horse breeding was advancing so that bigger and stronger warhorses were becoming available, producing specimens substantially larger than those types seen on the Bayeux Tapestry and early seals, which are sometimes small and slim.[126] A construction layer of the Anarchy-period castle at Trowbridge, Wiltshire, produced a horse bone (a distal right femur) of unusually massive size that was tentatively identified as that of a warhorse.[127] The equestrian figures that were *de rigueur* on twelfth-century seals provide additional evidence for subtle but important changes in cavalry apparel. That of Robert, Earl of Leicester, perhaps in use as early as 1118 and certainly by *c.* 1150 and one of the very earliest equestrian seals to survive, depicts Robert with a long shield wielding his lance overarm, whereas later figures have much shorter shields and hold swords.[128] Medieval horse armour in museum collections is much later in date although a reference to Richard I capturing 200 horses after the Battle of Gisors in 1198, 140 of which were 'covered in iron' (probably of mail construction), provides a tantalising suggestion that it was not entirely unknown in the twelfth century.[129]

Of the other main types of material culture associated with cavalry, horseshoes have been recovered from many different categories of archaeological site of the twelfth century, including urban and rural settlements as well as castles, in much greater numbers than any of the other categories of artefact considered here. More usually found as fragments, it is uncertain whether the shoes of warhorses can be identified specifically, as these items were manufactured in a wide range of sizes, perhaps with different forms for front and rear hoofs, and of narrower and thicker iron. What is clear is that twelfth-century horseshoes had nail holes of countersunk rather than rectangular form, as the latter type is unknown before *c.* 1200.[130] The other key cavalry artefact is the stirrup, which allowed the rider greater control of the horse and facilitated more effective use of weapons such as the couched lance. Intact stirrups are exceptionally rare, but copper alloy strap mounts (attaching the stirrup to the strap, to prevent wear on the leather) are known in quite large numbers, especially through metal-detected finds. There has been a tendency to attribute these to the eleventh century.[131] It is now established that their chronology extends to the middle years of the twelfth century, however, with examples sometimes depicting quasi-heraldic beasts and monsters and blending late Saxon/ Anglo-Scandinavian iconography with Romanesque designs.[132]

More diagnostic items of knightly material culture were spurs. In the eleventh and twelfth century the 'prick spur' (i.e. with a single point, used to control the horse) was in use, gradually giving way to the 'rowel spur' (incorporating a spiked wheel) in the thirteenth and early fourteenth centuries. Prick spurs were mainly manufactured of iron, but occasionally of copper alloy, and sometimes flushed over (or 'fusion-plated') with a thin coating of tin, which seems to have been a knightly prerogative and a technique not usually applied to other metalwork such as stirrups.[133] Forms from the middle of the twelfth century onwards are recognisable because they were tighter-fitting than before, with the

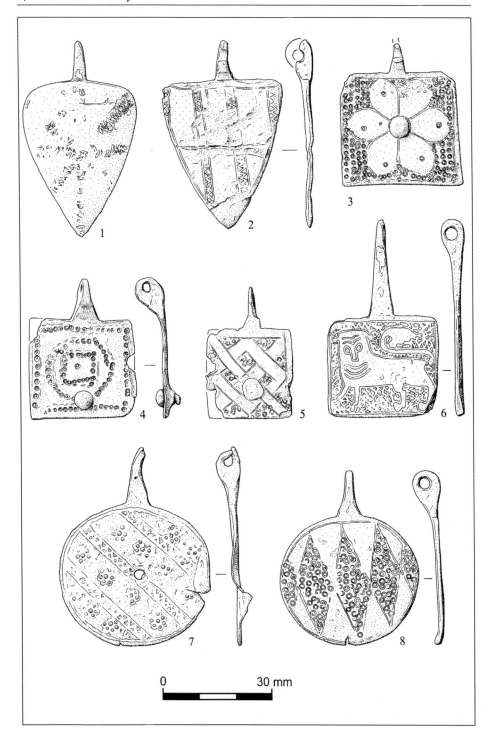

1   2   3

4   5   6

7   8

0 ————— 30 mm

Fig 6.5: *opposite* Twelfth-/early thirteenth-century copper alloy horse harness pendants from East Anglia: **(1)** shield-shaped, gilt, bearing an engraved rocker arm cross on saltire or possible escarbuncle (Attlebridge/Alderford/Swannington, Norfolk); **(2)** shield-shaped, gilt, bearing four engraved pales containing zig-zag lines (Emneth, Norfolk); **(3)** rectangular, bearing a sexfoil on a field of stamped annulets (Cawston, Norfolk); **(4)** rectangular, tinned, decorated with stamped annulets forming a square in circle within a border (Quidenham, Norfolk); **(5)** square, gilt, bearing a fret reserved on a field of stamped annulets (Euston, Suffolk); **(6)** rectangular, gilt, bearing a lion passant guardant on an engraved rocker-arm field (Withersdale/Mendham, Suffolk); **(7)** circular, gilt, with three bends containing zig-zag lines between multiple stamped sexfoils (Glandford (marginal), Norfolk); **(8)** circular, gilt, decorated with five lozenges in fess containing stamped annulets on a plain field (Stoke Holy Cross, Norfolk). Drawing by Steven Ashley.

'arms' (fitting around the wearer's ankles) curved rather than straight, while shorter 'necks' (the projection on which the point or 'goad' was mounted) became fashionable, as did more pronounced goads.[134] Good examples of clearly dateable mid-twelfth-century spurs come from a layer at Castle Acre, Norfolk, sealed no later than the 1140s.[135]

A rather less well-known but not uncommon type of medieval artefact associated with the mounted knight is the horse harness pendant (Plate 15 and Fig. 6.5). They provide subtle but important evidence for the changing image of the mounted warrior. The harness pendant was a small decorated plate, usually of copper alloy and typically only 2–4cm across, incorporating a loop from which it could be hung from the horse harness. Pictorial sources show that they hung in lines along the breast-band of the horse in particular, and could also decorate the rear strap and brow-band.[136] Although the majority of surviving examples date to the thirteenth and fourteenth century, it is now clear that the earliest armorial horse pendants date to the second and third quarters of the twelfth century,[137] developing from 'decorative dingle-dangles' of the eleventh century.[138]

Twelfth-century harness pendants (Fig. 6.5) are characterised by engraved or stamped decoration or gilding, with little or no evidence of enamelling at this stage, and by the thinness of the metal used. Early horse pendants are not necessarily simple in form; while the more common types in the twelfth century comprised circular, oval, almond-shaped or rectangular plates, more elaborate designs included ornate openwork and two-piece types, as well as scallop-shaped and cruciform pendants.[139] Finer twelfth-century harness pendants are small-scale pieces of Romanesque art in their own right. Some were clearly intended to facilitate heraldic or proto-heraldic display, for instance with Romanesque beasts and monsters posed in heraldic attitudes.[140] Horse pendants are a small but underestimated part of the knightly repertoire, highlighting the importance of decoration and display on even the tiniest items of military material culture. We should be cautious in attributing heraldic associations to early pendants and other decorative items of military apparel, however, as certain representations clearly had wide currency and are found in widely distributed locations.[141] Quite who owned these different types of pendant in the twelfth century remains rather more obscure, but the range seems wide enough to suggest that while some would have identified the armed retainers of lords of high or middling status, others would have proclaimed the emerging identities of more minor knightly families.

Military Training: The Tournament

The tournament of the twelfth century developed from its roots in military training into a spectacle and elite pursuit that drew condemnation by the Church. The 1130 Council of Clermont and 1139 Second Lateran Council both forbade tournaments, which critics saw as leading to mortal sin through the pursuit of vainglory.[142] Larger tournaments were indistinguishable from battle, which could itself have a strong theatrical dimension and be preceded by war games, especially during sieges. Differences in the material culture of war and tournament were subtle: mounted knights used the same lances they would in battle, but replaced the lance-head with a blunt version (a *coronal*) for 'friendly' tournaments.[143] The popularity of tournaments also provided a stimulus to the development of heraldry in the period.[144] Twelfth-century romances communicated the symbolism and ideology of the noble tournament, but their authors were well aware of the practicalities of its setting and conduct, as exemplified by the lengthy and dramatic tournament held outside Wallingford Castle, Oxfordshire, in Chrétien de Troyes's *Cligés*.[145]

Historians have long recognised that tournaments thrived in Stephen's reign, which contrasts with Henry II's efforts to regulate or prohibit what was perceived as a dangerous activity that then remained uncommon for the rest of the twelfth century.[146] There is a broader correlation between periods of weak government and the popularity of tournaments, which also proliferated in the reigns of Henry III and Edward II.[147] Evidence for tournaments in Stephen's reign comes primarily from chronicles, and we almost certainly underestimate the popularity of these events among the lower ranks of the aristocracy at a time when the knightly image was developing fast. Hugh Mortimer is recognised as the first English fatality of the tournament, killed some time during Stephen's reign at Worcester.[148] Henry of Huntingdon's account of a speech by the Bishop of Orkney before the Battle of the Standard (1138) compared the Scots' forces unfavourably to the English knights, who were said to be well-trained for battle because of their military exercises in peacetime.[149] In 1140 Ranulf, Earl of Chester was able to recapture Lincoln Castle with only three men-at-arms as the royal garrison was said to be elsewhere, engaged in military games.[150] Stephen was not entirely impotent in the face of aristocratic pressure to hold tournaments, however: in 1142 he cancelled a 'military festivity' planned by counts William of Aumale and Alan of Brittany to be held somewhere near York, as he wanted to avoid distractions from an impending campaign.[151]

Actual military clashes in the civil war could have tournament-like qualities. Stephen's troops indulged in war games among themselves at the siege of Ludlow in 1139; 'driven by their boastful strength,' these involved a large number of soldiers, and caused fatalities, and were only checked by the king's direct intervention.[152] The royalist opening moves of the Battle of Lincoln in 1141 had the air of a tournament, set somewhat theatrically against the backdrop of the hilltop walled city (see pgs 46–7), while the Angevins were perfectly capable of conducting eye-catching operations of their own. In his account of the early stages of the siege of Winchester, later in 1141, Henry of Huntingdon is explicit that choreographed war games took place instead of a full-blooded clash of arms: 'Conflicts took place every day, not in pitched battles but in the excursions of knightly manoeuvres. Valiant exploits were not unrecognisably confused as in the darkness of war, but the prowess and glory earned by individuals appeared in the open.'[153]

Summary

Knightly identity was evolving fast in the twelfth century, and it would be natural to assume that military material culture changed in parallel. Is this true? Outwardly, the mid-twelfth-century knight looked quite similar to the Norman warriors depicted in the Bayeux Tapestry, with some subtle differences. By the 1130s–40s the knight was a little better protected with mail covering more of his extremities. A slightly wider range of military personnel would have been armoured, and minor stylistic differences are distinguishable in showier swords, shields, spurs and scabbards. More important in the actual prosecution of warfare was the changing use of the crossbow, which saw widespread use alongside 'armour-piercing' bodkin-type arrowheads. The battles of the period were also the first major military clashes in England where heraldic display was visible – in particular on banners and shields, but also more subtly on horse harness pendants. These devices created new means of displaying knightly allegiance, rank and affinities to elite social networks. While many of the key developments in the material culture of war in the twelfth century concerned the apparel of mounted knights, it is striking that knights tended to fight on foot in pitched battles, while the characteristic mode of warfare of the period – the siege – saw mounted warriors play a marginal role in the actual prosecution of conflict.

Notes

1 Jones, R.W. 2010, 14–15.
2 Harvey 1970, 28–9.
3 Walker 1960, 209–10.
4 Morillo 1994, 191.
5 Jones, R.W. 2010, 15–16.
6 *Gesta Stephani* I, 66, Potter and Davis 1976, 132–3.
7 Isaac 1999.
8 Bisson 2008.
9 Boon 1988, 37–40.
10 Oksanen 2008, 267–8; Janin with Carlson 2013, 77–9.
11 William of Newburgh, *The History of English Affairs* I, 1, 2, Walsh and Kennedy 2007, 14–15.
12 Verbruggen 1997, 129–30.
13 Abels 2008.
14 Hosler 2013, 68–9.
15 France 2008, 3.
16 Crouch 2008.
17 Johns 2003, 40.
18 Slitt 2012, 2.
19 Johns 2003, 18–19.
20 For a general overview of Norman arms and armour, see Gravett 1993.
21 Crouch 1992, 149.
22 Dressler 2004, 14–15.
23 Lankester 2010, 115–17.
24 Rigold 1962–3, 94–5.
25 Lewis 2005, 144.
26 Engel 2002, 76.
27 Ailes 2008.
28 Nicolle 1988, 348–55.
29 Kendrick 1941. The piece is in the Burrell Collection owned by Glasgow Museums: Accession No. 5-6.139.
30 Wallace Collection S151.
31 Jones, R.W. 2010, 4–5.
32 The Portable Antiquities Scheme, www.finds.org.uk.
33 Boylston 2000.
34 Fiorato et al. 2000.
35 Ingelmark 2001.
36 Boylston 2000, 373.
37 Mitchell et al. 2006.
38 Foard and Morris 2012, 30, 32, 59. On the battle, see Strickland and Hardy 2011, 75–8.
39 Anon 1827, 639.
40 Eaves 2002, 325.
41 Keen 1984, 64–5. For a detailed description of the knighting of Geoffrey of Anjou by Henry I in 1128, see Bradbury 1990, 32.
42 On the challenges of approaching medieval swords through archaeology, see Halpin 1986, 183–5.
43 For examples from the River Thames, see Christie and Creighton 2013, 41–3.
44 Oakeshott 1991, 30–83.
45 Royal Armouries Collections IX.5610, found in the River Seine near Rouen,

and dating to between the eleventh and mid-twelfth century. See Richardson 2007, 83; Woosnam-Savage 2008.

46 DeVries and Douglas Smith 2012, 21.

47 Peirce 1990, 149–51.

48 Ashley and Biddle 2014.

49 Peirce 1990, 149–51; Oakeshott 1991, 30–83; 1964, 81–114.

50 deNeergaard 1987, 40.

51 Christie 2009, 330–1; PAS SUR-43C192.

52 Spencer 1961.

53 Goodall 2012, 343, 360–1.

54 Oakeshott 1991, 74.

55 Christie and Creighton 2013, 41–3; 432–6.

56 Oakeshott 1960, 201.

57 Oakeshott 1960, 200–23; Loades 2010, 122.

58 Strickland 1996b, 62–4.

59 Edwardson 1970.

60 Glasgow Museums A.1987.31. For the possibility that the A stands for *Angeli* ('Angels'), see Strickland 1996b, 64, Plate 3. See also Jones, R.W. 2010, 138.

61 Vance 1970, 31; van Emden 1995, 49, 57, 72.

62 Evison 1967. See also Christie and Creighton 2013, 42.

63 Strickland and Hardy 2001, 73–8.

64 *Gesta Stephani* I, 16, Potter and Davis 1976, 34–5.

65 Richardson and Sayles 1963, 74 n.

66 Biddle 1990b, 1078–9.

67 MacGregor 1975–6, 320; Musset 2005, 51. However, on doubts about the *Carmen de Hastingae Proelio*'s limitations as a source for the battle, see Davis 1978, 242.

68 MacGregor 1975–6, 320; 1985, 161.

69 Sensfelder 2007, 27.

70 *Chronicles of the Reigns of Stephen, Henry II and Richard I*, Howlett 1889, 173–4. See also Christie and Creighton 2013, 207.

71 Strickland 1996a, 358–9.

72 Bradbury 1985, 36; MacGregor 1985, 161; Musset 2005, 84 n.76.

73 See, for example, White 1974, 5; Croft 1996, 24.

74 The text refers to *ballistariorem et saggittariorem* ('crossbowmen and archers'). See Tanner 1990, 203. See also Contamine 1985, 274; Strickland 1996b, 72.

75 On crossbow remains generally, see Credland 1980. On the manufacture of crossbow nuts, see MacGregor 1985, 161; 1991, 367.

76 Bachrach 2004, 102.

77 Credland 1990, 1075–6.

78 Beresford 1987, 192. For revised dating, see Creighton 2005b, 21–7.

79 Renn 1960, 61.

80 Credland 1990, 1076.

81 Ward Perkins 1940, 65–73.

82 Jessop 1996.

83 Jessop 1997, 48.

84 Strickland and Hardy 2011, 26.

85 Mitchell et al. 2006, 150, 153.

86 Goodall 1987, 185–6, finds nos 183, 184. However, redating of the site puts this context firmly in the Anarchy period. For a summary of the redating, see Creighton 2005b, 24.

87 Goodall 1982, 235–6, finds nos 156–9.

88 Goodall, 1990a, 1073, find no. 4009.

89 Graham and Davies 1993, 89, finds nos 18–19.

90 Nicolle 1988, 340–2.

91 Daubney 2010.

92 *The Annals of Roger de Hoveden* I, trans. Riley 1853, 244.

93 William of Malmesbury, *Historia Novella* III, 43, King and Potter 1998, 87.

94 Strickland 1994, 73.

95 Cowper 2006, 46–50.

96 Biddle 1990c.

97 Peirce 1986, 156–7.

98 Blair 1959, 20.

99 Examples recoded through the

PAS include LANCUM-B10EC4 and WMID3622. See the Portable Antiquities Scheme, www.finds.org.uk.

100 Lewis 2005, 50–1.
101 Higham and Barker 2000, 99.
102 Peirce 1986, 155.
103 Mitchell et al. 2006, 153.
104 Peirce 1986, 158–9; Prestwich 1996, 18.
105 Henry, Archdeacon of Huntingdon, *Historia Anglorum* X, 8, Greenway 1996, 714–15.
106 Blair 1959, 25.
107 Blair 1959, 29; DeVries and Douglas Smith 2012, 71.
108 Prestwich 1996, 19.
109 Lewis 2005; 42–3, 48–50; 2010, 471–3.
110 Southwick 2006, 5.
111 Gravett 1993, 56.
112 Blair 1959, 30; Williams and Edge 2004, 123; Southwick 2006, 5.
113 Biddle 1990b, 1077.
114 Peirce 1986, 160.
115 Stroud 1999, 11.
116 Lewis 2005, 55.
117 Toolis 2004, 83–4.
118 Bennett 2003, 51.
119 Anderson 1908, 206–7. See also Bliese 1988.
120 Ailes 1990, 12.
121 Harvey and McGuiness 1996, 47.
122 Graham-Campbell 1992, 78.
123 DeVries and Douglas Smith 2012, 12–14. See also Strickland 1996b, 361.
124 Renn 1994, 188.
125 Nicolle 1988, 348.
126 Davis 1989, 21–2, 80–2. See also Graham-Campbell 1992, 78.
127 Graham and Davies 1993, 132.
128 Heslop 1984, 317.
129 Davis 1989, 21; Breiding 2005, 9.
130 Goodall 1990b, 1054.
131 In his corpus of late Saxon stirrup mounts, Williams dates these to a short period between the first quarter of the 11th century and 'around 1100 or not long after' (Williams 1997, 8).
132 Lewis 2007; Webley 2014, 354.
133 Jope 1956.
134 Ward Perkins 1940, 93–103; Ellis 1990, 1037. For examples of the period see, for example, Goodall 1987, 186, finds nos 166–70 from Goltho.
135 Ellis 1982, 230–3.
136 Ashley 2002, 4.
137 Ashley 2002, 27; Griffiths 2004, 62–3.
138 Graham-Campbell 1992, 87.
139 The Portable Antiquities Scheme database (www.finds.org.uk) records over 3,000 medieval harness pendants, including over 100 twelfth-century examples. For illustrative examples dated to the twelfth century, see SWYOR-31A700; SWYOR-F5EB75; NMS-314B02; NMS-026123; NMS-D7E903.
140 Ashley 2002, 28–9.
141 Baker 2015, 23–4.
142 Keen 1984; Tanner 1990, 200. See also Strickland 1996b, 73–4.
143 DeVries and Douglas Smith 2012, 14.
144 Bennett 2003, 51.
145 Tasker Grimbert and Chase 2011, 1–3.
146 Crouch 1992, 135–6; 2005, 9; Keen with Barker 1996, 83; Steane 1999, 155.
147 Barker 1986, 9; Barber and Barker 1989, 19.
148 Barker 1986, 7–8.
149 Henry, Archdeacon of Huntingdon, *Historia Anglorum* X, 8, Greenway, 714–15. See also Barker 1986, 8.
150 Barber and Barker 1989, 19.
151 Crouch 2005, 20.
152 *The Chronicle of John of Worcester* III, McGurk 1998, 267.
153 Henry, Archdeacon of Huntingdon, *Historia Anglorum* X, 19, Greenway, 740–1.

Chapter 7

Faith and Fortification: The Church

THE EVIDENCE of documents produced and curated by religious institutions has tended to dominate narratives of Stephen's reign; indeed, we have inevitably come to understand 'the Anarchy' largely through the prism of ecclesiastical writers. The medieval Church as an institution was a central pillar of society that influenced corporate identity and individual behaviour in different ways, although it was not a monolithic and immovable organisation but instead comprised myriad groups and personnel with varying perceptions of Christianity. This chapter combines analysis of the textual sources with archaeological and other material evidence to assess the consequences of the civil war for ecclesiastical institutions, communities and structures. The following account considers, in turn, churches, monasteries and bishops' palaces, to explore how the conflict impacted upon patterns of patronage and building, and to consider the place of these sites within the militarisation of the landscape.

Church and Civil War

Any consideration of the impact of 'the Anarchy' on the Church throws up some immediate contradictions.[1] From one perspective, this was a period of enormous turbulence and crisis for the Church, with bishops embroiled in the conflict, monastic lands seized and ravaged, and churches burned or fortified. Damage to church buildings and property is attested by the horror-struck reactions of chroniclers both in generic terms and through specific references to named institutions that were attacked or suffered collateral damage. A map of documented instances of church fortification and damage to ecclesiastical property

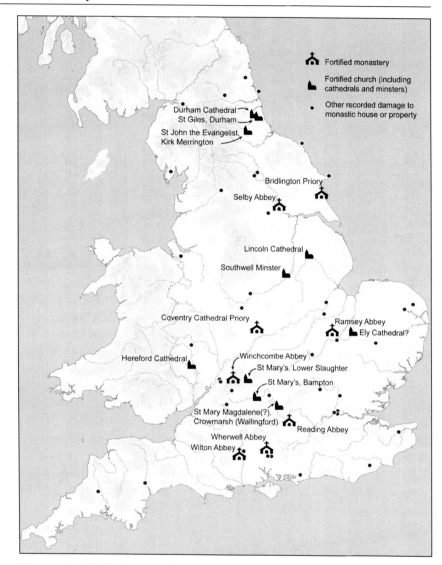

Fig. 7.1: Fortified ecclesiastical sites and damage to monastic property, *c.* 1135–53. Compiled from twelfth-century chronicles and other sources, with additional information provided by Callaghan 1974; 1978; Burton 2008a. Map work by Oliver Creighton.

is presented in Figure 7.1. What makes this level of damage especially remarkable is the fact that the Church was instrumental in the western European 'peace movement' of the eleventh and twelfth century that sought to suppress the excesses of war, including pillage and violence towards ecclesiastical property.[2] The paradox is that churches were targeted, seemingly as never before, in the very period in which knighthood was emerging as a Christian vocation and the ideals of chivalry were crystallising.[3] From another viewpoint, however, the mid-twelfth century saw a dramatic upsurge in religious patronage, especially through the foundation of houses of the new orders and gifts to established family monasteries. This was well understood at the time: for example, William of Newburgh comments that more monasteries were established in Stephen's reign than over the entire preceding century.[4]

Before reviewing the material evidence, it is useful to summarise the circumstances of the rift between King Stephen and his leading churchmen, which was one of the root causes of the conflict. Stephen's claim to the throne initially enjoyed widespread clerical backing, but within five years this had been significantly eroded and by the time of the king's appearance before a legate at Winchester in August 1139, his commitment to upholding the liberties of the Church was widely doubted.[5] The exact processes behind this breakdown in relations have been deconstructed by numerous scholars,[6] but most emphasise the event known as 'the arrest of the bishops' in June 1139 as decisive.[7] This infamous episode comprised a brawl between the representatives of three bishops – Roger of Salisbury, Alexander of Lincoln and Nigel of Ely – and members of a notable entourage during a meeting of the royal council in Oxford. Stephen placed the bishops under arrest on trumped-up charges and seized their strategically important castles. It appears that Stephen doubted the bishops' loyalty – an insecurity fuelled by the fact that he had angered his brother Henry of Blois by overlooking him for the appointment of Archbishop of Canterbury a year earlier. Henry had instead retained his position as Bishop of Winchester and growing fraternal animosity seems to have led to his summoning of Stephen to account for his actions before the legate. While no formal settlement was reached at the council, historians have generally viewed Winchester as a pyrrhic victory for Stephen, and the dissatisfaction of all parties is reflected in subsequent plans to petition Rome by both royal and ecclesiastical representatives. Perhaps most crucially, the council at Winchester displayed in a very public manner Stephen's resistance to submitting to clerical authority and proved pivotal in cementing the Church as a focus of opposition.[8]

Another important contextual element is the Crusade movement. The attack on Lisbon launched from Dartmouth in May 1147 attracted Crusaders from England (especially the south and east) but also

Scotland, Flanders, the Rhineland and Boulogne.[9] The expedition provided an outlet for demoralised English nobles, some of whom claimed the ecclesiastic protection of property due to Crusaders upon taking the cross.[10] But the success of this operation, testifying that England could be a launch pad for an international military action even in the depths of civil war, must be viewed against the Second Crusade's spectacular overall failure and its damage to papal esteem and Western Christianity in general. King Stephen also lost prestige for not participating in the Crusade, although he and his queen, both of whom came from famous early Crusading families, were generous and influential supporters of the Templars, who expanded dramatically in England during his reign.[11]

Militarisation of Churches

For much of the Anglo-Saxon period the spiritual needs of the laity were met by a system of minsters – centres which served federations of sub-districts spanning substantial territories. From the mid-ninth century, however, a more localised pattern of ecclesiastical provision emerged, and more permanent stone-built churches were constructed in significant numbers from the eleventh century onwards. Unlike the minsters, these new churches did not serve vast territories but were instead typically associated with single agrarian communities, villages and manors. The foundation of estate churches by local lords was the key motor of growth.[12] Church building continued apace into the twelfth century to the extent that of the 10,000 or so parish churches built in England by the sixteenth century, the majority of those which survive have a core datable to between *c.* 1050 and 1200.[13] A great deal of debate has focused on the scale and chronology of this so-called 'great rebuilding' of churches.[14] Local studies are increasingly showing that the Norman Conquest was not the main driver for this movement and that elite patronage and investment in parish churches was more protracted through the later eleventh and twelfth century; in the North Riding of Yorkshire, for instance, many parish churches show several different phases of rebuilding in the twelfth century, the rate of stone church building steadily increasing through the century.[15]

By the second quarter of the twelfth century, Anglo-Saxon features had either ceased to be used in rural churches or had been integrated into the Norman architectural repertoire. Typical plan forms ranged from single-cell structures to buildings with aisles, towers and transepts.[16] An excellent example of a 'typical' parish church of the mid-twelfth century is St Nicholas, Barfreston, Kent (Plate 16a). The external appearance of St Nicholas is that of a perfect two-cell church dating to *c.* 1170–85, although elements were rebuilt and replaced in the mid-nineteenth century. Especially characteristic of the mid-twelfth century is the lavish decorative sculpture, which 'displays a richness ... inversely proportional to the size of the building.'[17] Here as elsewhere it is the quality, positioning and iconography of carvings rather than the scale of the church that were vehicles conveying the wealth and power of the patrons – in this case the de Port family, who held the manor and were also sub-constables of Dover. Architectural sculpture provides the best means of identifying work of the mid-twelfth century and is discussed in more detail in Chapter 5. Only in very exceptional cases can archaeological dating pin a phase of church construction down to the decades around the civil war, although a clear example is St Mary in Kempley, Gloucestershire (Plate 16b), where dendrochronology has assigned timbers in the primary roof phase a combined felling date range of *c.* 1120–50, making it the earliest scientifically dated extant roof of any sort in Britain, and approximately contemporary to some of the famous frescoes within the church.[18] The manor of Kempley was in the hands of the powerful de Lacy family, who seem to have been responsible for the lavish building project in what was then, or would shortly become, one of the most bitterly contested regions in England.[19]

Fortified churches

The militarisation of churches was an especially prominent aspect of the civil war, being widely attested by chroniclers who decried the seizure and occupation of ecclesiastical buildings, the desecration of cemeteries and sometimes armed clashes in and around churches.[20] Damage to church property was also more or less endemic in the struggle for Normandy and its borders: in 1135, for example, Orderic Vitalis comments that the army of Geoffrey of Anjou had 'violated churches and cemeteries'; while at the siege of Falaise in 1138 they 'sacrilegiously broke into churches, defiled holy places, and stole consecrated vessels and vestments without fear of God.'[21] Such events were not just limited to wartime: the text of a charter of *c.* 1121 from the abbey of Savigny, near Lyons in France, provides an illuminating parallel of how a fortress built in defiance of the lord of the area, the abbey itself, caused grievance: Stephen de Varennes had made a castle out of a sheep house near the abbey, forcing the peasantry to do service to him and ravaging the estate, before the property was returned to the abbot and destroyed.[22]

Churches were also natural points for refugees to gravitate to. The *Gesta Stephani* records that displaced peasants constructed cottages around churches for protection in 1144.[23] At Winchcombe, Gloucestershire, the great fire of 1151, which destroyed the abbey's early records and precipitated a rebuilding campaign, was said to have broken out in timber huts built around the church, apparently for defence.[24] King Stephen compensated the cathedral church of Exeter for damage sustained during the siege of Exeter in 1136 by granting it land in the nearby royal manor of Colyton.[25] Whether this damage was caused by Stephen's household and men occupying the site as a headquarters or by the sequestration of foodstuffs, supplies and building materials for the siege, we do not know.[26]

All factions indulged in the appropriation and fortification of churches; the common factor was martial necessity. It overwhelmingly occurred during sieges and pressing military struggles, when moral concerns over breaching the sanctuary of a holy building were outweighed by the advantages of securing a pre-positioned stone strongpoint. That pious members of the knightly classes were willing to violate church property in a very visible way that totally transgressed accepted codes of martial conduct suggests extreme circumstances. Churches were invariably the most substantial and elevated structures in their localities and, where stone-built, relatively invulnerable to damage or destruction through burning. Their bell towers could have served as ready-made look-out positions from which to observe enemies and scan routes of approach for attacking or relieving forces, thereby removing the need to build a siege castle or campaign work *de novo* and saving labour, time and cost. But deeper psychological factors may also have been in play; fortifying a church and desecrating a community's graveyard was a provocative insult and a conspicuous demonstration of a lord's inability to protect his own people. By way of comparison, a similar mixture of motives explains damage to churches during the English Civil War of the mid-seventeenth century – symbolic defacement to demonstrate power, looting to obtain military essentials (such as metal for bullets) and vandalism by forces elated in victory or out of control following defeat.[27]

A particularly well-documented instance of a church turned Anarchy-period siege work is St Giles, Durham, which was vigorously contested in 1143 during the struggle for control of the diocese. Symeon of Durham describes how the bishop's men occupied the church, which was part of a hospital founded outside the city walls earlier in the twelfth century, after they were repelled in an advance on the city; it was later burned, along with the surrounding suburb, by men of the usurper of the bishopric, William Cumin.[28] The same struggle saw Cumin's soldiers defile Durham Cathedral and witnessed 'mailed men with drawn swords charging between the altars'; doors were broken down, ladders placed at the windows and the monks threatened.[29]

Several chroniclers claim that churches were converted into or used as castles, although how often this entailed the physical addition of fortified elements to buildings as opposed to their requisitioning and garrisoning is hard to tell. Some of the struggles in which churches feature were brief, while any elements added to them, such as ramparts, ditches or timber superstructures (especially on their towers), would have been swiftly removed in peacetime as aberrations. For example, a letter of Gilbert Foliot records that the church of St Mary in Lower Slaughter, Gloucestershire, was turned into a castle during the civil war.[30] The surviving structure has no pre-thirteenth-century fabric and we have no firm context for this action, although it may conceivably have been occupied to besiege the motte and bailey at nearby Upper Slaughter. Crucially, we should note once more that twelfth-century chroniclers used the word *castellum* flexibly to describe a variety of fortified sites and institutions, and we should not necessarily assume that a church transformed into a 'castle' would have resembled one physically. It is in this context that we might also interpret references such as Stephen allowing 'a castle to be made and a home of blood and war raised up' from an (un-named) church at Wallingford, Oxfordshire, in 1139 (see pg. 67). In such examples, the church structure might have been pressed into use as a headquarters or barrack block, but was in all probability not altered in any lasting manner.

Where a church was adapted as a military base, one or both of two strategies was followed: fortifying the tower and/or encircling the building with an earthwork. At Bampton, Oxfordshire, the 'castle' erected by the Empress's supporters in 1142 was 'right on the church tower, which had been built in olden times of wondrous form and with extraordinary skill and ingenuity.'[31] Excavations show that the present late thirteenth-century crossing tower was built over the eastern bay of an earlier nave, the west end of which seems to have been marked by a stair turret, thereby confirming the presence of the visually striking west tower, while the ancient minster stood within an enclosure that provided ready-made defences.[32]

The *Gesta Stephani* is also quite explicit that the tower of the cathedral church of Hereford was used as a fortification in 1140, when

Geoffrey Talbot's forces adapted it to counter royalist troops in the adjacent castle. The comment that Geoffrey 'turned a house of prayers and a place of atonement for souls to a confusion of strife and a haunt of war and blood' seems a generic expression of outrage, but the chronicler provides additional vivid detail on the consequences of the siege for Hereford's population:

> the earth of their kinsfolk's graveyard was being heaped up to form a castle-mound [*castelli sustollebatur uallum*] and they [the townsmen] could see, a cruel sight, the bodies of parents and relations, some half-rotten, some quite lately buried, pitilessly dragged from the depths; or because at one time it was visible that catapults [*balistas*] were being put up on the tower from which they had heard the sweet and pacific admonition of the bells, at another that missiles were being shot from it to harm the king's garrison.[33]

The Norman tower at Hereford Cathedral collapsed during the eighteenth century, but older depictions show that it was an unusual axial feature at the west end of the nave.[34] The cathedral also had two smaller towers over the east bays of the choir aisles, which would have been closer to the castle, although it was presumably the main tower that was fortified, so that siege engines could bombard the nearest part of the castle (the motte). It is unclear whether the graveyard that was disturbed was that of the cathedral,[35] or St Guthlac's, which adjoined the castle on Castle Green and where a shallow linear depression running SSW–NNE has been tentatively identified as the siege work ditch.[36] The minster church of St Guthlac had effectively been part of the castle complex since the mid-eleventh century, when the Norman fortification was squeezed into its precinct, highlighting how the fortification of ecclesiastical sites was not limited to the mid-twelfth century.

A second strategy for fortifying a church was to provide it with enclosing defences, as witnessed at Southwell Minster, Nottinghamshire (Fig. 7.2) in 1142, when a *vallum* around the church allowed a royalist force to put up stiff resistance against the men of William Paynel, who had taken Nottingham Castle.[37] Whether this was newly created or a reworking of an existing enclosure is uncertain: excavations within the grounds of the Minster Chambers, immediately north-west of the church, recorded part of a large ditch, 4m wide, running north–south on the edge of the minster graveyard and marking a significant early boundary, perhaps of pre-Conquest origin and partly silted by the twelfth century.[38] More closely archaeologically datable is

Fig. 7.2: Aerial view of Southwell Minster, showing the church within its precinct. Source: © English Heritage.

the fortification of the priory and cathedral church of St Mary's, Coventry, which was only partly complete when it was converted into a siege work against nearby Coventry Castle. Excavation recorded a filled-in ditch over 7.5m wide running under the nave and north aisle of the church and underlying the foundations of one of the piers; it contained deposits of twelfth-century Coventry ware, and a lack of silting denotes a short-lived feature soon backfilled.[39] Only the eastern part of the nave was built at the time and the ditch seems to have converted what was in effect a grand building site into a ringwork. This corroborates documented accounts of Robert Marmion's fortification of the site in 1142–43, described most dramatically by William of Newburgh, who explained how he met his comeuppance upon stumbling into a defensive ditch, breaking his thigh and having his head cut off by a soldier of the Earl of Chester, who held Coventry Castle.[40] A third and final example is Kirk Merrington, County Durham, which was fortified in 1143 by the men of William Cumin. A ditch or moat was partly complete when the church was attacked by the bishop's barons, forcing the defenders to retreat inside and resist from the tower 'and the bulwarks [*propugnacula*] they had constructed,' before it was taken by fire.[41]

    In a subtly different category are those castles built within or on the edges of cemeteries and those that enclosed churches within their outer defences. The Angevin castle at Cirencester, Gloucestershire, built in 1142 and burned by Stephen the same year, stood next to the abbey.[42] At Malmesbury, Wiltshire, Bishop Roger of Salisbury's castle was built on the edge of the monk's cemetery, 'not a stone's throw' from the church.[43] Malmesbury Castle was certainly no expedient work: situated at the neck of the promontory and dominating the former *burh*, it was militarily significant enough to be contested in 1139, 1144 and 1153, and remained active until the reign of John, who ordered it demolished and the site given over to the monks.[44] Particularly instructive is the case of the compact mid-twelfth-century motte-and-bailey castle at Repton, Derbyshire, which is undocumented and known only through excavation. Here, the castle incorporated the ancient Mercian minster church within its defences, just as a Viking fortress on the same site had done more than two and half centuries previously.[45] The north ward of the castle at Eaton Socon, Cambridgeshire, attributed a twelfth-century context, also sealed part of an extensive Saxo-Norman cemetery,[46] while at Red Castle, Thetford, Norfolk, a twelfth-century ringwork was superimposed over a cemetery and a small church.[47] Like Repton, the instances of church destruction and/or cemetery

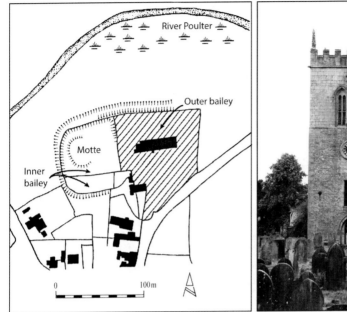

Fig. 7.3: Plan and photograph of St Mary's, Cuckney.
Photograph by Oliver Creighton; plan by Mike Rouillard.

desecration at Eaton Socon and Thetford are undocumented, suggesting that the catalogue of documented destruction inflicted on ecclesiastical property is not exhaustive. Another example of church appropriation for which no written record exists is Trowbridge Castle, Wiltshire, which possesses closely datable archaeological evidence of an Anarchy-period foundation. The castle incorporated a stone-built late Anglo-Saxon church within its inner bailey; the graveyard continued in use, albeit squeezed into a far smaller area, while part of the associated settlement was cleared to make way for the massive earthwork defences.[48] We have clear evidence of unusual modifications to the church building: a compact earth surface was deliberately laid over the original floor, which had a number of postholes cut into it, while low drystone walls were built against the insides of the nave walls; a coin of King Stephen from within the floor layer means that we can date these developments closely to the civil war.[49] While the purpose of these changes is uncertain – they conceivably speak of some temporary military function for the building – it is clear that a community's long-standing burial ground became far less accessible and effectively privatised within the powerful double defences of the castle.

Cuckney, Nottinghamshire, is another clear example of an Anarchy-period castle incorporating a church within its defences (Fig. 7.3). Occupying a naturally defensible position on marshy ground within a bend of the River Poulter, the parish church of St Mary's stood entirely within a rectangular outer bailey, isolated from the motte and inner bailey by a ditch. We have a clear documentary context for the castle's foundation: the Cartulary of Welbeck records that Thomas de Cuckney, a known Angevin sympathiser, built it, apparently *de novo*, during the 'old war'.[50] The church's earliest standing fabric is the south doorway, earlier than the nave and relating to a building episode of *c.* 1150.[51] However, underpinning work in 1951 revealed wall footings under the church's north arcade but also, remarkably, a mass burial of around 200 haphazardly packed males.[52] Is it fanciful to see this as a potential war grave of the period? Thomas de Cuckney certainly established the nearby Premonstratensian house of Welbeck as an act of penance; its foundation charter of *c.* 1153–54, which includes St Mary's at Cuckney as a gift, records the remarkable dedication 'for my soul and the souls of my father and my mother and my ancestors' but also 'of those whom I have unjustly plundered.'[53]

Monasteries: Patronage and Politics

One of the most striking features of medieval monastic history is the proliferation of new orders in the late eleventh and twelfth century. The monasticism that these orders represented was driven by a desire to return to primitive observances and apostolic poverty in a challenge to the established Benedictines and Cluniacs that created what some historians have termed a 'crisis of monasticism.'[54] Four orders transformed the twelfth-century monastic landscape in Britain: the Cistercians, Carthusians, Savigniacs and Tironensians. In the first three decades of the twelfth century, however, new foundations were dominated by the Augustinians, who had made their first appearance in England towards the end of the eleventh century. It is well established that Stephen's reign witnessed an explosion of new foundations: the total number of monastic houses in England and Wales increased by around 50%, with around 180 new establishments split very unevenly between the various orders.[55] Regional variations are apparent, however: the pattern of monastic foundation in East Anglia shows an early spurt in the first part of Stephen's reign but then a tailing off that continued into the reign of Henry II, suggesting a time lag before the effects of the conflict impacted on the trajectory of growth.[56]

The house of Tiron never gained a firm foothold, despite successful foundations in Scotland such as Kelso, while the Carthusians made little impact at this stage. With their organised and highly hierarchical structure, the Cistercians were the great success story with over 80 houses established after their first foundation in 1128, attracting fervent patronage especially but not exclusively from Angevin supporters and incorporating the order of Savigny from 1147.[57] The rise of the military order of the Templars mirrored that of the Cistercians, benefitting from royal favour and patronage in the first three decades of its existence in England (after 1128); the great growth in Hospitaller foundations came a little later, from the mid-1140s.[58] The rate at which Augustinian houses were founded slowed slightly during Stephen's reign, while the Benedictines emerged as the clear losers with barely a handful of new establishments. The Black Monks also suffered a disproportionate amount of war damage given the size and wealth of their houses, many of which lay in heavily contested zones. Figure 7.4 presents comparative plans of a sample of monastic houses across the various orders that were established in the early to mid-twelfth century, although, as discussed in detail below, ascertaining the earliest plans for these sites is extremely problematic.

Within this general framework, establishing the precise foundation dates of individual monastic houses in the 1130s, 1140s and early 1150s can be difficult.[59] Founding a monastic site was a protracted process as opposed to a single act, and political turmoil could accentuate delays in new foundations getting up and running. Waleran de Meulan's establishment of the Cistercian abbey of Bordesley in lands in the forest of Feckenham granted to him by Stephen and its endowment with especially lavish grants was an 'exercise in prestige' that closely followed his receipt of the earldom of Worcester in 1138.[60] Yet the foundation was in limbo in its early years: in the wake of the Battle of Lincoln (1141) a new charter was produced by the Empress Matilda, who thereafter claimed it as her own foundation.[61] While the uncertain political and tenurial conditions of the Anarchy actually boosted monastic patronage, other factors meant that the process of translating 'acts' of foundation into completed building complexes was far more drawn-out.

Our understanding of the plans of these foundations in their earliest phases is underdeveloped, although we can safely assume that many communities 'established' during the civil war had a precarious existence at first and that their sites would have appeared impermanent, with timber buildings a world away from the familiar image of the

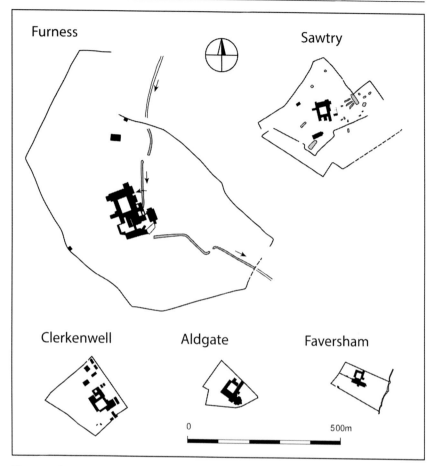

Fig. 7.4: Comparative plans of monasteries established in the early to mid-twelfth century. Map work by John Davey.

stone-built church and claustral complex. Excavations of earth-fast timber buildings from the earliest mid-twelfth-century phases of Fountains, North Yorkshire, and Sawley, Lancashire, afford something of the appearance of monastic houses at this nascent stage.[62]

Another important new trend in the pattern of monastic expansion during Stephen's reign is the foundation of houses by relatively lower-ranking families as well as more established dynasties. In Yorkshire, for example, tenants, wealthy sub-tenants and members of the knightly classes indulged in monastic foundation as these newly emboldened classes made their mark on local landscapes.[63] Houses of regular canons and nunneries were especially favoured by lower-ranking patrons. In London the Augustinian nunnery of St Mary Clerkenwell (Fig. 7.4) was one of three Augustinian nunneries founded in the city during Stephen's reign; it was established *c.* 1144 by a lay knight, Jordan de Bricet, and Muriel de Munteni, also responsible for founding the Hospital of St John of Jerusalem that lay adjacent.[64]

Stephen and/or his queen founded 11 monastic houses, split between the Augustinians, Templars, Savigniacs and Benedictines, dwarfing the total of two established by the Empress Matilda and her son Henry.[65] The pinnacle of Stephen's patronage was St Saviour's, Faversham, built from 1147 as the chapel royal and mausoleum of the house of Blois and colonised by Cluniac monks (Fig. 7.4).[66] St Saviour's was an especially grand and conspicuous foundation built in stone from the outset. Stephen's queen was buried there in 1152, his son Eustace in 1153 and the king himself in 1154.[67] Located on a tongue of land rising above the navigable waterway known as 'The Creek' and readily accessible via maritime routes, the abbey lay secure in the heartland of royalist territory. Excavation has revealed the plan of the large abbey church which survived mainly as chalk foundations covering an area roughly 113m by 24m, far exceeding the size of contemporary Cluniac priories such as Thetford and Castle Acre, Norfolk.[68] King Stephen also invested heavily in the Augustinian house of Holy Trinity Priory, Aldgate (Fig. 7.4), which had been founded in 1107–08 and grew into an impressive complex tucked into the north-east corner of London's city walls. Only fragments of the site which, like Faversham, served as a royal mausoleum, survive above ground today but its development can be reconstructed mainly from archaeological and historical study.[69] Investment in Holy Trinity in the mid-twelfth century saw it transformed into one of the finest churches in Norman England and another distinctively royal complex. The grand presbytery, where two of Stephen's children were buried and which may have had some form of giant order in its arcades, is placed around *c.* 1150.[70] Stephen also reputedly founded St Stephen's Chapel in Westminster Abbey, which projected out on the east side, facing the River Thames.[71] Such developments reflect Stephen's desire to display the greatness of his royal wealth and piety in London, helping to legitimise his power in the eyes of the capital's largely loyal population.

The famous Benedictine house of Glastonbury, Somerset, provides a particularly clear example of the impact of an influential and wealthy patron on the fabric of a monastery in the mid-twelfth century. Re-evaluation of 36 seasons of archaeological excavation undertaken between 1904 and 1979 reveals with some clarity the significant investment made by Henry of Blois during his abbacy, which commenced in 1126 and continued, despite his subsequent appointment as Bishop of Winchester in 1129, until his death in 1171.[72] The length of Henry's tenure saw him preside over the apogee of Norman Glastonbury; his patronage allowed consolidation of the monastic estate and included the commissioning of a new history, *De Antiquitate Glastonie Ecclesie*, written by William of Malmesbury.[73] Henry also invested heavily in the architecture of the abbey, John of Glastonbury detailing that he 'raised from their foundations the bell tower, chapter house, cloister, *lavatorium*, refectory, dormitory, the infirmary with its chapel, a beautiful and spacious place, an attractive gate of dressed stone, a great brewery and many stables for horses.'[74] Archaeology illuminates in particular detail Henry's development of the cloister walks, which surrounded a central garden space defined by a kerb, and perhaps a conduit house.[75]

Sponsorship of religious orders and the establishment of monasteries were deeply symbolic processes; these were 'citadels of prayer' intended for the benefit of the souls of the founders and their families and sometimes as dynastic mausoleums.[76] There is no doubt that the civil war saw patrons use monastic foundation to consolidate and demonstrate territorial power. In a period when tenurial rights and property ownership were often ambiguous, monastic foundation was a strategy that allowed a benefactor to make a public statement regarding control of land. A case in point is the Cluniac priory of St James, Exeter, founded by the staunch Angevin supporter Baldwin de Redvers c. 1141, the same year in which he was created Earl of Devon. Baldwin preferred to style himself 'Earl of Exeter,' and the new foundation enhanced his power base in the city where his principal castle also lay.[77] Another illustrative example of a site founded for an explicitly political purpose is Revesby, Lincolnshire, where William de Roumare, Earl of Lincoln, asked Rievaulx to settle a monastery next to his *caput* at Bolingbroke. The colony was established in 1143 but the initiative had been planned earlier, in 1141–42, when Roumare defected to the Angevins, and was clearly intended to announce his affiliation.[78] Monasteries became weapons in regional power plays. Ranulf, Earl of Chester advanced his ambition to control William d'Aubigny's honour of Belvoir, centred on Belvoir Castle, Leicestershire, by making claims over monasteries attached to it in a kind of 'spiritual siege warfare.'[79] In the far north of England, meanwhile, monasteries were founded and endowed as pseudo-colonial ventures by the Scots royal family,[80] as is the case with the Cistercian house of Holme Cultram, Cumbria, established on the Soloway Firth *c.* 1150 by Prince Henry, son of King David I.[81]

The 'twinning' of a castle with a monastic house established in close proximity was a popular seigneurial strategy of the period. Nearly half the 170 documented examples in England can in fact be dated to the twelfth century, which represented the climax of the phenomenon, many of them involving new Augustinian houses.[82] Even in the case of the Cistercian order, which specified that its houses should be secluded, Anarchy-period foundations such as Bordesley, Worcestershire (*c.* 1138), Vaudey, Lincolnshire (*c.* 1147), and Sawley, Lancashire (*c.* 1148), all lay close to the castles of their patrons and founders.[83] In Devon, Richard of Okehampton established a Cistercian house at Brightley, close to his castle, in the mid-1130s, although upon his death it moved to a more suitable location at Forde (formerly Devon, now Dorset), so here the rationale for a site close to the *caput* was temporary.[84] For the writer of *The Book of the Foundation of Walden Monastery*, Geoffrey de Mandeville, Earl of Essex founded a priory next to his ridgetop castle *c.* 1136–40 'for the benefit of the castle alone,' for the site was restricted and unsuitable, with infertile soil.[85] The establishment of a market and, in all probability, a fortified settlement adjacent to the earl's castle emphasises how the foundation of a monastery was but one element in a coordinated strategy of lordly aggrandisement (see also pg. 226). A rather different sort of religious establishment likely to have been founded by Geoffrey de Mandeville is Temple Church, located on a prominent site on the west bank of the River Fleet in London. Earl Geoffrey seems to have established the Temple *c.* 1140, when he was custodian of the Tower of London,[86] demonstrating once again how castle and religious foundation were complementary.

Some of these new monasteries were in effect monuments of penance; a handful of foundation charters specify that houses were established to atone for the war crimes of the patron or his family.[87] Insight into the sorts of spiritual pressures that lords could come under is provided by correspondence between the Cluniac bishop Gilbert Foliot and his uncle William de Chesney, a supporter of Stephen who held knight's fees in the south and East Midlands and rose to the position of Sheriff of Oxfordshire. Seen as a profiteer of the civil war, William was urged to make amends for the sake of his soul.[88] Charters of Geoffrey de Mandeville show his late attempts at restitution, including the restoration of properties and rights to beneficiaries such as St Martin le Grand and Holy Trinity Aldgate, London.[89]

An extension of this phenomenon is that some monasteries were established on the sites of deactivated castles, 'almost as if to purge the sin.'[90] Illustrative examples from the civil war and its immediate aftermath include the Augustinian priories established on the site of the Earl of Chester's motte and bailey at Repton, Derbyshire, c. 1153–59,[91] and Old Buckenham, Norfolk, established by William d'Albini c. 1146–51 on the site of the old castle that was abandoned and superseded by New Buckenham.[92] More remarkable still, the Cistercian house of Meaux, North Yorkshire, founded c. 1150, incorporated timbers recycled from the decommissioned castle of Montferrant, at nearby Birdsall.[93]

Cistercians and Savigniacs

Although the Cistercian expansion was well in train by the death of Henry I, during Stephen's reign the number of houses increased from five to 32 (or 45, if houses of the Savigniac order, incorporated in 1147–48, are included), the period 1145–50 marking the most dramatic period of growth during the order's entire history.[94] Supporters of the Angevin cause in particular were keen sponsors of the Cistercians, although shifting loyalties meant that this was not exclusively the case, and while King Stephen did not found any Cistercian houses, he confirmed the endowment of several, and others were established by known royalists.[95] The Cistercians were able to take advantage of the period's tenurial uncertainty and emerged in the 1140s and 1150s as the most fashionable order by which a patron could materialise his tenurial rights.[96] The expansion tailed off dramatically after 1154, which might be partly attributable to the establishment of peace, although on the wider international stage the criticism of the Cistercians following the catastrophic failure of the Second Crusade, promoted by Bernard of Clairvaux, was a major factor in the drying up of new foundations.

Precisely why the Cistercians were so successful has been a matter of debate, although an important factor, besides the order's efficient organisation, was the diverse nature of its patronage base, with expansion coming from the White Monks themselves, from archbishops and bishops, and from kings, barons and knightly families.[97] In terms of explaining the more specific spike in foundations during the civil war, it must be relevant that founding a Cistercian house represented less of an outlay than a Benedictine foundation, while certain foundations were intended as acts of atonement. William of Ypres, the most reviled mercenary in the civil war, was a benefactor, founding the Cistercian house of St Mary's in Boxley, Kent, from Clairvaux in 1141.[98] Sawtry Abbey, Cambridgeshire (Fig. 7.4) is another useful example. The abbey lay in the earldom of Huntingdonshire, which had been held from 1136 by Prince Henry, son of David I of Scots, but in 1138 was confiscated by King Stephen, who granted it to one of his men, Simon de Senlis II. As insurance against circumstances changing once again, de Senlis established the abbey in 1147 as a marker of the legitimacy of his tenure.[99]

Founded in Normandy in 1112, the Savigniac Order was characterised by similar ideals of purity and austerity to the Cistercians, with whom it merged in 1147 following a short, sharp burst of foundations in the duchy and in England that soon petered out.[100] The Savigniacs arrived in Britain in 1124 with the foundation of Tulketh, near Preston in Lancashire, which transferred to a more promising site at Furness, Cumbria (Fig. 7.4), in 1127.[101] By 1147 the Savigniacs had 14 houses in England and Wales, although very little architecture survives. One of the most influential advocates of the Savigniac houses was the Count of Boulogne and Mortain, who founded Furness in 1124; later, as King Stephen, he planted monks at Buckfast in Devon in 1136 and with his wife established Coggeshall, Essex, a few years later. As a prestigious patron and 'super magnate,' Stephen's favour contributed in no small measure to the great vogue for the Savigniacs in the first half of the 1130s. The early histories of the abbeys of Byland and Calder, and their problematic relationship with Furness, however, hint at many of the problems which plagued the order. In 1134 Furness sent a colony of 13 monks to settle on land at Calder, Cumbria, although the site was abandoned in 1137 after a devastating raid by the Scots. Upon returning to Furness, the monks were refused entry and cast adrift to wander the Pennines, eventually attracting the patronage of Roger de Mowbray and settling at Byland in 1143.[102] This exceptionally protracted process of establishing a house indicates how the loose character of the Savigniacs' organisation and the turmoil of the conflict counted against their success, in a manner quite unlike the Cistercians. The ultimate result of these problems was a petition from Abbot Serlo in 1147, requesting that the entire Savigniac congregation be accepted into the Order of Citeaux. Savigny was a monastic experiment that had failed. It is difficult to determine to what extent Stephen felt personal disappointment following the failure of the Savigniacs, but it is tempting to posit that these events may have served to add to his existing dissatisfaction with the Church more generally. Indeed, it may be significant that Stephen founded the great Cluniac abbey of St Saviour's, at Faversham in Kent, in the same year the Savigniacs were absorbed by the Cistercians.

The fate of the monasteries

Damage inflicted on monastic houses during the civil war is attested primarily through documentary references to estates and other property seized and wasted, and to abbeys and priories plundered, invaded, burned and fortified, although references are sometimes generic and the nature of the damage hard to ascertain.[103] Churches were also damaged on a large scale during sieges, as at Winchester in 1141, when two monasteries and 40 churches and were said to have been burned,[104] and punitive raids, such as Geoffrey de Mandeville's sack of Cambridge in 1143.[105] What looks like the opportunism of rampaging forces might conceal the deliberate targeting of ecclesiastical properties associated with a patron who was also an enemy. Exceptionally, at Fountains Abbey, North Yorkshire, excavators seem to have found direct physical evidence of the consequences of a sacking, in this case by the supporters of William Fitz Herbert, Stephen's nominee as Archbishop of York, in 1146. The first stone church was severely damaged by a fire concentrated in the south transept, of an intensity that discoloured the stone, while deposits of fallen wall plaster, mortar and window glass underlay new floor levels interpreted as evidence of the refurbishment that followed.[106]

In Cornwall, Reginald de Dunstanville, an illegitimate son of Henry I created Earl of Cornwall by the Empress in 1140, is said to have destroyed the tower of the canons of St Stephen's, Launceston.[107] The act seems to have been politically motivated: a charter of King Stephen issued in 1136 gave the priory authority to move to a new site at the ford over the River Kensey, so Earl Reginald was attacking a symbol of Stephen's patronage and favour, although he later atoned by supporting the newly relocated priory with generous endowments.[108] Indirect evidence of raids on monasteries is provided by records of reparations paid by transgressors through one-off or annual payments, grants of manors or new foundations as acts of penance.[109] This has led some commentators to suggest that war-damaged monastic houses may even have benefitted in the long term.[110] Each case was different, however, depending on local circumstances. *The Chronicle of Battle Abbey* reports that the abbey was unable to recover 'rightful possessions' that had been 'violently taken,' no matter how frequently complaints were made.[111] In other contexts, lords made their peace through generous gifts to multiple religious institutions: in Yorkshire, for example, Roger of Mowbray made grants to St Mary's and St Peter's, York, and to Selby Abbey between 1142 and *c.* 1154, to atone for wrongs including the exaction of castle works and illegal taxes.[112]

A remarkable letter of *c.* 1153 written by a monk from Fécamp on the north-east coast of France to his abbot, describes the desolation of the priory at Cogges, Oxfordshire, in particularly vivid detail:

> when I arrived at Cogges I found the house empty of goods and full of filth. On entering I was stupefied and aghast that if fear of ridicule and shame of precipitate flight had not forced me to stay, I should have returned immediately to Fécamp. There has certainly been more dishonour here than wealth, more misery than prosperity. I was most dispirited by the devastation of the place, the shame of dishonour, the scarcity of things and the ruin of the house.[113]

The letter goes on to lament pestilence and floods on the priory's lands, the death of horses, sheep, pigs and oxen, debt and a lack of farming equipment before begging the abbot of Fécamp to rehabilitate the priory and prevent its estates from becoming a wilderness. Cogges lay at the heart of one of the most bitterly contested regions in the civil war, its properties vulnerable to the depredations of field armies. While the monk's apocalyptic vision was clearly playing on biblical allusion, archaeological investigation at the priory site has provided very clear evidence of an energetic rebuilding campaign within a couple of decades of the dereliction. Excavations revealed a stone-built chamber block of *c.* 1150–80, which marked part of a renewal of Cogges, which had been established shortly before 1103 as a 'non-conventual' site, resembling a manor house rather than a claustral complex.[114]

The most severely war-damaged religious houses were those occupied by military forces. The great Benedictine fenland abbey of Ramsey, Huntingdonshire, provides an especially important case study of how the civil war could impact upon the fortunes of a major monastic establishment over the long and short term. The abbey was fortified by the forces of Geoffrey de Mandeville, Earl of Essex, who took advantage of an internal dispute between two rival abbots to seize the house and expel its monks in 1143; it was used a raiding base until the earl's death in late summer 1144 (see also pg. 261).[115] *The Book of the Foundation of Walden Monastery* is explicit that Geoffrey de Mandeville strengthened the abbey as a military site: 'he strongly fortified that most beautiful church, above and below, inside and out, not as a fortress for God but as a castle.'[116]

Booths Hill, a small motte and bailey immediately south of the Ramsey monastic complex, is identified as a work of this period, overlooking dry land to the south of the precinct but also an ancient routeway running west from Ramsey to the mother parish church of Bury.[117] Archaeological evidence suggests that the motte was only one element within a larger scheme of fortification. A large oval precinct enclosure can be reconstructed from earthworks and property boundaries (Fig. 7.5b), defining and defending what was a locally prominent island site sandwiched between Bury Fen to the south and Stocking Fen to the north, although it is not clear whether this pre- or postdates the motte.[118] Excavation within this enclosure, immediately east of the claustral complex, has revealed a twelfth-century phase of activity involving the reworking of a boundary marker running across the precinct interior as a defensive bank and ditch *c.* 4.6m wide; this was interpreted as protecting the abbey buildings and the lode (an artificial waterway used for trade and perhaps flood control).[119] Another phase of replanning closely followed this burst of activity as the abbots strove to re-establish the institution's wealth in the wake of the civil war: the great tower of the church was completed by Abbot Walter by the close of Stephen's reign and the claustral complex saw investment too, while within the replanned precinct, the outworks

Fig. 7.5: Comparative plans of monastic sites fortified in the civil war: **(a)** Reading; **(b)** Ramsey. Map work by Seán Goddard, based on Aston 2000; Spoerry et al. 2008.

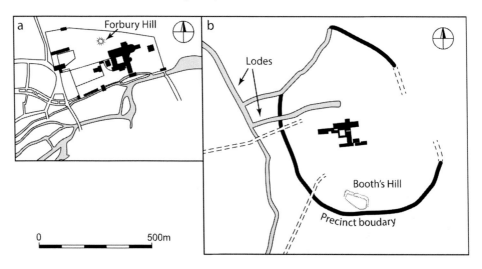

of the 'demilitarised' motte were later adapted as a fish pond at some point.[120] The economic growth and organisation of the abbey's estates were the subject of a seminal 1957 study by J. Ambrose Raftis, who identified the civil war as a catalyst for reorganisation that saw, in the short term, the alienation of lands and property, but then a dramatic rise in profits over the course of the twelfth century.[121] Extensive schemes of land improvement included investment in new causeways and waterways as well as the promotion of the settlement at the abbey gate, which received a market grant around 1200.[122] Other excavated evidence of Anarchy-period fortification of monasteries is lacking, although Forbury Hill, Reading (Fig. 7.5a), set within the precinct, is another likely 'monastic motte.'[123]

As twelfth-century writers were invariably monks, we should treat their horrified descriptions of the desolation of monasteries with caution. Given their wealth and suitability as *ad hoc* military bases, monasteries were certainly vulnerable to the type of warfare being waged, but chroniclers also embroidered their accounts, intermingling the reality of events with religious or political messages. The Ely chronicler explains that Bishop Nigel's castle of 'stone and cement' near Ely Cathedral collapsed due to the holy power of Saint Aethelthryth, forcing him to construct an alternative fortification.[124] More dramatic still is the account in *The History of the Monastery of Selby*, completed in 1174, of how the traumas of the civil war had prompted the abbey's founder-monk, St Germanus of Auxerre, to intercede through successive miracles. Of 35 miracles recorded in the *History*, 15 occurred in the period 1143–54; of these, most involved military personnel (including a soldier trying to break into the church and soldiers setting fire to the vill) or innocent victims of violence including hostages.[125] The catalyst was the construction of Selby 'castle,' established by Henry de Lacy in 1143 and besieged within a week by William of Aumale, Earl of York. No trace of any castle survives, although the statement that the besieging force 'found a secret way in through the offices of the monks,'[126] implies that it lay within the precinct or, more likely, represented a garrisoning of existing buildings. The geopolitical context of the 'castle' is clear: located some 19km north-east of Henry de Lacy's power base at Pontefract, on the very frontier of his lordship, his 'castle' at Selby would have overlooked a sharp bend in the River Ouse and dominated the passage of shipping to and from York, which lay upriver, while also threatening properties of the earl.[127]

Without evidence to the contrary, the fortification of monasteries likely often amounted to the garrisoning of troops within seized buildings, with features of the precinct used to sustain and accommodate field forces. This may have been the case with the so-called castle 'built' for 300 knights at Wherwell Priory, Hampshire, in 1141.[128] St Mary's Priory, Bridlington, was also 'converted' into a castle by the Earl of York in 1143, although there is no suggestion that this involved building works, nor that any great damage was done.[129] Likewise, while some accounts have Stephen building or strengthening a 'castle' at Wilton, Wiltshire, in 1142–43,[130] the detailed description of the struggle over the town in the *Gesta Stephani* makes it sound as if the king occupied the nunnery as a headquarters, to which some of his men fled upon being scattered by the forces of the Earl of Gloucester.[131] Any defence works probably entailed refurbishment of the *burghal* circuit rather than the erection of a 'castle' as such.

Bishops and Bishops' Palaces

Bishops played many varied roles in the civil war: they were both victims and perpetrators of violence, energetic castle builders and also sometimes peacemakers.[132] The distinction between bishops' palaces and castles was blurred; some sites could be both, depending on one's perspective, while non-defended complexes could be given a military makeover. As well as investing in defences, bishops could be active in the field of conflict and participants in, as well as victims of, siege warfare: for instance, the *Gesta Stephani* records how in 1147 the Bishop of Winchester reacted to the capture of one of his castles ('Lidelea') by gathering a great army and building two counter-castles to reduce the garrison by hunger.[133]

There was a boom in episcopal building projects in the years preceding the civil war; the investment in fortified bishops' palaces and castles that we see during the Anarchy was no new phenomenon. The building programme of the immensely powerful Roger, Bishop of Salisbury (bishop 1102–39) is especially notable for its scale. In Henry of Huntington's eyes, there was no more splendid site in the whole of Europe than Bishop Roger's castle at Devizes, Wiltshire.[134] The castle has seen no appreciable archaeological work and the site is heavily rebuilt, but its splendour may have had as much to do with the planned town at its foot and the great park that surrounded it, as the buildings and fortifications *per se*.[135] Bishop Roger also carried out major works at Old Sarum Cathedral and castles at Malmesbury, Wiltshire, Kidwelly, Carmarthenshire and Sherborne, Dorset.[136] At Sherborne, archaeological evidence illuminates in detail the sophistication of Bishop Roger's fortress-palace built between *c.* 1122 and 1135. The spacious and precisely planned complex comprised a central arrangement of buildings around a compact courtyard that featured a great tower provided with upper windows overlooking an accompanying deer park, set within a ward planned using geometrical principles. The large assemblage of carved stone attests especially high-quality and innovative craftsmanship.[137] As at Old Sarum, the central courtyard arrangement may reflect monastic influences but also the size and complexity of a major episcopal household. The ambition of a near-contemporary episcopal building programme for Roger's nephew or perhaps son, Bishop Alexander 'The Magnificent' of Lincoln, at Newark in Nottinghamshire from *c.* 1130 has likewise been illuminated by excavation. Earlier earth and timber defences were levelled completely in a massive earth-moving operation that created a level platform for a lavish new courtyard castle to transform the public image of episcopal power in the town.[138] Here castle building was closely associated with a programme of road diversion, bridge building and urban promotion and defence.[139]

By far the most important case study of a fortified bishop's residence of the civil war period, however, is Henry of Blois's palace of Wolvesey, Winchester, nestled in its own moated precinct in the south-east corner of the former Roman walls (Fig. 7.6: bottom). Such was the scale of Henry of Blois's transformation of the site into a vast complex, planned around a central courtyard in irregular form, that it stands out as a one-off building project – 'the most substantial residence of Romanesque England.'[140] Based on his extensive excavations of 1963–71, Martin Biddle's nuanced phasing of the site allows us to chart Henry's works in detail but should not disguise the fact that for the entire civil war period the palace was in effect a building site.[141] The West Hall, constructed for the second Norman bishop and Henry of Blois's predecessor, William Giffard, was the principal structure on the site when Henry was consecrated bishop in 1129. The new East Hall (*c.* 1135–38) was probably intended as the public and ceremonial heart of the complex, with the old West Hall then the focus for private apartments. The palace was encircled within a curtain wall (*c.* 1138–41), while further defensive elements, dated to the period following the siege and 'rout' of Winchester, were the garderobe turret on the south-east corner of the East Hall and a 'keep'-cum-kitchen (*c.* 1141–54) projecting out from its east side; the gatehouse facing the city was later still (*c.* 1158–71). Interpretation of the 'keep' (Plate 17) is especially problematic. An entry in the *Annales Monastici* for 1138 records that

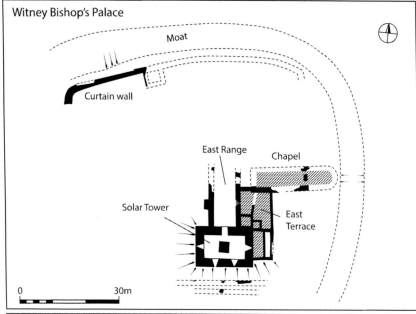

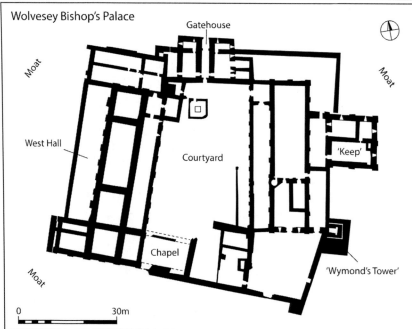

Fig. 7.6: Comparative plans of bishop's palaces fortified in the civil war. Map work by Seán Goddard, based on Biddle 1986; 1990a; Allen and Hiller 2002.

Henry built a 'house like a palace' (*domus quasi palatium*) with a 'very strong tower' (*turris fortissima*) at Winchester. One interpretation is that the tower lay on the separate site of the former royal palace west of the cathedral,[142] although an alternative reading of the excavated evidence puts the 'keep' structure earlier than the East Hall.[143] A building that might bear comparison was excavated on the site of the prior's lodging at Thetford Priory, Norfolk. Comprising a two-storey structure, 11m square and with a spine wall and at least one corner strengthened by a large buttress, it may date to the mid-twelfth century and has been styled as a 'proto-keep.'[144]

A second significant example of how an important episcopal residence evolved through the middle years of the twelfth century is Mount House, Witney, Oxfordshire (Fig. 7.6: top), another palace of the bishops of Winchester, although the precise dating of the various sub-phases is less clear-cut than at Wolvesey.[145] In the early years of the twelfth century the heart of the bishop's palace at Mount House comprised a rectangular solar tower and attached east range; this was transformed into an impressive complex in the mid- to late twelfth century through the addition of a chapel and a terrace running alongside the east range, and then a new garderobe range and the insertion of a central pier within the solar tower, perhaps to strengthen or heighten it. In apparently defensive measures, a clay mound was built around the tower, entailing the blocking of windows in its lower level and modifications to others to provide ventilation through a narrow tunnel (Fig. 7.7). The whole complex was also enclosed by a moat and a curtain wall with gatehouse. The addition of the east terrace, effectively forming a raised garden, can be seen in the context of an emerging interest in the integration of elite residences into their immediate landscape settings with garden designs that could also provide elevated opportunities to view the surroundings. Wolvesey Palace had a similar feature.[146]

Conflicts within the phasing evidence at Mount House mean that the precise dating of these twelfth-century upgrades is unclear. In particular, it is uncertain whether three coins of King Stephen found in backfilled deposits within the solar tower are residual.[147] It is quite possible that these refurbishments started before or during the civil war and extended into the peaceful period beyond. We should also note that despite apparent attempts to increase the site's defensibility, these works might not have been as effective as they seemed; the excavations showed that the moat was 10m wide and 2.6m deep on the north side of the complex but only 5.5m wide and 1.1m deep to the east, perhaps suggesting that it was primarily intended as a display of status, with the water feature at its widest where it faced the road, mill and settlement.[148] At the very least, the spectacular remains of Mount House highlight the ability of twelfth-century bishops to blend defence and high-quality living in complexes that rivalled those of the higher nobility.

The earliest buildings in the palace at Bishops Waltham, Hampshire, are also attributed to Bishop Henry, who seems to have been responsible for the curtain wall around the complex.[149] Nothing is known archaeologically of Henry of Blois's palace at Glastonbury, which probably underlies the early fourteenth-century abbot's hall.[150] The similarity of the fragments of exceptionally high-quality sculpture from Bishop Henry's work on the cloisters at Glastonbury Abbey to material from Wolvesey Palace suggests the existence of a coherent 'court style ... expressing a visual identity personal to Henry of Blois.'[151] Henry's palace at Glastonbury is likely to have been a similarly lavish structure. One suggestion is that it could have incorporated a

Fig. 7.7: Excavated and consolidated remains of the solar tower of the bishop's palace at Witney, showing modifications to the windows. Photograph by Oliver Creighton.

proto-keep comparable to Wolvesey and a similar excavated structure at Thetford Priory, Norfolk.[152]

Discussion: The Militarisation of Churches in Context

This synthesis of documentary and archaeological evidence for the fortification and destruction of churches should not deflect attention away from the underlying fact that, overall, the mid-twelfth century was a period of rapid ecclesiastical growth. To underline this point, we need to appreciate both the modest number of sites militarised, and the fact that this was not an entirely new phenomenon.

In terms of damage to monasteries, we might first question the representativeness of documentary evidence for ecclesiastical losses and reparations, and accept a likely bias in this data set towards the larger and wealthier houses. The uneven survival of written records is likely to skew further the geographical and chronological depiction of events in Figure 7.1. That said, the best estimate is that of a total number of a little over 500 monasteries and secular colleges, no more than 1–2% were occupied or fortified during the entire civil war, something in the region of 10–20% damaged (including their estates), and of these up to 45% may have received reparations.[153] Viewed over the *longue durée*, the impact of the damage is modest: unlike in the Viking period, monastic houses were not extinguished due to the ravages of war, and even in the case of those places such as Ramsey that were confiscated and fortified, monastic communities were able to reap rewards and plan afresh in the post-war years. The pattern that can be established also has a strong regional bias, with the Thames Valley, parts of the South and East Midlands, and Yorkshire representing the most severely affected areas. Other parts of the country heavily hit by the civil war, such as the south-west, paradoxically saw relatively little damage to church property as far as we can ascertain.

Ultimately, the total number of parish churches damaged or occupied is unknowable, although archaeological evidence confirms that not every case is attested in the documentary sources. Even so, the proportion of church sites damaged is likely to be far lower than the figure for monasteries, given the comparatively richer pickings that abbeys and priories presented. Equally, it is important to stress that the vast majority of bishops' palaces in the mid-twelfth century were probably not defended and that the well-documented activities of Roger of Salisbury and Henry of Winchester give a somewhat skewed idea of the role of defence in episcopal building projects. Further, it is clear that the disruptions of the civil war did not halt ambitious ecclesiastical building projects. Some very significant works extended into or spanned the conflict, such as Rochester Cathedral, which was significantly rebuilt in the two decades after 1137, when it was damaged by fire.[154] Rochester was tucked into a corner of England relatively unaffected by the civil war, but major work was also in progress during Stephen's reign at Ely, Exeter, Lincoln, Norwich and Romsey, while the chapter house of Durham Cathedral was built through the late 1130s. The sculptural evidence discussed in Chapter 5 casts another sort of light on the period's energetic church building. It is telling that perhaps the most oft-quoted line relating to Stephen's reign – the reference to Christ and his saints sleeping in the Anglo-Saxon Chronicle for 1137 – is followed by an account, usually ignored, of how, despite the evils of the period, Abbot Martin of Peterborough was still able to carry out improvements to the abbey's estates, including planting a vineyard and roofing the church.[155]

As another corrective to the chroniclers' outrage at the militarisation of churches, it is important to underline that integrating ecclesiastical buildings within defences was nothing new. It was entirely natural for most major twelfth-century castles to incorporate chapels for households and perhaps garrisons within their walls: for example, King Stephen endowed the chapel in Launceston Castle, Cornwall, with the annual sum of £5 after moving to the region to quell disturbances and retake castles.[156] The association between noble residence and private church had a long pre-Conquest ancestry. In the late Anglo-Saxon period, tower naves such as St Mary's in Broughton, Lincolnshire, had high-status secular as well as religious functions, and many were set within defended thegnly enclosures.[157] Equally, the western ends of major Norman churches could incorporate military architecture, as exemplified by Bishop Remigius's late eleventh-century donjon-like block in the west front of Lincoln Cathedral.[158] Another, different sort of post-Conquest example of an ecclesiastical site being used as a fortification is the action by forces loyal to William II against the rebellious Earl of Northumbria, Robert of Mowbray, in 1095. The earl fled to the monastery of St Oswin at Tynemouth following an unsuccessful attempt to enter Newcastle; he was able to resist the royal forces for six days before being wounded and captured, having sought sanctuary in the monastic church.[159] The conversion of churches and monasteries into fortifications was not therefore an anathema unique to the Anarchy, as chroniclers would have us believe.

The military circumstances of the Anarchy might well have ensured that the raising of fortifications on consecrated ground was more common than in the late eleventh and early twelfth century, but churches physically embraced within the 'private' defences of castles, usually in baileys or outer baileys, were common in the post-Conquest landscape, and ultimately perpetuated a late Saxon tradition of closely juxtaposed aristocratic residence and estate church.[160] The desecration of churchyards through castle building also had precedents in the Norman Conquest. At Barnstaple and Cambridge, for example, excavation shows how the defences of new urban castles cut through graveyards,[161] while at Norwich as many as six cemeteries are sealed beneath the Norman castle's defences.[162] At Worcester, Urse d'Abitot, Sheriff of Worcestershire incurred the displeasure of the Archbishop of York for erecting a castle that cut off part of the cathedral priory's cemetery at some point before September 1069.[163] Indeed, there is good reason to think that the period 1066–80 actually saw more intensive destruction to church fabric through castle building than the mid-twelfth century, although it went undocumented or is referred to only obliquely in the sources.

Summary

The war crimes against the Church catalogued by chroniclers and borne out to some extent in the archaeological record seemingly affected modest numbers of sites in specific geographical zones. Archaeological investigations have revealed clear signs of the militarisation of ecclesiastical sites, although in many contexts documentary evidence for the apparent transformation of a church into a castle suggests that the building was garrisoned rather than being converted into something physically resembling a castle. The civil war had a series of much longer-lasting impacts on the ecclesiastical world, however, in terms of creating the social and tenurial conditions and a spiritual environment where religious patronage became increasingly politicised and where lower-ranking members of the elite had the means and motivation to establish monasteries, which swelled in numbers as never before.

Notes

1 For an overview, see Holdsworth 1994.

2 Contamine 1985, 270–80.

3 Keen 1984, 48.

4 William of Newburgh, *The History of English Affairs* I, 16, 3, Walsh and Kennedy 1988, 78–9.

5 White 2000, 19–23; Bollerman and Nederman 2008, 434.

6 See, for example, Davis 1967, 31–5; Stringer 1993, 64; Bradbury 1996, 48–55.

7 *Contra* Yoshitake 1988; Matthew 2002, 92–3.

8 Bollerman and Nederman 2008, 441.

9 Tyerman 1988, 32–5; Bennett 2001.

10 Constable 1953, 261.

11 Nicholson 1993, 16–17; Gervers 1992, 199.

12 Morris 1989, 165–7; Blair 2005, 426, 498.

13 Fernie 2002, 208.

14 Gem 1988.

15 McClain 2011, 166–7.

16 Fernie 2002, 222; Plant 2003, 215.

17 Magrill 2009, 47.

18 Miles et al. 1999; Morley and Miles 2000. See also Morley 1985.

19 Jurica 2010, 203, 217.

20 Morris 1989, 250–2; Strickland 1996b, 86–8.

21 *The Ecclesiastical History of Orderic Vitalis* XIII, 13, 38, Chibnall 1978, Vol. VI, 454–5, 526–7.

22 Herlihy 1970, 230–2.

23 *Gesta Stephani* II, 78, Potter and Davis 1976, 152–3.

24 *Landbok Sive Registrum Monasterii de Winchelcumba* I, 83, ed. Royce 1892–1903, ii, xliii.

25 Cronne and Davis 1968, no. 285.

26 Higham and Henderson 2011, 143.

27 Carlton 1992, 276–8.

28 Symeon of Durham, *Libellus de exordio atque procurso istius, hoc est Dunhelmensis, ecclesie*, continuation, 7, trans. Rollason 2000, 296–7, 308–9.

29 Symeon of Durham, *Libellus de exordio*, continuation, 7, Rollason 2000, 296–7, continuation: variant section, 314–19.

30 Morey and Brooke 1965, 86.

31 *Gesta Stephani* II, 69, Potter and Davis 1976, 138–9.

32 Blair 1998.

33 *Gesta Stephani* I, 53, Potter and Davis 1976, 108–11. Other siege engines were also used by the men of Miles of Gloucester, who attacked the castle from a different side, presumably south of the River Wye. See also Shoesmith 1980, 58.

34 Morris 2000, 206–7.

35 Boucher et al. 2015, 10–11.

36 Shoesmith 1980, 4–5, 57–9, Fig. 2. See also Speight 2000, 270–1.

37 John of Hexham in Symeon of Durham, *Symeonis monachi opera omnia*, Arnold 2012, Vol. II, 311–12.

38 Elliott 2004, 52–3.

39 Rylatt and Mason 2003, 5, 16–19, 137.

40 William of Newburgh, *The History of English Affairs* I, 12, 2, Walsh and Kennedy 1988, 70–3. See also Henry, Archdeacon of Huntingdon, *Historia Anglorum* X, 22, Greenway 1996, 744–5.

41 Symeon of Durham, *Libellus de exordio*, continuation, 9, Rollason 2000, 306–9.

42 *Gesta Stephani* II, 69–70, Potter and Davis 1976, 138–41.

43 William of Malmesbury, *Historia Novella* II, 22, King and Potter 1998, 44–5.

44 Colvin et al. 1963 Vol. II, 734.

45 Biddle and Kjølbye-Biddle 1992, 37–8.

46 Lethbridge 1952, 56–8; Addyman 1965, 49–52.

47 Knocker 1967.

48 Graham and Davies 1993, 63–70.

49 Graham and Davies 1993, 69–70.

50 Stenton 1932, 199.

51 Pevsner and Williamson 1979, 110.

52 Barley 1951.

53 Colvin 1951, 64–5.

54 Burton 1994, 63.

55 Holdsworth 1994, 216. See Knowles 1963, Appendix XIII.

56 Pestell 2004, 161–2.

57 Hill 1968, 80–115; Burton 1994, 67–9.

58 Gervers 1992, 159–60.

59 Holdsworth 1994, 217.

60 Crouch 1986, 201.

61 Crouch 2000, 183. See also Greene 1992, 19–22.

62 Coppack 1998, 27.

63 Burton 1999, 191–3.

64 Sloane 2012, 17, 138–9.

65 Holdsworth 1994, 220.

66 Knowles and Hadcock 1971, 65.

67 Philp 1968, vii.

68 Telfer 1965, 1–3; Philp 1965, 22; 1968.

69 Schofield and Lea 2005.

70 Schofield and Lea 2005, 91–8, 144.

71 Steane 1999, 72.

72 Gilchrist and Green 2015.

73 Scott 1981. See also Gilchrist and Green 2015, 56, 59.

74 Carley 1985, 167. See also Gilchrist and Green 2015, 64, 124.

75 Gilchrist and Green 2015, 124, 154–64.

76 Holdsworth 1994, 224–6.

77 Orme 2014, 171.

78 Burton 1999, 116.

79 King 1990, 176–7.

80 Burton 2008, 18–21.

81 O'Meara 2013, 282–3.

82 Thompson 1986, 307. See also Pestell 2004, 199.

83 Fergusson 1984, 18; Thompson 1986, 311–17.

84 Higham 1977, 13.

85 *The Book of the Foundation of Walden Monastery* I, 6, ed. and trans. Greenway and Watkiss 1999, 7.

86 Park 2010, 74.

87 Examples include North Ferriby (*c.* 1140), Watton (*c.* 1150), Welbeck (*c.* 1153) and Sibton (*c.* 1150), and perhaps Alnwick (*c.* 1147) and Malton (*c.* 1150). See Callaghan 1978, 309–10.

88 Brooke and Morey 1967, 33–4.

89 Green 2015, 96–7.

90 Thompson 1986, 306.

91 Stroud 1999, 11–12; Knowles and Hadcock 1971, 171–2.

92 Liddiard 2000, 44. See also Thompson 1986, 312.

93 Fergusson 1984, 133. See also Higham and Barker 1992, 125–6.

94 Fergusson 1984, 16–18.

95 Burton 1999, 121–2; Burton and Kerr 2011, 41.

96 Burton 1986, 30–1; 1994, 73.

97 Burton 1994, 70–1.

98 Dobson and Edwards 2010, 100.

99 Stringer 1980, 325–34; 1994, 74.

100 Grant 1987, 111.

101 Fergusson 1984, 55–6, 126–7; Greene 1992, 47.

102 Poulle 1994, 164–6.

103 Callaghan 1974 catalogues 73 examples: 51 Benedictine houses, five Augustinian, three Cistercian, two Savigniac and 12 secular colleges.

104 Biddle 1976, 297–300.

105 *Gesta Stephani* II, 83, Potter and Davis 1976, 164–5.

106 Gilyard-Beer and Coppack 1986, 150, 154–6. See also Burton 2008, 24.

107 Hull 1987, xvi–xvii, xx.

108 Saunders 2006, 31–2.

109 Callaghan 1978.

110 Cronne 1970, 3.

111 *The Chronicle of Battle Abbey*, Searle 1980, 213.

112 Dalton 1994, 193.

113 Translated in Blair and Steane 1983, 47–8.

114 Blair and Steane 1983, 73, 104.

115 Page and Proby 1926, 379; Page et al. 1932, 191.

116 *The Book of the Foundation of Walden Monastery* I, 9, Greenway and Watkiss 1999, 17.

117 RCHME 1926, 209–10. See also Page and Proby 1926, 291–2.

118 Spoerry et al. 2008, 178–9.

119 Spoerry et al. 2008, 185–7.

120 Page and Proby 1926, 291–2; Page et al. 1932, 191.

121 Raftis 1957, 54–61, 86.

122 Page et al. 1932, 188; Oosthuizen 2012, 209–10.

123 This may or may not be the 'Reading castle' that Robert of Torigni records as being built by King Stephen and destroyed in 1153. See King 1983, 11; Spurrell 1995, 262.

124 *Liber Eliensis* III, 62, Fairweather 2005, 389.

125 *Historia Selebiensis Monasterii*, ed. and trans. Burton with Lockyer, lx–lxxiii. See also Burton 2008, 26–8; Dalton 2001, 139–40.

126 *Historia Selebiensis Monasterii*, Burton with Lockyer, 100–1.

127 Dalton 1994, 171–2; 2001, 133–7.

128 *Gesta Stephani* I, 65, Potter and Davis 1976, 130–1.

129 Callaghan 1974, 221; Dalton 1994, 162–4.

130 See, for example, Henry, Archdeacon of Huntingdon, *Historia Anglorum* X, 20, Greenway 1996, 740–1.

131 *Gesta Stephani* II, 73, Potter and Davis 1976, 146–9.

132 Holdsworth 1994, 212–15.

133 *Gesta Stephani* II, 109, Potter and Davis 1976, 208–11.

134 Henry, Archdeacon of Huntingdon, *Historia Anglorum* X, 10, Greenway 1996, 720–1.

135 See Creighton 2005b, Fig. 6.2.

136 Stalley 1971; Thompson 1998, 85–90; White and Cook 2015, 16–17.

137 White and Cook 2015, 124–8.

138 Marshall 2004a; King 2002, 11.

139 Marshall 2004a, 210; 2006, 260–1. See also King 1996, 11.

140 Emery 2006, 432.

141 Biddle 1986. See also Biddle 1969.

142 Biddle 1986, 10–11, 36.

143 Thompson 1992, 18–19.

144 Thompson 2001, 78–81. For the excavated evidence, see Wilcox 1987, 1, 3.

145 Allen and Hiller 2002.

146 Creighton 2009, 62–3, 174–5, 190–2.

147 Allen and Hiller 2002, 201–6.

148 Allen and Hiller 2002, 217.

149 Lewis 1985. See also Hughes 1989, 46.

150 Gilchrist and Green 2015, 423.

151 Baxter 2015, 357.

152 Gilchrist and Green 2015, 423.

153 Callaghan 1974; 1978.

154 McAleer 1999, 57, 83.

155 *Anglo-Saxon Chronicle*, Whitelock 1961, 200. See also Home 2015, 88–90.

156 Saunders 2006, 31.

157 Shapland 2008.

158 Gem 1986.

159 Barlow 1983, 354–5.

160 Creighton 2005b, 123–5.

161 Creighton 2005b, 121–3.

162 Shepherd Popescu 2009, 264–75.

163 Colvin et al. 1963, Vol. II, 888.

Chapter 8

Town, Village and Country

IN THE FINAL thematic chapter of this volume, the focus shifts to the evidence for towns, rural settlements and landscapes. In contrast with castles and siege works, which represent arguably the most conspicuous traces of the civil war in the English landscape, the influence of the conflict upon everyday urban and, especially, rural life is, as will be seen, far less tangible. Major towns were not spared from the flow of the conflict, but in terms of the archaeology of urbanism, the mid-twelfth century is a difficult and somewhat neglected area. Material culture from twelfth-century phases of settlements is typically scant and, again, we must employ an interdisciplinary approach in order to maximise our understanding. This chapter first investigates the different impacts of the conflict upon urban landscapes, with London and Winchester afforded particular attention given the key roles that these centres played, followed by an assessment of the conduct of sieges within and around towns and the evidence for the establishment of new towns and markets. The second half of the chapter turns to the archaeology of the countryside, questioning first whether the Anarchy influenced or affected settlement forms or agricultural regimes, before considering fortified villages and concluding with an overview of the overall evidence for landscape devastation during the conflict.

Major Urban Centres

The conflict of Stephen's reign occurred a good way along the trajectory of urbanisation in England. Against the general sweep of medieval urban history, it represented a relatively minor interruption of a period of sustained growth across *c.* 850–1300, bridging the preceding phase of Norman imposition and the great period of expansion and town foundation that followed. Besides the damaging effects of sieges, the uncertain political environment of the mid-twelfth century exacerbated strains and divisions within urban communities and stalled or damaged commercial growth. In this environment, political favour and location had a considerable bearing on the fortunes of major urban centres, no more so than in the contrasting experiences of London and Winchester.

London and Winchester

While London and its region saw little direct military action, the city still played a pivotal role in unfolding political events. Londoners had enthusiastically acclaimed Stephen as king in 1135 and he held his Christmas court there that year. The king's economic interests coincided with those of London's merchants; he was a local landowner and, being married to Matilda of Boulogne, controlled the ships of Boulogne that transported English wool to Flanders.[1] Later, following the Battle of Lincoln in 1141, the Empress Matilda's hurried flight from London in the face of the city's armed citizenry proved a watershed moment for the Angevin cause.[2] The connection between King Stephen and London was close, and there is a theory that the king intended to be buried in the city, within the impressive church of the Augustinian Holy Trinity Priory, Aldgate, which he had patronised and which had a special connection with his family.[3] Two of his children who had died in infancy, Baldwin and Matilda, were buried here at some point before 1147–48, and Stephen may have planned to be interred between them, near the altar, before circumstances changed and Faversham Abbey, Kent, became the venue for the royal mausoleum (for archaeological investigation of this site, see pg. 131).

The participation of London's militia in the campaigns of the 1140s was another reflection of the city's arch-royalist status. This force was effective in siege warfare: Londoners helped tip the balance at Winchester in 1141 and at Faringdon, Oxfordshire, in 1145.[4] All this was symptomatic of London's growing civic power; indeed, the events of Stephen's reign arguably laid the foundations for the city's establishment as a commune later in the twelfth century.[5] The 1140s also saw Stephen's financial administration gravitate away from Winchester towards London. The old capital of Wessex was no longer secure, nor convenient given the Angevin power base in the West Country and the progressive loss of Normandy, which removed Winchester's importance as a point for transiting treasure to and from the duchy.[6] This downgrading of Winchester as the locus of royal government is reflected clearly in the king issuing a far higher proportion of charters from London after 1142, and at some point before 1154 exchequer operations were transferred wholesale to London.[7]

For the vast majority of London's populace, however, everyday life continued more or less as usual. In the archaeological record we see little or no evidence of any dislocation in trade, nor any sign that lines of contact between city and hinterland were disrupted. There is possible evidence for one small hoard, deposited at Billingsgate *c.* 1141, seemingly at the peak of London's involvement in the conflict (see also pg. 149), although this evidence stands in contrast to the four likely hoards known from the decade after 1066.[8] We see no indications of any great hiatus in occupation, nor of breaks in building projects; indeed, the mid-twelfth century was positively a boom time for monastic foundations and patronage within and around the city (see pg. 199). In terms of London's fortifications, nothing is known of any improvements to its ancient former Roman city walls, and the main addition to its principal royal castle in the mid-twelfth century was non-military in nature: in 1147 Queen Matilda founded the hospital of St Katharine's on the edge of the castle precincts, initially for 13 poor people.[9]

In contrast, Winchester suffered more than any other major city as a consequence of the civil war, both directly and indirectly. Late in the summer of 1141 a drawn-out and high-stakes siege within a siege saw the Empress's forces attack both Bishop Henry of Blois's *castellum* (almost certainly the Norman palace in the centre of the city) and his *domus* (Wolvesey Palace, tucked into the south-east corner of the walls), while they themselves were assailed or blockaded by royalist units arrayed around the city. Figure 8.1 offers a reconstruction of events. Chroniclers claimed that over 40 churches were burned as well as St Mary's Abbey within the walls and Hyde Abbey without.[10] According to the *Gesta Stephani*, firebrands launched by the bishop's soldiers within his *castellum* were the source of the conflagration.[11] While archaeological excavations have found no direct evidence of catastrophic widespread burning, it would be difficult to distinguish such traces from those of large-scale fires common in medieval timber cities and, given the dispersal of the institutions affected, it is tempting to imagine a more limited firing than the chroniclers suggest.[12] Compounding the damage was a vicious sacking led by Londoners, who looted houses, cellars and churches.[13] The war-damaged royal palace in the city centre was gone by 1143, its site taken into the cathedral precinct.[14] Excavation has shown that at St Mary Magdalen, immediately east of the walled city, a short-lived 'secular' phase

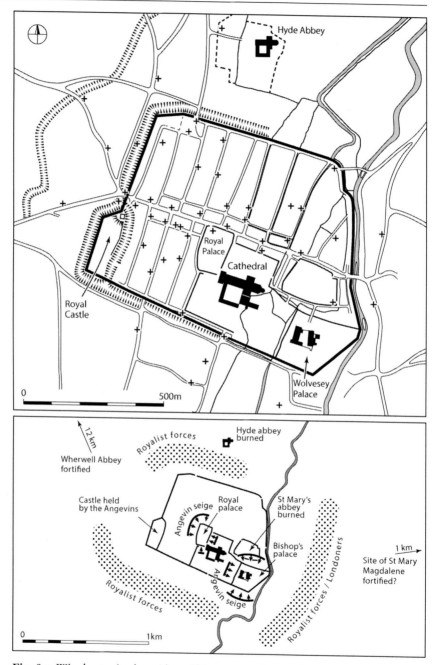

Fig. 8.1: Winchester in the mid-twelfth century: **(top)** urban topography; **(bottom)** stylised reconstruction of the 1141 siege, showing possible deployments of forces. Source: based on Biddle 1976, with additions. Drawing by Seán Goddard.

of activity in the mid-twelfth century saw a large square sunken structure resembling the base of a tower built on the hospital site, before its re-establishment *c.* 1150–70.[15] One interpretation is that the tower had some association with the 1141 siege, especially given its strategic situation on a hill overlooking the major London–Winchester route that was central in the struggle.

Something of the economic consequences of these events can also be gleaned through comparison of an important and detailed survey of the city of 1148 with another produced *c.* 1110.[16] This shows reduced revenues in the rental market, although any devastated zones had been rebuilt in the interval, and while many more properties were waste in 1148, these were not focused in the known siege-affected zones. In the longer term, as noted, the second half of the twelfth century saw the royal court and administration disengage with Winchester. As a result, the city soon fell from its second ranked position in the urban hierarchy, its mint decreasing in importance and archaeological evidence testifying to a declining volume of foreign trade. However, the siege probably accentuated rather than initiated a longer-term trend that was already in train.[17]

Jews and Jewries

A less obvious consequence of Stephen's reign for urban settlements but one with important long-term implications was the rapid establishment and expansion of Jewish enclaves in favoured centres. The Norman kings had a strategic interest in the Jews, who were in effect royal property. Jews were introduced initially from Rouen by William the Conqueror, primarily for their expertise in supplying plate to moneyers for coin minting and in money changing, and subsequently came to be valued as money lenders.[18] Our understanding of the growth of England's Jewries in Stephen's reign hinges on comparing scant documentation from the reign of Henry I (when London alone hosted a Jewish population) with that of Henry II, rather than direct evidence of Stephen's actions. It is nonetheless evident that Stephen's reign saw Jews settled in several provincial towns, especially those that boasted strong royal connections in the south and east of the country. The list is headed by Cambridge, Lincoln and Norwich, so that by 1159 ten other officially recognised Jewish enclaves existed.[19]

These Jewish settlements were deliberate implantations as opposed to *ad hoc* colonising ventures. The king's motive was presumably financial as he sought to tap into Jewish wealth in order to support grinding military campaigns and pay his mercenaries. By the late twelfth and early thirteenth century, when we are able to map the locations of Jewish quarters in towns and cities in more detail, it is clear that most lay under the protective shadows of royal fortresses, whose sheriffs and constables were charged with their oversight and protection.[20] This strategic placement of Jewish quarters is very likely traceable back to Stephen's reign. An illuminating episode is the 'St William' crisis of 1144, when a group of Norwich's Jews, accused of abducting, torturing and ritually crucifying a tanner's son, were supported by the sheriff, John de Chesney, who provided refuge from the mob in the royal castle and represented them in court.[21] Norwich's twelfth-century Jewry clustered immediately south-west of the castle, around one end of the market place, where the synagogue also lay, although by the thirteenth century Jewish properties were more widely scattered within the town.[22] The area features the last remaining secular Norman building in the city, the Music House, the earliest parts of which date to *c.* 1140–50 and which was certainly owned by a prominent Jewish family in the late twelfth century.[23] Although the numbers of Jews settled in twelfth-century English provincial towns were modest, this policy added a new dimension to the ethnic mix of urban centres, some of which – like Norwich – already possessed distinctive 'French' boroughs, thereby creating the potential for positive interaction but also friction between various groups.

Castles, sieges and urban defences

Many important towns suffered lengthy sieges in the civil war, and some faced several, including Hereford, Lincoln, Malmesbury and Wallingford. Intramural castles and their castellans were often the target rather than towns themselves, however, and sieges were sometimes prosecuted partly from within the urban area, as at Exeter in 1136 and Oxford in 1142. Loyalties could be complex, shifting and conflicting, so that the 'allegiance' of towns is a difficult area. The polarisation of royal and episcopal power within Winchester around the climactic 1141 siege, with palaces and castles forming the power bases of rival factions, is a particularly clear case in point (see above, pgs 221–3). Assaults on cities could be attacks on individuals; a successful sacking could humiliate a lord and proclaim his impotence. An obvious example is Robert, Earl of Gloucester's attack on Worcester in November 1139, as described by John of Worcester, which saw houses fired, prisoners taken and livestock stolen from the hinterland; visiting the city in the wake of the devastation, Waleran, Count of Meulan (the earl of the city) 'felt as if the damage had been done to himself.'[24]

Orderic Vitalis records several cases of urban populations actively participating in the conflict in Normandy. For instance, the men of Saint-Évroul attacked forces under Robert Bouet who were pillaging the town's hinterland, hanging seven of them in the aftermath, although the town was attacked in reprisal for this action and 84 properties were reported burnt.[25] The town of Écouché was burnt in a scorched earth policy by its own inhabitants when approached by Angevin forces, 'leaving only smoke and ashes.'[26] Recorded occasions of open conflict in English towns in the period is limited, however. The Battle of Lincoln (1141) took place outside the city walls but the city was brutally sacked 'according to the law that governs hostilities,' in the words of Henry of Huntingdon.[27] This is likely a reference to the 'right of storm' – a convention by which a town or fortress that had refused terms could be plundered.[28] The sacking probably caused more fatalities than the actual battle. The 1138 siege of Shrewsbury ended with the garrison savagely punished by King Stephen because of the unusual level of resistance they put up. The king took William fitz Alan's fortress by direct assault after filling the ditch with faggots of wood and using fire and a siege engine of unknown type to force the gate open, although, once again, it was the castle rather than the town that was the focus of the action.[29] At Hereford, the consequences of the devastating 1143 siege prompted a major ecclesiastical replanning of the town. In the aftermath of the attack on Hereford Castle launched from the cathedral, St Guthlac's was moved from its war-damaged site to a new position in the Bye Gate area outside the city walls, and its cemetery abandoned.[30]

Castles rather than towns were usually the focus of defensive investment, although very few new urban castles were built after the initial wave of Norman building in the period 1066–80.[31] The Anarchy represents a second and much more limited burst of urban castle building in England, although the majority of these sites were purely military installations built on the urban fringes, outside the usual framework of lordship, and quickly disappeared from townscapes, as at Exeter, Oxford and Wallingford, for example.[32] At Luton, Bedfordshire, the castle of the royalist mercenary Robert de Waudari was built in a peripheral position, *c.* 200m south of the historic core on a ridge which overlooked both the town and the road to London. Alongside this militaristic rationale for raising the castle in such a predatorial position, it may be significant that the castle avoided the site of the late Saxon/ Domesday manorial centre in the town centre (which became the site of a second castle in the early thirteenth century), perhaps because the king did not want his mercenary fortifying a traditional royal manor.[33]

Murage grants, through which kings permitted urban communities to raise funds for wall building, did not exist until the early thirteenth century. Assessing the extent to which towns were provided with defences in Stephen's reign, and whether these were maintained, is therefore problematic. Some important episcopal towns received defences in the mid-twelfth century as part of programmes of aggrandisement involving new castles. Devizes, Wiltshire,[34] and Newark, Nottinghamshire,[35] are the clearest examples, although in both cases these initiatives probably started before the civil war. At Devizes, the ditch was V-shaped, *c.* 5m deep and 9m across, but with no surviving bank.[36] Likely examples of towns or incipient boroughs embraced with ditched and ramparted defences in the late 1130s and 1140s are Castle Acre and Castle Rising, both in Norfolk, and Trowbridge, Wiltshire, although this is based on the morphological association of circuits with castles established or strengthened in the conflict. At Saffron Walden, Essex, the mid-twelfth-century castle's outer bailey embraced the church and market and seems in effect to have provided defences for an accompanying settlement. Excavation reveals a ditch up to 4.4m wide and 1.7m deep; the earthworks known as the 'Battle Ditches' or 'Repell Ditches' enclosing a rectangular area to the south of this ridge-top focus are usually dated to the early thirteenth century, although archaeological dating does not rule out the possibility that the twelfth-century town could have extended this far.[37] Where the bounds of the castle stopped and the town started was no doubt blurred in the mid-twelfth century, as was the distinction between small fortified boroughs and villages, some of which were similarly provided with defences that were in effect the outworks of adjacent castles, as discussed in the section on the rural landscape below.

An important example of a city where historical and archaeological sources align to confirm energetic work on urban defences during the civil war is Bath. The *Gesta Stephani* recounts in unusual detail the refurbishment in 1138 of Bath's ancient defences, which also enclosed a late Saxon *burh*, which lends support to the theory that the city's bishop was its author:

> The king after inspecting the circuit of the town and going all around it found it to be an impregnable position and admirably suited to resistance, and therefore he gave orders for the walls to be raised higher, the battlements made steeper, and a close and careful watch kept, with the assistance of a numerous garrison, to restrain the people of Bristol.[38]

So the soldiers whom the king had left in the town of Bath to attack the people of Bristol behaved with resolution and energy, strengthened wall and mounds impregnably by every device for resistance, kept armed watch in turn around the walls through the dead of night, and sometimes in that very silence of night went out of the walls and prepared ambushes in suitable spots.[39]

The alleged impregnability and ease of fortifying the city seem to reflect the fact that Bath was still embraced within its polygonal Roman walled circuit. However, archaeological evidence highlights that the mid-twelfth-century refurbishments focused on outworks rather than the enceinte itself. Excavations adjacent to the site of the north gate in 1980 showed that the twelfth-century defences followed the line of late Saxon outworks built in advance of the line of the crumbling Roman wall. The ditch was recut so that it was at least 3m deep and a metalled berm created behind the inferred position of a wall strengthened with a buttress. The aim was probably to create outworks flanking the gateway and the initiative may not have entailed reconstruction of the whole circuit.[40] The refurbishments have the flavour of securing a campaign base from which the rebellious stronghold of Bristol could be besieged and the territory around it devastated, rather than an investment in genuinely urban defences to protect a populace.

A comparable case of an Anglo-Saxon *burh* reused as a campaign castle is Cricklade, Wiltshire. Here, excavations in 1975 provided evidence for a late phase of refortification of the Anglo-Saxon rampart, which formed a rectangular perimeter against the River Thames, very much like Wallingford (see pg. 64). The refurbished system comprised a replacement palisade (represented by a palisade trench for massive timbers along the line of the former wall) and inner and (wide) outer ditches, and is consistently dated with pottery to the early/mid-twelfth century, which very likely reflects William of Dover's *castellum* of Cricklade 'constructed' in 1144.[41] This reminds us once again that contemporary chroniclers could describe a wide range of fortified installations with the word *castellum*. Towns could become castles: Wilton, Wiltshire, may be a similar case of a temporarily strengthened *burh* styled as a 'castle' by the chroniclers (see pg. 208), while the *burh* defences of Christchurch, Dorset, seem also to have been refurbished in the 1140s, to judge from excavated evidence.[42]

Charters, Markets and Planted Towns

Surveys of urban growth in medieval England have long recognised that King Stephen's reign coincided with a slackening in the rate of town foundation, before renewed expansion in Henry II's reign saw a flurry of new charters and the establishment of numerous small towns, mainly by local lords.[43] From documentary sources we know that charters for new boroughs and markets continued to be granted in the late 1130s and 1140s, although there is little to confirm that these new foundations developed characteristically urban functions before the upsurge in commercialisation in the thirteenth century. Another reflection of the economic slowdown can be found in the coin hoards of the 1140s, which often indicate a more limited range of places of issue than previously.[44] This suggests that trading networks had become more localised.

The economic fortunes of towns whose hinterlands straddled royal and Angevin spheres of influence may have suffered most acutely. In his magisterial survey of medieval town plantation, *New Towns of the Middle Ages* (1967), Maurice Beresford reckoned that the decade 1141–50 saw two new towns (1% of the medieval total) and 1151–60 seven (4% of the total), marking a short but noticeable trough in the overall rate of new town growth before rebounding to a more typical annual rate.[45] It is worth looking closely at those new towns and market centres that were planted during the civil war, although weaknesses in the dating evidence presents problems as in several cases the potential date range of foundation spans either the start or end of Stephen's reign.

Most royal grants of commercial privileges concerned places in the eastern counties, the king granting or confirming fairs to more than a dozen abbeys, priories and cathedrals.[46] The Empress granted fairs to St Frideswide's, Oxford, and Godstow Abbey, Oxfordshire.[47] Bishops were especially active agents in the commercialisation of the twelfth-century countryside through the promotion of new towns.[48] Devizes, Wiltshire, is well known as a plantation of Bishop Roger of Salisbury, established in 1135–39 with its park adjacent to the slightly earlier castle.[49] The development of urban settlement at Wells, Somerset, can be traced to the upturn in the fortunes of the monastic cathedral under the episcopate of Bishop Robert of Lewes (1135–66), who won the favour of King Stephen. The borough seems to have been planted in the late 1130s or 40s and the growth of its commercial functions is reflected by the extension of the fair from one to three days in the period.[50] Baldock, Hertfordshire, was a foundation of the Knights Templar, established soon after 1138–48, when Gilbert de Clare, first Earl Pembroke, granted the order a prime commercial site at an intersection of communications routes.[51]

More typically, however, new trading centres established in Stephen's reign were promoted by secular lords. Thurstan de Beauchamp, Earl of Warwickshire, obtained permission from the Empress to hold a Sunday market in his castle of Beaudesert (*ad castellum suum de Bellodeser*), Warwickshire, *c.* 1140.[52] A LiDAR survey of the site (Plate 18) shows well the inconvenient hilltop location of the castle: the vast outer bailey may well have accommodated the market. This arrangement was temporary, however, and by the 1220s the trading centre lay in Henley(-in-Arden) below.[53] New Buckenham, Norfolk, was also established close to a castle in the 1140s, in this case by William d'Albini, who acquired land from the Bishop of Norwich so that his new castle-town, which replaced an earlier *caput*, could be positioned where he wished.[54] A grand scheme of landscape design extended far beyond the new trading settlement, and his foundation was complemented by two parks, completing an integrated exercise in town and country planning.[55]

The market town of Saffron Walden, Essex (Fig. 8.2), provides an especially instructive case study of how castle plantation could be symbiotic with town growth in the mid-twelfth century. A crucial piece of evidence is the Empress's charter of 1141 to Geoffrey de Mandeville, Earl of Essex, giving him permission to move the market of Newport 'into his castle at Walden, with all the customs which better belonged to that market before then' (*in castellum suum de Waldena cum omnibus consuetudinibus que prius mercato illi melius pertinuerunt*).[56] This is the first documentary evidence for the castle and settlement. Geoffrey had probably recovered his family's manor of Walden, along with Great Waltham and Sawbridgeworth, early in Stephen's reign, perhaps in 1136, when he is said to have consecrated the cemetery of Walden Priory.[57] The writer of *The Book of the Foundation of Walden Monastery* also attributes the ennoblement of Walden Castle to Geoffrey,[58] and archaeological excavation confirms that the ridge-top donjon with concentric oval baileys, the outermost embracing a fortified market, was built in a single phase of construction in the early to mid-twelfth century.[59] All this points to an integrated seigneurial initiative of aggrandisement and economic investment in which the new donjon standing on the promontory of Bury Hill with the town at its foot and Walden Priory were both elements.[60] Even this most celebrated 'champion of Anarchy' had a keen eye on the economic potential of his estates.

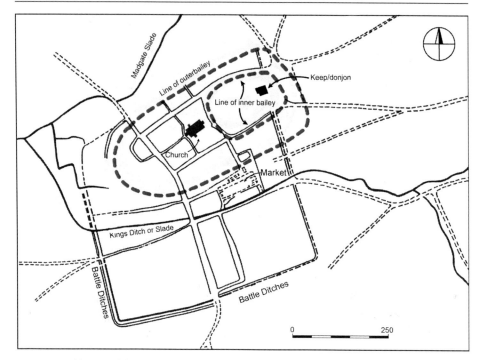

Fig. 8.2: Saffron Walden: plan of the medieval town, highlighting the principal features of twelfth-century topography.
Source: map based on Andrews et al. 2001, with additions from Lewis and Ranson 2013.

That castle and town could be close to the point of being indivisible in the mid-twelfth century is illustrated by the case of Mountsorrel, Leicestershire (Fig. 8.3). The first references to a settlement at Mountsorrel are in a charter of *c.* 1148 which mentions a 'village' (*villam*), and the famous treaty of *c.* 1149–53 between the Earl of Leicester, whose castle it was, and his rival the Earl of Chester, which mentions the 'borough and baileys' (*burgo et baliis*).[61] The grant of a market and fair is not recorded until 1292, although this appears to reinforce the existence of an extant urban institution.[62] Excavations within the medieval town at 13 The Market Place, and 1 and 3 Leicester Road (respectively north and north-north-east of Castle Hill) confirm that occupation commences in the twelfth century and show that plots were artificially raised and traversed by a network of drainage gulleys indicative of an unfavourable and poorly drained site, attributable both to the volume of surface run-off from Castle Hill and the proximity

Fig 8.3: Mountsorrel: aerial view of the castle overlooking the town. © English Heritage.

of the floodplain.[63] All the indications are, therefore, that Mountsorrel originated as a castle-dependent nucleus – a seigneurially forced nucleation on a poor but strategic site – with settlement and trading at the fortress's foot predating the formalisation of urban status.[64]

Not all new towns of the period were castle-dependent foundations. Hedon, East Yorkshire, was a port established *c.* 1138–48 by the Earl of Aumale on a creek leading to the River Humber, while Boroughbridge, North Yorkshire, in existence by *c.* 1145, was the result of the construction of a bridge over the River Ure.[65] The borough of (New) Thirsk, North Yorkshire, established by the

Mowbray family *c.* 1135–45, actually superseded the castle-gate village, which was rejected in favour of a site with greater potential on the opposite side of the Cod Beck river.[66]

Political favouritism continued to have a crucial bearing on the fates of towns in the immediate post-war years. The start of Henry II's reign saw an intense burst of urban charters that confirmed or extended earlier privileges. Royal favour is particularly apparent in the charter for Wallingford (1155), which recognised 'the service and great labour' of the population of an Angevin power base that had sustained three prolonged and bloody sieges. The liberties granted to the burgesses, including freedom from certain dues and favourable trading conditions, were such that, at the time, only London had a wider range of privileges.[67] In the 1150s Baldwin de Redvers, Earl of Devon and lord of the manor, excused his burgesses of Christchurch, Hampshire, from paying certain customary dues, including 'all market duties,' almost certainly for their loyalty during the civil war.[68] In contrast, the royal charter for Exeter (1154) effectively admonished the city by abolishing 'bad customs' introduced since the time of Henry I.[69]

The Rural Landscape: Impacts and Change

The evolution of England's medieval landscape has been an area of intense and protracted scholarly debate – perhaps more than any other subject explored by this volume. Disagreement persists over both the chronology of change detectable in the archaeology of the medieval countryside, and the appropriate means of explaining these developments. By far the greatest time and ink has been spent attempting to determine the origins of English villages and, in particular, to understanding why and when coalesced 'nucleated' villages accompanied by open fields came to characterise some parts of the country but not others.[70] Either side of a central zone of nucleated villages extending from the south coast to Northumberland, historic settlement was typically more dispersed and associated with more discrete field systems.[71] Although it now appears that at least a minority of villages were preceded by antecedent communities there is at least a general consensus that only from the ninth century did these settlements begin to assume their medieval morphological character, and that the process of nucleation extended far beyond the Norman Conquest, to *c.* 1200.[72]

Along with the restructuring and coalescence of existing settlements, other villages were established *de novo* – a process that also appears to have continued well into the twelfth century. In the north of England, for example, a number of 'row-plan' villages previously associated with the imposition of strict Norman lordship in the wake of the 'Harrying of the North,' appear to date to the twelfth century when subject to excavation.[73] Rural communities also continued to settle and cultivate more physically marginal landscapes. Thus, in East Anglia, for example, settlements shifted from well-drained river valleys to the peripheries of large commons on interfluvial floodplains, in a pattern recognised as early as the tenth century but which persisted into the mid-twelfth century.[74] The continued reclamation of wetlands went hand in hand with further settlement growth, as recognised in several parishes in Lincolnshire,[75] and in the marshlands of Norfolk, where occupation – previously restricted to naturally raised, silted-up channels known as 'roddons' – expanded along the network of droveways from the twelfth century.[76]

It is clear that the overall extent of royal forest diminished during Stephen's reign. Forest administration was not fully maintained, while rights and tracts of land were granted away in royal *acta*, sometimes to garner political support, so that many of the extensions of the forests under Henry I were lost and only restored in Henry II's reign.[77] Detailed local studies reveal that this situation did not apply universally, however. Thus, in Nottinghamshire, the arch-royalist William Peverel used his strong position to help enforce forest law over a more extensive area than in 1135.[78] Charters also make clear that in certain local contexts Stephen guarded his forest rights closely, for instance by being specific about permissible assarts – although this can also be interpreted as reversing previous slippages of control.[79]

The civil war therefore occurred towards the end of a protracted period – perhaps as much as four centuries in duration – during which the settlements and agricultural arrangements of medieval England were crystallising. It is, however, acutely difficult to identity in the archaeo-logical record the impact of the civil war upon such longer-term trends, and as is the case for much material culture from the period, there is certainly no distinctive 'Anarchy event horizon' in the rural landscape. This lack of archaeological signature should perhaps not come as a surprise, especially considering how the Norman Conquest is equally hard to detect in the physical fabric of everyday life in the countryside.[80] The central issue for the study of both the Anarchy and the Conquest is that archaeological sequences cannot be dated sufficiently precisely to allow correlation with historically attested events in either period.

Although unambiguous material indicators of the conflict have proved imperceptible to existing research, the archaeological evidence can nevertheless shed light on landscape developments datable to the twelfth century in certain instances. The investigation and characterisation of rural life are particularly assisted by the proliferation of small-scale, local pottery-producing centres from the late eleventh century (see pg. 124). The introduction of such wares brings into focus for the first time many rural communities in northern and western England, which were virtually aceramic throughout the early medieval period.[81] In more densely settled landscapes, the twelfth century is witness to the establishment of secondary centres, partly because of manorial fragmentation, as visible at places such as West Cotton, near Raunds, Northamptonshire.[82]

Another potential route into chronologies of settlement development through the period is the now sizable and ever-expanding data set of dendrochronological dates for the timber components of rural buildings. Numbers of twelfth-century dates are small in comparison to later periods, but one notable trend concerns dates for aisled buildings: when these are calculated as a percentage of the total number of tree-ring dates in each half-century, the period *c.* 1150–99 has more than four times the number of examples than the period *c.* 1100–49, and the figure for tree-ring-dated open halls is similarly much higher for the second half of the twelfth century.[83] This cements the notion of the later twelfth century as the crucial threshold for the spread of timber-framed buildings.[84] Nevertheless, any notion that the transition from 'earth-fast' methods of construction (where principal posts were set in postholes) to more complex timber-framing technologies (where the building's strength and stability relies on jointing) was smooth and rapid requires revision, however; the pattern on the ground is much more complex, with a wide variety of coeval building technologies in use at any point.[85] It is also to the period *c.* 1150–1200 that we can date the earliest surviving domestic stone-built structures in the English countryside, such as Boothby Pagnell Manor House in Lincolnshire and Hemingford Grey Manor House in Cambridgeshire, although the attribution of these as 'first floor halls' now seems wrong.[86]

The clearest cases of rural settlement change in the mid-twelfth century are associated with castles, partly as their lords were the agents of change, but also because excavation of these sites provides us firm chronological pegs around which archaeologists have been able to piece together sequences. Middleton Stoney, Oxfordshire, the castle of Richard de Camville in the mid-twelfth century (Fig. 4.7: bottom right), is a particularly clear example. De Camville was part of a coterie of advisors close to King Stephen; he was a tenant-in-chief of estates in Berkshire and Oxfordshire before 1135 but rose dramatically up the social ladder to become a figure of national importance as one of Stephen's favoured 'new men.'[87] Excavation and survey in the parish of Middleton Stoney provide vivid insights into how such a rise in status might be manifested in the rural landscape. A new castle tower was surrounded by a rubble plinth capped with clay, making it appear to stand upon an elevated motte; its construction coincided with that of a new parish church, whose earliest fabric dates to the same period, at a time which also saw the reorientation of the settlement pattern, with the village moved to the new site and the road network replanned around the castle-church nucleus. A park and market were licensed later, in 1201.[88]

Several other schemes of landscape reorganisation that accompanied the construction of new castles in the mid-twelfth century seem likely to have included the creation of new parks, although these units tended to be documented later. The most important examples (already discussed) are Castle Acre and Castle Rising, Norfolk, and Castle Hedingham, Essex (see pgs 104–10). The addition of a planned core to an earlier settlement nucleus is another possible sequence, as evidenced at 'Goltho,' Lincolnshire. This seems to have been an initiative of the de Kyme lords when the manor was reunited following subdivision into three separate holdings after 1066; their scheme of aggrandisement extended to the establishment of a small Gilbertine priory and reconstruction of the manorial site as a compact motte and bailey.[89]

The imposition of castles on rural settlements – as opposed to their growth from manorial sites within them – is unusual across the medieval period as a whole; most known examples can be attributed an Anarchy-period context.[90] The classic case in point is Burwell, Cambridgeshire, while the nearby Cambridgeshire sites of Swavesey and Rampton bear comparison (see pgs 272–3). At nearby Eaton Socon, Cambridgeshire, the defensive earthworks of a substantial ringwork were similarly superimposed upon a Saxo-Norman settlement or perhaps a thegnly site, and there is evidence that wattle and daub buildings were flattened and burned to make way for the castle; the sequence has also been attributed a mid-twelfth-century date.[91]

The role of castles as bases for exacting taxes from rural populations, as attested by the chroniclers, compounds our view of these sites as predatory. It is less apparent whether castle lords were able to extract taxes from rural populations because of the fact that they possessed a castle, or whether the fortification simply functioned in administrative matters like a non-defended manorial site. The process of tax collection could have been perfectly peaceful, and the phenomenon was nothing new. In the immediate post-Conquest decades, Domesday Book shows how new Norman overlords quickly imposed taxes on the peasantry, which may be one of the main reasons why the value of many manors rose between 1066 and 1086, especially in southern England.[92] Overall, we urgently need to get over the inherently negative view of the impact of Anarchy-period castles on the landscape that is enshrined in the words of the archaeologist Brian Hope-Taylor who, reporting on one of the first excavations of one of these sites, saw them as 'raw wounds on the body of England.'[93]

Defended villages

Defended villages were rare in medieval England. In virtually all known cases, fortifications around settlements were effectively outworks of castles as opposed to truly communal defences in the manner of walled towns.[94] There is good evidence that a significant number of these sites date to the twelfth century rather than the immediate post-Conquest period. At Ascot D'Oilly, in the parish of Ascot-under-Wychwood, Oxfordshire, the especially well-preserved earthworks of a rectangular village enclosure are attached to a small motte-and-bailey castle, which was probably built during the civil war by Roger d'Oilly II and has yielded twelfth-century material (Fig. 8.4: top).[95] The bank of the enclosure, which seems to have embraced a unit of peasant crofts, stands around 1m high, with an external ditch; the morphological evidence suggests that it is contemporary with the castle.[96] The site of Boteler's (or Oversley) Castle, near Alcester, Warwickshire (Fig. 8.4: middle), presents evidence for a defended castle-village of the period in a different way, as here the existence of an attached settlement was completely unknown prior to excavation in advance of road construction in 1992–93.[97] The castle, built for Ralph Boteler, a vassal of the Earl of Leicester, is first documented in the foundation deeds of Alcester Abbey in 1139–40; the settlement seems to have been planned slightly later, probably in the 1140s. It lay within a vast (c. 235 × 215m) semi-circular outer bailey defended by a ditch up to 6.7m wide and 2.7m deep, with an internal rampart. The entire site was abandoned by c. 1225. That the attached settlement had an economic base that was partly non-agricultural (with evidence of steel manufacture, for example) points towards a specialist economy symbiotically linked to the castle.[98]

How often similar sequences are repeated elsewhere is difficult to say, as early phases are obscured where settlements continue to

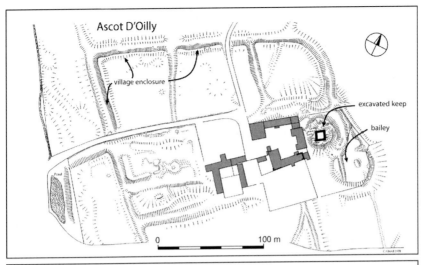

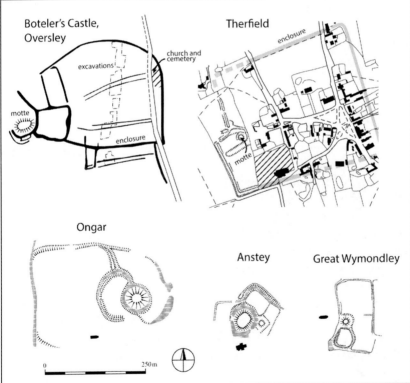

Fig. 8.4: Plans of defended villages and castles.
Source: based on Creighton 2004; Bond 2001; Creighton
and Rippon forthcoming. Drawing by Oliver Creighton.

be occupied. There is certainly a blurred distinction between outer baileys and enclosures around villages or small boroughs. Both Ascot D'Oilly and Boteler's Castle bear comparison to Ongar, Essex (Fig. 8.4: bottom), where excavation indicates the earliest phase of the settlement, which lay within a curving enclosure west of the castle measuring c. 200 × 300m, to have been laid out in the mid-twelfth century.[99] The twelfth-century town took the form of a linear settlement either side of High Street, which ran north–south through the defensive enclosure, a major topographical feature whose ditch measured between 13.75 and 15.50m wide.[100] Other relevant sites that may bear evidence of small-scale schemes of seigneurial property protection during the mid-twelfth century include Therfield, Hertfordshire (Fig. 8.4: middle), where excavation has sampled the village enclosure and revealed defences of similar proportions to those of the small adjoining motte and bailey.[101] Hertfordshire has a concentration of defended castle-villages, with other clear examples at Anstey and Great Wymondley, which have also been posited as Anarchy-period sites (Fig. 8.4: bottom).[102] Caution is needed, however, as the earthworks of settlement enclosures attached to Norman castles can look very much like manorial paddocks created around sites *after* their demilitarisation. A further possibility is that some of the vast baileys formed where castles were superimposed upon prehistoric hillforts were intended to enclose settlements or populations, as at sites such as Castle Combe in Wiltshire and Almondbury in West Yorkshire, which featured a small hilltop borough by the later medieval period (see pg. 99).

A final important but little-known example of a defended medieval village with good evidence of mid-twelfth-century origins is the Nottinghamshire village of Wellow (Fig. 8.5). The settlement plan is still girdled with the bank and rock-cut ditch of an earthwork known as the Gorge Dyke, forming a diamond-shaped perimeter around a clearly planned settlement comprising units of equally sized plots, and is highly unusual as the only recognised example of a medieval defended village in England without a castle.[103] This earthwork, measuring up to 2.5m above the base of its ditch, is larger than the sorts of bank that divide many deserted Midland medieval villages from their open fields, and geophysical survey suggests that it has a masonry core.[104] Parts of the intramural zone have never been built upon; several zones preserve ridge and furrow, which clearly underlies the village bank. An external green north of the village seems to be an early or original feature.

All lines of evidence suggest that the village was a latecomer to the landscape: Wellow is not listed in Domesday Book and was originally

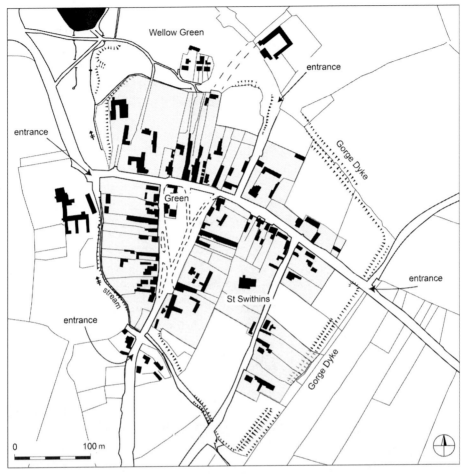

Fig. 8.5: Plan of the defended village of Wellow.
Map work by Steven Trick, incorporating
information in Barley 1957.

a chapelry, sitting in the south-west corner of the original parish.
The place name is first recorded in 1207, as *Welghag*, a compound of
Old English *wielle* and *haga*, meaning 'an enclosure near a spring,'[105]
highly apposite for the village's location on a tributary of the River
Maun that is canalised around the dyke. The most likely period for the
creation of Wellow as a nucleated village is the middle of the twelfth
century, when it was a possession of the Cistercian abbey of Rufford, a
daughter house of Rievaulx founded *c.* 1145 by Gilbert de Gaunt, Earl
of Lincoln. That land in the surrounding area was cleared under the

direction of the clerics is indicated by a cartulary entry of *c.* 1145–53 recording compensation to the local population; the settlements of Cratley, Rufford and Grimston seem to have been cleared to create a *tabula rasa* and to centralise the previously dispersed population.[106] Whether the settlement dates to the civil war or its immediate aftermath is impossible to say, and we should be careful in linking the fact that the village was defended with the disturbances of the conflict. While the Gorge Dyke would have provided a degree of protection, given that Cistercian landowners probably lie behind its creation, it is significant that it also forms a water management system. The village was probably primarily developed as an economic venture to maximise revenues from the estate. As with the other examples of fortified villages, the lords' motives were probably as much about bringing populations under tighter control as protecting them from lawlessness.

Landscape Devastation? Mapping the Impact of War

As seen, the direct impacts of the civil war upon England's landscape are extremely difficult to identify through the archaeological evidence of settlements, structures and artefacts alone. The techniques of environmental archaeology hold a certain potential to illuminate large-scale episodes of medieval landscape devastation, although this is yet to be realised. In terms of the potential 'off-site' signatures of ravaging and damage to the agricultural base through military action, sharp drops in arable production could feasibly be detectable in pollen cores, as could horizons of charcoal dust related to burning. 'On-site' evidence could also indicate episodes of intense burning, although both areas come with their challenges. The sampling intervals employed in palaeoenvironmental analysis and the vagaries of radiocarbon dating, which lacks the precision to relate specific ecological changes to historical events, mean that such relatively short-term changes in land use cannot be identified or dated with precision. Another significant issue is that post-medieval drainage of fenland areas, which produce excellent evidence for environmental change in prehistory, and desiccation of the uppermost layers of peat, mean that little or no twelfth-century material is likely to survive.

The wasting of enemy lands was a tactic widely used during the civil war. Commanders targeted the agricultural base quite deliberately, to punish adversaries, to crush morale and to deny resources to enemy forces. The conflict must also have seen widespread collateral damage as armies lived off the land and soldiers ransacked property. The chronicler of the *Gesta Stephani* recounts on several occasions how burning, pillaging and military action transformed the landscape into desert, and Gloucestershire, Wiltshire and the Cambridgeshire fens were hotspots of destruction.[107] In addition to its economic implications for armies and populations, devastation of the landscape clearly had a profound psychological impact not just on victims but also potential future victims, and was a key weapon of fear and intimidation.[108]

Further insight into the geographical spread and severity of destruction can be gleaned by mapping references to landscape devastation and relating this data set to the somewhat fragmentary material record. Previous attempts to plot landscape devastation during the Anarchy have been relatively broad-brush.[109] By mapping documented episodes of violence and viewing their distribution alongside other evidence for conflict, such as castles and sieges (see Chapter 3; Figs 3.1a–c and 3.5) and hoards (see Chapter 5; Fig. 5.5), we can start to develop a much more nuanced national picture of the impact of the war. Accordingly, Figures 8.1a–b map known and likely areas of landscape devastation for the early (1135–41) and later (1142–54) parts of the conflict.

Such an approach demonstrates that, during the first half of Stephen's reign, the southern and western parts of the country were particularly affected. The war during this first phase was perhaps most keenly felt in the Angevin heartland of the West Country, as well as in the Thames Valley. Wessex saw similar concentrated upheavals in the first half of the conflict, with Winchester a key strategic centre for both sides. Levels of devastation in Wales and on the borderlands with England are almost certainly grossly under-represented in the sources. Notable, however, is a band of devastation to the east of the Pennines, running from North Yorkshire to the Scottish Borders. Such a pattern is largely a result of forays into English territory by King David of Scots and his allies, who sought to undermine royal authority, particularly in the early part of Stephen's reign. We should be careful not to assume that areas subject to military action and, indeed, conquest necessarily suffered economically in the longer term. The economic fortunes of Cumbria and Northumbria probably rose in the late 1130s, sitting on the edge of King David of Scots's 'English empire' and benefitting from the knock-on commercial effects of the silver mining bonanza.[110] While David's creation of this transitory Scoto-Northumbrian realm was once viewed by historians as a doomed adventure, it is now increasingly seen as having come close to fundamentally redrawing the map of British political geography.[111]

The key zone of the Thames Valley – the heartland of English kingship, symbolically and strategically vital, rather than some separatist or peripheral region – continued to be especially bitterly contested in the second half of the war. The conflict in this area does not appear to have spread as extensively as previously, however, and counties such as Gloucestershire, Somerset and Worcestershire were generally subject to fewer episodes of devastation. Action was instead more concentrated in a corridor extending roughly from Bristol to Oxford. Hampshire was again the focus of activity in the latter part of Stephen's reign, with the south Wessex coast affected more significantly than before. Particularly devastating was Stephen and Eustace's scorched earth policy when campaigning against Henry of Anjou in Wessex in the autumn of 1149. Ravaging the districts around Devizes, Marlborough and Salisbury, they sought to 'plunder and destroy' Angevin lands and 'set fire to the crops and every other means of supporting human life and let nothing remain anywhere' so that 'under this duress, reduced to the extremity of want, they [the Angevins] might at last be compelled to yield and surrender.'[112] In the north of England, County Durham and Yorkshire continued to provide the stage for numerous scenes of conflict, but events became more tightly focused over time and Scottish armies held back from large-scale campaigns. Perhaps the most significant shift in the geographical emphasis of conflict in the second half of Stephen's reign was toward central and eastern England, which had escaped largely unscathed in the earlier part of the war. The fenland rebellion of Geoffrey de Mandeville (see Chapter 9) saw East Anglia take centre stage in the early 1140s, but the Midlands were also considerably more affected than before.

The influence of the conflict upon developments in the countryside is exceptionally difficult to demonstrate in detail (see above), but it is notable that areas of both nucleated and dispersed village were at times affected. The twelfth-century civil war is one of several histor-ically attested periods of landscape devastation that could have created opportunities for village planning. The war clearly did not result in mass upheaval of settlement structure, and if horizons of post-war planning are to be found it is in localised patterns. In Somerset, for example, it has been suggested that there could be a correlation between medieval villages showing morphological evidence of Continental-style *solskifte* ('sun division') – a system by which open field systems and accompanying settlements could be planned in regular form – and castles known or suspected to have seen action during the civil war, the implication being that lords of the period could have indulged in settlement planning.[113]

While this assessment represents a useful index of the geographical concentration of the conflict over time, the interpretation of the written evidence is far from straightforward, and historians have contested the extent to which a state of 'anarchy' is demonstrated by the texts. A number of scholars have sought to bring into question the suitability of the term to describe the period, and doubt whether the degree of violence and disorder was in any way peculiar to Stephen's reign.[114] Those arguing a more minimalist viewpoint have often cited the continued functioning of royal government, as well as the flourishing of the Church and the proliferation of monasticism.[115] It has also been suggested that many of the sources paint a deliberately negative picture of contemporary conditions, extrapolating isolated episodes of local violence in order to depict a nation crippled by war.[116]

An important corrective to such minimalist interpretations has been provided by Hugh Thomas, who counters that the bleak picture painted by chroniclers does in fact reflect historical reality.[117] In addition to demonstrating the limited effectiveness of Stephen's government, Thomas argues that much of the evidence relating to increased Church prosperity is actually anecdotal in nature. He further argues that historians have been guilty of the same process of extrapolation for which twelfth-century chroniclers are criticised, that scholars have cited any sign of normality as evidence for a society unaffected by the civil war. Moving beyond the critique of minimalist approaches, Thomas provides a useful comparison between violence recorded during Stephen's reign and that documented during the supremacies of Henry I and Henry II, the result being a measure of conflict spanning the duration of the twelfth century.[118] While a greater concentration of violent episodes certainly falls within Stephen's reign, these are *recorded* events and cannot be taken as a definitive gauge of actual levels of violence. Differential geographical coverage by chroniclers introduces one biasing factor, which is compounded by uncertainty over the terminology used in the sources.

Also highly relevant here is Catherine Clarke's application of 'trauma theory,' to argue that twelfth-century historians were sufficiently affected by the horrors of 'the Anarchy' to stray from literary norms in their accounts of the period and the events leading up to it. The magnitude of atrocity and suffering was arguably so far removed from normality as to defy direct representation, and writers turned to metaphor and coded literary discourse to grapple with fractured

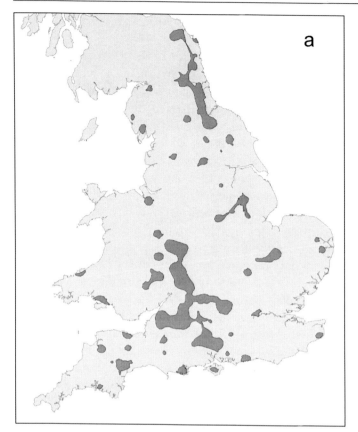

Fig. 8.6: Areas of attested landscape devastation during the civil war:
(a) *above* 1135–41; (b) *opposite* 1142–54; (c) *page 246* waste in the pipe roll of
1155–56, as a percentage of Danegeld, by county (counties in white not covered).
Map work by Steven Trick and Duncan Wright: (a) and (b) based on a database
of twelfth-century chronicles, © Anarchy? War and Status Project; (c) based
on the 1155/56 pipe roll (Hunter 1844; data reproduced in White 1985, 45;
Amt 1993, 139).

history. Generalised but horrific accounts of human suffering in the
Peterborough Chronicle continuations, John of Worcester's addition of
wonders and portents into his chronicle and William of Newburgh's
collection of troubling supernatural stories in chapters 27 and 28 of his
History of English Affairs all speak of traumatised experience beyond
the reach of conventional narrative.[119] Supporting evidence can be found
in descriptions of the horrors of war in the miracle stories of Stephen's
reign,[120] *The History of the Monastery of Selby* providing especially
colourful examples (see pg. 207).

Further debate has surrounded the use of the term 'waste' (*vastare*) and the extent to which its appearance in the sources, particularly the pipe rolls, truly represents devastation of the landscape. Whether or not documented 'waste' can be considered an indicator of landscape devastation as a result of military action is not an issue restricted to the Anarchy and its aftermath, and offers comparable challenges to those studying the impact of the Norman Conquest and the 'Harrying of the North.'[121] Many researchers have pointed to evidence in the first surviving pipe roll for Henry II, from the exchequer year 1155–56, and the large exemptions for 'waste' in the collection of Danegeld, especially in the midland counties, as evidence of the continued impact of the conflict (Fig. 8.6c).[122] There are, however, difficulties with such a straightforward interpretation, and scholars have raised numerous concerns regarding gaps in the records and administrative circumstances that would have

resulted in exemption of Danegeld.[123] In this context, it is notable that there is little clear correlation between the distribution of waste in the pipe rolls and the overall pattern of the most heavily devastated regions in the civil war. If the waste in the pipe rolls reflects devastation from military campaigns (as well as related famine and pestilence), then the actions in question must have been the campaigns by Henry of Anjou at the very end of the conflict, in 1153, which hit these areas, especially Warwickshire – the greatest hotspot of waste – particularly hard (see Fig. 2.1b: bottom right).[124] This area would have had far less time to recover than other regions battered earlier in the war. If any other category of evidence suggests that this zone suffered the depredations of war it is the hoard evidence, which shows a clustering in this general area of the country against a background noise of hoard deposition that tends to be far more focused towards eastern England (see pgs 145–50).

In terms of the civil war's overall demographic impact, we are inevitably in the realms of educated guesswork. By way of comparison, the total war dead for the British civil wars of the mid-seventeenth century, both direct and indirect, is estimated at 3.7% of the population in England, 6% in Scotland and 41% in devastated Ireland.[125] Although this conflict was half as long as the civil war of Stephen's reign, the fighting was without doubt more intense and deadly, with many more large-scale battles. By contrast, the twelfth-century civil war was marked by far greater damage to the agricultural base through the ravaging of field armies, and the duration of the conflict compounded its effects. While any estimate of the English population loss during the conflict of 'the Anarchy' is speculative in the extreme, it would not be fanciful to reckon on a figure of 2–3%, followed by rapid recovery.

Summary

Despite the almost 20-year duration of the civil war, its impacts on both landscapes and townscapes had very significant geographical biases. It comes as no surprise that there was, generally speaking, a greater impact upon urban rather than rural life, as urban castles, fortified towns and their hinterlands were the focus of numerous sieges and counter-sieges. Yet behind the image of a slowdown in urban growth, lords were investing in new town plantations, invariably alongside their fortified centres and often as components within more comprehensive schemes of aggrandisement. Tracing the impact of the Anarchy on the rural landscape of England is a more difficult proposition. The twelfth century represents the end stages of a protracted period in which the settlement pattern was crystallised, but the influence of the war upon villages and agricultural regimes is indiscernible through material remains alone. Examples of defended villages may reflect the responses of lords and communities to the uncertain political conditions, but the dating evidence does not allow firm correlations to be made. Documentary sources catalogue landscape devastation carried out by armies on both sides throughout the conflict, but the geographical extent and duration of its impact are contested by researchers. What can be said with greater assurance is that the war had a strong geographical bias, with certain regions, most notably the West Country and Thames Valley, the focus of regular and damaging upheaval. Elsewhere, urban and rural populations are likely not to have been too heavily affected by the ebb and flow of the conflict, where the political and military fortunes of the social elite did not impinge on everyday life.

Notes

1 Brooke 1975, 33–44.

2 On the loyalty of Londoners during the conflict, see Truax 1996.

3 Schofield and Lea 2005, 148.

4 Clark 2010, 236–8. According to the *Gesta Stephani*, the arrival of an 'invincible band of Londoners' (*inuicta Londoniensium caterua*) at Winchester in 1141 tipped the balance of forces and prompted the decisive royalist attack on Matilda's army. The Londoners also joined the savage sack of the city and its churches (*Gesta Stephani* I 65, Potter and Davis 1976, 129–33). Henry of Huntingdon recounts that in 1145 Stephen led a 'formidable and numerous army of Londoners' (*Lundoniensium terribilem et numerosum adduxit exercitum*) that violently stormed the Earl of Gloucester's new castle at Faringdon, Oxfordshire (*Historia Anglorum* X, 23, Greenway 1996, 746–77). This action was a turning point in the war in that it severed communications between the Angevin heartland around Gloucestershire and the outposts in the Thames Valley (Stenton 1932, 247). Londoners were also present with Stephen at the climactic siege of Wallingford in 1152–3 (*Gesta Stephani* I, 117, Potter and Davis 1976, 226–7).

5 Brooke 1975, 34–9.

6 Green 1992.

7 Green 1992, 110–11; Yoshitake 2015, 63–6.

8 Stott 1991, 300–2.

9 Keevil 2004, 8.

10 Biddle 1976, 297–300, 318–19, 329. See also Chibnall 1991, 112–14.

11 *Gesta Stephani* I 65, Potter and Davis 1976, 130–1.

12 Biddle 1976, 389–90.

13 *Gesta Stephani* I 67, Potter and Davis 1976, 134–7.

14 Biddle 1976, 299–301.

15 Roffey 2012, 203, 211.

16 Biddle 1976, 370–1.

17 Biddle 1976, 489–508.

18 Abulafia 2011, 256–7.

19 Streit 1993, 177, 181; Hillaby 2003, 20–4.

20 Richardson 1960, 110–11. See also Creighton 2005b, 147.

21 Yarrow 2006, 130.

22 Lipman 1967; Shepherd Popescu 2009, 376–7, 961.

23 Smith 1997.

24 *The Chronicle of John of Worcester* III, McGurk 1998, 275. See also Crouch 1986, 46–7; Liddiard 2005a, 107–9.

25 *The Ecclesiastical History of Orderic Vitalis* XIII, 23, Chibnall 1978, Vol. VI, 461–2.

26 *The Ecclesiastical History of Orderic Vitalis* XIII, 26, Chibnall 1978, Vol. VI, 466–7.

27 Henry, Archdeacon of Huntingdon, *Historia Anglorum* X, 18, Greenway 1996, 739. See also Strickland 1996b, 222, 281.

28 Strickland 1996b, 222.

29 *The Ecclesiastical History of Orderic Vitalis* XIII, 37, Chibnall 1978, Vol. VI, 520–3; *The Chronicle of John of Worcester* III, McGurk 1998, 250–1.

30 Shoesmith 1980, 59; Barrow 2000, 27–9; Boucher et al. 2015, 10.

31 Creighton 2005b, 133–51.

32 Creighton 2005a, 276, 283.

33 Abrams and Shotliff 2010, 401.

34 Creighton 2005b, 155, 193; Creighton and Higham 2005, 83, 158, 257.

35 Marshall 2004a, 210; King 2002, 11.

36 Haslam 1977–78.

37 Bassett 1982, 23–4, 71, 74, 77; Andrews and Mundy 2002, 265–6; Ennis 2005a, 204; Lewis and Ranson 2013, 36–9.

38 *Gesta Stephani* I 30, Potter and Davis 1976, 43.

39 *Gesta Stephani* I 33, Potter and Davis 1976, 47.
40 O'Leary 1981, 14–15, 24.
41 Haslam 2003.
42 Haslam 2009, 107.
43 Griffiths 2011, 169.
44 King 2002, 16. See also pg. 148.
45 Beresford 1967, 331, 336.
46 Beverley Minster, East Yorkshire; St Augustine's, Canterbury; St John's, Colchester; Crowland Abbey, Lincolnshire; Eye Priory, Suffolk (at Bawsey, Norfolk); Great Bricett Priory, Suffolk; Kirkham Priory, North Yorkshire; Lincoln Cathedral (at Sleaford, Lincolnshire); Norwich Cathedral; Nostell Priory, West Yorkshire (and another at Woodkirk in Morley); Walden Priory, Essex; Winchester Cathedral; and Wymnondham Priory, Hertfordshire. See Cronne and Davis 1968, nos 44, 99, 162, 217, 252, 287, 291, 421, 476, 616, 621, 622, 914, 952, 974.
47 Cronne and Davis 1968, nos 369, 645.
48 King 1996, 10–14.
49 Beresford 1967, 504–5.
50 Shaw 1993, 24–7.
51 Beresford 1967, 452–3.
52 Cronne and Davis 1968, no. 597.
53 Salzman and Styles 1945, 45, 208.
54 Beresford 1967, 382, 467; Liddiard 2000, 58.
55 Liddiard 2005b, 39–40, 43.
56 Cronne and Davis 1968, no. 274. See also Bassett 1982, 19.
57 *The Book of the Foundation of Walden Monastery*, Greenway and Watkiss 1999, 4–5.
58 *The Book of the Foundation of Walden Monastery* I, 6, Greenway and Watkiss 1999, xv–xvi.
59 Bassett 1982, 26–7; 48–61; Lewis and Ranson 2013, 36–9.
60 Wareham 2005.
61 King 1980a, 6–7.
62 Beresford 1967, 462–3; Letters 2013.
63 Lucas 1987.
64 Creighton 1997, 31.
65 Beresford 1967, 510–11, 523–4.
66 Beresford 1967, 189, 518–19.
67 Keats-Rohan 2009, 63.
68 Page 2005, 170–71.
69 Campbell 2000, 66–7.
70 See, for example, Lewis et al. 1997; Rippon 2008; Williamson 2013.
71 See, for example, Gray 1915; Rackham 1986; Roberts and Wrathmell 2000.
72 Jones, R. 2010; Wright 2015.
73 See, for example, Austin 1987; Sherlock 2004; Daniels 2009.
74 Wade-Martins 1980; Davison et al. 1990; Williamson 2013 158–9.
75 See, for example, Hallam 1965.
76 Silvester 1988.
77 Young 1979, 11–12, 18–19; Amt 1993, 173.
78 Crook 1994, 333–4, 337–8.
79 Amt 1993, 173.
80 Creighton and Rippon forthcoming.
81 Austin 1987, 69–71.
82 Chapman 2010.
83 Meeson 2012, 60–1.
84 Walker 1999.
85 Meeson 2012, 60. See also Meeson and Welch 1993.
86 Emery 2007, 29–32. On the question of whether such structures were self-contained 'first-floor halls,' as traditionally thought, or chamber blocks that operated in tandem with (lost) ground-floor halls, see Blair 1993.
87 Amt 1993, 50–1.
88 Rahtz and Rowley 1984, 12–14, 156–7. See also Rowley 1972, 123.
89 Creighton 2005b, 24–5. 'Goltho' is given in inverted commas because it is likely that the site is medieval Bullington.
90 Creighton 2005b, 198–202; Creighton and Higham 2005, 79.
91 Addyman 1965; Lethbridge 1952.
92 See Creighton and Rippon 2016.
93 Hope-Taylor 1956, 249.

94 Creighton 2004. See also Creighton 2005b, 212–14.

95 Bond 2001. On excavations at the castle site (Jope and Threlfall 1959), see pg. 236.

96 Bond 2001, 59.

97 Jones et al. 1997.

98 Jones et al. 1997, 9–10.

99 Ennis 2011.

100 Ennis 2011, 126.

101 Biddle 1964, 65.

102 Renn 1971, 5; Bond 2001, 67–8.

103 Creighton 2005b, 212; Creighton and Higham 2005, 79. Although there is a ringwork castle site within the parish (Jordan's Castle), it is physically distant from the settlement, lying 800m north-east of the village. See Crook 2008.

104 The only excavation of the defences, a test pit dug on their eastern part in 1994, showed the bank to comprise red clay, 0.53m thick, with a buried ploughsoil beneath. A single pottery sherd was found in the upper part of the clay layer, which was broadly dated to the medieval period (Notts HER No. L11536).

105 Gover et al. 1940, 64. The Domesday entry for 'Creilage' is sometimes equated with Wellow, though it more likely corresponds to the nearby deserted village of Cratley.

106 Barley 1957; Crook 2008, 143.

107 The comparison of the landscape to a desert is made three times in 1139 and once each in 1143, 1143–44, 1146 and 1146–47. See *Gesta Stephani* I, 42, 44, 45, II, 78, 83, 95, 104, Potter and Davis 1976, 91, 95, 97, 153, 165, 187, 199.

108 Thomas 2008, 150.

109 See Roberts and Wrathmell 2002, Fig. 6.8.

110 Blanchard 2002, 39–41. See also Barrow 1985, 18.

111 Stringer 1997. See also Oram 2006, ch. 3.

112 *Gesta Stephani* II, 114, Potter and Davis 1976, 218–19.

113 Aston 1985, 93–5.

114 Stringer 1993, 4; White 2000, 323–7; Bradbury 1996, 190–3; Crouch 2000, 1–7; Matthew 2002, 127–33.

115 See, for example, Matthew 2002, 32–4.

116 Stringer 1993, 86; White 2000, 326.

117 Thomas 2008.

118 Thomas 2008, maps 2 and 4.

119 Clarke 2004; 2008; 2009.

120 Thomas 1999.

121 See, for example, Wightman 1975, 55–71; Matthews 2003, 53–70.

122 Davis 1903; Amt 1991; Thomas 1998, 150–1 and map 10.

123 White 1985; 2000, 154–7.

124 Hollister 1974, 237; 1993, 82. See also Bradbury 1996, 190–1.

125 Carlton 1992, 212.

Chapter 9

Anarchy on the Fen Edge: Case Study of the Isle of Ely

I N A PERIOD with more than its fair share of infamous characters, Geoffrey II de Mandeville, Earl of Essex from 1140, is perhaps the most disreputable of all. In J.H. Round's 1892 biography *Geoffrey de Mandeville*, the earl was 'the great champion of anarchy,'[1] the quintessential robber baron whose allegiance shifted as he sold and resold himself to the highest bidder. Authors since have been tempted into portraying him as 'the poster boy of England's "anarchy."'[2] Historians have unsurprisingly focused on Geoffrey's remarkable political career; debate has centred on the extent of his loyalty, his motives and the reasons for his downfall, the evidence hinging on charters whose dating has been vigorously contested.[3] Rather less attention has focused on the realities on the ground of Geoffrey's military involvement in the civil war – most notably, his rebellion and fenland campaign of 1143–44 that ended with his death, and a programme of castle building and aggrandisement that mirrored his meteoric rise – and its impact upon the landscape.[4] Accordingly, this case study considers the conflict landscape of the Isle of Ely and its surrounding district, which was the focus not only of Geoffrey de Mandeville's revolt but also two earlier operations, by King Stephen in 1140 and by Geoffrey and Earl Gilbert of Pembroke in 1142. Three campaigns in four years ensured that the fenland region was one of the most heavily affected in the entire civil war. The Anglo-Saxon Chronicle's generalised description of Stephen's reign as 19 winters 'when Christ and his saints slept' – perhaps the most oft-quoted snippet of primary documentary evidence for the chaos of the civil war – was written by a Peterborough monk and may well draw on local experiences of the conflict rather than capturing the situation in England more generally.[5]

This case study presents a narrative account of the three fenland campaigns of the 1140s against the background of William I's famous struggle in the same area against Hereward the Wake in 1070–71. It reconstructs the main military movements and events as a basis for examining the archaeological evidence for the network of castles that loomed large in and around this unusually complex conflict landscape.

The Isle of Ely: Context and Background

The Isle of Ely (Fig. 9.1) was a natural locus for rebellion. Today it is a 'dry island,' but it was once completely surrounded by wetland. It was freed from its physical isolation after large-scale drainage schemes in the post-medieval period.[6] In the later medieval period, the mosaic of waterways, rivers and reclaimed land provided some of England's richest agricultural land, and valuable fisheries and salterns, over which the region's monasteries vied for control.[7] Causeways, low rises and promontories were critically important for military control of this fenland landscape, which presented unusual challenges for commanders. Archaeology has shown that strategic networks of enclosures related to causeways were present by late prehistory, as exemplified by the Wardy Hill 'system' on the north of the Isle.[8] Somewhat paradoxically, while concerns of defence, war and social status have been central to prehistorians' research on the fens, study of the documented conflict landscapes of the eleventh and twelfth centuries is comparatively poorly developed.

In the early medieval period, the fens were seen as a liminal or intermediate zone, lying on the periphery of political and spiritual jurisdiction. During the Middle Saxon period, the zone developed as the interface between the Mercians, the East Anglians and, to a lesser extent, the Anglians. A series of early monasteries was constructed by the Mercians and East Angles on either side of the fens; Mercian kings founded a network of minsters along the western fen edge between Peterborough and Crowland from the middle of the seventh century, while East Anglian claims to the lowlands were forwarded by the development of Ely and Soham.[9] In addition to their political marginality, the wetlands were also viewed as ideologically peripheral; the life of Saint Guthlac describes how at the end of the seventh century the hermit chose a tumulus in the Cambridgeshire fens as his spiritual desert but was beleaguered by evil spirits, terrible cohorts of foul spirits and monsters.[10] While the twelfth-century chroniclers of fenland monasteries were keen to assert the pleasant and productive

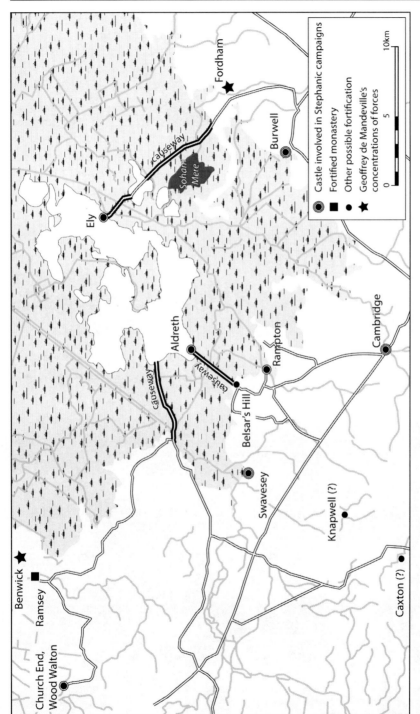

Fig. 9.1: Reconstruction of the Isle of Ely in the mid-twelfth century and the principal castles involved in the Stephanic campaigns. Drawing by Seán Goddard and Duncan Wright.

qualities of the landscapes they inhabited, such devices only served to demonstrate the economic and spiritual accomplishment of taming these regions.[11] In the case of Ely, the ultimate fame and success of the abbey (Fig. 9.2), which became a cathedral in 1109, were heightened by its isolated topographical setting, so that this was recognised as a 'holy island' as well as a liminal zone.

Documentary sources are useful in providing an insight into how Ely and its surrounding fenland were understood in the twelfth century, but it is the archaeological evidence that is most informative when attempting to reconstruct the character of settlement and land use on the Isle. The city of Ely itself has been described as 'purely

Fig 9.2: Ely Cathedral. Photograph by Oliver Creighton.

rural' in the late eleventh century, and even 'largely rural, though with marked urban beginnings' in the mid-thirteenth.[12] This strict division between 'rural' and 'urban' may not be entirely helpful, however, and it is clear that the minster at Ely was already stimulating settlement growth in the eighth century, various outlying dependent farms developing to sustain the needs of the clerical community. Polyfocal settlement patterns such as these may leave a less substantial individual archaeological signatures, but together their economic output would have been significant and their yields would have proved attractive to commanders seeking to sustain their troops. Elsewhere on the Isle, Domesday Book records manors at Haddenham, Little Thetford and Wilburton among others, and by the twelfth century it was probably as settled as the fen edge, which archaeological and written sources indicate was increasingly populated from the eighth century onwards.[13]

Assault on Ely: 1070–71, 1140 and 1142

That the Isle of Ely presented unique opportunities for occupying forces and severe challenges for those attempting to attack it is exemplified by William I's protracted campaign against Hereward the Wake in 1070–71, which was instrumental in cementing the Isle's enduring image as a rebel bastion. The king's operation stalled in the face of the rebels' occupation of a marshland archipelago landscape dotted with lakes and criss-crossed by treacherous fast-flowing streams disguised by reed beds. The all-important causeways that provided access to the island (see Fig. 9.1) were narrow, hindering cavalry movements and thus nullifying a key Norman strength.[14] Naval operations were rare in the Anglo-Norman military system, but the Anglo-Saxon Chronicle makes it clear that William's campaign employed both a 'land force' and 'naval force,' and Florence of Worcester says that the king stormed the Isle using *butescarls* – Anglo-Saxon royal marines.[15]

Having finally captured the island and crushed the rebellion after several failed attacks across the Aldreth causeway, parts of which were apparently built anew, William enhanced the already considerable natural strength of the Isle by erecting two fortifications that featured prominently in the campaigns of the 1140s. That William 'allocated a site for a fortress within the monks' precincts' at Ely in 1071, to be built by people of the shires of Cambridge, Huntingdon and Bedford, shows us that the fortification of ecclesiastical sites was not restricted to the Anarchy.[16] He also garrisoned a fortress at

Aldreth, which commanded the southern causeway onto the island and was to prove militarily the more important of the two sites. The centrality of the causeway and fortification at Aldreth (*Alreheðe* or *Alhereðe* in the *Liber Eliensis*, or *Book of Ely*) to control of the island is clear. Forming part of a long-distance route linking Cambridge and Ely known as the Portway, it was one of only three overland access points onto the Isle before the draining of the fens, and the most direct point of access from the south. On the Isle's eastern side, the Stuntney Causeway connected it to the village of Soham, and to the west the Earith Causeway traversed Haddenham Fen.[17] The significance of the Portway as an arterial route was enduring: archaeological evidence confirms that the Aldreth causeway has prehistoric origins,[18] and the crossing over the Great Ouse at Aldreth High Bridge, 1.2km south-west of Aldreth village, is the only medieval bridge in the county outside of Cambridge.[19]

The importance of Aldreth Castle and causeway is one of many areas of similarity between William the Conqueror's campaign of 1070–71 and those of the 1140s, and over time these events blurred together in memory. It is surely no coincidence that Geoffrey Gaimar's famous poem, *Estoire des Engleis*, which details the exploits of Hereward the Wake, was composed in the late 1140s. Gaimar was probably influenced by the recent and ongoing events of the Anarchy, drawing upon knowledge of twelfth-century guerrilla warfare to construct an outlaw narrative in which Hereward's noble actions and values made a powerful statement about the corruption of the present.[20] This folkloric image of the Isle as a marshland fortress was essential to the conceptual construction of it as a special place.[21] This was magnified further by the events of the 1140s.

We can reconstruct only the essentials of King Stephen's assault on Ely in January 1140, which saw Bishop Nigel dramatically driven from his see. Nigel had rebelled in 1139, holding Devizes Castle, a property of his uncle, Bishop Roger of Salisbury, against the king. Stephen had turned on Nigel following Bishop Roger's death: in the words of Henry of Huntingdon, the king's 'feelings of hatred ... had now extended to his [Roger's] kin.'[22] The rebellion saw the Isle of Ely militarised once again, although the compiler of the *Liber Eliensis* is at pains to stress that the island's two fortifications were both initiatives of Bishop Nigel; he had positioned at Ely 'a very strong fortress ... built of stone and cement' which, due to the holy power of Aethelthryth, kept collapsing, and constructed another wooden fortress surrounded with a rampart 'near the river.'[23] While the latter is clearly a reactivation of the castle at Aldreth on the southern causeway, it is unclear whether the bishop's fortification at Ely was a rebuilding of William I's earlier castle or was an early version of the bishop's palace attached to the cathedral (Fig. 9.2). Investigation of the surviving motte and bailey known as Cherry Hill in the corner of Cathedral Park has revealed no sign of stonework; the castle was certainly abandoned as a fortification by the thirteenth century, when its mound supported the monks' windmill, and it was probably decommissioned and pulled down by Henry II, which may explain the lack of ditch around the motte.[24]

King Stephen used amphibious warfare to storm Ely via the Aldreth route from the south, having first paused to reconnoitre 'the wonderful and unconquerable fortifications of the place.'[25] Employing a chain of boats laid side by side and surmounted with a platform of wicker hurdles, he created a pontoon bridge so that mounted knights could cross a stretch of shallow water.[26] That Stephen's plan of attack was identical to William I's 70 years earlier shows the restrictive effects of fenland geography on military strategy, although there may be symbolic undertones in how the king followed the Conqueror's example, and chroniclers may have conflated the two actions. The accounts of Stephen's attack in the *Gesta Stephani* and the *Liber Eliensis* suggest that there was a landing place on raised ground to the south of Aldreth, separated from the Isle's shoreline by open water.[27] The place name Aldreth means 'landing-place by the alders.'[28] As has been demonstrated, the causeway was a feature of long-standing significance and Stephen's actions must indicate repair or refurbishment of its northern extremity.[29] The rapid entry of the royal army onto the Isle triggered a rout in which many soldiers were wounded and others captured, and Bishop Nigel fled westward 'like a hireling' to join the Empress in Gloucestershire.[30] The king secured the island by garrisoning his own troops in the castle at Aldreth once the bishop's knights had been ejected.[31]

The second, and rather more scantily documented, Anarchy-period campaign on the Isle occurred early in 1142, when the king dispatched Geoffrey de Mandeville and Gilbert, Earl of Pembroke with a troop of soldiers to again disperse Bishop Nigel's supporters, who were using the island as a muster point. The political context of this expedition was Stephen's reassertion of his rights in the wake of his release from captivity in November 1141, keen to nip another potential fenland uprising in the bud.[32] The action was briefer than in 1140: 'arriving in haste,' the earls put the 'common soldiery' to flight but captured the knights and paraded them to Ely on horseback, suggesting that the attack once again came through Aldreth across the causeway.[33] Outstaying any unlikely welcome, Geoffrey soon turned on the monks, 'raging and threatening their death and the laying waste of the holy place' and forcing them to petition the king. Stephen instructed that the monks should be allowed to hold their estates peacefully, and forced Geoffrey's commanders to return rents owed to them.[34] The earl's presence was temporary; within months Bishop Nigel was restored peacefully, taking control of his bishopric 'together with the fortress of Aldreth,' and set about righting perceived wrongs.[35]

In all these events, the principal 'fighting castle' of the Isle and the strategic key to the island was Aldreth; chroniclers consistently associated possession of Aldreth Castle with control of Ely itself. The compiler of the *Liber Eliensis* tended to differentiate the *praesidium* at Ely, which lay within the bounds of the abbey, from the fortification at Aldreth, which was more usually identified with the word *castellum*.[36] The *Gesta Stephani* does not name Aldreth Castle as such but the vivid description of the fortification's landscape setting is sufficiently detailed to suggest an eyewitness account: it was 'a castle, wondrously set, long since, right in the water in the middle of the opening of the track.'[37] Despite this precise geographical information, the location of Aldreth Castle remains to be clearly identified. No earthwork within or near the village of Aldreth presents itself and the fortification – evidently a timber castle, perhaps a ringwork – may have been built over.

Another possibility is that the documented castle of Aldreth can be equated with the 'hill' fort known as Belsar's Hill, commanding the landward (southern) approach to the 3.5km-long causeway. Belsar's Hill is an oval fortified enclosure, located on a slight spur extending northward into the fens. Before enclosure in the mid-nineteenth century, access onto the causeway from this direction skirted around the perimeter of the fort's ramparted and ditched defences.[38] First recorded in the early thirteenth century, the place name is apparently derived from the Old French *bel assis* ('well seated/placed') and the site is traditionally identified as the point of departure for William the Conqueror's attack on Ely.[39] It is unlikely that such an inherently strategic location was not garrisoned or even refurbished in the three campaigns of the twelfth century. Belsar's Hill is a univallate enclosure of Iron Age form, and any medieval military occupation phase would have reused it as a bridgehead with considerable potential given that the eroded bank still stands *c.* 2m high and that it was originally circumvallated with a moat.[40] Although geophysical survey does not reveal any internal features that may relate to twelfth-century fortification, such elements are likely to have been focused around the bridgehead part of the enclosure, which was largely destroyed during construction of a modern trackway. Other than the castles, archaeological evidence for the campaigns is minimal to non-existent. Groups of spearheads dredged from the rivers and drainage channels around the Isle of Ely, including from the strategically important crossing at Braham Dock, have been claimed as evidence of William the Conqueror's campaign here,[41] but would be indistinguishable from types used in the mid-twelfth century.

1143–44: Geoffrey de Mandeville's Fenland Campaign

The peace on the Isle lasted little more than a year. The catalyst for further upheaval was Geoffrey de Mandeville's dramatic arrest by the king at court in St Albans in September 1143, which coincided with Bishop Nigel's absence in Rome, where he sought to petition the Pope. Having been transported to London, Earl Geoffrey was forced to give up his castles of Pleshey and (Saffron) Walden, both in Essex, as well as the Tower of London, of which he was the constable, in return for his life and liberty.[42] Historians have debated the king's motives, which were not transparent. In the eyes of the chroniclers, Geoffrey had acted with presumptuous quasi-royal authority and a rumour surfaced that he was plotting for the Angevin cause, while Stephen might also have held a personal grudge relating to Geoffrey's treatment of his son Eustace's wife, Constance, during the king's captivity. Quite why Stephen delayed his decisive action against the earl is less clear.[43] Another factor in Stephen's move against Geoffrey must have been the military value of the earl's castles which, in the words of the *Gesta Stephani*, were 'built round the city' of London.[44] In the wrong hands, they could tip the balance of power.

At this point it is worth summarising the extent of Geoffrey de Mandeville's territorial power in 1143. The de Mandevilles' hereditary power base had been focused in central and north-west Essex, where Geoffrey I de Mandeville had received a large and valuable block of estates around Pleshey, which became the *caput* of the de Mandeville honour and the venue for the honorial court.[45] The motte-and-bailey castle here was powerfully defended and an attached semi-circular enclosure of 16 hectares embraced an attendant settlement planted in the late eleventh or early twelfth century.[46] Geoffrey II de Mandeville had gained the resumption of the manors of Walden, along with Great

Waltham and Sawbridgeworth, early in Stephen's reign, perhaps in 1136, and rapidly transformed Walden into the new *caput* of his holdings, complete with the triumvirate of new stone castle, priory and market, the settlement at the foot of the castle enclosed with ditched defences (for full discussion, see pg. 110).[47]

The chronology of the four charters through which Geoffrey rose dramatically to the peak of his influence (two of Stephen, usually identified as S1 and S2, and two of the Empress, M1 and M2) has been subject to intense debate. While this has an important bearing on interpretations of Geoffrey's allegiance and motivation, the state of his power base at the time of his downfall and rebellion in 1143 can be reconstructed securely.[48] Having been made Earl of Essex by Stephen in 1140, by which stage he had also regained his ancestral constableship of the Tower of London,[49] Geoffrey's political ascent elevated him to the status of a 'super earl.'[50] The Empress's first charter, which is generally dated to midsummer 1141, recognised Geoffrey's right to the earldom and granted him the hereditary shrievalty and chief justiciarship of Essex along with other properties.[51] Later that summer the Empress granted him additional lands and honours, including the lands of his grandfather Eudo de Ryes and Eudo's office of royal *dapifer* (steward),[52] while Stephen's second charter in Christmas 1141 gave Geoffrey further generous grants and lands and granted him constableship of the Tower.[53] Geoffrey's much more modest new timber castle at South Mimms, Hertfordshire, appears to have served primarily as a hunting seat rather than as a fortification of strategic value: lying on the very edge of de Mandeville's estates and those of St Albans, it was also just hidden out of view from the cathedral town on a 'false crest' (see pgs 100–1 for full discussion).[54]

The outbreak of the rebellion

Entering into open rebellion following his release from captivity in autumn 1143, Geoffrey took advantage of the power vacuum on Ely. According to the *Liber Eliensis*, the men guarding the Isle 'gave admittance' to the earl, putting the fortifications at Ely and Aldreth under his control, although a later mandate of the Pope to the Archbishop of England in favour of Bishop Nigel recorded in the same source says that Geoffrey 'forcibly usurped the Isle of Ely … and took possession of certain fortresses on it,' distributing estates among his followers.[55] Geoffrey had prior knowledge of the area's defences from his 1142 campaign and he would have been well aware of these sites' strategic importance. The *Waltham Chronicle* also provides details of a mini civil war between Geoffrey and William d'Aubigny, Earl of Arundel, which can probably be dated to late 1143. William seems to have been the aggressor: he had fired houses on one of Geoffrey's manors and plundered his estates, in revenge for which the Earl of Essex attacked the vill of Waltham, on the border between their spheres of influence, and burned down houses, including that of the Waltham chronicler himself.[56] The brethren of Waltham responded to this desecration by taking down the holy cross – a ritual act of protest known as the 'humiliation of the saints' in which a holy cross was laid on the ground until restitution was forthcoming.[57]

While the chronology of Geoffrey's movements during the rebellion is difficult to reconstruct in detail, an initial target was Ramsey Abbey, west of the Isle, to which he moved by boat.[58] Taking advantage of a dispute between Abbot Daniel, who had been installed by the king, and his displaced predecessor Walter, Earl Geoffrey expelled the monks and used the abbey as a castle and raiding base after plundering the church of its treasure and relics.[59] Henry of Huntingdon claimed to have personally observed the walls of the abbey church and cloister exuding blood,[60] while the *Chronicle of Ramsey Abbey* records how de Mandeville's troops refused to leave the fortified abbey and threatened the abbot with murder, while he in turn burned their tents.[61] On this occasion there is good reason to think that the monastic complex at Ramsey was physically defended by Geoffrey's men, with a motte ('Booths Hill') superimposed into the precinct,[62] rather than that the abbey's 'conversion' into a castle implying only that it was garrisoned (for full discussion, see pg. 206). Geoffrey's actions opened the floodgates for others to wreak havoc on Ramsey's estates: a letter of Archbishop Theobald that can probably be dated to 1143 contains a mandate to Robert Foliot, Walter de Wahull and others to desist from their depredations of the abbey.[63] It is for these actions that Geoffrey was excommunicated and, crucially, it is within this context that we should interpret the chroniclers' accounts of his rebellion, the fact that Geoffrey died unabsolved amplifying Stephen's ultimate success in the campaign.[64]

Another de Mandeville raid early in the campaign targeted Cambridge, plundering then firing churches in the city and its hinterland but not occupying the settlement.[65] The state of Cambridge's fortifications rendered it vulnerable; the city's pre-Conquest ditched defences were not remodelled until the thirteenth century, and the royal motte and bailey, not yet renewed in stone, formed the principal defensive structure.[66] The sheriff was still receiving 'allowance for waste' in

1156.[67] St Ives, Cambridgeshire (formerly Huntingdonshire), seems also to have been raided.[68]

Geoffrey and his commanders then sought to consolidate their position by militarising the district with fortified positions, not all of which can be equated with castles. He garrisoned Benwick, north-east of Ramsey, 'at the very crossing point of the waters,' and then usurped and secured Fordham, on the opposite (south-east) side of the Isle, with a 'strong band of knights.'[69] The geostrategic value of both locations is clear. While the heartland of the rebellion was the Isle itself, Geoffrey's key bases were around its peripheries, safeguarding the causeway routes in and out of the island. Fordham secured the link to real or potential allies in East Anglia, in particular Hugh Bigod, and could also have controlled access from the south onto Stuntney Causeway, while Benwick was the link to Ramsey. Geoffrey's forces controlled another castle, this one perhaps purpose-built, at (Wood) Walton, to the south-west of Ramsey, as documented fleetingly in the *Chronicle of Ramsey Abbey* (for discussion of the site's archaeology, see below, pg. 274). Upon Geoffrey's death later in the campaign, his eldest and illegitimate son, Ernulf de Mandeville, consented to withdraw his soldiers from Ramsey Abbey 'to the castle of Walton, which he had built' (*qui castellum quoddam fecerat apud Waltone*).[70] This reminds us that Geoffrey was not acting alone and that his forces were dispersed. His son commanded a separate detachment and another was led by William de Say, husband of his sister Beatrice, who might have instigated the attack on Ramsey.[71] Other lieutenants are remembered by the chroniclers for their comeuppance: Reimer, leader of a contingent of infantry, was set adrift on the sea and sucked into a whirlpool after the war, while an unnamed cavalry commander dashed his brains out falling from his horse.[72] That separate infantry and cavalry commanders are named might reflect the existence of a marshal and constable.[73]

With de Mandeville' forces moving like 'a spider in its web,'[74] the region's broken geography ensured that the earl could not readily be brought to battle when Stephen arrived in the district early in 1144. To the military historian John Beeler, the actions of Geoffrey de Mandeville and Stephen's military response in 1143–44 were a case study of the sophistication of medieval generalship.[75] We may overestimate Geoffrey's strategic gifts, however. *The Book of the Foundation of Walden Monastery* specifies that the earl 'first assailed manors, villages and other things belonging to the king's estates,'[76] and it is worth considering the extent to which his actions were driven by opportunism and vindictiveness against the king as much as overarching strategy. The earl made no effort to regain his castles and estates, as far as we can tell; his occupation at Ramsey exploited the fact that Abbot Walter had been replaced with the Stephanic loyalist Daniel; the raid on Cambridge targeted an obvious royal property; and the base at Fordham took over another valuable royal estate.[77] The consequences of the campaign for the region are not in doubt:

> For twenty or thirty miles there was no ox, no ploughman to be found tilling the smallest piece of land. One could scarcely buy the tiniest measure [of corn] for two hundred pence, and, so great was the human disaster that followed from the scarcity of bread that, throughout the lanes and streets, people lay dead in hundreds and thousands, swollen like [wine]skins, and their corpses were left unburied for the wild beasts and birds.[78]

Another vivid allusion to the devastation is Gervase of Canterbury's description of Geoffrey's journey to Burwell: *en route* he stopped to rest due to the heat and the green grass wilted beneath him and did not recover for another year.[79] The language is derived from Mark 4:6 ('when the sun came up, the plants were scorched, and they withered because they had no root'), emphasising the illegal nature of de Mandeville's rebellion and justifying his status as outlaw and excommunicate.

The impact of warfare on agricultural production would have been particularly pronounced on the fens because of the finely balanced mixed farming economies typical of these townships. While the diverse resources of the fens had attracted significant levels of settlement from the prehistoric period, even in the twelfth century only limited areas of land were suitable for arable and these zones were reliant on a drainage system to produce successful yields.[80] A lack of maintenance or damage to this system of channels could quickly tip a wide area into disaster.[81] The campaign had longer-term consequences too. The mid-twelfth century was a watershed in the organisation of Ramsey Abbey's estates: either as a direct result of Geoffrey de Mandeville's exactions or due to post-war reconstruction, the abbey's properties were alienated. According to J. Ambrose Raftis, in his monumental economic history of the abbey, 'the beginning of this decadence in manorial policy must likely be sought in the Civil War.'[82]

1144: Stephen's intervention

The context of Stephen's programme of castle building against Geoffrey in 1144 is summarised in the *Gesta Stephani*: 'the king, in a judicious attempt to hinder his wonted raids in the same region, built castles in suitable places (*locis oportunis*) and, after garrisoning them adequately for resistance to the devastators of the country, turned in another direction to deal with other affairs of the realm.'[83] In meeting this threat, Stephen had to depart from the standard Anglo-Norman strategy of closely blockading a foe with small siege castles. In this context the enemy could not be seen and the king's presence could not be maintained with small garrisons in ringworks. Instead a network of campaign fortresses much larger in extent and more permanent in presence was necessary. This programme of castle building is probably the clearest example of a unified strategy in pursuit of a single military objective from any context in medieval England.[84] Whether Stephen's network of castles was intended to 'ring' the Isle of Ely[85] is another matter; rather, they blocked specific causeways and overlooked thoroughfares while forming a screen that isolated the heartland of de Mandeville's rebellion from his estates and nearest allies, with local factors influencing the location of each installation. Further afield, a transferral of knights' dues to perform castle guard at the royal castle at Norwich to the town of Bury St Edmunds can be dated no more closely than 1139–46, but may indicate a further security response.[86]

Further historical references to the castles built by Stephen are fleeting and occur only in the context of Geoffrey's death after receiving a fatal wound at Burwell, Cambridgeshire. The *Liber Eliensis* is unsurprisingly inward-looking and silent on castles outside the Isle.[87] The fullest account of the events at Burwell is provided by Gervase of Canterbury. He describes how Geoffrey's death occurred after he had hurried to the siege of the castle of Burwell (*castelli de Burwelle*), which had been built by the king; in an act of impetuosity he removed his helmet and was struck in the head by an arrow.[88] The *Chronicle of Ramsey Abbey* provides little additional detail but confirms that the castle of Burwell was newly built (*de nova fuerat constructum*) and that the archer (*Sagittarius*) who fired the fatal arrow at Geoffrey de Mandeville was one of those 'inside the castle' (*intra castellum*).[89] The wound proved fatal and he died at Mildenhall, 15km north-east of Burwell, perhaps attempting to withdraw to his allies in the east. It is important to underline that while it is clear from these historical sources that the castle at Burwell was a *de novo* construction, no chronicler makes any reference to the fortification being unfinished or attacked while still being constructed, as is sometimes asserted.[90] Burwell Castle is a site of exceptional significance for our understanding of twelfth-century warfare and castle building. In a period when correlating

Fig 9.3: Burwell Castle under archaeological survey in 2014, showing the medieval spoil heaps on the edge of the unfinished castle earthworks. Photograph by Oliver Creighton.

documented castles with actual evidence on the ground is hazardous in the extreme, here we have a site whose date of construction seems crystal clear, but also where conditions of archaeological preservation are excellent, the castle earthworks standing under pasture on the edge of Burwell village (Fig. 9.3). A full account of the site's archaeology is therefore the centrepiece of the following account of the castles of the campaign.

Burwell: an unfinished campaign castle

The earthwork remains of Burwell Castle (Figs 1.3 and 9.3) are located in the south-western part of Burwell village, approximately 120m west of the parish church of St Mary's, in a paddock known as Spring Close. While the written sources furnish us with the barest details of the castle's construction, archaeological evidence provides information on the character of twelfth-century castle building and the nature of pre-castle and post-castle developments, as well as insight into the military and symbolic purposes of the fortification.

Burwell was a central place in the communication network of the south-eastern fen edge: the castle site occupied a low island alongside the main thoroughfare to Stuntney Causeway, while the village lay at the head of a lode connecting to the River Cam that seems to have been constructed in Roman period.[91] But the royal castle builders may also have been aware of Burwell's importance as the location of the meeting place for the Staploe hundred. The place name Staploe and cognate terms are mentioned in documents relating to Burwell from the twelfth century, and is derived from the Old English *stapol-hoh*, which refers to a projection of land with a pillar or post on it.[92] *Stapol* names are associated with both assembly points and early cult centres.[93] Such assembly points were often assimilated into the administrative network of Anglo-Saxon royal government, and by the time Burwell is first referenced in documentary sources it is as the centre of a private estate

Fig 9.4: Results of geophysical survey at Burwell Castle:
(a) *below* resistivity; (b) *opposite* resistivity interpretation; (c) *page 268* magnetometry; (d) *page 269* magnetometry interpretation. Source: © Anarchy? War and Status Project; map work by Steven Trick and Michael Fradley.

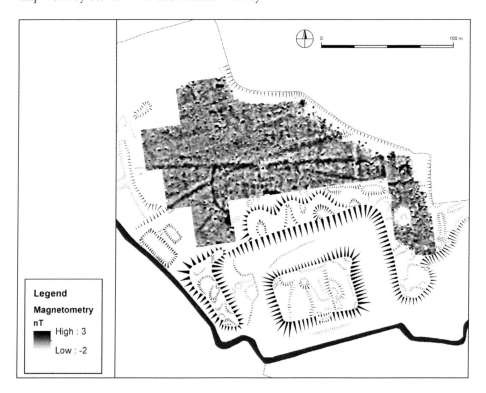

held by the *thegn* Aelfgar. The exact location of Aelfgar's residence, which was granted to Ramsey Abbey in 990 along with his estate, cannot be certain, but place name evidence forwards Spring Close as the likeliest candidate. The *burh* in the place name Burwell ('*burh* by the spring or well'),[94] may well refer to Aelfgar's residence. Spring Close seems the prime contender as the site of the thegnly court, as there is still a spring adjacent to St Mary's church in an area shown by archaeological investigation to be delineated by an enclosure that is likely to represent the remnants of Aelfgar's precinct. The feature survives partly as an earthwork and is traceable as a geophysical anomaly (Fig. 9.4), delimiting an oval precinct around the castle site and church (see also Fig. 1.3). An earlier phase of activity is indicated by a likely Roman temple complex identified by geophysical survey as lying beneath the castle. This can be seen on the magnetometry plot (Fig. 9.4c–d) as a square or rectangular feature projecting northward from the castle earthworks, and provides a likely explanation for the large volumes of Roman material recovered on early excavations of the site.[95]

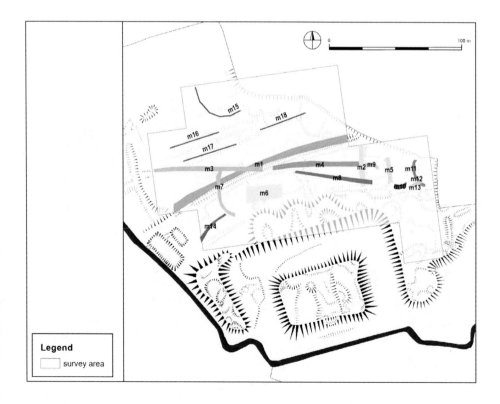

Thus by the time Stephen and his commanders arrived in the region in the 1140s, Burwell already had a long and prestigious history as a central place of great significance, and control of it may have been synonymous with power and authority over the locality. The form of the site, as revealed by detailed topographic and geophysical survey,[96] and excavations by T.C. Lethbridge in the 1930s,[97] is worth summarising in detail. The enclosure at Burwell Castle consists of a raised sub-rectangular platform measuring around 30m by 60m, orientated east-north-east by west-south-west on its long axis (Figs 9.4 and 9.5). It is surrounded by a large rectangular ditch up to 30m in width, its base 4–6m below the platform. This central platform appears to have been furnished with a rectangular tower measuring 6.4m x 4.8m internally and possessing stone-built foundations. It is likely that this structure was integrated into a stone curtain wall that extended around all sides of the castle mound. Dating these structural elements

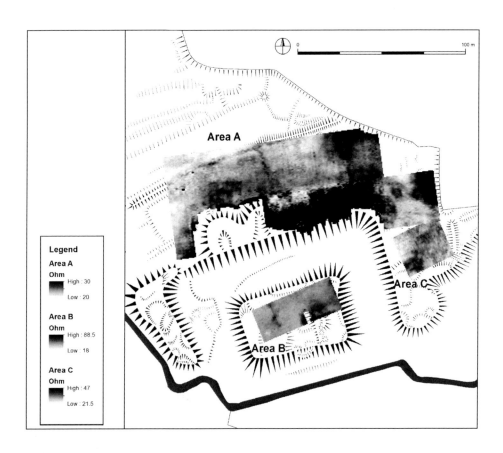

to a specific chronological period requires caution, and is complicated by the later use of the central castle platform as the site of a chapel and the residence of the Abbot of Ramsey. Excavating the stone-built tower and walls, Lethbridge was nevertheless confident that they represented Anarchy-period features that were only later adapted and enhanced in order to meet the needs of the clerical site.[98]

Despite being furnished with at least the initial foundations of stone defences, the archaeological evidence demonstrates that castle building at Burwell ceased before completion. A series of large irregular mounds situated along the outer western and northern sides of the castle (Figs 9.3 and 9.5) are spoil heaps derived from material excavated from the castle ditches. It seems that the original intention of the builders was to subsequently remove this spoil as part of the construction process, given that sections of the mounds overlook the central castle platform.[99] Earthworks immediately north of the

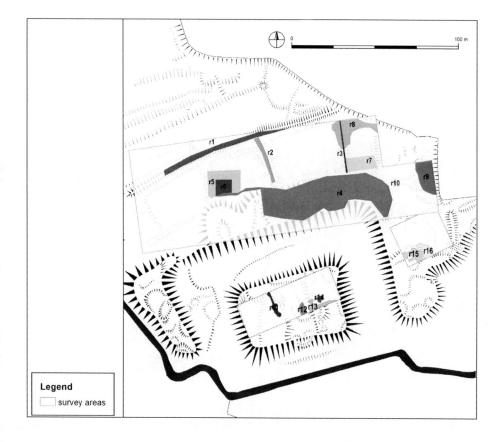

Legend

□ survey areas

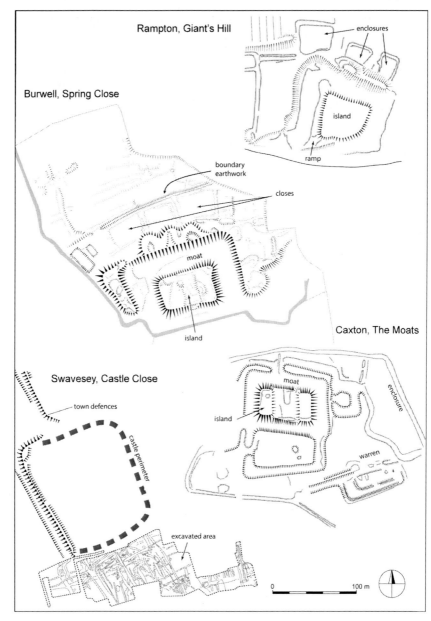

Rampton, Giant's Hill

enclosures

Burwell, Spring Close

island

ramp

boundary
earthwork

closes

moat

island

Caxton, The Moats

Swavesey, Castle Close

moat

enclosure

town defences

island

castle perimeter

warren

excavated area

0   100 m

Fig 9.5: Comparative plans of castle sites at Burwell, Caxton, Rampton and Swavesey. Source: Swavesey based on Spoerry 2005; Caxton on RCHME Cambs I 1968; others sites are original surveys © Anarchy? War and Status Project.

Fig 9.6: Reconstruction of Burwell Castle under construction in 1143–44, showing its likely imposition within a thegnly precinct incorporating the church. Drawing by Richard Parker.

spoil mounds are generally regarded as tofts and crofts abandoned when castle construction commenced.[100] These features do not project underneath the castle as earlier investigations asserted, however, but are instead bounded to the south by banks and scarps which also form the northern extent of the castle complex. Furthermore, the earthwork forms are not typical of a medieval toft and croft arrangement and geophysics show no evidence of internal occupation within the contended house plots. Rather, the network of enclosures bears closer comparison to Middle Saxon and later examples excavated at West Fen Road, Ely, and it is possible that at Burwell these elements represent paddocks of mixed function associated with the thegnly residence, bounded along their northern extent by the bank and ditch of the precinct.[101] It is therefore likely that the castle at Burwell was inserted into a pre-existing thegnly *curia*, in a process recognised at other elite Late Saxon residences such as Goltho, Lincolnshire and Trowbridge, Wiltshire (see pgs 97–8).[102] A reconstruction of the castle under construction, and supplanting this putative thegnly power base, is offered in Figure 9.6.

Other Stephanic campaign castles

The reference in the *Gesta Stephani* to King Stephen building multiple castles against Geoffrey de Mandeville has prompted archaeologists and historians to identify several other sites in the region as products of the campaign.[103] Three candidates bear serious scrutiny: Rampton, Caxton Moats and Swavesey (all Cambridgeshire) (Fig. 9.5; for locations see Fig. 9.1), as detailed below. Others are far less compelling as they stand too far from the locus of operations. On the grounds of a superficial morphological resemblance to Burwell, the sites of Eaton Socon, Cambridgeshire, and Weeting, Norfolk, have been suggested to date from the operation,[104] as has Lidgate, Norfolk, which overlooks the Icknield Way but takes the form of a motte and bailey, the latter enveloping the churchyard.[105] Some or all of these castles will have mid-twelfth-century origins or phases, but none can confidently be identified as part of Stephen's strategy.

The site of Giant's Hill, Rampton (Fig. 9.5), has been identified by several commentators as one of King Stephen's campaign castles, largely due to the monument's similar form to that at Burwell and the earthwork's strategic setting close to the southern end of the Aldreth causeway.[106] Close study of the earthworks at Rampton reveals some important distinctions, however, as the form bears traces of its later adaptation as a moated manorial site of the de l'Isle family, and excavators digging foundations for a spigot mortar emplacement in 1942 found rubble and bricks which they believed most likely dated from the fifteenth century.[107] Giant's Hill does possess a central mound surrounded by a ditch, although of trapezoidal form and smaller than Burwell. The ditch is partially blocked at its south-west corner by an earthwork ramp that is presumably related to the site's construction and hints that the castle may have been unfinished. Earthworks to the north of this main complex previously identified as a pre-castle settlement seem more likely to be related to later manorial structures. The focus of twelfth-century, and probably earlier, occupation instead appears to have been located between Giant's Hill and the church of All Saints, 150m to the west, as earthworks typical of medieval settlement are bounded to the north by apparently contemporaneous ridge and furrow.

The second site is 'The Moats' at Caxton (Fig. 9.5), an isolated position within a shallow valley but with views over the old Roman Road of Ermine Street. The ground plan of the principal moat is a carbon copy of Burwell, with a rectangular moated island of identical proportions and platforms raised at either end in the same manner.

The resemblance is too close to be coincidental and could suggest that Stephen's engineers and builders were working to a common blueprint, although it may well have been a manorial centre before the mid-twelfth century and was certainly redeveloped as one in the later medieval centuries. Evidence for the site's adaptation as a later moated manorial residence is apparent in the system of associated paddocks, enclosures, fish ponds and a warren, and in the fourteenth century the site was the dower house for the manor.[108]

The third possible addition to Stephen's campaign castles is the fortification at Swavesey known as Castle Close, occupying a rectangular enclosure on the west side of the town's ditched defences and apparently planned over open fields (Fig. 9.5).[109] There is a tradition that this was a later medieval castle of the Zouch family.[110] This is mistaken, as the fortification was disused by *c.* 1200, when it was incorporated into the town defences and flood defence system.[111] The castle has also been attributed an Anarchy-period date,[112] although an immediate post-Conquest context cannot be ruled out. The strategic context is significant, as Swavesey was a dock and small port in the twelfth century, the castle occupying a low island jutting out into the fenland. The town plan suggests that castle building blocked off one of the roads (the route now known as Taylor's Lane), which was diverted around it. Excavation of a large area to the south of the castle in the late 1990s showed that the insertion of the castle coincided with a major rearrangement of settlement topography and the replacement of early drainage ditches with more permanent boundaries,[113] thereby paralleling the disruptive impact of the castle at Burwell.

Campaign castles of Geoffrey de Mandeville

Besides Ramsey Abbey, the only fortification in the Ely area associated with Geoffrey de Mandeville for which we have direct archaeo-logical evidence is the site known as Castle Hill at (Wood) Walton, Huntingdonshire (Plate 19), to which Geoffrey's son Ernulf withdrew at the end of the campaign. The castle was one component within a dispersed and fluid medieval settlement pattern on the fen edge: the shrunken hamlet of Church End, within which the castle earthworks are set, lies 600m north-north-east of the parish church, while the larger focus of Wood Walton lies *c.* 2km to the south of the castle and also displays evidence of shrinkage.[114] In the medieval period the low promontory of Castle Hill projected out into the fenland to the north. The fenland canal known as 'Monk's Lode' terminates immediately to the west, although this seems to have been first cut in the late twelfth century by the clerics of Sawtry Abbey, by which point the castle was probably disused.[115]

The castle earthworks at Church End are part of an unusual and clearly multiphase complex including fish ponds and relict cultivation remains.[116] Phasing is presented in the inset of Plate 19. At the crest of the hill, the core of the castle site comprises a partial ringwork, which was either left unfinished or was else slighted, with a section of ditch infilled and its bank levelled. A large sub-oval enclosure running around the base of the hill and measuring *c.* 180m east–west by *c.* 120m north–south is part of an earlier feature rather than the bailey enclosure it has sometimes been identified as. This may well represent a pre-castle manorial enclosure, in the manner of Burwell, and both earthwork and geophysical survey demonstrate that the unit was subdivided, perhaps indicative of individual tenement plots or paddocks of a similar form to examples excavated at nearby Cottenham, where a radial network of enclosures was developed around a focal point as early as the seventh century.[117] It is by no means certain that the ringwork was constructed *de novo* by the de Mandevilles; it may alternatively have been established by the de Bolebec family, who held the manor of Walton from 1086 until 1134, or the de Sellas, who seized and claimed the manor early in the civil war.[118] On balance, an Anarchy-period fortification of an extant manorial compound seems the most likely scenario. The castle's decommissioning after the fenland campaign removed a symbol of political rebellion, while the establishment of Sawtry Abbey in the neighbouring manor was part of the same very public strategy of restoring order to a devastated zone through religious endowment by a man loyal to the king, Simon de Senlis.[119]

Another diminutive timber castle whose construction has been attributed to this period is the motte at Knapwell, Cambridgeshire, which was an estate on the southern fringes of Ramsey Abbey's holdings (Fig. 9.1).[120] Standing within shrunken village earthworks near the parish church and overlooking a ford, the motte, no more than 2m high and without a bailey, is one of the tiniest examples that can be reliably identified as such. Although it is undocumented, excavation in the 1920s uncovered St Neots ware, which went out of use *c.* 1200.[121] Whether the site was built by the Abbot of Ramsey as an exercise in property protection or by Geoffrey de Mandeville as an outpost is, however, impossible to judge.[122]

Summary

Its wealth and isolation, combined with a rebel heritage, explain the prominent place of the Isle of Ely during the Anarchy. Yet the Isle's experience in the civil war was also unusual. The 1143–44 campaign in particular was a guerrilla operation without any recorded pitched battles or, especially, the sieges that were so characteristic of the period. In some senses the fenland campaigns of the 1140s appear something of a sideshow, self-contained and removed from other events, yet the impact of the conflict on the fens was also unusually severe. Even in the context of a war in which the ravaging of estates was endemic, the fenlands suffered especially high levels of devastation to their fragile agricultural base. The 1143–44 campaign saw the largest programme of royal castle building recorded in the civil war, all keyed into local landscapes and frequently superimposed within earlier sites, as revealed by archaeological evidence.

Notes

1 Round 1892, 226.

2 Watkins 2015, 65.

3 See Davis 1964; 1988a; 1988b; Prestwich 1988a; 1988b.

4 For a summary account of the fenland campaign in its political context see Salzman 1948, 386–8. See also Beeler 1966, 136–42; Bradbury 1996, 127–32.

5 Darby 1977, 12.

6 Barrowclough 2010.

7 Coles and Hall 1998, 68–78; Spoerry 2005, 85–93.

8 Evans 2003, 253–70.

9 Keynes 2003, 10–12; Roffe 2005, 284–6.

10 *Vita Sancti Guthlaci* XXXI, ed. and trans. Colgrave 1985.

11 See, for example, Kelly 2009, 4.

12 Pugh 1953, 34.

13 See, for example, Wright 2010; 2015, 105.

14 *Liber Eliensis* II, 104–10, Fairweather 2005, 209–38.

15 Morillo 1994, 59, 119–20.

16 *Liber Eliensis* II, 111, Fairweather 2005, 229–30. See also Colvin et al. 1963, 21, 24–5, 41.

17 Smail 1972.

18 Evans 2003, 263; Wilkes and Elrington 1978, 30–6, 47–8.

19 Ravensdale 1974, 22.

20 Jones, T.S. 2010, 84.

21 Evans and Hodder 2006, 453.

22 Henry, Archdeacon of Huntingdon, *Historia Anglorum* X, 12, Greenway 1996, 722–5.

23 *Liber Eliensis* III, 62, Fairweather 2005, 389. The wording is potentially ambiguous and can also be read to suggest that another fortification near the river was built or strengthened *in addition* to the castle of Aldreth, which was 'restored' and 'placed under guard' (see, for example, Renn 1968). This seems unlikely given that all other accounts suggest only two fortifications on the Isle.

24 Pugh 1953, 28–30.

25 *Gesta Stephani* I, 47, Potter and Davis 1976, 98–9.

26 *Gesta Stephani* I, 47, Potter and Davis 1976, 98–101; *Liber Eliensis* III, 62, Fairweather 2005, 388–90.

27 The *Liber Eliensis* states that 'the king put in at Aldreth. There he collected boats together and, placing wicker hurdles on top of them, made the shallow water passable for knights on horseback' (III, 62, Fairweather 2005, 389) while the *Gesta Stephani* reports: 'and when at length a bridge had been skilfully constructed in this way over the boats, he and his men quickly came to the shores of the island beyond. But when the water had been crossed by this device there still remained some muddy fens, in which a shallow ford, suitable for crossing, was secretly shown to the king' (I, 47, Potter and Davis 1976, 100–1).

28 Reaney 1943, 232.

29 An archaeological exploration at Aldreth High Bridge in 1930 which sought the location of the battle where William the Conqueror's soldiers had met with disaster, found no evidence of the conflict in terms of artefacts, but reported a 'medieval landing place' here, comprising bundles of sedge secured by stakes driven into the peat. See Lethbridge 1931, 156.

30 *The Chronicle of John of Worcester* III, McGurk 1998, 280–1.

31 *Liber Eliensis* III, 64, Fairweather 2005, 390.

32 Round 1892, 161, 411. See also King 2010 176–80.

33 *Liber Eliensis* III, 69, Fairweather 2005, 394–5.

34 *Liber Eliensis* III, 69–71, Fairweather 2005, 393–4.

35 *Liber Eliensis* III, 73, Fairweather 2005, 396–7.

36 Davison 1967.

37 *Gesta Stephani* I, 47, Potter and Davis 1976, 98–9. See also Davis 1962, 217.

38 See Kenney and Oswald 1996.

39 Reaney 1943, 174.

40 Kenney and Oswald 1996; Evans 2003, 255–6, 263.

41 Lethbridge and O'Reilly 1934, 90–3.

42 *Gesta Stephani* II, 81–2, Potter and Davis 1976, 160–3; Henry, Archdeacon of Huntingdon, *Historia Anglorum* X, 21, Greenway 1996, 742–5; William of Newburgh, *The History of English Affairs* I, 11, 3, Walsh and Kennedy 1988, 68–9.

43 King 2010, 193–5. See also Bradbury 1996, 129–30.

44 *Gesta Stephani* II, 81, Potter and Davis 1976, 160–1.

45 Wareham 2005, 118.

46 Williams 1977, 1, 5, 241.

47 *The Book of the Foundation of Walden Monastery*, Greenway and Watkiss 1999, xv–xviii.

48 Here the chronology of Davis 1964 is followed. See also Prestwich 1988a; 1988b; Davis 1988a; 1988b. See also Green 2015.

49 Cronne and Davis 1968, no. 273.

50 Crouch 2000, 182.

51 Cronne and Davis 1968, no. 274. See also Raymond Powell 2005, 115.

52 Cronne and Davis 1968, no. 275. See also Raymond Powell 2005, 115.

53 Cronne and Davis 1968, no. 276. See also Round 1892, 136–62.

54 Kent et al. 2013.

55 *Liber Eliensis* III, 82–3, Fairweather 2005, 403–5.

56 *The Waltham Chronicle* 30, ed. and trans. Watkiss and Chibnall 1994, 79–81.

57 Watkiss and Chibnall 1994, 80 n.1.

58 *The Book of the Foundation of Walden Monastery* I, 6, Greenway and Watkiss 1999, 16–17.

59 *Chronica Abbatiae Ramesiensis*, 410–11, ed. Macray 1886, 328–34. See also William of Newburgh, *The History of English Affairs* I, 11, 3, Walsh and Kennedy 1988, 68–9; *Gesta Stephani* II,

83, Potter and Davis 1976, 164–5. For a discussion, see King 2010, 198–9.

60 Henry, Archdeacon of Huntingdon, *Historia Anglorum* X, 22, Greenway 1996, 745.

61 *Chronica Abbatiae Ramesiensis*, 411, Macray 1886, 330.

62 Hall 1992, 48.

63 *Cartularium Monasterii de Rameseia*, ed. Hart and Lyons I 1884, 106. See also Farrer 1925, 62.

64 Davis 1967, 85.

65 *Gesta Stephani* II, 83, Potter and Davis 1976, 164–5.

66 RCHME Cambridge 1959, 304–7.

67 Roach 1959, 5 n.58.

68 Round 1892, 212–13.

69 *Liber Eliensis* III, 82, Fairweather 2005, 44. Benwick and Fordham have occasionally been listed as the site of 'lost' castles of Geoffrey de Mandeville. See Renn 1968, 50, 190; King 1983, 40; Lowerre 2005, 231, 233.

70 *Chronica Abbatiae Ramesiensis*, ed. Macray 1886, 332.

71 *The Book of the Foundation of Walden Monastery* I, 9, Greenway and Watkiss 1999, 14–17.

72 Henry, Archdeacon of Huntingdon, *Historia Anglorum* X, 22, Greenway 1996, 747; William of Newburgh, *The History of English Affairs* I, 11, 6, Walsh and Kennedy 1988, 70–1.

73 Prestwich 1996, 12.

74 King 2010, 197.

75 Beeler 1963, 7–9.

76 *The Book of the Foundation of Walden Monastery* I, 9, Greenway and Watkiss 1999, 17.

77 Fletcher 2002, 395.

78 *Liber Eliensis* III, 82, Fairweather 2005, 403.

79 Gervase of Canterbury, Stubbs, Vol. I, 1879, 128.

80 Wright 2010, 18; 2015, 105.

81 Darby 1940, 145.

82 Raftis 1957, 86.

83 *Gesta Stephani* II, 84, Potter and Davis 1976, 164–5.

84 Creighton 2005b, 59.

85 King 2010, 197.

86 Douglas 1932, no. 64, 83–4; see also no. 183, 160–1.

87 The details of Geoffrey's death at Burwell, off the island, receive little attention. The *Liber Eliensis* states that 'Geoffrey … perished at the hands of the king's army' (III, 86, Fairweather 2005, 409).

88 Gervase of Canterbury, Stubbs, Vol. I, 1879, 128.

89 *Chronica Abbatiae Ramesiensis*, Macray, 1886, 331–2. *The Book of the Foundation of Walden Monastery* styles the place where Geoffrey received his fatal wound as *oppidulum in Burwella*, translated as the 'small castle of Burwell' (I, 6, Greenway and Watkiss 1999, 16–17). *The Waltham Chronicle* has it that he 'received a mortal wound outside the castle of Burwell which he had been assiduously attacking' (30, Watkiss and Chibnall 1994, 81). Other sources do not mention where Geoffrey was wounded. In the words of Henry of Huntingdon, Earl Geoffrey 'was the only one to fall' 'among the serried ranks of his own men' (*Historia Anglorum* X, 22, Greenway 1996, 745), while William of Newburgh has him 'attacking an enemy castle … closely surrounded by a band of his troops' (I, 11, 5, Walsh and Kennedy 1988, 68–9). The *Gesta Stephani* is far less specific, stating only that Geoffrey was 'at length surrounded by the king's men and laid low' (*Gesta Stephani* II, 84, Potter and Davis 1976, 166–7).

90 See, for example, King 1983, 39.

91 Allen Archaeology 2007.

92 Reaney 1943, 187.

93 Blair 1995; 2013; Meaney 1997.

94 Reaney 1943, 188.

95 Wright et al. 2016.

96 Wright et al. 2016.

97 Lethbridge 1936.

98 Lethbridge 1936, 129.

99 RCHME 1972, 40–2.

100 For an example of this hypothesis see Malim 2001.

101 Mortimer et al. 2005; Mudd and Webster 2011.

102 Beresford 1987; Graham and Davies 1993.

103 See Creighton 2005b, 59. See also Lowerre 2005, 231–8.

104 Renn 1968, 50.

105 Creighton 2005b, 123; Liddiard 2005b, 39.

106 Brown and Taylor 1977, 97–9.

107 Seymour 2000.

108 RCHME Cambs. I 1968, 41; Salzman 1948, 21–2; Bolton et al. 1973, 26.

109 Lowerre 2005, 233–4.

110 Reaney 1943, 173. The site is also recorded as Castle Hill and Castle Croft.

111 Wright and Lewis 1989, 380–1.

112 Maekawa 1997, 245–6; Sayer 2009, 144; Spoerry 2005, 95–9.

113 Spoerry 2005, 95–9; Sayer 2009, 139–41.

114 Hall 1992, 38–40.

115 Hall 1992, 33, 40.

116 RCHME 1926, 298; Brown and Taylor 1978, 63.

117 Mortimer 2000.

118 Brown and Taylor 1978.

119 Stringer 1980.

120 Wright and Lewis 1989, 333.

121 Hurst 1956, 53.

122 RCHME Cambs. I 1968, 160–3; Taylor 1979, 127–8.

Chapter 10

The Twelfth-Century Civil War in Context: Assessment and Reassessment

A LONG-STANDING FOCUS for historical debate on King Stephen's reign concerns whether or not the epithet 'the Anarchy' is appropriate for the period. The pendulum of opinion has swung between maximalist and minimalist viewpoints with sharply different understandings of the scale, intensity and impact of the conflict and of the degree to which royal government broke down. If nothing else, 'the Anarchy' makes a useful distinction from the 'English Civil War,' which is universally understood as the crisis of the mid-seventeenth century. Scholars have also assessed the characters and achievements of the main historical figures of the period – primarily King Stephen, his cousin and nemesis the Empress Matilda and the king's younger brother Bishop Henry of Blois. Other debate has centred on the attitudes and agency of the Church and the aristocracy during the conflict, and considered how these institutions were transformed by it. Without doubt, the concept of the 'Anarchy' of the twelfth century was in need of deconstruction and critical examination, but it is unclear how much further debate can develop if it remains focused on essentially the same body of documentary source material. Accordingly, this volume has attempted to draw together the full range of archaeological and material evidence – comprising sites, landscapes and artefacts – alongside new spatial presentations and understandings of documentary sources to afford a rather different perspective on the civil war and its era. Both direct and indirect evidence for the nature and impact of the conflict have been considered at different scales, from individual items of portable material culture to buildings, to nationwide patterns of conflict events. What does this reassessment provide?

Using the Archaeology

This body of archaeological and other material evidence – old and new – does not and cannot contribute evenly to all the different areas of debate about Stephen's reign and the so-called 'Anarchy.' Archaeologists have sometimes applied the labels 'the Anarchy' and 'Anarchy-period' rather loosely and often inappropriately. The period has sometimes been used as a convenient chronological peg from which to hang interpretations and around which site chronologies have been based, sometimes without due caution. At the most basic level, archaeological evidence can of course serve to illuminate something of the background against which historical events took place – the appearance of castles built and the topographies of cities besieged, for example – in order to lend context, colour and sometimes tangible concrete detail to established narratives. Archaeology can also play a role in helping us come more closely to grips with some of the period's prominent personalities. A clear case in point is the ability of large-scale excavation to illuminate building projects commissioned by the twelfth century's great and good, and to cast new light on their careers and cultural connections. The investigation of Henry of Blois's palace of Wolvesey in Winchester provides an exemplar. Numismatic evidence also provides us with an indirect route to understanding the agency and political affiliations of rulers, wannabe rulers and major magnates in the period. However, these approaches can underestimate the full value of archaeological enquiry that has the capacity not only to feed into historical debates and flesh out time-honoured narratives, but also to open up fresh angles of enquiry and bring new understandings to the period.

That said, there is no avoiding the problem that the ever-present issue of dating makes interpretation of the archaeological evidence base immensely challenging. Taken in isolation, many different types of archaeological evidence, from the grassed-over earthworks of supposed 'adulterine' castles through to portable artefacts such as decorative scabbard chapes or harness pendants found through metal-detecting, are more or less impossible to attribute to the precise period of the civil war without other contextual information, circumstantial evidence and detailed argument based on better understood parallels. The medieval archaeologist's favoured tool for dating – pottery – presents especially complex issues as the mid-twelfth century not only saw England's pottery industries undergo massive and widespread upheaval, but also intricate variation between the experiences of different regions. The main trends witnessed the disappearance of the late Saxon urban industries and the emergence of networks of rural pottery production centres that became progressively commercialised through the twelfth century. Quite simply, from ceramics assemblages alone it is almost impossible to positively place an excavated site within the decades of the civil war in virtually any part of Britain. In a more general sense, it is also crystal clear that 'the Anarchy' is not clearly identifiable as an event horizon in the archaeological record of pottery, even in the most heavily and directly contested settlements and regions.

One particular area where archaeology has relatively little to offer at present is in terms of direct material evidence for the most immediate impacts and consequences of the actual fighting. For example, we have no certain examples of excavated mass graves from the small number of pitched battles of the period (although the battlefield of Northallerton (1138) presents excellent potential for the future). Evidence for war-damaged buildings and property is not unsurprisingly minimal and usually problematic, although St Mary's Priory and Cathedral, Coventry, provides a dramatic example of an ecclesiastical site transformed into a counter-castle. Similarly, excavations at Fountains Abbey have recovered clear and well-dated physical evidence of the site's sacking and burning by a war band. In contrast, environmental sequences as yet provide no independent evidence for the burning, wasting and destruction of the agricultural base in the countryside, while skeletal analyses from excavated cemeteries do not show stress within populations, although studies of sufficient scale are still awaited. In all these areas it is questionable whether the events of 'the Anarchy' actually created a clear and detectable archaeological signature; indeed, it would be naïve to look for one given the noted challenges of close dating. In parallel with research into Anglo-Saxon warfare, the vast majority of archaeological evidence relating to 'the Anarchy' instead reflects the militarisation of society and only very rarely actual conflict.

A more general critique of archaeological approaches to the civil war can be levelled at the enduring tendency of archaeologists to interpret chroniclers' accounts too literally and to search for physical correlates of 'things' described without sufficient understanding of the literary conventions, stock phrases and sometimes religious allusions that contemporary writers used. A prime case in point is that the *castellum* as described by chroniclers and the physical reality as investigated by archaeologists can be quite different things. Twelfth-century chronicles represent literature as well as history and we should be very careful about taking descriptions of 'castles' in the civil war at face value; the word *castellum* could refer to a wide variety of militarised features, ranging from walled cities to garrisoned churches and monasteries, and was even deployed to describe topographical features of the landscape itself. A parallel issue concerns churches and church property documented as 'damaged' during the civil war: it is often not clear whether this relates to physical action or instead implies financial harm, such as through the exaction of taxes. In the face of the numerous challenges inherent in the archaeological evidence for twelfth-century conflict, the material is much more valuable when understood and contextualised at a landscape-wide scale.

Reading Warfare

In terms of evidence for the conduct of war, the interpretations advanced here stress that elements of martial choreography were present in a conflict that is most commonly associated with chaos and destruction. Siege castles are a prime source of evidence. These frequently misunderstood sites had important visual and psychological functions as icons of royal presence that symbolised the risk run by rebels and rivals. Siege castles were instrumental in a mode of warfare that could be protracted, as the detailed case study of the three sieges of Wallingford – not one of which involved a direct attack on the castle or town – makes very clear. Archaeology also reinforces the notion that the mid-twelfth century saw subtle but significant changes in military apparel; for example, the battlefields and sieges of the Anarchy saw heraldry become visible in conflict for the first time. Elements of apparel, such as scabbards and harness pendants, became showier and the domination of siege warfare saw archers increase in importance, and bodkin-style armour-piercing arrowheads used on a large scale, perhaps for the first time. Knightly identity was also changing rapidly and was negotiated and symbolised through a repertoire of material culture including swords and gilded spurs.

In other ways, however, the mid-twelfth century saw little innovation in the way that warfare was actually prosecuted. Many of the features of the civil war singled out by horrified chroniclers were characteristic of established Anglo-Norman ways of waging war, the devastation of territories by field armies who lived off the land being the most obvious example. Another clear example is that the employment of mercenaries was not new; their depredations were probably exaggerated by chroniclers prejudiced against foreign soldiers of fortune who lay outside the knightly classes, and they continued to be used to great effect in the later armies of Henry II. Only the extent to which churches were militarised stands out as unusual in the broader history of Anglo-Norman conflict, although, as seen, in the mid-twelfth century, adapting a church or even a cathedral into a castle did not necessarily involve adding defences to its physical fabric.

It is important to view the violence of the civil war in perspective. By and large, the codified rules of Anglo-Norman warfare, enmeshed within an emerging culture of chivalry, remained intact. The overall military landscape was as much characterised by the avoidance of battle as large-scale set-piece clashes of arms. Sieges, which constituted the default way of waging war, usually constituted long-term stand-offs; few involved decisive assaults and many were concluded through negotiation. This has major implications for the archaeological study of medieval conflict: if we restrict our understanding of conflict to battle-fields, we gain a distorted view of contemporary warfare. Environments readily characterised as landscapes of war can also be seen variously as landscapes of negotiation and peaceable power. It has been shown how devices such as baronial treaties saw magnates attempting to restrict fighting and the ravages of war out of self-interest. In this sense, castles could be symbols of armed neutrality as much as war-fighting machines. Allegiance to one side or the other in the civil war was not necessarily absolute, and a neutral but armed stance represented a sophisticated response to political turmoil. The Battle of the Standard/Northallerton (1138) is unique as a set-piece clash of exceptional ferocity and intensity, marked by an unusually high death toll. Performances of violence on the battlefield included tournament-like jousts, and the principal aim of most clashes was to capture and ransom rather than to kill high-status opponents, as witnessed at the Battle of Lincoln and the Rout of Winchester (both 1141). Given all these considerations, it is difficult to estimate the total population loss as a direct or indirect result of the civil war, but it was likely no more than 2–3%, a demographic blip, to be followed by rapid recovery and accelerating population growth into the late twelfth century and beyond.

Landscape Mapping

In these ways and others, analysing conflict at a landscape-wide level can make a telling contribution to the debate about the utility of the label 'the Anarchy' for the period. Mapping of documented conflict events makes very evident how geographically limited the conflict really was. To a large extent, military events were focused in a war zone stretching from the Cotswolds in the north to the south coast, and from Wallingford in the east to Bristol and Gloucester in the west. While the wealthiest areas of the south-east of the country remained very firmly under royalist control, for a not insignificant period of time during the 1140s and early 1150s this zone was in effect a small dysfunctional Angevin state, with its own system of urban centres and ports, and with marches or borderlands to the north and east. The evidence of coins and minting centres can help us map the shape, extent and economic reach of this zone. The focus of the conflict in the central south-west is significant: this was also a battle for a region that had been the traditional heartland of English kingship – the royal enclave of Wessex and the Thames Valley – from the late Saxon period onwards. In the Midlands and the north, a more complex and shifting mosaic of interests characterised by high levels of magnate governance remains more challenging to map. There is good evidence that the economic fortunes of Cumbria and Northumbria were positively boosted as they became part of David of Scots's 'English empire' and reaped the commercial benefits of the silver mining boom in the late 1130s.

The archaeological record for the twelfth century is perhaps most informative when examining change over the *longue durée*. It is important to stress that we see underlying continuity in many areas; as is the case with the Norman Conquest, the civil war saw no hiatus in the rhythms of everyday life for the vast majority of people, as indicated by the evidence of pottery, burial, building technologies and fieldscapes, for example. Twelfth-century portable material culture has been very poorly represented in the archaeological literature, although there are signs that this is changing. The establishment of churches great and small continued and perhaps even accelerated. Other ecclesiastical buildings were extended or provided with the lavish and fantastic sculptural decoration that was such a hallmark of the period, including the often grotesque beakheads that embodied the mid-twelfth-century *zeitgeist*.

The precise historical-archaeological evidence of the coinage provides the most vivid insight into economic disturbance and dislocation:

the minting landscape saw unprecedented change; hoards provide a barometer of insecurity (in the sense that the war saw higher levels of the non-recovery of hoards, rather than more hoards being deposited); and the coins themselves show evidence of declining standards of weight if not always fineness. Coin hoards also suggest that trading patterns were more localised than before. This disruption to the economy through the general climate of instability, uncertain or confused property rights and specific military episodes such as the ravaging of estates, would outwardly seem to indicate that the mid-twelfth century was not a period of growth, although we have to balance this against the clear archaeological and other evidence for energetic investment by lords, not only in their own residences but also in ecclesiastical foundations.

Particularly striking is how the atmosphere of civil war boosted monastic foundation, as lords sought to define their territorial authority and to show allegiance to political networks. Monastic foundation was popularised among the knightly classes, who invariably endowed houses of the new religious orders, including many nunneries. The communities of many such small-scale establishments lived precarious existences at first and the initial level of investment could be modest. Their foundation constituted a statement of piety and sometimes atonement but also, fundamentally, served to stamp the mark of local families on local landscapes. At the level of the parish church, the evidence points towards the 'great rebuilding' accelerating into the mid-twelfth-century through energetic patronage. For some regions the evidence of grave slabs provides a window into how the identities of these local lords were negotiated, and the mid- to late twelfth century was once again a high point of activity and investment. Turning to the rural landscape, archaeological evidence usually lacks the precision to date convincingly episodes of settlement planning and reorganisation to the period of the civil war as opposed to the later twelfth-century period of economic rebuilding and renewed growth. There are good reasons, though, to think that some instances of settlement planning reflected the agency of newly emboldened manorial lords and, indeed, it is into the later twelfth century that some of the hallmark features of the elite medieval landscape emerge, including mill mounds, fish ponds and deer parks.

Lordly Culture: Image and Reality

It has also been underlined that archaeological evidence indicates the mid-twelfth century as a watershed in myriad ways and at a variety of levels. Of fundamental importance is the rapidly transforming nature of lordly identity through the period, which has ramifications in the material evidence. One particular archaeological contribution is the ever-growing number of twelfth-century artefacts found through metal-detecting, including elite objects such as harness pendants and lead seal matrices. We see changes to the lordly image evidenced in the material culture through early forms of heraldry on military apparel, although this is a controversial area. It is also evident through the development of seals, and the fact that some issues of baronial coinage – for instance those of William of Aumale, of Robert, Earl of Gloucester and of his son William, Earl of Gloucester – drew on seal-like designs, reflecting an area of interface between the two categories of evidence.

An irony is that the image of the mounted knight proclaimed on seals, and which was also celebrated and developed through a burgeoning tournament culture that got going in the 1130s and '40s, was crystallising during a period that saw cavalry play a very limited role in actual military actions. Instead, knights tended to fight as dismounted infantry on the rare occasions when set-piece battles were conducted, and contributed relatively little to the success or failure of sieges. It is crucial to underline that these changes in the power and imagery of lordship were not a sudden and radical departure from the norm. Rather, these developments were part of a long-term process that saw the presence of lords and their authority over populations gradually ratcheted up; it is just that Stephen's reign saw seigneurial power tightened an extra notch or two, to a new level. Far from being a phenomenon of the mid-twelfth century, or even since the Norman Conquest, the trend towards the growing coercive power of lordship can be traced back into the ninth and tenth centuries.

A good part of the reason why a holistic approach to the landscape of twelfth-century England is challenging is that castles have been isolated from these debates about the evolution of lordship and lordly identity. This is largely a by-product of the prominence that chroniclers gave to castles, which were invariably portrayed as weapons of war, so that their full range of functions and meanings have been underestimated for the period of the civil war. Castles established in the Anarchy need to be understood within the context of important changes to the lordly image and seigneurial identity if they are to be rescued from the caricature of being nasty, brutish (and tall). While undoubtedly installations with military potential, it seems unthinkable that castles were not themselves also essential elements within the making of the seigneurial image. Too often, castle studies have seen interpretations polarised between perspectives stressing 'status and symbolism' and others with a focus on 'security and defence.' Detailed examination of the different contexts of castle building during the civil war reveals that these two dimensions were irrevocably entwined.

Crucially, the 1130s, 1140s and 1150s actually saw far more *variety* in castle construction than before, even if royal castle building (at least of fortified residences as opposed to campaign works) ground to a total halt. The multifarious contexts for 'Anarchy-period' castle building ranged from military works that lay entirely outside the manorial system through to massive stone donjons of major magnates, especially newly elevated earls. It is striking that the largest-scale donjons of the period – sites such as Castle Rising, Castle Acre and Hedingham – lay in the more secure easterly regions and did not stand alone as seigneurial initiatives. Rather, in each case the castles were component parts of larger schemes of landscape reorganisation involving new or replanned settlements, churches and parks. This pattern is mirrored at a smaller scale by parish-wide initiatives undertaken by lords with local profiles at places such as 'Goltho' and Middleton Stoney. As far as we can judge from the available archaeological evidence, many of these more local castle power bases reused earlier centres of significance, including thegnly enclosures attached to estate churches. Invariably the label 'adulterine' is misleading; castles of the civil war were not anarchic blots on the landscape but phases in the cultural stratigraphy of given localities. The most instructive example is King Stephen's campaign castle at Burwell, left part-built when its *raison d'être* was removed by the death of Geoffrey de Mandeville while besieging it. To conceptualise even this site as an 'Anarchy-period' field monument is wrong, however: Stephen's campaign castle reused a thegnly enclosure, which itself in all probability perpetuated a pre-Christian fen edge ritual site, while the castle was later turned into a chantry chapel.

It is also to the mid-twelfth century that we can most likely date many of the so-called *burgus* enclosures attached to castles, with rural populations settled or resettled within earth and timber defences, as at places such as Ascot D'Oilly and Boteler's Castle. The Nottinghamshire village of Wellow provides a rare but instructive example of a defended village that stood independent of a castle, but whose origins seem to relate to a mid-twelfth century episode of reorganisation. This phenomenon of defended villages might represent the 'archaeology of fear' during a period of instability, or it might alternatively reflect seigneurial agency, as lords tightened their grip on rural populations, although again it is worth underlining that we are dealing with a handful of examples. Another important trend was the frequent use of visually prominent hilltop sites, not just for castles, but also as centres for urban growth, as exemplified by the sites of Mountsorrel and Beaudesert, or mints, as in the case of Castle Combe. These sites and others can be understood as looming lordly edifices that proclaimed a new form of seigneurial identity and confidence to wider populations. Such sites need not be understood in isolation but as elements in a seigneurial package. In terms of the archaeology of lordship, this was a period of image-making as much as warmongering.

While these trends during the 19 years of the civil war saw an aristocratic revolution in England, at a far broader scale the emerging seigneurial culture was temporarily more akin to the European mainstream and to the situation in contemporary France in particular. In France, a mountain of historiography is devoted to exploring the relationship between a breakdown of central authority in the tenth and eleventh centuries and the emergence of locally based power structures with castellans at their core, and the parallels are worth taking seriously. The phenomenon of magnate and civic coinages seen on the Continent was also for a while translated to an English context. An irony is that in England the civil war ended with a settlement in favour of a dynasty firmly rooted in Continental Europe, but which pursued a traditional strong English approach to monarchy.

A Watershed?

It is only by examining the events of the civil war with reference to the periods before and after that we are able to get any real sense of its impact and effects on society and landscape. In several spheres it seems clear that the events of the conflict did not themselves somehow initiate dramatic change but acted to influence processes that were already in train. The emergence of independently minded lesser aristocrats from the shadow of their overlords is one obvious example of a movement stirring before Stephen's reign, but one that was accelerated by the sociopolitical climate of civil war. Another example is the impact of the conflict on the Cistercian expansion: the White Monks were in the early stages of their colonisation when the conflict began, but it created a whirlwind of social and political factors that provided an impetus to monastic expansion at a crucial moment. To speculate what would have happened to the order in England and Wales without the civil war is to stray into the realm of counterfactual history, but it is evident that the conflict was a major factor in the speed and geographical breadth of the Cistercian expansion.

Another example concerns the competing status of London and Winchester as key centres of royal government in the twelfth century. At the point of Stephen's accession, Winchester was in decline and London in the ascendancy, but the civil war proved a decisive point in the geography of royal government. After Stephen's reign, government was centred on London, and the boost to the city's fortunes and status as a result of the civil war ultimately underlay its rise to commune status at the end of the twelfth century. We see parallels in other spheres: the middle years of the twelfth century were demonstrably a boom time for sculpture and the art of the late Romanesque, but the civil war provided a nudge that sent it in particular directions. So too, episcopal palaces had reached high levels of ostentation and sophistication earlier in the twelfth century with hallmark building projects such as Old Sarum and Sherborne, but Stephen's reign provided a hothouse environment that saw the construction of the most ambitious Romanesque palace of all, Henry of Blois's site of Wolvesey, Winchester. Less obvious is the impact of Stephen's reign on the history of medieval England's Jewish population, which was previously centred in London but expanded to enclaves attached to important royal castles such as Norwich during the civil war.

Overall, it is tempting to portray the middle decades of the twelfth century as more of a watershed than the Norman Conquest in terms of the organisation of the English landscape. It is worth considering that many of the supposed landscape signatures of the Norman Conquest actually date to more than 80 years later, including the widespread foundation of local castles by lords of the manor and huge towers by greater magnates; the massive wave of monasteries of reformed orders; and the 'great rebuilding' of parish churches in the Romanesque style. The twinning of lordly *caput* and ecclesiastical foundation, so synonymous with the imposition of Norman power, was another hallmark of the period. This period also saw the quintessential image of Norman military might – the mounted knight – celebrated in material culture and the emergence of heraldic devices on the battlefield. In this sense, the peak of the Normanisation of the English landscape came several generations after the Conquest. Consideration of these research themes and others can help extricate studies of the twelfth-century civil war from the 'anarchy or not?' debate. In conclusion: the mid-twelfth century is best regarded *not* as an age of anarchy but as an *age of transition*.

Appendix

Key Sites to Visit

THIS APPENDIX provides a brief gazetteer of key sites associated with the 'Anarchy' that can be visited. Arranged by region, it includes details on site location and accessibility. Given the sheer number of places involved in a civil war that extended over almost 20 years, this is not a comprehensive list, but is intended to indicate to the reader locations where tangible and broadly dateable remains can be seen, as well as conflict landscapes that are accessible.

Southern and South-West England

Danes Castle, Exeter (SX919933) is a small ringwork siege castle almost certainly built by King Stephen against Rougemont Castle, which lies on the opposite side of Longbrook Valley to the south (although the view is blocked by Exeter Prison). The earthworks were landscaped after the site was excavated in the early 1990s and are fully and freely accessible. The best-preserved siege castle of the civil war is, however, the ringwork and bailey known as 'The Rings' at **Corfe, Dorset** (SY956820), located on a publicly accessible site immediately south of the great castle, with spectacular views of the latter. The site has never been excavated but the earthworks are impressive and show evidence of modification as a platform for gunpowder artillery in the English Civil War.

Winchester, Hampshire contains numerous sites of significance from the period; the foremost is **Wolvesey Palace** (SU484290), in the south-east corner of the city walls, which preserves extensive remains associated with Bishop Henry of Blois. **Farnham Castle, Surrey** (SU83724732), preserves excellent evidence of Henry of Blois's castle in the form of the excavated remains of a tower sealed within the motte, itself surrounded by a later shell keep. Both sites are managed heritage attractions with entrance fees.

Nothing remains of **Malmesbury Castle, Wiltshire**, although the abbey which it adjoined displays some of the finest late Romanesque sculpture in Britain (ST933874). Located approximately 1.5km south of Malmesbury (ST94058578), and probably constructed in order to besiege the town and castle, is the ringwork of Cam's Hill. Although on private property, a public footpath passes to the north of the monument, from which there are good views of the earthworks. Akin to Malmesbury, most of the other main Angevin castles in the West Country have unimpressive or heavily rebuilt remains, including Bristol and the two important Wiltshire sites of Trowbridge (the site of which is entirely built over) and Devizes (although the street plan fossilises the layout of the twelfth-century new town). **Ludgershall Castle, Wiltshire** (SU263511), to which the Empress Matilda fled in 1141 after the Angevins' military reverse at Winchester, preserves only stubs of masonry from internal buildings within the substantial earthworks of a double ringwork. The site is freely accessible. In terms of its standing remains, **Sherborne Castle, Dorset** (ST648167), is the best preserved bishop's castle of the twelfth century, comprising a courtyard complex within earthwork defences built for Bishop Roger of Salisbury, set within a former lake. The excavated and consolidated remains of Bishop Roger's palace and cathedral can be seen at **Old Sarum, Wiltshire** (SU 137327). Both are managed sites with entrance fees.

Nestled on the banks of the River Thames, the town of **Wallingford, Oxfordshire**, and its environs represent one of the most important and most accessible conflict landscapes of the period. The grassed-over earthworks of the castle (SU610896) take up a vast area, although the twelfth-century fortress was a more compact unit centred on the grassed-over motte. Most parts of the site are freely accessible. Of the multiple siege castles built against Wallingford, only the site of one is secure: Stephen's Mount, Crowmarsh, on the opposite side of the river, now buried beneath the housing development of King Stephen's Close (SU613894). The great bridge over the Thames was also fortified in the period and the riverside landscape contested during the three separate sieges. Wallingford Bridge, which preserves a few twelfth-/thirteenth-century arches, also affords excellent views over the Thames-edge landscape where the important 1153 peace negotiations took place.

St Mary, Kempley, Gloucestershire (SO669312), one of the finest mid-twelfth-century small parish churches in Britain, preserves spectacular wall frescoes of the same period. At **Hereford**, the castle site (SO510398) is unimpressive and the cathedral tower which supported siege engines is replaced by a later structure. An especially impressive site on the borders is **Kilpeck, Herefordshire** (SO444304), well-known for the mid-twelfth-century sculpture on the parish church, which stands adjacent to a castle site and associated planned settlement.

Eastern England

Arundel Castle, West Sussex (TQ018073), where the Empress stayed after landing in England in 1139 is a popular tourist attraction but little can be gleaned of the twelfth-century castle, which was heavily rebuilt in later centuries.

    Burwell Castle, Cambridgeshire (TL587660), is the most fully preserved fortification built by King Stephen and occupies an easily accessible site next to the church. On the north side of the castle, which survives as a complex of well-defined earthworks under grass and scrubland, the spoil heaps excavated from the moat can be seen, as well as the underlying earthwork remains of a pre-existing settlement. Of the other likely campaign castles of the same period, **Giant's Hill, Rampton** (TL430680), is the most impressive and accessible. While the gatehouse is the main vestige of **Ramsey Abbey, Cambridgeshire**, possible evidence of the site's fortification by Geoffrey de Mandeville can be seen in the form of **Booths Hill** (TL292848), an overgrown earthwork on the edge of the abbey precinct, which may be an Anarchy-period motte. Good examples of the small mottes of the civil war period, unsurprisingly unimpressive, are **Knapwell, Cambridgeshire** (TL336631), and **Therfield, Hertfordshire** (TL331371).

    At **Faversham Abbey, Kent**, little remains of the monastery where King Stephen was buried, other than part of a gatehouse; large areas of the former abbey are under school playing fields. To the north is the creek where Stephen's body was reputedly deposited after the Dissolution. **St Nicholas, Barfreston, Kent** (TR264501), gives an excellent impression of a small parish church of the mid-twelfth century.

    At **Castle Acre Castle, Norfolk** (TF813148), the mid-twelfth-century phases of the de Warennes' great castle can be seen in the substantial excavated remains. The site needs to be appreciated within the context of the neighbouring fortified settlement and priory, which were elements within a contemporary lordly landscape. **Castle Rising, Norfolk** (TF666246), preserves the squat but impressive mid-twelfth-century donjon of the Albini family, which was left partly unfinished. The parish church shows spectacular contemporary Romanesque sculpture. The centrepiece of **Castle Hedingham, Essex** (TL787358), is the great mid-twelfth-century donjon of the earls of Oxford, set within impressive earthworks.

The Midlands and the North

Besides the large surviving motte, another important standing vestige of the earlier phases of **Oxford Castle, Oxfordshire** (SP509061), is St George's Tower, a massive square pre-Conquest stone tower incorporated into the Norman defences. It may or not be fanciful to see this as the structure through which the Empress escaped down onto the frozen Thames in the winter of 1142. Motte-like earthworks that contained small lordly towers can be seen at **Middleton Stoney** (SP532232) and **Ascot D'Oilly** (SP301190) (both Oxfordshire). **St Mary the Virgin, Iffley, Oxfordshire** (SP527035), is slightly later than the civil war, but preserves probably the most spectacular architectural sculpture in a twelfth-century parish church.

The battlefield of the **Battle of the Standard** (or Northallerton) is not easily accessible; the battlefield monument (SE360977) is located in a layby on the east side of the busy A167 Northallerton to Darlington road, although the centre of the action was probably further to the south. Better views of the battlefield can be obtained from Brompton Lane, further to the east. The battlefield of the **Battle of Lincoln** almost certainly lies west of the city and is largely built over; excellent views over the terrain can be obtained from the walls of the castle.

The castle of **Mountsorrel, Leicestershire** (SK582149), which features in the famous treaty between the earls of Chester and Leicester, survives as a rather confused series of earthworks, heavily disturbed by mining, although it offers excellent views over the accompanying castle-town. **Southwell Minster, Nottinghamshire** (SK702538), contains excellent Romanesque carvings although no evidence can be seen of the site's fortification in the civil war.

Among Yorkshire's many fine and impressive castles, examples with clear evidence that they were built or strengthened during the civil war are few. **Castle Hill, Almondbury** (SE15251407), just outside Huddersfield, is open and accessible and the earthworks show clearly the adaptation of a prehistoric hillfort into a motte and bailey. The siege castle adjacent to Pickering Castle, known as **Beacon Hill** (SE792844), may be an Anarchy-period work, although it could equally be later; its earthwork was adapted as a Royal Observer Corps bunker. The parish church of St John the Baptist at **Adel, West Yorkshire** (SE275402), preserves remarkable Romanesque sculpture and beakhead ornament.

The village of **Bishopton, County Durham** (NZ366208), contains one of England's best preserved motte-and-bailey earthworks, built or strengthened in the mid-twelfth century. Of the borderland castles contested during Stephen's reign, the most impressive with works of the period is **Norham, Northumberland** (NT906474), with its imposing rectangular donjon.

Bibliography

Primary Sources

Anglo-Saxon Chronicle, ed. D. Whitelock, 1961. London: Eyre and
   Spottiswoode.
The Book of the Foundation of Walden Monastery, ed. and trans.
   D. Greenway and L. Watkiss, 1999. Oxford: Clarendon Press.
Cartularium Monasterii de Rameseia, ed. W.H. Hart and P.A. Lyons, 3 vols,
   Rolls Series 79, 1884–93. London: Longman.
Chronica Abbatiae Ramesiensis (The Chronicle of Ramsey Abbey), ed.
   W.D. Macray, Rolls Series 83, 1886. London: Longman.
Chronicle of Battle Abbey, ed. and trans. E. Searle, 1980. Oxford: Clarendon
   Press.
*Chronicles of the Reigns of Stephen, Henry II and Richard I. Vol. IV:
   The Chronicle of Robert of Torigni*, ed. R. Howlett, 1889. London:
   HMSO.
Richard fitzNigel, *Dialogus de Scaccario, The Dialogue of the Exchequer*,
   ed. and trans. E. Amt, 2007. Oxford: Clarendon Press.
Gervase of Canterbury, *The Historical Works of Gervase of Canterbury,
   Volume 1: The Chronicle of the Reigns of Stephen, Henry II, and
   Richard I*, ed. W. Stubbs, 2 vols, Rolls Series 73, 1879–80. London:
   Longman.
Gesta Stephani, ed. and trans. K.R. Potter, with introduction and notes by
   R.H.C. Davis, 1976. Oxford: Clarendon Press.
Henry, Archdeacon of Huntingdon, *Historia Anglorum, The History of the
   English People*, ed. and trans. D. Greenway, 1996. Oxford: Clarendon
   Press.
*Historia Ecclesie Abbendonensis: The History of the Church of Abingdon,
   Volume II*, ed. J. Hudson, 2002. Oxford: Clarendon Press.
Historia Selebiensis Monasterii: The History of the Monastery of Selby, ed. and
   trans. J. Burton with L. Lockyer, 2013. Oxford: Oxford University Press.
John of Worcester, *The Chronicle of John of Worcester, Volume III: The
   Annals from 1067 to 1140*, ed. and trans. P. McGurk, 1998. Oxford:
   Clarendon Press.

Landbok Sive Registrum Monasterii de Winchelcumba, ed. D. Royce,
　1892–1903. Exeter: William Pollard.

*Liber Eliensis: A History of the Isle of Ely from the Seventh Century to the
　Twelfth*, ed. and trans. J. Fairweather, 2005. Woodbridge: The Boydell
　Press.

Orderic Vitalis, *The Ecclesiastical History of Orderic Vitalis*, ed. and trans.
　M. Chibnall, 6 vols, 1969–90. Oxford: Clarendon Press.

Pipe Rolls, *The Great Rolls of the Pipe for the Second, Third, and Fourth
　Years of the Reign of King Henry the Second, AD 1155, 1156, 1157, 1158*,
　ed. J. Hunter. London: Record Commission.

Roger of Hoveden, *The Annals of Roger de Hoveden, Comprising the
　History of England and of Other Countries of Europe from A.D. 732 to
　A.D. 1201, Volume I*, trans. H.T Riley, 1853. London: H.G. Bohn.

Symeon of Durham, *Symeonis monachi opera omnia*, ed. T. Arnold, 2 vols,
　2012. Cambridge: Cambridge University Press.

Symeon of Durham, *Libellus de exordio atque procurso istius, hoc est
　Dunhelmensis, ecclesie, Tract on the origins and progress of this the church
　of Durham*, trans. D.W. Rollason, 2000. Oxford: Clarendon Press.

Vita Sancti Guthlaci (Felix's Life of Saint Guthlac), ed. and trans.
　B. Colgrave, 1985. Cambridge: Cambridge University Press.

*The Waltham Chronicle: An Account of the Discovery of Our Holy Cross at
　Montacute and its Conveyance to Waltham*, ed. and trans. L. Watkiss
　and M. Chibnall, 1994. Oxford: Clarendon Press.

William of Malmesbury, *Historia Novella*, ed. E. King, trans. K.R. Potter,
　1998. Oxford: Clarendon Press.

William of Newburgh, *The History of English Affairs, Book I*, ed. and trans.
　P.G. Walsh and M.J. Kennedy, 1988. Warminster: Aris and Phillips.

William of Newburgh, *The History of English Affairs, Book II*, ed. and
　trans. P.G. Walsh and M.J. Kennedy, 2007. Oxford: Aris and Phillips.

Secondary Sources

Abels, R. 2008: 'Household men, mercenaries and Vikings in Anglo-Saxon
　England', in J. France (ed.), *Mercenaries and Paid Men: The Mercenary
　Identity in the Middle Ages*. Leiden: Brill, 143–65.

Abrams, J. and Shotliff, D. 2010: 'The remains of Robert de Waudari's
　adulterine castle, Castle Street, Luton', *Bedfordshire Archaeology* 26,
　387–404.

Abulafia, A.S. 2011: 'The Jews', in J. Crick and E. Van Houts (eds), *A Social
　History of England 900–1200*. Cambridge: Cambridge University Press,
　256–64.

Addyman, P.V. 1965: 'Late Saxon settlements in the St Neots area I: The
　Saxon settlement and Norman castle at Eaton Socon', *Proceedings of the
　Cambridge Antiquarian Society* 58, 38–73.

Ailes, A. 1990: 'Heraldry in twelfth-century England: The evidence', in

D. Williams (ed.), *Proceedings of the 1988 Harlaxton Symposium.*
Woodbridge: The Boydell Press, 1–16.

Ailes, A. 2008: 'The knight's alter ego: From equestrian to armorial seal', in
N. Adams, J. Cherry and J. Robinson (eds), *Good Impressions. Image
and Authority in Medieval Seals.* London: British Museum, 8–11.

Aitchison, N.B. 1988: 'Roman wealth, native ritual: Coin hoards within and
beyond Roman Britain', *World Archaeology* 20.2, 270–84.

Alcock, N.W., and Buckley, R.J. 1987: 'Leicester Castle: The great hall',
Medieval Archaeology 31, 73–9.

Allan, J.P. 1984: *Medieval and Post-Medieval Finds from Exeter, 1971–1980.*
Exeter: Exeter City Council and the University of Exeter.

Allen Archaeology. 2007: *Archaeological Evaluation Report: Trial Trenching
on Land to the North-West of 60 Reach Road, Burwell, Cambridgeshire.*
Unpublished report: Allen Archaeological Associates.

Allen, M. 2002: 'English coin hoards, 1158–1544', *British Numismatic Journal*
72, 24–84.

Allen, M. 2006: 'The English coinage of 1153/4–1158', *British Numismatic
Journal* 76, 242–302.

Allen, M. 2007: 'Henry II and the English coinage', in C. Harper-Bill and
N. Vincent (eds), *Henry II: New Interpretations.* Woodbridge: The
Boydell Press, 257–77.

Allen, M. 2011: 'Mints and money in Norman England', *Anglo-Norman
Studies* 34, 2–21.

Allen, M. 2012a: *Mints and Money in Medieval England.* Cambridge:
Cambridge University Press.

Allen, M. 2012b: 'The mints and moneyers of England and Wales,
1066–1158', *British Numismatic Journal* 82, 54–120.

Allen, M. 2014: 'Coinage and currency under William I and William II', in
R. Naismith, M. Allen and E. Screen (eds), *Early Medieval Monetary
History: Studies in Honour of Mark Blackburn.* Farnham: Ashgate,
85–112.

Allen, T.G. and Hiller, J. 2002: *The Excavation of a Medieval Manor House
of the Bishops of Winchester at Mount House, Witney, Oxfordshire.*
Thames Valley Landscapes Monograph 13. Oxford: Oxbow.

Amt, E.M. 1991: 'The meaning of waste in the early pipe rolls of Henry II',
Economic History Review 44.2, 240–8.

Amt, E.M. 1993: *The Accession of Henry II in England: Royal Government
Restored 1149–1159.* Woodbridge: The Boydell Press.

Anderson, A.O. 1908: *Scottish Annals from English Chroniclers A.D. 500 to
1286.* London: D.N. Nutt.

Andrew, W.J. 1937: 'The die for Stephen's coinage in the Guildhall Museum,
and secondary evidence there of an unpublished penny of Henry I',
British Numismatic Journal 22, 29–34.

Andrews, D.D., Mundy, C. and Walker, H. 2002: 'Saffron Walden: The
topography of the southern half of the town and marketplace', *Essex
Archaeology and History* (3rd series) 33, 221–73.

Anon. 1827: 'Domestic occurrences', *Gentleman's Magazine* 97.1, 637–9.

Archibald, M. 1984: 'Coins', in G. Zarnecki (ed.), *English Romanesque Art 1066–1200: Hayward Gallery, London 5 April–8 July 1984*. London: Weidenfeld and Nicolson, 320–41.

Archibald, M.M. 1991: 'Dating Stephen's first type', *British Numismatic Journal* 61, 9–22.

Archibald, M.M. 2001: 'The Lion coinage of Robert Earl of Gloucester and William Earl of Gloucester', *British Numismatic Journal* 71, 71–86.

Archibald, M.M. 2003: 'Early medieval coinage (1066–1279)', *British Numismatic Journal* 72, 76–88.

Archibald, M.M., Lang J.R.S. and Milne, G. 1995: 'Four early medieval coin dies from the London waterfront', *Numismatic Chronicle* 155, 163–200.

Armitage, E.S. 1912: *The Early Norman Castles of the British Isles*. London: Murray.

Ashley, S. 2002: *Medieval Armorial Horse Furniture in Norfolk*. East Anglian Archaeology Report 101. Dereham: Norfolk Museums and Archaeology Service.

Ashley, S. 2015: 'Anglo-Norman elite objects from castle and countryside', in C. Lapiche, J.A. Davies, J-M Levesque and A. Riley (eds), *Castles and the Anglo-Norman World*. Oxford: Oxbow, 281–98.

Ashley, S. and Biddle, M. 2014: 'Recent finds of late twelfth- or early thirteenth-century sword and dagger pommels associated with the Crusades', in S. Ashley and S. Marsden (eds), *Landscapes and Artefacts: Studies in East Anglian Archaeology Presented to Andrew Rogerson*. Oxford: Archaeopress, 199–210.

Ashwin, T. 2001: 'Middleton Mount: Excavations in and around the eastern bailey of Middleton Castle by Andrew Rogerson', *Norfolk Archaeology* 43.3, 645–56.

Astill, G. 1978: *Historic Towns in Berkshire: An Archaeological Appraisal*. Reading: Berkshire Archaeological Trust.

Aston, M. 1985: 'Rural settlement in Somerset: Some preliminary thoughts', in D. Hooke (ed.), *Medieval Villages: A Review of Current Work*. Oxford University Committee for Archaeology Monograph 5. Oxford: Oxford University Committee for Archaeology, 81–100.

Aston, M. 2000: *Monasteries in the Landscape*. Stroud: Tempus.

Austin, D. 1987: 'The medieval settlement and landscape of Castle Eden, Peterlee, County Durham: Excavations 1974', *Durham Archaeological Journal* 3, 57–78.

Bachrach, B.S. 1985: 'Some observations on the military administration of the Norman Conquest', *Anglo-Norman Studies* 8, 1–25.

Bachrach, D.S. 2004: 'Crossbows for the king: The crossbow during the reigns of John and Henry III of England', *Technology and Culture* 45.1, 102–19.

Baker, J. 2015: 'The earliest armorial harness pendants', *The Coat of Arms* 229, 1–24.

Barber, R. and Barker, J. 1989: *Tournaments: Jousts, Chivalry and Pageants in the Middle Ages*. Woodbridge: The Boydell Press.

Barker, J.R.V. 1986: *The Tournament in England 1100–1400*. Woodbridge: The Boydell Press.

Barley, M.W. 1951: 'Cuckney church and castle', *Transactions of the Thoroton Society of Nottinghamshire* 4, 26–9.

Barley, M.W. 1957: 'Cistercian land clearances in Nottinghamshire: Three deserted villages and their moated successor', *Nottinghamshire Medieval Studies* 1, 75–89.

Barlow, F. 1983: *William Rufus*. Berkeley and Los Angeles: University of California Press.

Barrow, G.W.S. 1985: *The Stenton Lecture 1984. David I of Scotland (1124–1153): The Balance of New and Old*. Reading: University of Reading.

Barrow, G.W.S. 1994: 'The Scots and the North of England', in E. King (ed.), *The Anarchy of Stephen's Reign*. Oxford: Clarendon Press, 231–53.

Barrow, J. 2000: 'Athelstan to Aigueblanche', in G. Aylmer and J. Tiller (eds), *Hereford Cathedral: A History*. London: Hambledon Press, 21–47.

Barrowclough, D. 2010: 'Expanding the horizons of island archaeology. Islandscapes imaginary and real, Ely: The case of the dry island', *Shima: The International Journal of Research into Island Cultures* 4.1, 27–46.

Bassett, S.R. (ed.) 1982: *Saffron Walden: Excavations and Research 1972–1980*. Chelmsford Archaeological Trust Report 2, CBA Research Report 45. London: Council for British Archaeology.

Bassett, S.R. 1985: 'Beyond the edge of excavation: The topographical context of Goltho', in H. Mayr-Harting and R.I. Moore (eds), *Studies in Medieval History Presented to R.H.C. Davis*. London: Hambledon, 21–39.

Bates, D. 1997: 'The prosopographical study of Anglo-Norman royal charters', in K.S.B. Keats-Rohan (ed.), *Family Trees and the Roots of Politics: The Prosopography of Britain and France from the Tenth to the Twelfth Century*. Woodbridge: The Boydell Press, 89–102.

Baxter, R. 2015: 'Romanesque carved stones', in R. Gilchrist and C. Green, *Glastonbury Abbey: Archaeological Investigations 1904–79*. London: Society of Antiquaries, 347–58.

Baxter, R. and Harrison, S. 2002: 'The decoration of the cloister at Reading Abbey', in L. Keen and E. Scarff (eds), *Windsor: Medieval Archaeology, Art and Architecture of the Thames Valley*. British Archaeological Association Conference Association Conference Transactions 25. Leeds: British Archaeological Association, 302–12.

Bedos-Rezak, B.M. 2011: *When Ego Was Imago: Signs of Identity in the Middle Ages*. Leiden: Brill.

Beeler, J. 1963: 'Towards a re-evaluation of English medieval generalship', *Journal of British Studies* 3.1, 1–10.

Beeler, J. 1966: *Warfare in England 1066–1189*. Ithaca: Cornell University Press.

Bennett, M. 2001: 'Military aspects of the conquest of Lisbon, 1147', in J. Phillips and M. Hoch (eds), *The Second Crusade: Scope and Consequences*. Manchester: Manchester University Press, 71–89.

Bennett, M. 2003: 'Why chivalry? Military "professionalism" in the twelfth century: The origins and expressions of a socio-military ethos', in D.J.B. Trim (ed.), *The Chivalric Ethos and the Development of Military Professionalism*. Leiden and Boston: Brill, 41–64.

Beresford, G. 1975: *The Medieval Clay-Land Village: Excavations at Goltho and Barton Blount*. Society for Medieval Archaeology Monograph 6. London: Society for Medieval Archaeology.

Beresford, G. 1987: *Goltho: The Development of an Early Medieval Manor c. 850–1150*. London: Historic Buildings & Monuments Commission for England.

Beresford, M. 1967: *New Towns of the Middle Ages: Town Plantation in England, Wales and Gascony*. London: Lutterworth.

Biddle, M. (ed.) 1976: *Winchester in the Early Middle Ages: An Edition and Discussion of the Winton Domesday*. Oxford: Clarendon Press.

Biddle, M. (ed.) 1990a: *Artefacts from Medieval Winchester. Part II: Object and Economy in Medieval Winchester*. Winchester Studies 7. Oxford: Clarendon Press.

Biddle, M. 1964: 'The excavation of a motte and bailey Castle at Therfield, Herts', *Journal of the British Archaeological Association* 27, 53–91.

Biddle, M. 1969: 'Wolvesey: The *domus quasi palatium* of Henry de Blois in Winchester', *Chateau Gaillard* 3, 28–36.

Biddle, M. 1986: *Wolvesey, the Old Bishop's Palace, Winchester*. London: Historic Buildings and Monuments Commission for England.

Biddle, M. 1990b: 'Crossbow boltheads', in M. Biddle (ed.), *Artefacts from Medieval Winchester. Part II: Object and Economy in Medieval Winchester*. Winchester Studies 7, Part II. Oxford: Clarendon Press, 1076–80.

Biddle, M. 1990c: 'Stone projectile balls', in M. Biddle (ed.), *Artefacts from Medieval Winchester. Part II: Object and Economy in Medieval Winchester*. Winchester Studies 7, Part II. Oxford: Clarendon Press, 1068–70.

Biddle, M. and Kjølbye-Biddle, B. 1992: 'Repton and the Vikings', *Antiquity* 66, 36–51.

Bisson, T.N. 2008: 'The lure of Stephen's England: *tenserie*, Flemings, and a crisis of circumstance', in P. Dalton and G.J. White (eds), *King Stephen's Reign (1135–54)*. Woodbridge: The Boydell Press, 171–81.

Blackburn, M. 2005: 'Penny of William of Aumale, Earl of York', *The Art Fund Review*, 66.

Blackburn, M.A.S. 1990: 'Coinage and currency under Henry I: A review', *Anglo-Norman Studies* 13, 49–81.

Blackburn, M.A.S. 1994: 'Coinage and currency', in E. King (ed.), *The Anarchy of King Stephen's Reign*. Oxford: Clarendon Press, 145–205.

Blair, C. 1959: *European Armour circa 1066 to circa 1700*. New York: Macmillan.

Blair, J. 1981: 'William Fitz Ansculf and the Abinger motte', *Archaeological Journal* 138, 146–8.

Blair, J. 1993: 'Hall and chamber: English domestic planning 1000–1250', in G. Meirion-Jones and M. Jones (eds), *Manorial Domestic Buildings in England and Northern France*. Society of Antiquaries Occasional Paper 15. London: Society of Antiquaries, 1–21.

Blair, J. 1995: 'Anglo-Saxon pagan shrines and their prototypes', *Anglo-Saxon Studies in Archaeology and History* 8, 1–28.

Blair, J. 1998: 'Bampton: An Anglo-Saxon minster', *Current Archaeology* 14, 124–30.

Blair, J. 2005: *The Church in Anglo-Saxon Society*. Oxford: Oxford University Press.

Blair, J. and Steane, J. 1982: 'Investigation at Cogges, Oxfordshire, 1979–81: The priory and the parish church', *Oxoniensia* 47, 37–126.

Bliese, J.R.E. 1988: 'Aelred of Rievaulx's rhetoric and morale at the Battle of the Standard, 1138', *Albion*, 543–56.

Bollermann, K, and Nederman, C.J. 2008: 'King Stephen, the English church, and a female mystic: Christina of Markyate's Vita as a neglected source for the council of Winchester (August 1139) and its aftermath', *Journal of Medieval History* 34.4, 433–44.

Bolton, D. K., Duncombe, G.R., Dunning, R.W., Kermode, J.I., Rowland, A.M., Stephens, W.B. and Wright, A.P.M. (eds) 1973: *The Victoria History of the County of Cambridge and the Isle of Ely, Volume 5*. London: Victoria County History.

Bond J. 2001: 'Earthen castles, outer enclosures and the earthworks at Ascot d'Oilly castle, Oxfordshire', *Oxoniensia* 66, 43–69.

Bonney, D.J. and Dunn, C.J. 1989: 'Earthwork castles and settlement at Hamstead Marshall, Berkshire', in M. Bowden, D. Mackay and P. Topping (eds), *From Cornwall to Caithness: Some Aspects of British Field Archaeology, Papers Presented to Norman V. Quinnell*. British Archaeological Reports 209. Oxford: British Archaeological Reports, 173–82.

Boon, G.C. 1988: *Coins of the Anarchy 1135–54*. Cardiff: National Museum of Wales.

Borrie, M.A.F. 1970: 'A sealed charter of the Empress Matilda', *British Museum Quarterly* 34.3–4, 104–7.

Boucher, A., Craddock-Bennett, L. and Daly, T. 2015: *Death in the Close: A Medieval Mystery*. Edinburgh: Headland Archaeology.

Boylston, A. 2000: 'Evidence for weapon-related trauma in British archaeological samples', in M. Cox and S. Mays (eds), *Human Osteology in Archaeology and Forensic Science*. Cambridge: Cambridge University Press, 357–80.

Bradbury, C.W. 1990: 'Sword pieces', in M. Biddle (ed.), *Artefacts from Medieval Winchester. Part II: Object and Economy in Medieval Winchester*. Winchester Studies 7, Part II. Oxford: Clarendon Press, 1080–2.

Bradbury, J. 1985: *The Medieval Archer*. Woodbridge: The Boydell Press.

Bradbury, J. 1990: 'Geoffrey V of Anjou, count and knight', in

C. Harber-Bill and R. Harvey (eds), *The Ideals and Practice of Medieval Knighthood III*. Woodbridge: The Boydell Press, 21–38.

Bradbury, J. 1992: *The Medieval Siege*. Woodbridge: The Boydell Press.

Bradbury, J. 1996: *Stephen and Matilda: The Civil War of 1139–53*, Stroud: Sutton.

Bradbury, J. 1998: 'The civil war of Stephen's reign: Winners and losers', in M. Strickland (ed.), *Armies, Chivalry and Warfare in Medieval Britain and France. Proceedings of the 1995 Harlaxton Symposium*. Stamford: Paul Watkins, 115–32.

Bradley, R. 1990: *The Passage of Arms: An Archaeological Analysis of Prehistoric Hoards and Votive Deposits*. Cambridge: Cambridge University Press.

Braun, H. 1934: 'Some notes on Bungay Castle', *Proceedings of the Suffolk Institute of Archaeology and History* 22.1, 109–19.

Breiding, D.H. 2005: 'Horse armor in medieval and Renaissance Europe: An overview', in S. Pyhrr, D.J. LaRocca and D.H. Breiding (eds), *The Armored Horse in Europe 1480–1620*. New York: Metropolitan Museum of Art, 8–18.

Brooke, C.N.L. 1975: *London 800–1216: The Shaping of a City*. Berkeley and Los Angeles: University of California Press.

Brooke, C.N.L. and Morey, A. (eds) 1967: *The Letters and Charters of Gilbert Foliot, Abbot of Gloucester (1139–48), Bishop of Hereford (1148–63) and London (1163–87)*. Cambridge: Cambridge University Press.

Brooke, G.C. 1916: *A Catalogue of English Coins in the British Museum: The Norman Kings*, 2 vols. London: The British Museum.

Brown, A.E. and Taylor, C.C. 1977: 'Cambridgeshire earthwork surveys, II: Rampton: Giant's Hill', *Proceedings of the Cambridge Antiquarian Society* 67, 97–9.

Brown, A.E. and Taylor, C.C. 1978: 'Cambridgeshire Earthwork Surveys III', *Proceedings of the Cambridge Antiquarian Society* 68, 59–75.

Brown, G. 2008: *Richmont Castle, East Harptree: An Analytical Earthwork Survey*. Unpublished report: English Heritage.

Brown, R.A. 1989: *Castles from the Air*. Cambridge: Cambridge University Press.

Burton, J. 1986: 'The foundation of Cistercian houses', in C. Norton and D. Park (eds), *Cistercian Art and Architecture in the British Isles*. Cambridge: Cambridge University Press, 24–39.

Burton, J. 1994: *Monastic and Religious Orders in Britain 1000–1300*. Cambridge: Cambridge University Press.

Burton, J. 1999: *The Monastic Order in Yorkshire, 1069–1215*. Cambridge: Cambridge University Press.

Burton, J. 2008: 'Citadels of god: Monasteries, violence, and the struggle for power in northern England, 1135–1154, *Anglo-Norman Studies* 31, 17–30.

Burton, J. and Kerr, J. 2011: *The Cistercians in the Middle Ages*. Woodbridge: The Boydell Press.

Callaghan, T. Jr. 1974: 'The impact of anarchy on English monasticism, 1135–1154', *Albion* 6.3, 218–32.

Callaghan, T. Jr. 1978: 'Ecclesiastical reparations and the soldiers of "the Anarchy"', *Albion* 10.4, 300–18.

Cameron, K. 1961: *English Place-Names*. London: Batsford.

Campbell, J. 2000: Power and authority 600–1300', in D. Palliser (ed.), *The Cambridge Urban History of Britain. Volume I, 600–1540*. Cambridge: Cambridge University Press, 51–78.

Carley, J.P. 1985: *The Chronicle of Glastonbury Abbey: An Edition, Translation and Study of John of Glastonbury's 'Cronica sive Antiquitates Glastoniensis Ecclesie'*. Woodbridge: Boydell and Brewer.

Carlton, C. 1992: *Going to the Wars: The Experience of the British Civil Wars 1638–1651*. London: Routledge.

Carman, J. and Carman P. 2012: 'Walking the line between past and present: Doing' phenomenology on historic battlefields', in H. Cobb, O.J.T. Harris, C. Jones and P. Richardson (eds), *Reconsidering Archaeological Fieldwork: Exploring On-Site Relationships between Theory and Practice*. New York: Springer, 97–112.

Casey, J. 1980: *Understanding Ancient Coins*. London: Batsford.

Castor, H. 2010: *She-Wolves: The Women Who Ruled England before Elizabeth*. London: Faber & Faber.

Cathers, K. 2002: 'Markings on the land' and early medieval warfare in the British Isles', in P. Doyle and M.R. Bennett (eds), *Fields of Battle: Terrain in Military History*. Dordrecht: Klewer Academic Publishers, 9–17.

Cherry, J. 1997: 'Medieval and post-medieval seals', in D. Collon (ed.), *7000 Years of Seals*. London: British Museum Press, 124–42.

Chibnall, M. 1991: *The Empress Matilda: Queen Consort, Queen Mother and Lady of the English*. Oxford: Blackwell.

Christelow, S. M. 1996: 'A moveable feast? Itineration and the centralization of government under Henry I', *Albion* 28.2, 187–228.

Christie, N. (ed.) 2009: 'Medieval Britain and Ireland in 2008', *Medieval Archaeology* 53, 327–82.

Christie, N. and Creighton, O.H., with Hamerow, H. and Edgeworth, M. 2013: *Townscapes in Transformation. From Burh to Borough: The Archaeology of Wallingford, AD 800–1400*. Society for Medieval Archaeology Monograph 35, Leeds: Society for Medieval Archaeology.

Clark, A. 1889: *Survey of the Antiquities of the City of Oxford Composed in 1661–6 by Anthony Wood. Volume I: City and Suburbs*. Oxford: The Oxford Historical Society at the Clarendon Press.

Clark, J. 2010: 'Londoners at arms: From the Viking wars to the Wars of the Roses', *Transactions of London and Middlesex Archaeological Society* 61, 235–43.

Clarke, C.A.M. 2004: 'Crossing the Rubicon: History, authority and civil war in twelfth-century England', in L. Ashe and I Patterson (eds), *War and Literature*. Cambridge: D.S.W. Brewer, 61–83.

Clarke, C.A.M. 2008: 'Writing civil war in Henry of Huntingdon's *Historia Anglorum*', *Anglo-Norman Studies* 31, 31–48.

Clarke, C.A.M. 2009: 'Signs and wonders: Writing trauma in twelfth-century England', *Reading Medieval Studies* 35, 55–77.

Claughton, P. 2003: 'Production and economic impact: Northern Pennine (English) silver in the 12th century', *Proceedings of the 6th International Mining History Congress, September 26–29, 2003, Akabira City, Hokkaido, Japan* (Akabira City, 2003), 146–9.

Claughton, P. 2011: 'Mineral resources', in J. Crick and E. Van Houts (eds), *A Social History of England 900–1200*. Cambridge: Cambridge University Press, 56–65.

Coad, J.G. 1983: 'Recent work at Castle Acre Castle', *Château Gaillard* 11, 55–67.

Coad, J.G. and Streeten, A.D.F. 1982: 'Excavations at Castle Acre Castle, Norfolk, 1972–77: Country house and castle of the Norman earls of Surrey', *Archaeological Journal* 139, 138–301.

Coad, J.G., Streeten, A.D.F. and Warmington, R. 1987: 'Excavations at Castle Acre castle, Norfolk, 1975–1982: The bridges, lime kilns, and eastern gatehouse', *Archaeological Journal* 144, 256–307.

Cole, M. 1994: *Merdon Castle, Hursley, Hampshire. Report on Geophysical Survey, 1994*. Ancient Monuments Laboratory Report. Unpublished report: English Heritage.

Coles, J. and Hall, D. 1998: *Changing Landscapes: The Ancient Fenland*. Cambridge: Cambridgeshire County Council and Wetland Archaeology Research Project.

Coles, S. 2004: 'Excavation at Castle Street, Luton: The site of Robert de Waudari's Castle', *Bedfordshire Archaeology* 25, 201–7.

Collard, M. 1988: 'Excavations at Desborough castle, High Wycombe, 1987', *Records of Buckinghamshire* 30, 15–41.

Colvin, H.M. 1951: *The White Canons in England*. Oxford: Clarendon Press.

Colvin, H.M., Brown, R.A. and Taylor, A.J. 1963: *The History of the King's Works, Volumes I and II: The Middle Ages*. London: HMSO.

Constable, G. 1953: 'The Second Crusade as seen by contemporaries', *Traditio* 9, 213–79.

Contamine, P. 1984: *War in the Middle Ages*. Oxford: Blackwell.

Coppack, G. 1998: *The White Monks: The Cistercians in Britain 1128–1540*. Stroud: Tempus.

Cotter, J. 1997: *A Twelfth-Century Pottery Kiln at Pound Lane, Canterbury: Evidence for an Immigrant Potter in the Late Norman Period*. Canterbury Archaeological Trust Occasional Paper No 1. Canterbury: Canterbury Archaeological Trust.

Coulson, C. 1993: 'Specimens of freedom to crenellate by licence, *Fortress* 10, 3–15.

Coulson, C. 1994a: 'Freedom to crenellate by licence: An historiographical revision', *Nottingham Medieval Studies* 38, 86–137.

Coulson, C. 1994b: 'The castles of the Anarchy', in E. King (ed.), *The Anarchy of King Stephen's Reign*. Oxford: Clarendon Press, 67–92.

Coulson, C. 1995: 'The French matrix of the castle-provisions of the Chester-Leicester *Conventio*', *Proceedings of the Battle Conference on Anglo-Norman Studies* 17, 65–86.

Coulson, C. 2003: *Castles in Medieval Society: Fortresses in England, France, and Ireland in the Central Middle Ages*. Cambridge: Cambridge University Press.

Cowper, M. 2006: *Cathar Castles: Fortresses of the Albigensian Crusade 1209–1300*. Oxford: Osprey.

Crafter, T.C.R. 1998: 'A re-examination of the classification and chronology of the *cross-and-crosslets* type of Henry II', *British Numismatic Journal* 68, 42–63.

Credland, A.G. 1980: 'Crossbow remains', *Journal of the Society of Archer-Antiquaries* 23, 12–19.

Credland, A.G. 1990: 'Crossbow nut', in M. Biddle (ed.), *Artefacts from Medieval Winchester. Part II: Object and Economy in Medieval Winchester*. Winchester Studies 7, Part II. Oxford: Clarendon Press, 1074–6.

Creighton, O.H. 1997: 'Early Leicestershire castles: Archaeology and landscape history', *Transactions of the Leicestershire Archaeological and Historical Society* 71, 21–36.

Creighton, O.H. 2000: 'Early castles in the medieval landscape of Wiltshire', *Wiltshire Archaeological and Natural History Magazine* 93, 105–19.

Creighton, O.H. 2004: '"The rich man in his castle, the poor man at his gate": Castle baileys and settlement patterns in Norman England', *Chateau Gaillard* 21, 25–36.

Creighton, O.H. 2005a: 'Castles and castle-building in town and country', in C. Dyer and K. Giles (eds), *Medieval Town and Country 1100–1500*. Society for Medieval Archaeology Monograph 22. Leeds: Society for Medieval Archaeology, 275–92.

Creighton, O.H. 2005b: *Castles and Landscapes: Power, Community and Fortification in Medieval England*. London: Equinox.

Creighton, O.H. 2009: *Designs upon the Land: Elite Landscapes of the Middle Ages*. Woodbridge: The Boydell Press.

Creighton, O.H. and Higham, R.A. 2005: *Medieval Town Walls: An Archaeology and Social History of Urban Defence*. Stroud: Tempus.

Creighton, O.H. and Rippon, S.J. forthcoming 2016. 'Conquest, colonisation and the countryside: Archaeology and the mid-11th- to mid-12th- century rural landscape', in C.C. Dyer and D. Hadley (eds), *Archaeology and the Norman Conquest*. Society for Medieval Archaeology Monograph. Leeds: Society for Medieval Archaeology.

Croft, S. 1996: *Strategies of Arms Control: A History and Typology*. Manchester: Manchester University Press.

Cronne, H.A. 1970: *The Reign of Stephen, 1135–54: Anarchy in England*. London: Weidenfeld and Nicholson.

Cronne, H.A. and Davis, R.H.C. (eds) 1968: *Regesta Regum Anglo-Normannorum 1066–1154. Volume III.* Oxford: Clarendon Press.

Crook, D. 1994: 'The archbishopric of York and the extent of the forest in Nottinghamshire in the twelfth century', in G. Garnett and J. Hudson (eds), *Law and Government in Medieval England and Normandy: Essays in Honour of James Holt.* Cambridge: Cambridge University Press, 325–40.

Crook, D. 2008: 'Jordan Castle and the Foliot family of Grimston, 1225–1330', *Transactions of the Thoroton Society of Nottinghamshire* 112, 143–58.

Crouch, D. 1986: *The Beaumont Twins: The Roots and Branches of Power in the Twelfth Century.* Cambridge: Cambridge University Press.

Crouch, D. 1990: *William Marshal: Court, Career and Chivalry in the Angevin Empire 1147–1219.* London: Longman.

Crouch, D. 1992: *The Image of Aristocracy in Britain, 1000–1300.* London: Routledge.

Crouch, D. 1994: 'The March and the Welsh Kings', in E. King (ed.), *The Anarchy of Stephen's Reign.* Oxford: Clarendon Press, 255–89.

Crouch, D. 2000: *The Reign of Stephen, 1135–1154.* Harlow: Pearson Education.

Crouch, D. 2005: *The Tournament.* London and New York: Hambledon and Continuum.

Crouch, D. 2008: 'William Marshal and the Mercenariat', in J. France (ed.), *Mercenaries and Paid Men: The Mercenary Identity in the Middle Ages.* Leiden: Brill, 15–32.

Cumberpatch, C. and Roberts, I. 2013: 'A Stamford ware pottery kiln in Pontefract: A geographical enigma and a dating dilemma', *Medieval Archaeology* 57, 111–50.

Dalton, P. 1992: '*In NeutroLatere:* The armed neutrality of Ranulf II Earl of Chester in King Stephen's reign', *Anglo-Norman Studies* 14, 39–59.

Dalton, P. 1994: *Conquest, Anarchy and Lordship: Yorkshire 1066–1154.* Cambridge: Cambridge University Press.

Dalton, P. 2001: 'Ecclesiastical responses to war in King Stephen's reign: The communities of Selby Abbey, Pontefract Priory and York Cathedral', in P. Dalton, C. Insley and L.J. Wilkinson (eds), *Cathedrals, Communities and Conflict in the Anglo-Norman World.* Woodbridge: The Boydell Press, 131–49.

Dalton, P. 2005: 'Sites and occasions of peacemaking in England and Normandy, c. 900–c. 1150', *The Haskins Society Journal* 16, 12–26.

Dalton, P. and White, G.J. (eds) 2008: *King Stephen's Reign (1135–1154).* Woodbridge: Boydell Press.

Daniels, R. 2009: 'The deserted medieval village of High Worsall, North Yorkshire', *Durham Archaeological Journal* 18, 67–98.

Darby, H.C. 1940: *The Medieval Fenland.* Cambridge: Cambridge University Press.

Darby, H.C. 1977: *Medieval Cambridgeshire.* Cambridge: Oleander Press.

Daubney, A. 2010: 'Medieval copper-alloy mace-heads from England, Scotland and Wales', in S. Worrell, G. Egan, J. Naylor, K. Leahy and M.J. Lewis (eds), *Portable Antiquities Scheme Conference: A Decade of Discovery*. British Archaeological Reports, British Series, 520. Oxford: Archaeopress, 194–200.

Davis, H.W.C. 1903: 'The anarchy of Stephen's reign', *English Historical Review* 18, 630–41.

Davis, H.W.C. (ed.) 1913: *Regesta Regnum Anglo-Normannorum I*. Oxford: Clarendon.

Davis, R.H.C. 1962: 'The authorship of the *Gesta Stephani*', *English Historical Review* 77, 209–32.

Davis, R.H.C. 1964: 'Geoffrey de Mandeville reconsidered', *English Historical Review* 79, 299–307.

Davis, R.H.C. 1967: *King Stephen, 1135–1154*. London: Longman.

Davis, R.H.C. 1978: 'The Carmen de Hastingae Proelio', *English Historical Review* 93.367, 241–61.

Davis, R.H.C. 1988a: 'Geoffrey de Mandeville: A final comment', *English Historical Review* 103, 967–8.

Davis, R.H.C. 1988b: 'The treason of Geoffrey de Mandeville: A comment', *English Historical Review* 103, 313–17.

Davis, R.H.C. 1989: *The Medieval Warhorse: Origin, Development and Redevelopment*. London: Thames and Hudson.

Davison, A., Fenner, A. and Fenner, A. 1990: *The Evolution of Settlement in Three Parishes in South-East Norfolk*. Dereham: Norfolk Archaeology Unit and Norfolk Museum Service.

Davison, B.K. 1967: 'Burwell and Ely Castles', *Archaeological Journal* 124, 214–58.

Davison, B.K. 1972: 'Castle Neroche: An abandoned Norman fortress in south Somerset', *Transactions of the Somerset Archaeological and Natural History Society* 116, 16–58.

de Laborderie, O., Maddicott, J.R. and Carpenter, D.A. 2000: 'The last hours of Simon de Montfort: A new account', *English Historical Review* 115.461, 378–412.

deNeergaard, M. 1987: 'The decoration of medieval scabbards', in J. Cowgill, N. de Neergaard and N. Griffiths, *Medieval Finds from Excavations in London: 1. Knives and Scabbards*. London: HMSO.

DeVries, K. and Douglas Smith, R. 2012: *Medieval Military Technology*, 2nd ed. Toronto: University of Toronto Press.

Dewey, J. and Dewey, S. (eds) 2005: *1155 and All That: Wallingford's 850-Year Old Charter*. Wallingford: Pie Powder Press.

Dixon, P. 2008: 'The influence of the White Tower on the great towers of the twelfth century' in E. Impey (ed.), *The White Tower*. New Haven and London: Yale University Press, 243–75.

Dixon, P. and Marshall, P. 2003: 'The Great Tower at Hedingham Castle: A reassessment', in R. Liddiard (ed.) *Anglo-Norman Castles*. Woodbridge: The Boydell Press, 297–306.

Dobson, B. and Edwards, E. 2010: 'The religious houses of Kent, 1220–1540', in S. Sweetinburgh (ed.), *Later Medieval Kent, 1220–1540*. Woodbridge: The Boydell Press, 79–110.

Dodd, A. (ed.) 2003. *Oxford Before the University: The Late Saxon and Norman Archaeology of the Thames Crossing, the Defences and the Town*. Thames Valley Landscapes Monograph 17. Oxford: Oxford Archaeology.

Dolley, M. 1966: *The Norman Conquest and the English Coinage*. London: Spink.

Douglas, D.C. (ed.) 1932: *Feudal Documents from the Abbey of Bury St. Edmunds*. London: British Academy.

Doyle, P and Bennett, M.R. (eds) 2002: *Fields of Battle: Terrain in Military History*. Dordrecht: Klewer Academic Publishers.

Dressler, R.A. 2004: *Of Armor and Men: The Chivalric Rhetoric of Three English Knights' Effigies*. Aldershot: Ashgate.

Dyer, C.C. 2002: *Making a Living in the Middle Ages: The People of Britain 850–1520*. New Haven and London: Yale University Press.

Dyer, C.C. and Hadley, D. (eds) forthcoming 2016: *Archaeology and the Norman Conquest*. Society for Medieval Archaeology Monograph.

Eaves, I. 2002: 'Arms, armour and militaria', in I. Roberts (ed.), *Pontefract Castle: Archaeological Excavations 1982–86*. Yorkshire Archaeology 8. Leeds: West Yorkshire Archaeological Service, 324–55.

Edwardson, A.R. 1970: 'The Fornham sword', *Proceedings of the Suffolk Institute of Archaeology* 32.1, 87.

Egan, G. 1998: *The Medieval Household: Daily Living c. 1150–c. 1450. Finds from Excavations in London 6*. London: The Stationary Office.

Elliott, L. 2004: 'Excavations at the Minster Chambers, Southwell, Nottinghamshire', *Transactions of the Thoroton Society of Nottinghamshire* 107, 41–64.

Ellis, B. 1982: 'Spurs', in J. Coad and A. Streeten, 'Excavations at Castle Acre Castle, Norfolk, 1972–77', *Archaeological Journal* 139, 138–301.

Ellis, B. 1990: 'Spurs', in M. Biddle (ed.), *Artefacts from Medieval Winchester. Part II: Object and Economy in Medieval Winchester*. Winchester Studies 7, Part II. Oxford: Clarendon Press, 1037–54.

Ellis, P. 2000: *Ludgershall Castle, Wiltshire: A Report on the Excavations by Peter Addyman, 1964–1972*. Devizes: Wiltshire Archaeological and Natural History Society.

Emery, A. 2006: *Greater Medieval Houses of England and Wales, 1300–1500: Volume 3, Southern England*. Cambridge: Cambridge University Press.

Emery, A. 2007: *Discovering Medieval Houses in England and Wales*. Princes Risborough: Shire.

Engel, U. 2002: 'The Bayeux tapestry and all that: Images of war and combat in the arts of medieval England', in B. Korte and R. Schneider (eds), *War and the Cultural Construction of Identities in Britain*. Amsterdam: Rodopi, 61–92.

Ennis, T. 2005: 'The *magnum fossatum* at Saffron Walden: Excavations at Elm Grove, off Goul Lane 2001', *Essex Archaeology and History* (3rd series) 36, 204–7.

Ennis, T. 2011a: 'A medieval site at Chipping Ongar: Excavations at 127–129 High Street, 2007', *Essex Archaeology and History* (4th series) 2, 124–67.

Ennis, T. 2011b: 'Investigations on the medieval defences of Walden Castle, Saffron Walden, 2005–2009', *Essex Archaeology and History* (4th series) 2, 98–106.

Evans, C. 2003: *Power and Island Communities: Excavations at the Wardy Hill Ringwork, Coveney, Ely*. East Anglian Archaeology 103. Cambridge: Cambridge Archaeological Unit.

Evans, C. and Hodder, I. 2006: *Marshland Communities and Cultural Landscapes, The Haddenham Project Volume 2*. Cambridge: McDonald Institute for Archaeological Research.

Everson, P. 1988: 'What's in a name? "Goltho", Goltho and Bullington', *Lincolnshire History and Archaeology* 23, 93–9.

Everson, P. 1990: 'The problem of Goltho', *Medieval Settlement Research Group Report* 5, 9–14.

Everson, P. and Brown, G. 2010: 'Dr Hoskins I presume? Field visits in the footsteps of a pioneer', in C.C. Dyer and R. Jones (eds). *Deserted Villages Revisited*. Hatfield: University of Hertfordshire Press, 46–63.

Evison, V.I, 1967: 'A sword from the Thames at Wallingford Bridge', *Archaeological Journal* 124, 160–89.

Farrer, W. 1925: *Honors and Knights' Fees: An Attempt to Identify the Component Parts of Certain Honors and to Trace the Descent of the Tenants of the Same Who Held by Knight's Service Or Serjeanty from the Eleventh to the Fourteenth Century*. Manchester: Manchester University Press.

Fergusson, P. 1984: *Architecture of Solitude: Cistercian Abbeys in Twelfth-Century England*. Princeton: Princeton University Press.

Fernie, E. 2002: *The Architecture of Norman England*. Oxford: Oxford University Press.

Fiorato V., Boylston A. and Knüsel, C. (eds) 2000: *Blood Red Roses. The Archaeology of a Mass Grave from the Battle of Towton, AD 1461*. Oxford: Oxbow.

Fletcher, A.J. (ed.) 2002: *The Victoria History of the County of Cambridge and the Isle of Ely, Volume 10*. London: Oxford University Press for The Institute of Historical Research.

Foard, G, 2012: *Battlefield Archaeology of the English Civil War*. British Archaeological Reports (British Series 570). Oxford: Archeopress.

Foard, G. and Morris, R. 2012: *The Archaeology of English Battlefields: Conflict in the Pre-Industrial Landscape*. CBA Research Report 168. York: Council for British Archaeology.

France, J. 2008: 'Introduction', in J. France (ed.), *Mercenaries and Paid Men: The Mercenary Identity in the Middle Ages*. Leiden: Brill, 1–13.

Fulford, M. 1985: 'Excavations on the sites of the amphitheatre and forum-basilica at Silchester, Hampshire: An interim report', *Antiquaries Journal* 65.1, 39–81.

Fulford, M. 1989: *The Silchester Amphitheatre: Excavations of 1979–85*. Britannia Monograph Series 10. London: Society for the Promotion of Roman Studies.

Garnett, G. 2007: *Conquered England: Kingship, Succession and Tenure*. Oxford: Oxford University Press.

Gem, R. 1986: 'Lincoln Minster: *ecclesia pulchra, ecclesia fortis*', in T.A. Heslop and V.A. Sekules (eds), *The British Archaeological Association Conference Transactions for the Year 1982, VIII: Medieval Art and Architecture at Lincoln Cathedral*. London: British Archaeological Association, 9–28.

Gem, R. 1988: 'The English parish church in the eleventh and early twelfth centuries: A great rebuilding', in J. Blair (ed.), *Minsters and Parish Churches: The Local Church in Transition, 950–1200*. Oxford: Oxbow, 21–30.

Gervers, M. 1992: 'Donations to the Hospitallers in England in the wake of the Second Crusade', in M. Gervers (ed.), *The Second Crusade and the Cistercians*. New York: St. Martin's Press, 155–61.

Gilchrist, R. 2012: *Medieval Life: Archaeology and the Life Course*. Woodbridge: The Boydell Press.

Gilchrist, R. and Green, C. 2015: *Glastonbury Abbey: Archaeological Investigations 1904–79*. London: Society of Antiquaries.

Gillingham, J. 1992: 'Conquering the barbarians: War and chivalry in twelfth-century Britain', *Haskins Society Journal* 4, 67–84.

Gilyard-Beer, R. and Coppack, G. 1986: 'Excavations at Fountains Abbey, North Yorkshire, 1979–80: The early development of the monastery', *Archaeologia* 108, 147–88.

Goddard, E.H. 1930: 'The mount at Great Somerford', *Wiltshire Archaeological Magazine* 45, 88–9.

Good, G.L. 1996: 'Bristol castle keep: A re-appraisal of the evidence and a report on the excavations in 1989', *Bristol and Avon Archaeology* 13, 17–45.

Goodall, I.H. 1982: 'Iron objects', in J. Coad and A. Streeten, Excavations at Castle Acre Castle, Norfolk, 1972–77', *Archaeological Journal* 139, 138–301.

Goodall, I.H. 1987: 'Objects of iron', in G. Beresford, *Goltho: The Development of an Early Medieval Manor c.850–1150*. London: Historic Buildings and Monuments Commission for England, 177–87.

Goodall, I.H. 1990a: 'Arrowheads', in M. Biddle (ed.), *Artefacts from Medieval Winchester. Part II: Object and Economy in Medieval Winchester*. Winchester Studies 7, Part II. Oxford: Clarendon Press, 1070–4.

Goodall, I.H. 1990b: 'Horseshoes', in M. Biddle (ed.), *Artefacts from Medieval Winchester. Part II: Object and Economy in Medieval*

Winchester. Winchester Studies 7, Part II. Oxford: Clarendon Press, 1054–67.

Goodall, I.H. 2012: *Ironwork in Medieval Britain: An Archaeological Study.* Society for Medieval Archaeology Monograph 31. Leeds: Society for Medieval Archaeology.

Gover, J.E.B, Mawer, A. and Stenton, F.M. 1940: *The Place-Names of Nottinghamshire.* English Place-Name Society 17. Cambridge: Cambridge University Press.

Graham, A.H. and Davies, S.M. 1993: *Excavations in the Town Centre of Trowbridge, Wiltshire 1977 and 986–1988: The Prehistoric and Saxon Settlements, the Saxo-Norman Manorial Settlement, and the Anarchy Period Castle.* Salisbury: Wessex Archaeology.

Graham-Campbell, G. 1992: 'Anglo-Scandinavian equestrian equipment in eleventh-century England', *Anglo-Norman Studies* 14, 77–89.

Grant, L. 1987: 'The architecture of the early Savigniacs and Cistercians in Normandy', *Anglo-Norman Studies* 10, 111–43.

Gravett, C. 1993: *Norman Knight 950–1204 AD.* London: Osprey.

Gray, H.L. 1915: *English Field Systems.* Cambridge: Harvard University Press.

Green, J.A. 1990: *English Sheriffs to 1154.* London: HMSO.

Green, J.A. 1992: 'Financing Stephen's war', *Anglo-Norman Studies* 14, 91–114.

Green, J.A. 1997: *The Aristocracy of Norman England.* Cambridge: Cambridge University Press.

Green, J.A. 2006: *Henry I: King of England and Duke of Normandy.* Cambridge: Cambridge University Press.

Green, J.A. 2015: 'The charters of Geoffrey de Mandeville', in P. Dalton and D. Luscombe (eds), *Rulership and Rebellion in the Anglo-Norman World, c. 1066–c. 1216.* Farnham: Ashgate, 91–110.

Green. J.A. 1997: 'Family matters: Family and the formation of the Empress's party in south-west England', in K.S.B. Keats-Rohan (ed.), *Family Trees and the Roots of Politics: The Prosopography of Britain and France from the Tenth to the Twelfth Century.* Woodbridge: The Boydell Press, 147–64.

Greene, J.P. 1992: *Medieval Monasteries.* London: Leicester University Press.

Greenway, D. and Watkiss, L. (ed. and trans.) 1999: *The Book of the Foundation of Walden Monastery.* Oxford: Clarendon Press.

Griffiths, D. 2011: 'Towns and their hinterlands', in J. Crick and E. Van Houts (eds), *A Social History of England 900–1200.* Cambridge: Cambridge University Press, 152–78.

Griffiths, N. 2004: 'Harness fittings and associated fittings', in J. Clark (ed.), *The Medieval Horse and its Equipment, c.1150–c.1450.* Woodbridge: The Boydell Press, 61–71.

Hadley, D.M. 2011: 'Ethnicity and acculturation', in J. Crick and E. Van Houts (eds), *A Social History of England 900–1200.* Cambridge: Cambridge University Press, 235–46.

Hall, D.N. 1992: *The Fenland Project No. 6: The South-Western Cambridgeshire Fens.* East Anglian Archaeology No 56. Cambridge: Cambridgeshire Archaeology Committee.

Hallam, E.M. 1982: 'Royal burial and the cult of kingship in France and England, 1060–1330', *Journal of Medieval History* 8.4, 359–80.

Hallam, H.E. 1965: *Settlement and Society: A Study of the Early Agrarian History of South Lincolnshire.* Cambridge: Cambridge University Press.

Halpin, A. 1986: 'Irish medieval swords *c.* 1170–1600', *Proceedings of the Royal Irish Academy* 86C, 183–230.

Hamilton Thompson, A. 1912: *Military Architecture in England During the Middle Ages.* Oxford and London: Oxford University Press.

Harvey, P.D.A. and McGuiness, A. 1996: *A Guide to British Medieval Seals.* London: The British Library and Public Record Office.

Harvey, S. 1970: 'The knight and the knight's fee in England', *Past and Present* 49, 3–43.

Haskins, C.H. 1927: *The Renaissance of the Twelfth Century.* Cambridge: Harvard University Press.

Haslam, J. 2009: 'The development of late-Saxon Christchurch, Dorset, and the Burghal Hidage', *Medieval Archaeology* 53, 95–118.

Haslam, J. 1977–78: 'The excavation of the defences of Devizes', *Wiltshire Archaeological Magazine* 72–3, 59–65.

Haslam, J. 2003: 'Excavations at Cricklade, Wiltshire, 1975', *Internet Archaeology* 14. http://dx.doi.org/10.11141/ia.14.1

Helmerichs, R. 1993: 'King Stephen's Norman itinerary', *Haskins Society Journal* 5, 89–97.

Henig, M. 2008: 'The re-use of ancient intaglios set in medieval personal seals, mainly found in England: An aspect of the Renaissance of the 12th century', in N. Adams, J. Cherry and J. Robinson, *Good Impressions: Image and Authority in Medieval Seals.* London: British Museum, 25–34.

Henry, F. and Zarnecki, G. 1957–58: 'Romanesque arches decorated with human and animal heads', *Journal of the British Archaeological Association*, 20–1, 1–35.

Herlihy, D. (ed.) 1970: *The History of Feudalism.* New York, Evanston and London: Harper and Row.

Heslop, T.A. 1984: 'Seals', in G. Zarnecki (ed.), *English Romanesque Art 1066–1200. Hayward Gallery, London 5 April–8 July 1984.* London: Weidenfeld and Nicolson, 298–319.

Heslop, T.A. 1991: 'The seals of the twelfth-century Earls of Chester', *Journal of the Chester Archaeological Society* 71, 179–97.

Heslop, T.A. 1994: *Norwich Castle Keep: Romanesque Architecture and Social Context.* Norwich: Centre of East Anglian Studies.

Hicks, L. 2013: 'The concept of the frontier in Norman chronicles: a comparative approach', in K. Stringer and A. Jotischky (eds), *Norman Expansion: Connections, Continuities and Contrasts.* Farnham: Ashgate, 143–64.

Higgott, T. 1998: 'Is Newbury's medieval castle at Hamstead Marshall?', *Transactions of the Newbury District Field Club* 14.2–3, 28–9.

Higham, R.A. 1977. 'Excavations at Okehampton Castle, Devon. Part I: The motte and keep', *Proceedings of the Devon Archaeological Society* 35, 1–42.

Higham, R.A. 1982: 'Early castles in Devon, 1068–1201', *Château Gaillard* 9–10, 101–16.

Higham, R.A. 1988: 'Devon castles: An annotated list', *Proceedings of the Devon Archaeological Society* 46, 142–9.

Higham, R.A. 2013: 'William the Conqueror's siege of Exeter in 1068', *Report and Transactions of the Devonshire Association for the Advancement of Science, Literature and the Arts* 145, 93–132.

Higham, R.A. 2015: *Shell-Keeps Revisited: The Bailey on the Motte?* Daventry: Castle Studies Group.

Higham, R.A. and Barker, P. 2000: *Hen Domen, Montgomery: A Timber Castle on the English-Welsh Border: A Final Report.* Exeter: Exeter University Press.

Higham, R.A. and Barker, R.A. 1992: *Timber Castles.* London: Batsford.

Higham, R.A. and Henderson, C.G. 2011: 'Danes Castle, Exeter: Excavations 1992–3', *Proceedings of the Devon Archaeological Society* 69, 125–56.

Hill, B.D. 1968: *English Cistercian Monasteries and their Patrons in the Twelfth Century*, Urbana: University of Illinois Press.

Hill, J.W.F. 1948: *Mediaeval Lincoln.* Cambridge: Cambridge University Press.

Hillaby, J. 2003: 'Jewish colonisation in the twelfth century', in P. Skinner (ed.), *Jews in Medieval Britain: Historical, Literary and Archaeological Perspectives.* Woodbridge: The Boydell Press, 15–40.

Hinton, D.A. 2005: *Gold and Gilt, Pots and Pins: Possessions and People in Medieval Britain.* Oxford: Oxford University Press.

Holdsworth, C. 1994: 'The Church', in E. King (ed.), *The Anarchy of King Stephen's Reign.* Oxford: Clarendon Press, 207–29.

Hollister, C.W. 1974: 'Stephen's Anarchy', *Albion* 6, 233–9.

Hollister, C.W. 1993: 'The magnates of Stephen's reign: Reluctant anarchists', *Haskins Society Journal* 5, 77–87.

Hollister, C.W. 2001: *Henry I.* New Haven and London: Yale University Press.

Holt, J.C. 1994: '1153: The treaty of Winchester', in E. King (ed.), *The Anarchy of King Stephen's Reign.* Oxford: Clarendon Press, 291–316.

Home, M. 2015: *The Peterborough Version of the Anglo-Saxon Chronicle: Re-writing Post-Conquest History.* Woodbridge: The Boydell Press.

Hope-Taylor, B. 1950: 'The excavation of a motte at Abinger in Surrey', *Archaeological Journal* 107, 15–43.

Hope-Taylor, B. 1956: 'The Norman motte at Abinger, Surrey, and its wooden castle', in R.L.S. Bruce-Mitford (ed.), *Recent Archaeological Excavations in Britain.* London: Routledge and Kegan Paul, 223–49.

Hoskins, W.G. 1956: 'Seven deserted village sites in Leicestershire', *Transactions of the Leicestershire Archaeological and Historical Society* 32, 36–51.

Hosler, J.D. 2007: *Henry II: A Medieval Soldier at War, 1147–1189*. Leiden: Brill.

Hosler, J.D. 2013: *John of Salisbury: Military Authority of the Twelfth-Century Renaissance*. Leiden and Boston: Brill.

Hughes, M. 1989: 'Hampshire castles and the landscape 1066–1216', *Landscape History* 11, 27–60.

Hughes, M.K. and Diaz, H.F. 1994: 'Was there a "Medieval Warm Period", and if so, where and when?', *Climatic Change* 26.2–3, 109–42.

Hulme, R, 2007–8: 'Twelfth century great towers: The case for the defence', *Castle Studies Group Journal* 21, 209–29.

Hurst, J.G. 1956: 'Saxo-Norman pottery in East Anglia', *Proceedings of the Cambridge Antiquarian Society* 49, 43–70.

Hurst, J.G. 1962–3: 'White Castle and the dating of medieval pottery', *Medieval Archaeology* 6–7, 135–55.

Impey, E. (ed.) 2008: *The White Tower*. New Haven and London: Yale University Press.

Ingelmark B.E. 2001: 'The skeletons', in B. Thordman, O. Norlund and B.E. Ingelmark (eds), *Armour from the Battle of Visby, 1361. Vol. 2*. Union City: Chivalry Bookshelf (reprinted from Vitterhets Historie och Antikvitets Akademien, Stockholm, 1939), 149–209.

Isaac, S. 1999: 'The problem with mercenaries', in D. Kagay and A. Villalon (eds), *The Circle of War in the Middle Ages*. Woodbridge: The Boydell Press, 101–10.

Ivens, R.J. 1983: 'Deddington Castle, Oxfordshire: A summary of excavations 1977–1979', *South Midlands Archaeology: CBA Group 9 Newsletter* 13, 34–41.

Ivens, R.J. 1984: 'Deddington Castle, Oxfordshire, and the English honour of Bayeux', *Oxoniensia* 49, 101–19.

Janin, H. with Carlson, U. 2013: *Mercenaries in Medieval and Renaissance Europe*. Jefferson: McFarland & Company.

Jervis, B. 2014: *Pottery and Social Life in Medieval England*. Oxford: Oxbow.

Jessop, O. 1996: 'A new typology for the study of medieval arrowheads', *Medieval Archaeology* 40, 192–205.

Jessop, O. 1997: 'European iron arrowheads: Evidence for their techno-logical development and geographical distribution', in G. de Boe and F. Verhaeghe (eds), *Rural Settlements in Medieval Europe: Papers of the Medieval Europe Brugge 1997 Conference, Volume 6*. Zellik: A.A.P. Rapporten 6, 43–9.

Johns, S.M. 2003: *Noblewomen, Aristocracy and Power in the Twelfth-Century Anglo-Norman Realm*. Manchester: Manchester University Press.

Johnson, C. and Cronne, H.A. (eds) 1956: *Regesta Regum Anglo-Norman-norum 1066–1154. Volume II, 1100–1135*. Oxford: Clarendon Press.

Jones, C., Eyre-Morgan, G., Palmer, S. et al. 1997 'Excavations in the outer enclosure of Boteler's Castle, Oversley, Alcester, 1992–3', *Transactions of the Birmingham and Warwickshire Archaeological Society* 101, 1–98.

Jones, M., Stocker, D., and Vince, A. 2003: *The City by the Pool: Assessing the Archaeology of the City of Lincoln*. Lincoln Archaeological Studies 10. Oxford: Oxbow.

Jones, R. 2010: 'The village and the butterfly: Nucleation out of chaos and complexity', *Landscapes* 11.1, 25–46.

Jones, R.L.C. 1999: 'Fortifications and sieges in Western Europe, c. 800–1450', in M. Keen (ed.), *Medieval Warfare: A History*. Oxford: Oxford University Press, 163–85.

Jones, R.W. 2010: *Bloodied Banners: Martial Display on the Medieval Battlefield*. Woodbridge: The Boydell Press.

Jones, T.S. 2010: *Outlawry in Medieval Literature*. New York: Palgrave Macmillan.

Jope, E.M. and Threlfall, R. 1959: 'The twelfth-century castle at Ascot Doilly, Oxfordshire: Its history and excavation', *Antiquaries Journal* 39, 219–70.

Jope, E.M. 1956: 'The tinning of iron spurs: A continuous practice from the tenth to the seventeenth century', *Oxoniensia* 21, 35–42.

Jope, E.M. 1963: 'The regional cultures of medieval Britain', in I.L.L. Foster and L. Alcock (eds), *Essays in Honour of Cyril Fox*. Routledge & Kegan Paul, 327–50.

Jurica, A.R.J. 2010: *The Victoria History of the County of Gloucester. Volume 12*. Woodbridge: Boydell and Brewer for the Institute of Historical Research.

Kahn, D. 1992: 'Anglo-Saxon and early Romanesque frieze sculpture in England', in D. Kahn (ed.), *The Romanesque Frieze and its Spectator*. London: Harvey Miller, 61–74.

Kapelle, W.E. 1979: *The Norman Conquest of the North: The Region and its Transformation, 1000–1135*. London: Croom Helm.

Kealey, E.J. 1974: 'King Stephen: Government and anarchy', *Albion* 6.3, 201–17.

Keats-Rohan, K.S.B. 2009: 'The genesis of the honour of Wallingford', in K.S.B. Keats-Rohan and D.R. Roffe (eds), *The Origins of Wallingford: Archaeological and Historical Perspectives*. British Archaeological Reports (British Series 494). Oxford: Archeopress, 52–67.

Keats-Rohan, K.S.B. 2012: 'Through the eye of the needle: Stigand, the Bayeux Tapestry and the beginnings of the *Historia Anglorum*', in D. Roffe (ed.), *The English and their Legacy, 900–1200. Essays in Honour of Ann Williams*. Woodbridge: The Boydell Press, 159–74.

Keats-Rohan, K.S.B. 2015a: 'Fortunes of war: Safe-guarding Wallingford castle and honour 1135–60', in P. Dalton and D. Luscombe (eds), *Rulership and Rebellion in the Anglo-Norman World, c. 1066–c. 1216*. Farnham: Ashgate, 125–39.

Keats-Rohan, K.S.B. 2015b: '"Most securely fortified": Wallingford castle 1071–1540', in K.S.B. Keats-Rohan, N. Christie and D. Roffe (eds),

Wallingford: The Castle and the Town in Context. Farnham: Ashgate, 34–115.

Keefe, T.K. 1990: 'Place-date distribution of royal charters and the historical geography of patronage strategies at the court of King Henry II Plantagenet', *Haskins Society Journal* 2, 179–88.

Keen, M. 1984: *Chivalry.* New Haven and London: Yale University Press.

Keen, M. with Barker, J. 1996: 'The medieval English kings and the tournament', in M. Keen (ed.), *Nobles, Knights and Men-at-Arms in the Middle Ages.* London and Rio Grande: Hambledon, 83–99.

Keevill, G. 2004: *The Tower of London Moat: Archaeological Excavations 1995–9.* London: Historic Royal Palaces.

Kelleher, R. 2011: 'Interpreting single finds in medieval England: The secondary lives of coins', in N. Holmes (ed.), *Proceedings of the XIV International Numismatic Congress, Glasgow, Vol II.* Glasgow: International Numismatic Council, 1492–9.

Kelleher, R. 2012: *Coins, Monetisation and Re-use in Medieval England and Wales: New Interpretations Made Possible by the Portable Antiquities Scheme.* Durham University: Unpublished PhD thesis.

Kelleher, R. 2015: *A History of Medieval Coinage in England.* Witham: Greenlight Publishing.

Kelly, S.E. 2009: *Charters of Peterborough Abbey.* Anglo-Saxon Charters 14. Oxford: Oxford University Press (The British Academy).

Kendrick, T.D. 1941: 'The Temple Pyx', *Antiquaries Journal* 21, 161.

Kenney, J. and Oswald, A. 1996: 'Belsar's Hill, Willingham, Cambridgeshire: A survey by the Royal Commission on the Historical Monuments of England', *Proceedings of the Cambridge Antiquarian Society* 84, 5–14.

Kent, J., Renn, D. and Streeten, A. 2013: *Excavations at South Mimms Castle, Hertfordshire 1960–91.* London and Middlesex Archaeological Society Special Paper 16. Lavenham: Lavenham Press.

Keynes, S. 2003: 'Ely Abbey 672–1109', in P. Meadows and N. Ramsay (eds), *A History of Ely Cathedral.* Woodbridge: The Boydell Press, 3–58.

King, D.J.C. 1966: 'Ringworks of England and Wales', *Château Gaillard* 3, 90–127.

King, D.J.C. 1983: *Castellarium Anglicanum.* Millwood: Kraus International.

King, E. (ed.) 1994: *The Anarchy of King Stephen's Reign.* Oxford: Clarendon Press.

King, E. 1980a: 'Mountsorrel and its region in King Stephen's reign', *Huntingdon Library Quarterly* 44.1, 1–10.

King, E. 1980b: 'The parish of Warter and the castle of Galchlin', *Yorkshire Archaeological Journal* 52, 55–8.

King, E. 1990: 'The foundation of Pipewell Abbey, Northamptonshire', *Haskins Society Journal* 2, 167–77.

King, E. 2000: 'Stephen of Blois, count of Mortain and Boulogne', *English Historical Review* 115, 271–96.

King, E. 2002: 'Economic development in the early twelfth century', in R. Britnell and J. Hatcher (eds), *Progress and Problems in Medieval England*. Cambridge: Cambridge University Press, 1–22.

King, E. 2006: 'The *Gesta Stephani*', in D. Bates, J. Crick and S. Hamilton (eds), *Writing Medieval Biography 750–1250. Essays in Honour of Frank Barlow*. Woodbridge: The Boydell Press, 195–206.

King, E. 2007: 'The accession of Henry II', in C. Harper-Bill and N. Vincent (eds), *Henry II: New Interpretations*. Woodbridge: The Boydell Press, 24–46.

King, E. 2010: *King Stephen*. London and New Haven: Yale University Press.

King, J.F. 1995: 'The parish church at Kilpeck reassessed', in D. Whitehead (ed.), *Medieval Art, Architecture and Archaeology at Hereford*. British Archaeological Association Conference Transactions 15. Leeds: British Archaeological Association, 82–93.

Knocker, G.M. 1967: 'Excavations at Red Castle, Thetford', *Norfolk Archaeology* 34, 119–86.

Knowles, D. 1963: *The Monastic Order in England: A History of its Development from the Times of St. Dunstan to the Fourth Lateran Council, 940–1216*, 2nd ed. Cambridge: Cambridge University Press.

Knowles, D. and Hadcock, R.N. 1971: *Medieval Religious Houses: England and Wales*. London: Longman.

Kusaba, Y. 1993: 'Henry of Blois, Winchester, and the twelfth-century renaissance', in J. Crook (ed.), *Winchester Cathedral: Nine Hundred Years, 1093–1993*. Chichester: Phillimore, 69–80.

Laban, G. 2011: *Land at the Street, Lister Wilder Site, The Street, Wallingford, Crowmarsh OX10 8EB: An Archaeological Evaluation Report*. Unpublished report: Museum of London Archaeology.

Laban, G. 2013: 'Evidence for a Stephanic siege castle at the Lister Wilder Site, The Street, Crowmarsh Gifford', *Oxoniensia* 78, 189–211.

Lankester, P. 2010: 'The thirteenth-century military effigies in the Temple Church', in R. Griffith-Jones and D. Park (eds), *The Temple Church in London: History, Architecture, Art*. Woodbridge: The Boydell Press, 93–134.

Latimer, P. 2015: 'How to suppress a rebellion: England 1173–74', in P. Dalton and D. Luscombe (eds), *Rulership and Rebellion in the Anglo-Norman World, c. 1066–c. 1216*. Farnham: Ashgate, 163–77.

Le Maho, J. 2000: 'Fortifications de siège et « contre-châteaux » en Normandie (XIe–XIIe siècles)', *Château Gaillard* 19, 181–9.

Le Patourel, H.E.J. 1976: *The Norman Empire*. Oxford: Clarendon Press.

Leah, M. 1993: 'Excavations and watching brief at Castle Acre, 1985–86', *Norfolk Archaeology* 41.4, 494–507.

Leeds, E.T. 1936: 'An adulterine castle on Faringdon Clump, Berkshire', *Antiquaries Journal* 16, 165–78.

Leeds, E.T. 1937: 'An adulterine castle on Faringdon Clump, Berkshire. Second report', *Antiquaries Journal* 17, 294–8.

Lethbridge, T.C. 1931: 'An attempt to discover the site of the Battle of Aldreth', *Proceedings of the Cambridge Antiquarian Society* 31, 155–6.

Lethbridge, T.C. 1936: 'Excavations at Burwell Castle, Cambridgeshire', *Proceedings of the Cambridge Antiquarian Society* 36, 121–33.

Lethbridge, T.C. 1952: 'Excavations of the Castle Site known as "The Hillings" at Eaton Socon, Bedfordshire', *Proceedings of the Cambridge Antiquarian Society* 4, 48–61.

Lethbridge, T.C. and O'Reilly, M.M. 1934: 'Archaeological notes', *Proceedings of the Cambridge Antiquarian Society* 34, 88–93.

Lewis, C. 1989: 'Paired mottes in East Chelborough, Dorset', in M. Bowden, D. Mackay and P. Topping (eds), *From Cornwall to Caithness: Some Aspects of British Field Archaeology, Papers Presented to Norman V. Quinnell*. British Archaeological Reports (British Series 209). Oxford: British Archaeological Reports, 159–73.

Lewis, C. and Ranson, C. 2011: *Archaeological Excavations in Mount Bures, Essex, 2011*. Unpublished report: McDonald Institute for Archaeological Research, Access Cambridge Archaeology.

Lewis, C. and Ranson, C. 2013: *Archaeological Excavations in Saffron Walden, 2013*. Unpublished report: McDonald Institute for Archaeological Research, Access Cambridge Archaeology.

Lewis, C., Mitchell-Fox, P., and Dyer, C. 1997: *Village, Hamlet and Field: Changing Medieval Settlements in Central England*. Macclesfield: Windgather Press.

Lewis, E. 1985: 'Excavations in Bishop's Waltham, 1967–78', *Proceedings of the Hampshire Field Club and Archaeological Society* 41, 81–126.

Lewis, M.J. 2005: *The Archaeological Authority of the Bayeux Tapestry*. British Archaeological Reports (British Series 404). Oxford: British Archaeological Reports.

Lewis, M.J. 2007: 'A new date for 'Class A, Type 11A' stirrup-strap mounts, and some observations on their distribution', *Medieval Archaeology* 51, 178–84.

Lewis, M.J. 2010: 'Questioning the authority of the Bayeux Tapestry', *Cultural and Social History* 7.4, 467–84.

Liddiard, R. 2000: *'Landscapes of Lordship': Norman Castles and the Countryside in Medieval Norfolk, 1066–1200*. British Archaeological Reports (British Series 309). Oxford: British Archaeological Reports.

Liddiard, R. 2005a: *Castles in Context: Power, Symbolism and Landscape, 1066 to 1500*. Bollington: Windgather.

Liddiard, R. 2005b: 'The castle landscapes of Anglo-Norman East Anglia: A regional perspective', in C. Harper-Bill (ed.), *Medieval East Anglia*. Woodbridge: The Boydell Press, 33–51.

Liddiard, R. and Wells, F. 2008: 'The Little Park at Castle Hedingham, Essex: A possible late medieval pleasure ground', *Garden History* 36.1, 85–93.

Lieberman, M. 2010: *The Medieval March of Wales: The Creation and Perception of a Frontier, 1066–1283*. Cambridge: Cambridge University Press.

Lilley, K.D. 1999: 'Urban landscapes and the cultural politics of territorial control in Anglo-Norman England', *Landscape Research* 24.1, 5–23.

Lilley, K.D. 2000: '"Non urbe, non vico, non castris": Territorial control and the colonization and urbanization of Wales and Ireland under Anglo-Norman lordship', *Journal of Historical Geography* 26.4, 517–31.

Lipman, V.D. 1967: *Jews of Norwich*. London: The Jewish Historical Society of England.

Loades, M. 2010: *Swords and Swordsmen*. Barnsley: Pen & Sword Military.

LoPrete, K. 2007: *Adela of Blois: Countess and Lord (c.1067–1137)*. Dublin: Four Courts Press.

Lowerre, A.G. 2005: *Placing Castles in the Conquest: Landscape, Lordship and Local Politics in the South-Eastern Midlands, 1066–1100*. British Archaeological Reports (British Series 385). Oxford: British Archaeological Reports.

Lucas, J. 1987: 'Excavations in a medieval market town: Mountsorrel, Leicestershire', *Transactions of the Leicestershire Archaeological and Natural History Society* 62, 1–7.

MacGregor, A. 1975–6: 'Two antler crossbow nuts and some notes on the early development of the crossbow', *Proceedings of the Society of Antiquaries of Scotland* 107, 317–32.

MacGregor, A. 1985: *Bone, Antler, Ivory and Horn: Technology of Skeletal Materials Since the Roman Period*. Beckenham: Croom Helm.

MacGregor, A. 1991: 'Antler, bone and horn', in J. Blair and N. Ramsay (eds), *Medieval Industries*. London: Hambledon Press, 355–78.

Mack, R.P. 1966: 'Stephen and the anarchy 1135–1154', *British Numismatic Journal* 35, 38–112.

Maekawa, K. 1997; 'A deserted medieval village and the formation of a fortified town in Cambridgeshire, England', in G. de Boe and F. Verhaeghe (eds), *Rural Settlements in Medieval Europe: Papers of the Medieval Europe Brugge 1997 Conference, Volume 6*. Zellik: A.A.P. Rapporten 6, 243–52.

Magrill, B. 2009: 'Figurated corbels on Romanesque churches: The interface of diverse social patterns represented on marginal spaces', *Canadian Art Review* 34.2, 43–54.

Malim, C. 2001: *Burwell Castle, Cambridgeshire: Information Pack*. Cambridge: Cambridgeshire County Council.

Manby, T.G. 1968: 'Almondbury Castle and hill fort', *Archaeological Journal* 125, 352–54.

Marshall, P. 2004a: 'Improving the image: The transformation of Bailey into Courtyard at the 12th-century Bishops' castle at Newark, Nottinghamshire', *Château Gaillard* 21, 203–14.

Marshall, P. 2004b: 'Lincoln castle: The architectural context of the medieval defences', in P. Lindley (ed.), *The Early History of Lincoln Castle*. Lincoln: Occasional Papers in Lincolnshire History and Archaeology, 53–65.

Marshall, P. 2006: 'Three urban castles and their communities in the East Midlands: Lincoln, Nottingham and Newark', *Château Gaillard* 22, 259–65.

Matthew, D. 2002: *King Stephen*. London: Hambledon and London.

McAleer, J.P. 1999: *Rochester Cathedral 604–1650: An Architectural History*. Toronto: University of Toronto Press.

McClain, A. 2007: 'Medieval cross slabs in North Yorkshire: Chronology, distribution, and social implications', *Yorkshire Archaeological Journal* 79, 155–93.

McClain, A. 2011: 'Local churches and the conquest of the North: Elite patronage and identity in Saxo-Norman Northumbria', in D. Petts and S. Turner (eds), *Early Medieval Northumbria: Kingdoms and Communities, AD 450–1100*. Turnhout: Brepols, 151–78.

McClain, A. 2012: 'Theory, disciplinary perspectives and the archaeology of later medieval England', *Medieval Archaeology* 56, 131–70.

Meaney, A.L. 1997: 'Hundred meeting-places in the Cambridge region', in A.R. Rumble and A.D. Mills (eds), *Names, Places and People: An Onomastic Miscellany in Memory of John McNeal Dodgson*. Stamford: Watkins, 195–240.

Meeson, B. 2012: 'Structural trends in English medieval buildings: New insights from dendrochronology', *Vernacular Architecture* 43, 58–75.

Meeson, R.A. and Welch, C.M. 1993: 'Earthfast posts: The persistence of alternative building techniques', *Vernacular Architecture* 24.1, 1–17.

Metcalf, D.M. 1998: *An Atlas of Anglo-Saxon and Norman Coin Finds, c. 973–1086*. London and Oxford: Royal Numismatic Society and Ashmolean Museum.

Miles, D.W.H., Worthington, M.J. and Groves, C. 1999: *Tree Ring Analysis of the Nave Roof, West Door and Parish Chest of St Mary, Kempley, Gloucestershire*. Ancient Monuments Laboratory Report. Unpublished report: English Heritage.

Mitchell, P.D., Nagar, Y and Ellenblum, R. 2006: 'Weapon injuries in the 12th Century Crusader garrison of Vadum Iacob Castle, Galilee', *International Journal of Osteoarchaeology* 16, 145–55.

Moorhouse, S.A. 1981: 'The medieval pottery industry and its markets', in D. Crossley (ed.), *Medieval Industry*. CBA Research Report 40. London: Munsell, 96–125.

Morey, A. and Brooke, C.N.L. 1965: *Gilbert Foliot and his Letters*. Cambridge: Cambridge.

Morillo, S. 1994: *Warfare under the Anglo-Norman Kings 1066–1135*. Woodbridge: The Boydell Press.

Morley, B.M. 1985: 'The nave roof of the church of St Mary, Kempley, Gloucestershire', *The Antiquaries Journal*, 65, 101–11.

Morley, B.M. and Gurney, D. 1997: *Castle Rising, Norfolk*. East Anglian Archaeology Report 81. Dereham: East Anglian Archaeology.

Morley, B.M. and Miles, D.W. 2000: 'The nave roof and other timberwork at the church of St Mary, Kempley, Gloucestershire: Dendrochronological dating', *The Antiquaries Journal* 80, 294–6.

Morris, C. 1978: '*Equestris ordo*: Chivalry as a vocation in the twelfth century', in D. Baker (ed.), *Religious Motivation: Biographical and Sociological Problems for the Church Historian*. Oxford: Blackwell for the Ecclesiastical History Society, 87–96.

Morris, R. 1989: *Churches in the Landscape*. London: J.M. Dent & Sons.

Morris, R.K. 2000: 'The architectural history of the medieval cathedral church', in G. Aylmer and J. Tiller (eds), *Hereford Cathedral: A History*. London: Hambledon Press, 203–40.

Mortimer, R. 2000: 'Village development and ceramic sequence: The middle to late Saxon village at Lordship Lane, Cottenham, Cambridgeshire', *Proceedings of the Cambridge Antiquarian Society* 89, 5–34.

Mortimer, R. Roderick, R. and Lucy, S. 2005: *The Saxon and Medieval Settlement at West Fen Road, Ely: The Ashwell Site*. East Anglian Archaeology 110. Cambridge: East Anglian Archaeology.

Mudd, A. and Webster, M. 2011: *Iron Age and Middle Saxon Settlements at West Fen Road, Ely, Cambridgeshire: The Consortium Site*. British Archaeological Report (British Series 538). Oxford: Archaeopress.

Musset, L. 2005: *The Bayeux Tapestry*. Woodbridge: The Boydell Press.

Myres, J.N.L. 1932: 'Three unrecognised castle mounds at Hamstead Marshall', *Transactions of the Newbury District Field Club* 6, 114–26.

New, E.A. 2010: *Seals and Sealing Practices: Archives and the User No. 11*. London: British Records Association.

New, E.A. 2013: 'Lleisionap Morgan makes an impression: Seals and the study of medieval Wales', *Welsh History Review* 29.3, 327–50.

Newson, J. 2013: 'Beakhead decoration on Romanesque arches in the Upper Thames Valley', *Oxoniensia* 78, 71–86.

Nicholson, H. 1993: *Templars, Hospitallers and Teutonic Knights: Images of the Military Orders, 1128–1291*. London: Leicester University Press.

Nicolle, D.C. 1988: *Arms and Armour of the Crusading Era, 1050–1350*, 2 vols. New York: Kraus International Publications.

Nieus, J.-F., 2015: 'The early career of William of Ypres in England: A new charter of King Stephen', *English Historical Review* 130.544, 527–45.

North, J.J. 1963: *English Hammered Coinage. Volume 1: Early Anglo-Saxon–Henry III, c. 650–1272*. London: Spink & Son Ltd.

O'Leary, T.J. 1981: 'Excavations at Upper Borough Walls, Bath, 1980', *Medieval Archaeology* 25, 1–30.

O'Meara, D. 2013: 'Scant evidence of great surplus: Research at the rural Cistercian monastery of Holme Cultram, Northwest England', in M. Groot, D. Lentjes and J. Zeiler (eds), *Barely Surviving or More than Enough? The Environmental Archaeology of Subsistence, Specialisation and Surplus Food Production*. Leiden: Sidestone Press, 279–96.

O'Neil, B.H. St J. 1936: 'Coins and archaeology in Britain', *Archaeological Journal* 92, 64–80.

Oakeshott, E. 1960: *The Archaeology of Weapons: Arms and Armour from Prehistory to the Age of Chivalry*. London: Lutterworth.

Oakeshott, E. 1964: *The Sword in the Age of Chivalry*. London: Lutterworth.

Oakeshott, E. 1991: *Records of the Medieval Sword*. Woodbridge: The Boydell Press.

Oddy, W.A., La Niece, S. and Stratford, N. 1986: *Romanesque Metalwork: Copper Alloys and their Decoration*. London: British Museum.

Oksanen, E. 2008: 'The Anglo-Flemish treaties and Flemish soldiers in England 1101–1163', in J. France (ed.), *Mercenaries and Paid Men: The Mercenary Identity in the Middle Ages*. Leiden: Brill, 261–73.

Oosthuizen, S. 2012: 'Cambridgeshire and the peat fen: medieval rural settlement and commerce, c. AD 900–1300', in N. Christie and P. Stamper (eds), *Medieval Rural Settlement: Britain and Ireland, AD 800–1600*. Oxford: Windgather, 206–24.

Oram, R. 2006: *Domination and Lordship: Scotland, 1070–1230*. Edinburgh: Edinburgh University Press.

Oram, R. 2008: *David I: The King Who Made Scotland*. Stroud: Tempus.

Orme, N. 2014: 'St James Priory, Exeter', *Devon Archaeological Society Proceedings 72*, 171–85.

Page, M. 2005: 'The origins of towns in medieval Hampshire: The case of Alton', *Proceedings of the Hampshire Field Club and Archaeological Association 60*, 170–4.

Page, W. and Proby, G. 1926: *The Victoria History of the County of Huntingdon, Volume 1*. London: St Catherine Press.

Page, W. and Round, J.H. (eds) 1907: *The Victoria History of the County of Essex, Volume 2*. London: Archibald Constable.

Page, W., Proby, G. and Inskip Ladds, S. 1932: *The Victoria History of the County of Huntingdon, Volume 2*. London: St Catherine Press.

Palliser, D.M. 1993: 'Domesday Book and the "Harrying of the North"', *Northern History 29*, 1–23.

Palliser, D.M., Slater, T.R. and Dennison, E.P. 2000: 'The topography of towns 600–1300', in D.M. Palliser (ed.), *The Cambridge Urban History of Britain Volume 1: 600–1540*. Cambridge: Cambridge University Press, 153–86.

Park, D. 2010: 'Medieval burials and monuments', in, R. Griffith-Jones and D. Park (eds), *The Temple Church in London: History, Architecture, Art*. Woodbridge: The Boydell Press, 67–91.

Parnell, G. 1993: *The Tower of London*. London: Batsford and English Heritage.

Patterson, R.B. 1991: 'Bristol: An Angevin baronial capital under royal siege', *Haskins Society Journal 3*, 171–81.

Peirce, I. 1986: 'The knight, his arms and armour in the eleventh and twelfth centuries', in C. Harper-Bill and R. Harvey (eds), *The Ideals and Practice of Medieval Knighthood. Papers from the First and Second Strawberry Hill Conferences*. Woodbridge: The Boydell Press, 152–64.

Peirce, I. 1990: 'The development of the medieval sword, c. 850–1300', in

C. Harper-Bill and R. Harvey (eds), *The Ideals and Practice of Medieval Knighthood. Papers from the Fourth Strawberry Hill Conference.* Woodbridge: The Boydell Press, 139–58.

Pestell, T. 2004: *Landscapes of Monastic Foundation: The Establishment of Religious Houses in East Anglia c.650–1200.* Woodbridge: The Boydell Press.

Pevsner, N., and Williamson, E. 1979: *The Buildings of England: Nottinghamshire*, 2nd ed. Harmondsworth: Penguin.

Philp, B. 1965: 'The excavations at the royal abbey at Faversham', in W. Telfer, *Faversham Abbey and its Last Abbot, John Caslock.* Faversham: The Faversham Society, 21–5.

Philp, B. 1968: *Excavations at Faversham, 1965: The Royal Abbey, Roman Villa and Belgic Farmstead.* Kent Archaeological Research Group Research Report 1. Bromley: Kent Archaeological Rescue Unit.

Plant, R. 2003: 'Ecclesiastical architecture, *c.* 1050 to *c.* 1200', in C. Harper-Bill and E. van Houts (eds), *A Companion to the Anglo-Norman World.* Woodbridge: The Boydell Press, 215–53.

Postan, M.M. 1972: *The Medieval Economy and Society: An Economic History of Britain 1100–1500.* Berkeley and Los Angeles: University of California Press.

Poulle, B. 1994: 'Savigny and England', in D. Bates and A. Curry (eds), *England and Normandy in the Middle Ages.* London: Hambledon Press, 159–68.

Pounds, N.J.G. 1990: *The Medieval Castle in England and Wales: A Social and Political History.* Cambridge: Cambridge University Press.

Prestwich, J.O. 1988a: 'Geoffrey de Mandeville: A further comment', *English Historical Review* 103, 960–6.

Prestwich, J.O. 1988b: 'The treason of Geoffrey de Mandeville', *English Historical Review* 103, 283–312.

Prestwich, M. 1996: *Armies and Warfare in the Middle Ages: The English Experience.* Yale: Yale University Press.

Prior, S.J. 2007: 'Strategy, symbolism and the downright unusual: The archaeology of three Somerset castles', in M. Costen (ed), *People and Places: Essays in Honour of Mick Aston.* Oxford: Oxbow, 76–89.

Pritchard, F. 1991: 'Small finds', in A. Vince (ed.), *Aspects of Saxo-Norman London: II Finds and Environmental Evidence.* London and Middlesex Archaeological Society Special Paper 12. London: London and Middlesex Archaeological Society, 120–278.

Public Record Office 1968: *Guide to Seals in the Public Record Office*, 2nd ed. London: HMSO.

Pugh, R.B. (ed.) 1953: *The Victoria History of the County of Cambridge and the Isle of Ely, Volume 4.* London: The University of London Institute of Historical Research by the Oxford University Press.

Purton, P.F. 1998: 'The siege castles at Arundel', *Postern* 8, 13–14.

Purton, P.F. 2006: 'The myth and the mangonel: Torsion artillery in the Middle Ages', *Arms & Armour* 3.1, 79–90.

Purton, P.F. 2010: *A History of the Early Medieval Siege, c. 450–1220, Vol. 1.* Woodbridge: The Boydell Press.

Rackham, O. 1986: *The History of the British Countryside.* London: Dent.

Raftis, J.A. 1957: *The Estates of Ramsey Abbey: A Study in Economic Growth and Organization.* Toronto: Pontifical Institute of Mediaeval Studies.

Rahtz, S. and Rowley, T. 1984: *Middleton Stoney: Excavation and Survey in a North Oxfordshire Parish 1970–1982.* Oxford: Oxford University Department for External Studies.

Rakoczy, L. 2008: 'Out of the ashes: Destruction, reuse and profiteering in the English Civil War', in L. Rakoczy (ed.), *The Archaeology of Destruction.* Newcastle upon Tyne: Cambridge Scholars Publishing, 261–86.

Rashleigh, J. 1849–50: 'Descriptive list of a collection of coins of Henry I and Stephen, discovered in Hertfordshire', in 1818', *The Numismatic Chronicle and Journal of the Numismatic Society* 12, 138–65.

Ravensdale, J.R. 1974: *Liable to Floods: Village Landscape on the Edge of the Fens, AD 450–1850.* London: Cambridge University Press.

Raymond Powell, W. 2005: 'The Norman government of Essex 1066–1154', *Essex Archaeology and History* (3rd series) 36, 110–17.

RCAHMW 1991: *An Inventory of the Ancient Monuments in Glamorgan: Volume III: Medieval Secular Monuments. The Early Castles, From the Norman Conquest to 1217.* Cardiff: HMSO.

RCHME 1926: *An Inventory of the Historical Monuments in Huntingdonshire.* London: HMSO.

RCHME 1959: *An Inventory of the Historical Monuments in the City of Cambridge,* 2 vols. London: HMSO.

RCHME 1968–72: *An Inventory of the Historical Monuments of Cambridgeshire,* 2 vols. London: HMSO.

Reaney, P.H. 1943: *The Place-Names of Cambridge and the Isle of Ely.* English Place-Name Society Vol. 19. Cambridge: Cambridge University Press.

Reece, R. 1981: 'The "Normal" Hoard', *PACT* 5, 299–308.

Renn, D.F. 1959: 'Mottes: A classification', *Antiquity* 33, 106–12.

Renn, D.F. 1960: 'The keep of Wareham Castle', *Medieval Archaeology* 4, 56–68.

Renn, D.F. 1968: *Norman Castles in Britain.* London: Baker.

Renn, D.F. 1971: *Medieval Castles in Hertfordshire.* Chichester: Phillimore.

Renn, D.F. 1994: 'Burhgeat and gonfanon: Two sidelights from the Bayeux Tapestry', *Anglo-Norman Studies* 16, 187–98.

Reynolds, N. 1975: 'Investigations in the Observatory Tower, Lincoln Castle', *Medieval Archaeology* 19, 201–05.

Riall, N. 2003: 'The new castles of Henry de Blois as bishop of Winchester: The case against Farnham, Surrey', *Medieval Archaeology* 47, 115–29.

Richardson, H.G. 1960: *The English Jewry under the Angevin Kings.* London: Methuen.

Richardson, H.G. and Sayles, G.O. 1963: *The Governance of Mediaeval England from the Conquest to Magna Carta*. Edinburgh: Edinburgh University Press.

Richardson, T. 2007: 'New acquisitions by the Royal Armouries', *Arms and Armour* 4.1, 83–4.

Rigold, S.E. 1962–3: 'The Anglian cathedral of North Elmham, Norfolk', *Medieval Archaeology* 6–7, 67–108.

Rippon, S. 2008: *Beyond the Medieval Village: The Diversification of Landscape Character in Southern Britain*. Oxford: Oxford University Press.

Roach, J.P.C. (ed.) 1959: *The Victoria History of the County of Cambridge and the Isle of Ely, Volume 3*. London: Oxford University Press for the Institute of Historical Research.

Roberts, B.K., and Wrathmell, S. 2000: *An Atlas of Rural Settlement in England*. London: English Heritage.

Roberts, B.K., and Wrathmell, S. 2002: *Region and Place: A Study of English Rural Settlement*. London: English Heritage.

Roffe, D. 2005: 'The historical context', in A. Crowson, T. Lane, K. Penn and D. Trimble (eds), *Anglo-Saxon Settlement on the Siltland of Eastern England, Lincolnshire*. Archaeology and Heritage Reports No. 7. Sleaford: Heritage Trust of Lincolnshire, 264–88.

Roffey, S. 2012: 'Medieval leper hospitals in England: An archaeological perspective', *Medieval Archaeology* 56, 203–33.

Rogers, R. 1992: *Latin Siege Warfare in the Twelfth Century*. Oxford: Clarendon Press.

Rogerson, A. and Ashley, S. 2011: 'Some medieval gaping-mouth beast buckles from Norfolk and elsewhere', *Medieval Archaeology* 55, 299–302.

Rogerson, A. and Ashley, S. 2013: 'A selection of finds from Norfolk recorded in 2013 and earlier', *Norfolk Archaeology* 46.4, 554–68.

Round, J.H. 1888: 'Danegeld and the finance of Domesday', in P.E. Dove (ed.), *Domesday Studies, Vol I*. London: Longman, 77–142.

Round, J.H. 1892: *Geoffrey de Mandeville: A Study of the Anarchy*. London: Longman, Green & Co.

Rowley, T. 1972; 'First report on the excavations at Middleton Stoney castle, Oxfordshire, 1970–71', *Oxoniensia* 37, 109–36.

Rowley, T. 1997: *Norman England*. London: Batsford and English Heritage.

Rylatt, M. and Mason, P. 2003: *The Archaeology of the Medieval Cathedral and Priory of St Mary, Coventry*. Coventry: Coventry City Council.

Sabin, D. and Donaldson, K. 2007: *Castle Combe Geophysical Survey for Wiltshire County Council*. Unpublished report: Archaeological Surveys, Castle Combe.

Salmon, J. 1946: 'Beakhead ornament in Norman architecture', *Yorkshire Archaeological Journal* 36, 349–57.

Salzman, L.F. (ed.) 1948: *A History of the County of Cambridge and the Isle of Ely: Volume 2*. London: The University of London Institute of Historical Research by the Oxford University Press.

Salzman, L.F. and Styles, P. (ed.) 1945: *The Victoria History of the County of Warwick, Volume 3*. London: The University of London Institute of Historical Research by the Oxford University Press.

Saunders, A. 1980: 'Lydford Castle, Devon', *Medieval Archaeology* 24, 123–86.

Saunders, A. 2006: *Excavations at Launceston Castle, Cornwall*, Society for Medieval Archaeology Monograph 24. Leeds: Maney.

Saxl, F. 1954: *English Sculptures of the Twelfth Century*. London: Faber and Faber.

Sayer, D. 2009: 'Medieval waterways and hydraulic economics: Monasteries, towns and the East Anglian fen', *World Archaeology* 41.1, 134–50.

Schofield, J. and Lea, R. 2005: *Holy Trinity Priory, Aldgate, City of London*. Museum of London Archaeology Service Monograph 24. London: Museum of London Archaeology Service.

Scott, J. 1981: *The Early History of Glastonbury: An Edition, Translation and Study of William of Malmesbury's De antiquitate Glastonie Ecclesie*. Woodbridge: Boydell and Brewer.

Scrope, G.P. 1852: *History of the Manor and Ancient Barony of Castle Combe*. London: Privately published.

Seaman, R.J. 1978: 'A re-examination of some hoards containing coins of Stephen', *British Numismatic Journal* 48, 58–72.

Sensfelder, J. 2007: *Crossbows in the Royal Netherlands Army Museum*. Delft: Eburon.

Seymour, L. 2000: *A Monument in its Landscape: Giant's Hill, Rampton, Cambridgeshire*. Unpublished report.

Shapland, M. 2008: 'St Mary's, Broughton, Lincolnshire: A thegnly tower-nave in the late Anglo-Saxon landscape', *Archaeological Journal* 165, 471–519.

Shaw, D.G. 1993: *The Creation of a Community: The City of Wells in the Middle Ages*. Oxford: Oxford University Press.

Shepherd Popescu, E. 2009: *Norwich Castle: Excavations and Historical Survey, 1987–98. Part I: Anglo-Saxon to c.1345*. East Anglian Archaeology Report 132. Norwich: Norfolk Museums and Archaeology Service.

Sherlock, S.J. 2004: 'Excavations at the Well House, Long Marston, North Yorkshire, *Yorkshire Archaeological Journal* 76, 113–34.

Shoesmith, R. 1980: *Hereford City Excavations. Volume 1, Excavations at Castle Green*. CBA Research Report 36. York: Council for British Archaeology.

Silvester, R.J. 1988: *The Fenland Project Number 3: Marshland and the Nar Valley*. Cambridge: Cambridge Archaeological Committee.

Slade, C.F. 1960: 'Wallingford castle in the reign of Stephen', *Berkshire Archaeological Journal* 58, 33–43.

Slitt, R. 2012: 'The boundaries of women's power: Gender and the discourse of political friendship in twelfth-century England', *Gender and History* 24.1, 1–17.

Sloane, B. 2012: *The Augustinan Nunnery of St Mary Clerkenwell, London: Excavations 1974–96*. MOLA Monograph 57. London: Museum of Archaeology.

Smail, R. 1972: 'The Aldreth Causeway', *Cambridgeshire Local History Council Bulletin* 27, 10–19.

Smith, R. 1997: *The Music House*. Norwich: Vernacular Architect Group Conference Papers.

Southwick, L. 2006: 'The great helm in England', *Arms and Armour* 3.1, 5–77.

Speight, S. 1995: 'Four more early medieval "castle" sites in Nottinghamshire', *Transactions of the Thoroton Society of Nottinghamshire* 99, 65–72.

Speight, S. 2000: 'Castle warfare in the *Gesta Stephani*', *Château Gaillard* 19, 269–74.

Spencer, B.W. 1961: 'Two additions to the London Museum', *Transactions of London and Middlesex Archaeological Society* 20.4, 214–17.

Spoerry, P. 2005: 'Town and country in the medieval fenland', in C. Dyer and K. Giles (eds), *Medieval Town and Country 1100–1500*. Society for Medieval Archaeology Monograph 22. Leeds: Society for Medieval Archaeology, 85–110.

Spoerry, P., Atkins, R., Macaulay, S. and Shepherd Popescu, E. 2008: 'Ramsey Abbey, Cambridgeshire: Excavations at the site of a fenland monastery', *Medieval Archaeology* 52, 171–210.

Spurrell, M. 1995: 'Containing Wallingford Castle, 1146–53', *Oxoniensia* 60, 257–70.

St John Hope, W.H. 1901–03: 'Notes on a third Great Seal of King Stephen', *Proceedings of the Society of Antiquaries of London* (second series) 19, 60–3.

Stalley, R.A. 1971: 'A twelfth-century patron of architecture: A study of the buildings erected by Roger, Bishop of Salisbury 1102–1139', *Journal of the British Archaeological Association* (third series) 34, 62–83.

Stalley, R.A. 2012: 'Diffusion, imitation and evolution: The uncertain origins of "beakhead" ornament', in J. Franklin, T.A. Heslop and C Stevenson (eds), *Architecture and Interpretation: Essays for Eric Fernie*. Woodbridge: The Boydell Press, 111–27.

Stamper, P.A. 1984: 'Excavations on a mid-twelfth century siege castle at Bentley, Hampshire', *Proceedings of the Hampshire Field Club and Archaeological Association* 40, 81–9.

Steane, J. 1999: *The Archaeology of the Medieval English Monarchy*. London: Routledge.

Stenton, F.M. 1932: *The First Century of English Feudalism, 1066–1166*. Oxford: Clarendon Press.

Stewart, P. 1978: 'Historical implications of the regional production of the dies under Ethelred II', *British Numismatic Journal* 48, 35–51.

Stott, P. 1991: 'Saxon and Norman coins from London', in A. Vince (ed.), *Aspects of Saxo-Norman London: II Finds and Environmental*

Evidence. London and Middlesex Archaeological Society Special Paper 12. London: London and Middlesex Archaeological Society, 279–325.

Streit, K.T. 1993: 'The expansion of the English Jewish community in the reign of King Stephen', *Albion* 25.2, 177–92.

Strickland, M. 2011: 'Henry I and the Battle of the Two Kings: Brémule, 1119', in D. Crouch and K. Thompson (eds), *Normandy and its Neighbours, 900-1250: Essays for David Bates*. Turnhout: Brepols, 77–116.

Strickland, M.J. 1989: 'Securing the north: Invasion and the strategy of defence in twelfth-century Anglo-Scottish warfare', *Anglo-Norman Studies* 12, 177–98.

Strickland, M.J. 1994: 'Against the Lord's anointed: Aspects of warfare and baronial rebellion in England and Normandy, 1075-1265', in G. Garnett and J. Hudson (eds), *Law and Government in Medieval England and Normandy. Essays in Honour of James Holt*. Cambridge: Cambridge University Press, 56–79.

Strickland, M.J. 1996a: 'Military technology and conquest: The anomaly of Anglo-Saxon England', *Anglo-Norman Studies* 19, 353–82.

Strickland, M.J. 1996b: *War and Chivalry: The Conduct and Perception of War in England and Normandy, 1066-1217*. Cambridge: Cambridge University Press.

Strickland, M.J. and Hardy, R. 2011: *The Great Warbow: From Hastings to the Mary Rose*. Sparkford: Haynes Publishing.

Stringer, K. 1980: 'A Cistercian archive: The earliest charters of Sawtry Abbey', *Journal of the Society of Archivists* 6, 325–34.

Stringer, K.J. 1993: *The Reign of Stephen: Kingship, Warfare and Government in Twelfth-century England*. London and New York: Routledge.

Stringer, K.J. 1997: 'State-building in twelfth-century Britain: David I, King of Scots, and northern England', in J.C. Appleby and P. Dalton (eds), *Government, Religion and Society in Northern England 1000-1700*. Stroud: Sutton, 40–62.

Stroud, G. 1999: *Derbyshire Extensive Urban Survey Archaeological Assessment Report: Repton*. Derby: Derbyshire County Council.

Stubbs, W. 1874–78: *The Constitutional History of England in its Origin and Development, Vol. 1*. Oxford: Clarendon Press.

Swanson, R.W. 1999: *The Twelfth-Century Renaissance*. Manchester: Manchester University Press.

Swanton, M. (ed and trans.) 2000: *The Anglo-Saxon Chronicles*. London: Pheonix.

Tamburr, K. 2007: *The Harrowing of Hell in Medieval England*. Cambridge: D.S. Brewer.

Tanner, N.P. (ed.) 1990: *Decrees of the Ecumenical Councils* (Original text established by G. Alberigo [et al.] in consultation with H. Jedin). London: Sheed and Ward.

Tarver, W.T.S. 1995: 'The traction trebuchet: A reconstruction of an early medieval siege engine', *Technology and Culture* 36.1, 136–67.

Tasker Grimbert, J. and Chase, C.J. (trans.) 2011: *Chrétien de Troyes in Prose: The Burgundian Erec and Cligés*. Cambridge: D.S. Brewer.

Taylor, A. 1978: *Anglo-Saxon Cambridgeshire*. Cambridge: Oleander Press.

Taylor, C.C. 1979: *Roads and Tracks of Britain*. London: Dent.

Telfer, W. 1965: *Faversham Abbey and its Last Abbot, John Caslock*. Faversham Paper 2. Faversham: The Faversham Society.

Thomas, H.M. 1999: 'Miracle stories and the violence of Stephen's reign', *Haskins Society Journal* 13, 111–24.

Thomas, H.M. 2008: 'Violent disorder in King Stephen's England: A maximum argument', in P. Dalton and G.J. White (eds), *King Stephen's Reign, 1135–1154*. Woodbridge: The Boydell Press, 139–70.

Thompson, M.W. 1960: 'Recent excavations in the keep of Farnham Castle, Surrey', *Medieval Archaeology* 4, 81–94.

Thompson, M.W. 1967: 'Excavations in Farnham Castle Keep, Surrey, England, 1958–60', *Château Gaillard* 2, 100–05.

Thompson, M.W. 1986: 'Associated monasteries and castles in the Middle Ages: A tentative list', *Archaeological Journal* 143, 305–21.

Thompson, M.W. 1992: 'Keep or country house? Thin-walled Norman 'proto-keeps', *Fortress* 12, 13–22.

Thompson, M.W. 1998: *Medieval Bishops' Houses in England and Wales*. Aldergate: Ashgate.

Thompson, M.W. 2001: *Cloister, Abbot and Precinct in Medieval Monasteries*. Stroud: Tempus.

Thompson, M.W. 2004: 'The early topography of Lincoln castle', in P. Lindley (ed.), *The Early History of Lincoln Castle*. Society for Lincolnshire History and Archaeology Occasional Papers 12. Lincoln: Society for Lincolnshire History and Archaeology, 23–9.

Toolis, R. 2004: '"Naked and unarmoured": A reassessment of the role of the Galwegians at the Battle of the Standard', *Transactions of the Dumfriesshire and Galloway Natural History and Antiquarian Society* 78, 79–92.

Truax, J.A. 1996: 'Winning over the Londoners: King Stephen, the Empress Matilda, and the politics of personality', *Haskins Society Journal* 8, 43–61.

Tyerman, C. 1988: *England and the Crusades, 1095–1588*. Chicago: University of Chicago Press.

van Emden, W. 1995: *La Chanson de Roland*. London: Grant & Cutler Ltd.

Vance, E. 1970: *Reading the Song of Roland*. Englewood Cliffs: Prentice-Hall, Inc.

Verbruggen, J.F. 1997: *The Art of Warfare in Europe during the Middle Ages*. Woodbridge: The Boydell Press.

Vince A.G., Lobb, S.J., Richards, J.C. and Mepham, L. 1997: *Excavations in Newbury 1979–1990*. Wessex Archaeology Report 13. Salisbury: Wessex Archaeology.

Vince, A. 2005: 'Ceramic petrology and the study of Anglo-Saxon and later medieval ceramics', *Medieval Archaeology* 49, 219–45.

Vince, A. and Jenner, A. 1991: 'The Saxon and early medieval pottery of London', in A. Vince (ed.), *Aspects of Saxo-Norman London, II: Finds and Environmental Evidence*. London and Middlesex Archaeological Society Special Paper 12. London: London and Middlesex Archaeological Society, 19–119.

Vince, A.G. 1981: 'The medieval pottery industry in southern England: 10th to 13th centuries', in H. Howard and E.L. Morris (eds), *Production and Distribution: A Ceramic Viewpoint*. British Archaeological Reports (International Series 120). Oxford: British Archaeological Reports, 309–22.

Vincent, N. 2015: 'The seals of King Henry II and his court', in P. Schofield (ed.), *Seals and their Context in the Middle Ages*. Oxford: Oxbow, 7–33.

Wade-Martins, P. 1980: *Fieldwork and Excavation on Village Sites in Launditch Hundred*. East Anglian Archaeology 10, Norwich: East Anglian Archaeology.

Walker, D. 1060: 'The "honours" of the Earls of Hereford in the twelfth century', *Transactions of the Bristol and Gloucestershire Archaeological Society* 79, 174–211.

Walker, J. 1999: 'Late-twelfth and early-thirteenth-century aisled buildings: A comparison', *Vernacular Architecture* 30.1, 21–53.

Ward Perkins, J.B. 1940: *London Museum Medieval Catalogue*. London: HMSO.

Wareham, A. 2005: *Lords and Communities in Early Medieval East Anglia*. Woodbridge: The Boydell Press.

Warren, W.L. 1973: *Henry II*. London: Methuen.

Watkins, C. 2015: *Stephen: The Reign of Anarchy*. London: Allen Lane.

Webley, R. 2014: 'Stirrup-strap mounts', *Medieval Archaeology* 58, 353–6.

Wessex Archaeology 2009: *Radcot, Oxfordshire: Archaeological Evaluation and Assessment of Results*. Unpublished report: Wessex Archaeology.

Wessex Archaeology 2011: *Groby Old Hall Groby, Leicestershire: Archaeological Evaluation and Assessment of Results*. Unpublished report: Wessex Archaeology.

West, F.J. 1999: 'The colonial history of the Norman Conquest', *History* 84, 219–36.

West, J. 2007: 'A taste for the antique? Henry of Blois and the arts', *Anglo-Norman Studies* 30, 213–30.

White, G.J. 1985: 'Were the Midlands "wasted" during Stephen's reign?', *Midland History* 10, 26–46.

White, G.J. 1990: 'The end of Stephen's reign', *History* 75.243, 3–22.

White G.J. 2000: *Restoration and Reform, 1153–1165: Recovery from Civil War in England*. Cambridge: Cambridge University Press.

White, Lynn Jr 1974: 'Technology assessment from the stance of a medieval historian', *The American Historical Review* 79.1, 1–13.

White, P. and Cook, A. 2015: *Sherborne Old Castle, Dorset: Archaeological Investigations 1930–90*. London: Society of Antiquaries of London.

Wilcox, R. 1987: 'The Thetford Cluniac Priory excavations 1971–4', *Norfolk Archaeology* 40, 1–18.

Wilkes, J.J. and Elrington, C.R. (eds) 1978: *A History of the County of Cambridge and Isle of Ely, Volume 7: Roman Cambridgeshire*. London: Oxford University Press for The Institute of Historical Research.

Williams, A. and Edge, D. 2004: 'Great helms and their development into helmets', *Glaudius* 24, 123–34.

Williams, F. 1977: *Pleshey Castle, Essex (XII–XVI Century): Excavations in the Bailey, 1959–1963*. British Archaeological Reports (British Series 42). Oxford: British Archaeological Reports.

Williams, D. 1997: *Late Saxon Stirrup-Strap Mounts: A Classification and Catalogue*. York: Council for British Archaeology.

Williams, T.J.T. 2015: 'Landscape and warfare in Anglo-Saxon England and the Viking campaign of 1006', *Early Medieval Europe* 23, 329–59.

Williamson, T. 2004: *Shaping Medieval Landscapes: Settlement, Society, Environment*. Macclesfield: Windgather Press.

Wilson, D.M. and Hurst, D.G. 1968: 'Medieval Britain in 1967', *Medieval Archaeology* 12, 155–211.

Wood, R. 2014: 'Romanesque sculpture at Quenington and South Cerney', *Transactions of the Bristol and Gloucestershire Archaeological Society* 132, 97–124.

Woosnam-Savage, R.C. 2008: 'He's armed without that's innocent within: A short note on a newly acquired medieval sword for a child', *Arms & Armour* 5.1, 84–95.

Wright, A.P.M. and Lewis, C.P. 1989: *A History of the County of Cambridge and the Isle of Ely, Volume 9*. London: The University of London Institute of Historical Research.

Wright, D.W. 2010: 'Restructuring the 8th-century landscape: Planned settlements, estates and minsters in pre-Viking England', *Church Archaeology* 14, 15–26.

Wright, D.W. 2015: *Middle Saxon Settlement and Society*. Oxford: Archaeopress.

Wright, D.W. and Fradley, M. 2013: 'Decoding an elite landscape: Power and patronage at Hailes, Gloucestershire', *Church Archaeology* 17, 29–36.

Wright, D.W., Creighton, O.H. and Fradley, M. 2015a: 'The ringwork at Cam's Hill, near Malmesbury: Archaeological investigation and landscape assessment', *Wiltshire Archaeological Magazine* 108, 105–18.

Wright, D.W., Creighton, O.H., Trick, S. and Fradley, M. 2015b: 'Fieldwork in conflict landscapes: Surveying the archaeology of 'the Anarchy', *Medieval Archaeology* 59, 313–19.

Wright, D.W., Creighton, O.H., Trick, S. and Fradley, M. 2016: 'Power, conflict and ritual on the fen-edge: The Anarchy-period castle at Burwell, Cambridgeshire and its pre-Conquest landscape', *Landscape History* 37.1, 25–50.

Wright, D.W. and Creighton, O.H. (eds) forthcoming: *Castles, Siegeworks*

and Settlements: Surveying the Archaeology of the Twelfth Century, Oxford: Archaeopress.

Yarrow, S. 2006: *Saints and their Communities: Miracle Stories in Twelfth-Century England*. Oxford: Oxford University Press.

Yoshitake, K. 1988: 'The arrest of the bishops in 1139 and its consequences', *Journal of Medieval History* 14.2, 97–114.

Yoshitake, K. 2015: 'The place of government in transition: Winchester, Westminster and London in the mid-twelfth century', in P. Dalton and D. Luscombe (eds), *Rulership and Rebellion in the Anglo-Norman World, c. 1066–c. 1216*. Farnham: Ashgate, 61–75.

Young, C.J. 2000: *Excavations at Carisbrooke Castle, Isle of Wight, 1921–1996*. Wessex Archaeology Report 18. Salisbury: Wessex Archaeology.

Young, C.R. 1979: *The Royal Forests of Medieval England*. Leicester: Leicester University Press.

Zarnecki, G. 1970: *Romanesque Sculpture at Lincoln Cathedral*, 2nd revised ed. Lincoln Minster Pamphlets No. 2. Lincoln: Lincoln Minster.

Zarnecki, G., Holt, J. and Holland, T. (eds) 1984: *English Romanesque Art 1066–1200. Hayward Gallery, London 5 April–8 July 1984*. London: Weidenfeld and Nicolson.

Index

Note: Places are indexed in historic counties before the 1974 local government reorganisation. Page numbers in **bold** refer to a figure or plate.

Abbotsbury (Dorset) **5**
Abinger (Surrey) 88–90, **89**
Adeliza of Louvain, wife of Henry I 20, 25
adulterine castles 80, 82–4, 91, 92, 102, 112, 116n10, 122, 280, 287
agreements see treaties and agreements
agriculture 8, 16, 17, 28, 68, 219, 233, 236, 240, 247, 252, 263, 275, 281
Alan, Count of Brittany and Earl of Richmond and Earl of Cornwall 86, 181
Alderford, Norfolk **178–9**
Aldgate, London 132, **198**, 199, 201, 220
Aldreth (Cambs.) 255–8, 260, 272
Alexander, Bishop of Lincoln 25, 129, 187, 209
alien priories 18
Almondbury (W Yorks.) 99, 238
Alnwick (Northumb.) 16, 217n87
ambushes 21, 39, 40, 227
amphibious warfare 39, 257
amphitheatres 57, 86, 94–5, 131
Anarchy, the
    chronology 19–30
    historiography/definition of 3–7, 279, 289

animal bones see zooarchaeology
Anstey (Herts.) **237**, 238
archers and archery 46, 49, 68, 73, 155, 161, 162, 168–71, 264, 282
Argentan, Normandy, France 21
aristocracy 7, 13, 15, 127, 180, 279
armies 30, 37–9, 42, 48, 62, 73, 154–7, 163, 205, 240–1, 242, 247, 282–3
    see also cavalry; infantry; mercenaries; militias; sergeants
armour 11, 35, 42, 46, 146, 155, 157–9, 162–3, 165, 168, 171, 172–3, 174, 177, 181, 182, 282
    see also mail
arms and armour 157–80
    see also archers and archery; armour; axes; bows; crossbows and crossbowmen; daggers; helmets; lances; maces; scabbards; spears and spearmen; swords
Arques, Pas-de-Calais, France 52
arrest of the bishops 24–5, 134, 187
arrowheads 8, 11, 101, 120, 160, 169–71, 182, 282
    see also bows, archers and archery; crossbows and crossbowmen

artillery (trebuchets, etc) *see* siege engines
Arundel (Sussex) **5**, 16, 25, 53, **54**, 60, 65, 157, 261, 292
Ascot D'Oilly (Oxon.) 102, **103**, 122, 236, **237**, 238, 287, 293
Ashby-de-la-Zouch (Leics.) 148, 149
Astall (Oxon.) **Plate 9**
Attlebridge, Norfolk **178–9**
atrocities 7, 4, 243
Aughton (E Yorks.) 130
Augustinians 19, 95, 196, 197, 199, 201, 202, 220
axes 161, 165, 172

baileys *see* mottes; ringworks
Baldwin de Redvers, Earl of Devon 22, 31, 59, 78n134, 91, 200, 232
Baldwin fitz Gilbert 175
Baldwin, son of King Stephen 132, 133, 220
ballistas *see* siege engines
Bamburgh (Northumb.) 53, 77n82, 143, **144**
Bampton (Devon) **5**, **41**, 61
Bampton (Oxon.) **5**, 191
banners 45, 61, 134, 135, 167, 175, 182
Barfleur, Normandy, France 29
Barfreston (Kent) **161**, 189, **Plate 16**
Barley Pound (Hants.) 58, 61, 69, 78n150, 87
Barnard Castle (Durham) 16
Barnstaple (Devon) **5**, 91, 215
Barwick upon Elmet (Northumb.) 99
Bath (Som.) **5**, 25, 49, **140**, 142, 226–7
battlefields 40–7
    see also Northallerton, Battle of; Lincoln, Battle of; Wilton, Battle of; Winchester, siege/rout of
Bayeux tapestry 90, 159, 169, 172, 173–4, 175, 176, 181
beakheads 129–31, 284, 293
Beaudesert (Warwicks.) 229, 288, **Plate 18**

Bedford 5, 24, 27, 56, 72, 140, 255
Belsar's Hill (Cambs.) 258–9
Belvoir (Leics.) 14, 86, 200
Benedictines 15, 19, 108, 196, 197, 199, 202, 205
Bentley (Hants.) **54**, 58, 122
Benwick (Cambs.) 262, 277n69
Berkeley (Glos.) 5
Berkhamsted (Herts.) 50, 65
Beverley (E Yorks.) 82, 155, 249n46
Bigod family 91
bishops 6, 18, 20, 21, 24, 25, 29, 42, 129, 134, 185, 187, 190–1, 194, 202, 208–13
bishops' palaces 208–13, 221
Bishopsteignton (Devon) **Plate 9**
Bohun family 115
borders 2, 19, 20, 21, 24, 30, 32, 38–9, 49, 64, 189, 241, 261, 284, 292, 294
Bordesley (Worcs.) 152n87, 197, 201
Boroughbridge (N Yorks.) 231
boroughs 15–16, 99, 112, 131, 138, 142, 146, 224, 226, 228–32, 238
    see also towns and urbanism
Boteler's Castle (Warwicks.) 236–8, **237**, 287
Boulogne, County of 20, 21, 188, 220
Bourgthéroulde, Normandy, France 169
bows 49, 56, 163, 168–71, 181
Box (Wilts.) 145, 148
Boxley (Kent) 203
Bramber (Sussex) **140**, 142
Brecon **5**
Brémule, Normandy, France 42, 53, 169
Breteuil, Normandy, France 42
Brian fitz Count, Lord of Wallingford 25, 65, 69, 78n134
bridges 65, 68, 70–1, 73–4, 82, 101, 109, 209, 231, 256, 257, 258, 259, 291
Bridlington (E Yorks.) **186**
Bridport (Dorset) **5**

Bristol (Glos.) **5**, 15, **140**, 284, 242, 131

   Angevin centre, as a 24, 25, 38, 85, **144**, 242

   castle 48, 85, 291

   rebellions and sieges 24, 48, 85, 226–7

   Stephen imprisoned at 26

Buckingham **140**, 142

Bungay, Suffolk 25, 50

burhs 15, 63–5, 194, 226–7, 267

burial mounds 92

burials 13, 95, 131–3, 159, 161–2, 173, 195, 196, 284

Burtuna (probably Purton, Wilts.) **5**

Burwell (Cambs.) **10**, 98, 100, 168, 235, 263, 264, 265–71, **265**, **266**, **267**, **268**, **269**, **270**, **271**, 272, 273, 274, 277n89, 287, 292

Bury St Edmunds (Suffolk) 127, **140**, **144**, 158, 264

butescarls 255

Calder (Cumbria) 203

Cambridge **5**, **140**, **144**, 166, 204, 215, 223, 255, 256, 261, 263

Canterbury (Kent) 125, **140**, **144**, 145

Carcassonne, Aude, France **51**

Cardiff (Glam.) **140**, 142, **144**, 145, 148, 156

Cardigan 40

Carisbrooke (IOW) 84

Carlisle (Cumb.) 21, 24, 28, 104, 143, **144**

Cary *see* Castle Cary

castellans 25, 31, 224, 288

Castellum de Silva (unlocated) *see* Castle of the Wood

Castle Acre (Norfolk) **103**, 105, **107**, 108–10, 136, **170**, 171, 179, 199, 226, 235, 287, 292

Castle Cary (Som.) **5**, 24, 49, **54**, 61, 86

Castle Combe (Wilts.) 98–9, **144**, 145–6, 238, **Plate 7**

Castle Hedingham (Essex) *see* Hedingham

Castle Neroche (Som.) 111

Castle of the Wood (unlocated, possibly Silchester, Hampshire) **5**, 86, 94

Castle Rising (Norfolk) **103**, 105–6, **106**, **140**, 142, 226, 235, 287, 292

castles *see* adulterine castles; curtain walls; donjons, mottes; ringworks; siege castles

casualties 40, 56, 74, 160–2

cathedrals 15, 18, 85, 98, 126, 129, 130, 131, 159, 192–4, 207, 208, 211, 214, 215, 221, 225, 228, 254, 257, 260, 281, 283, 291

cavalry 69, 155, 172, 176–80, 255, 262, 286

Cawston, Norfolk **178–9**

Caxton (Cambs.) **270**, 272–3

cemeteries 95, 97, 189, 194, 215, 225, 229, 281

Cerney, South (Glos.) **5**, 129

chapels 57, 85, 132, 199, 200, 211, 214, 269, 287

charters 2, 4, 6, 62, 69, 73, 78n149, 83, 99, 104, 110, 134, 152n87, 189, 196, 197, 201, 204, 220, 228–30, 232, 233, 251, 260

Châteauroux, Indre, France 42

Chester 15, **140**

Chichester (Sussex) 18, **140**

children 20, 132, 133, 164, 172, 199, 220

chivalry 36, 154, 156, 187, 283

Christchurch (Hants.) **5**, 227, 232

Church, the 11, 21, 25, 35–6, 169, 180, 185–8, 215, 243, 279

churches

   twelfth-century 185–9

   fortification of 185–96, 213–15

   see also cathedrals; chapels

Cirencester (Glos.) **144**, 194

Cistercians 19, 196–204, 239–40, 288

city walls *see* town defences

civil war, the English/British (mid-seventeenth-century) *see* English Civil War
Clare family 136, 175
Clerkenwell, London **198**, 199
Cluniacs 19, 109, 131, 196, 199, 200, 201, 203
Coed-y-Wenallt (Glam.) 148, 156
Cogges (Oxon.) 205
Coggeshall (Essex) 203
coifs 174
coins and coinage 7, 8, 9, 11, 65, 78n134, 99, 108, 119, 121, 126, 136–50, 156, 195, 211, 223, 228, 235, 284–5, 286, 288
    moneyers 78n134, 136, 137, 138, 139, 143, 145, 156, 223
    see also hoards and hoarding; mints
Colchester (Essex) **140**
Colyton (Devon) 190
Copford (Essex) **Plate 13**
Corbridge (Northumb.) 143, **144**
Corfe (Dorset) **5**, **54**, **55**, **59**, 290, **Plates 1, 4**
counter castles 51, 53, 208, 281
    see also siege castles
Coventry (Warwicks.) **5**, 27, **54**, 61, **186**, 194, 281
Cricklade (Wilts.) **5**, 48, **144**, 227
crossbows and crossbowmen 49, 163, 168–71, 181, 183n74, 183n75
Crowmarsh (Gifford) (Oxon.) **5**, **55**, 57, 58, 67–74, 114, **186**, 291
crusades 27, 28, 35, 162, 164, 187–8, 201
Cuckney (Notts.) **195**, 195–6
Cumin, William 191, 194
curtain walls 51, 84, 109, 209, 211, 212, 268

daggers 165
danegeld 244–6
Dartmouth (Devon) 27, 187
David I, King of Scots 2, 21, 28, 30, 38, 43, 45, 50, 143, 201, 203, 241, 284

Deddington (Oxon.) 111
deer 101, 109, 120
deer parks *see* parks
designed landscapes 92, 108, 208, 209, 211, 229, 235, 287
    see also gardens; parks
demesne 17
demography *see* population
dendrochronology 188, 189, 234
Derby 137, **144**, 145, 146
Desborough (Bucks.) 99–100
devils 87, 129
Devizes (Wilts.) **5**, 25, 49, 61, 116n17, **144**, 208, 226, 228, 242, 256, 291
dismounting 45, 47, 155, 176, 286
Domesday Book 14, 15, 17, 105, 168, 225, 236, 238, 250n105, 255
donjons 94, 104–10, 114, 115, 130, 142, 214, 229, 287, 292, 293, 294
Dorchester (Dorset) **144**
Dorchester-upon-Thames (Oxon.) 18
Dover (Kent) 21, 30, 39, 50, 104, **140**, 142, 189
Downton (Wilts.) **5**
Drax (E Yorks.) 30
Dublin, Ireland 56
Dudley (Worcs.) **144**
Dunstanville family 99
Dunster (Som.) 24, **54**, 61, 78n134
Dunwich (Suffolk) **140**
Durham 21, **140**, 141, 142, 143, **144**, **186**, 190, 191, 214
Durham, Bishop of 190
Dursley (Glos.) **5**

earls and earldoms 21, 28, 31, 81, 105, 110, 140, 145, 197, 203, 257, 260, 287
East Chelborough (Dorset) 47, **54**, 56
East Harptree (Som.) 99
Eaton Socon (Cambs.) 194–5, 235, 272
Edward I, King of England 42
Edward II, King of England 2, 3, 180
effigies 131, 133, 158–9, 174

Eleanor of Aquitaine 29, 32
Ely (Cambs.) **5**, 25, **186**, **254**, 254–5
    Isle of 11, 14, 38, 85, 251–75
Emneth, Norfolk **178–9**
Empress, the *see* Matilda
English Bicknor (Glos.) 130
English Civil War 3, 40, 57, 59, 112,
    162, 190, 279, 290
environmental archaeology 102, 240
Eustace, son of King Stephen 20, 23,
    28, 29, 73, 132, 199, 242, 259
Euston, Suffolk **178–9**
Évreux, Normandy, France 53
excommunication 261, 263
execution 48, 73, 92
Exeter (Devon) **5**, **9**, 10, 18, 22, 31,
    41, 48, 49, 50, **54**, **55**, 57, 62, 84,
    116n17, **140**, 142, 168, **170**, 190,
    200, 214, 224, 225, 232, 290,
    Plate 4
Eye (Suffolk) **140**, **144**, 249n46

fairs 228, 230
Falaise, Normandy, France 21, 189
Faringdon (Oxon.) **5**, 27, **54**, 60–1,
    122, 220, 248n4
Farnham (Surrey) 102, **103**, 111, 290
Faversham (Kent) 30, 131–2, **132**,
    198, 199, 204, 220
fieldworks 52
finger-rings *see* rings
Flemish 23, 31, 39, 40, 156–7
food and diet 71, 102, 121, 190
Forde (Devon) 201
Fordham (Cambs.) 262, 263, 277n69
Fordington (Dorset) **Plate 15**
forests 115, 197, 233
Fornham (Suffolk) **158**, 162, 167
frontiers *see* borders
funerary monuments 121, 131
Furness (Cumbria) **198**, 203

Galclint (unlocated) 86
Galwegians 24, 45–6, 162, 175
games and gaming pieces 128, 160,
    176

gardens 92, 102, 200, 211
garrisons 39, 48, 49, 53, 56, 58, 61, 65,
    67, 68, 69, 71, 73, 84, 86, 155, 156,
    168, 172, 181, 191, 192, 207, 208,
    214, 215, 225, 226, 255, 257, 258,
    261, 262, 264, 282
Garthorpe (Lincs.) 92
Gasny, Normandy, France 53
gatehouses 109, 111, 209, 211, 292
Geoffrey II de Mandeville, Earl of
    Essex 251–2
    castle-building 100–1, 104, 110,
    124, 205, 229, 259–60, 261
    commercial initiatives 110, 201,
    229
    death 131, 159, 168, 287
    ecclesiastical patronage 131, 201,
    263, 264
    family 259–60
    historiography 4, 251
    revolts 10, 26–7, 204, 242, 251–2,
    257–75, 292
    see also Burwell; Pleshey;
    Rampton; Saffron Walden;
    South Mimms; Tower of
    London
Geoffrey Talbot 25, 192
Geoffrey, Count of Anjou 6, 20, 23,
    27, 29, 31, 49, 56, 182n41, 189
geophysical survey 58, 59, 61, 70,
    71, 72, 86, 99, 238, 258, 266, 267,
    268, 271, 274
Gesta Stephani 4, **5**, 49, 57, 61, 64,
    65, 67, 68, 70, 72, 81, 84, 85, 86,
    94, 111, 155, 190, 191, 208, 221,
    226, 241, 257, 258, 259, 263, 272
Giddersdale (E Yorks.) 86
Gilbert fitz Richard de Clare, Earl
    of Hertford 136
Gilbert de Clare, Earl of Pembroke
    229
Gilbert Foliot 191, 201
Gilbertines 235
Glastonbury (Som.) 126, 199–200,
    212
Glandford, Norfolk **178–9**

Gloucester 5, 19, 25, 26, 46, 131, **140,**
144, 159, 284
Goltho (Lincs.) **96,** 96–8, 169, **170,**
171, 235, 271, 287
gonfanons 136, 159, 176
Gower (Glam.) **5, 35,** 40
graves *see* cemeteries; funerary
monuments; mass graves
Great Rollright (Oxon.) **Plate 9**
great towers *see* donjons
Great Wymondley (Herts.) **237,** 238
Groby (Leics.) 103, 114
Gumley (Leics.) 92

Hailes Camp (Glos.) 99, **Plate 7**
halls 57, 88, 94, 97, 105, 110, 209, 211,
212, 234
Hamstead Marshall (Berks.) **54, 55,**
60, **Plate 4**
harness pendants 127, 160, 179–80,
182, 280, 282, 286
Harptree (Som.) **5**
Harrowing of Hell 129
Harrying of the North 150, 233,
245
Hastings (Sussex) 13, 40, **140,** 150,
168, 169
Hedingham (Essex) **103,** 105, **106,**
107, 108, 237, 287, 292–3
Hedon (E Yorks.) **140,** 142
helmets 135, 146, 154, 157, 159, 173–4,
175, 176, 264
Hembury (Devon) 100
Hen Domen (Mont.) 173
Henry de Lacy 99, 207
Henry de Tracy 91
Henry I, King of England 2, 6,
20–1, 25, 29, 65, 83, 111, 131, 139,
202, 204, 223, 232, 233, 243
death and burial of 20–1, 131,
139
war/rebellions and 42, 48, 49, 53,
60, 243
itinerary 19, 23
ecclesiastical patronage 130
coinage 139, 149

Henry II, King of England (and as
Henry of Anjou) 2, 3, 6, 20, 30,
49, 91, 115, 143, 196, 223, 243,
245
coinage 143, 144, 146
military campaigns 27, 28–9, 30,
31, 42, 49, 157, 242, 246, 283
revolt against 3, 49, 91, 149
seals 134
sieges 64, 71, 72, 155
slighting of castles 83, 111–2, 114,
257
Henry III, King of England 3, 180
Henry of Blois, Bishop of
Winchester 20, 21, 26, 126–7,
187, 199–200, 213, 279
Abbot of Glastonbury 126,
199–200, 212
arts, and the 126–7
castles 100, 102, 221, 290
coinage 126, 146
palaces 209–13, 280, 289
seal 135
see also Glastonbury Abbey;
Winchester, Wolvesey Palace;
Witney
Henry of Huntingdon 6, 18, 44, 50,
68, 70, 72, 111, 173, 181, 225,
256, 261
Henry V, Holy Roman Emperor
20
Henry, son of David I King of
Scots and Earl of Huntingdon
and Northumberland 45, 46,
50, 201, 203
heraldry 136, 138, 145, 146, 164, 173,
175, 177, 179–80, 182, 282, 286,
289
Hereford 5, 16, 24, 25, **140, 186,**
191–2, 224, 225, 291
Hereward the Wake 252, 255, 256
hillforts 98–100, 115, 145, 238, 293
hoards and hoarding 11, 121, 127,
137, 138, 139, 140, 145, 146–50,
156, 221, 228, 241, 246, 285
Holme Cultram (Cumbria) 200–1

horses 48, 50, 58, 134, 135, 172, 173, 176–80, 182, 200, 205, 257, 262
horseshoes 177
Hospitallers *see* Knights Hospitaller
hospitals 69, 73–4, 149, 190, 221, 223
hostages 61, 62, 73, 207
Huddersfield (W Yorks.) 99, 293
Hugh Bigod, Earl of Norfolk 25, 27, 262
Hugh Mortimer 180–1
Humphrey de Bohun, 97
hunting 101, 108, 109, 124, 128, 133, 169, 170, 260
   lodges 101, 260
Huntingdon 56, **140**, **144**

Ilchester (Som.) **140**, **144**
illicit castles *see* adulterine castles
infantry 29, 45–7, 155, 172, 262, 286
Ingarsby (Leics.) 92–3, **93**
invasions 24, 29, 30, 32, 38, 43, 146
Ipswich (Suffolk) **140**, **144**, 145
Ireland 14, 56, 87, 129, 247
Isle of Purbeck (Dorset) 38
itineraries 8, 19, 22–3

John de Chesney 224
John, King of England 2, 3, 77n89, 83, 91, 114, 115, 157, 194
jousting 46, 161, 180–1, 283

keeps *see* donjons
Kelso (Roxburgh) 197
Kempley (Glos.) 189, 291, **Plate 16**
Kidwelly (Carm.) 208
Kilpeck (Herefords.) 131, 292
kingship 2, 15, 19–20, 30, 38, 134, 136, 138, 139, 242, 284
Kirk Merrington (Durham) **186**, 194
Knapwell (Cambs.) 274, 292
knights and knighthood
   apparel 154, 155, 159–60, 162, 163–8, 173, 175, 176–81
   dubbing/knighting 28, 163

effigies 131, 133, 158–9, 174
image/identity 31, 35, 48, 73, 135, 154, 159, 163, 175, 180, 181–2, 187, 190, 282–3, 289
in battle 29, 42, 45–7, 48, 66, 69, 73, 155, 157, 168, 169, 181, 190, 208, 257, 262, 286, 289
knights' fees 135, 201
knight service 155
religious patronage 198, 199, 203, 285
Knights Hospitaller 197
Knights Templar 188, 197, 199, 228

Lacy family 99, 189
lances 46, 134, 135, 159, 176, 177, 180
landscape
   impact of the Anarchy upon the 240–7
   see also rural settlement; villages
latrines 102
Launceston (Cornwall) 16, **140**, 141, 204, 214
Launde (Leics.) 92
laws of war 34–8, 74, 190, 282
leather 149, 164, 165, 174, 177
Leicester 49, 88, 112, **140**, **144**, 145
Lewes (Sussex) **140**
licensing of castles 83–4
Lidelea (unlocated) **5**, **54**, 61, 69, 86, 208
Lincoln **5**, 15, 18, 25, 27, 43, 45–7, 48, 50, **54**, 86, 98, 110, 129, **140**, **144**, 145, 149, 157, 161–2, 166–7, 181, **186**, 214, 223, 224, 249n46
   Battle of Lincoln 25–6, 34, 43–7, 134, 145, 156, 162, 163, 172, 175, 181, 197, 220, 225, 283, 293
Linton (Kent) 149
Lisbon, Portugal 27, 187
Loddiswell (Devon) 100
London **5**, 14, 18, 19, 26, 65, **140**, 219, 220–1, 223, 232, 259, 260, 289
   archaeological sites and assemblages 128, 139, 149, 165

defences and castles 104–5, 221,
    259
ecclesiastical sites 131, 132–3, 159,
    160, 199, 201, 221
economy, trade and mint 124, 125,
    138, 139, 145, 146, 149, 220–1,
    232
royal government and 15, 21,
    220–1, 289
Stephen and 21, 220–1, 289
Matilda (the Empress) and 26
militia 27, 69–70, 155, 220, 248n4
Louis VI, King of France 23
Louis VII, King of France 27, 29
Lower Slaughter (Glos.) **186**, 191
Ludgershall (Wilts.) 26, 121, 291
Ludlow (Salop.) 46, 50, **54**, 56, 61,
    181
Luton (Beds.) 90, 114, 225, **Plate 5**
Lydford (Devon) 103

maces 172
Magna Carta 83, 157
mail 42, 135, 154, 157, 158, 159, 160,
    171, 172–3, 174, 176, 177, 181,
    191
Maldon (Essex) **140**
Malmesbury (Wilts.) **5**, 42, 47, 49,
    54, 55, 58, 72, 78n125, 116n17,
    140, **144**, 194, 208, 224, 291
mangonels *see* siege engines
manor houses 97, 108, 112, 115, 205,
    234
markets 16, 110, 123–5, 150, 201, 207,
    224, 226, 228–32, 235, 260
Marlborough (Wilts.) **5**, **144**, 145,
    242
Mary, daughter of King Stephen
    132, 220
mass graves 46, 162, 174, 281
Matilda of Boulogne, queen of King
    Stephen
    death 29, 132
    marriage to Stephen 20, 220
    military role 39
    religious patronage 221

Matilda, daughter of Henry I ('the
    Empress')
    Angevin figurehead and leader 1,
        2, 20–8, 31, 38, 64, 65, 115, 157,
        204, 220, 221, 257, 279, 280
    campaigns 25–6, 60, 291, 292, 293
    charters 6, 104, 152n87, 197, 228,
        229, 260
    castles 86, 191, 292
    coinage 137, 142, 145, 148
    death and burial 28
    historiography 6, 7
    itinerary 19, 23
    landing in England 25, 30
    marriages 20
    religious patronage 197, 199
    role model, as a 157
    seal 136
    sieges 25, 26, 60, 65, 68, 221, 293
Matilda, daughter of King Stephen
    132
Maude *see* Matilda
Meaux (N Yorks.) 202
Mendham, Suffolk **178–9**
mercenaries 31, 39, 74, 90, 148, 155,
    156–7, 162, 163, 168, 202, 223,
    225, 283
metalwork 91, 127–8, 177
Middleton (Norfolk) 98
Middleton Stoney (Oxon.) 102, 103,
    107, 115, 234–5, 287, 293
Miles de Beauchamp (of Bedford) 24
militaria *see* arms and armour
militias 45, 155, 220
mills and milling 58, 92, 212, 257,
    285
mints 9, 15, 65, 78n134, 99, 121,
    136–50, 223, 284–5, 288
miracles and miracle stories 207, 244
moats 65, 92, 97, 112, 115, 209, 211,
    258, 272–3, 292
monasteries and priories
    foundation and patronage of
        196–204
    fortification/militarisation of
        204–8, 213–15

see also Augustinians;
  Benedictines; Cluniacs;
  Cistercians; Gilbertines;
  Knights Hospitaller; Knights
  Templar; Savigniacs
Montacute (Som.) 14
Montreuil-en-Bellay,
  Maine-et-Loire, France 49, 56
mottes
  construction and refurbishment
    52, 56, 84, 85, 88–100, 206–7,
    236, 259, 261, 274
  dating of 91–2, 122, 272, 274
  excavation 56, 57, 88–91, 94–104,
    122, 173, 174, 194, 257
  other landscape features
    misidentified as 57, 91–4
  paired 56, 60, 110
  re-use of earlier features 92, 94,
    100, 145, 194, 206
  sieges and siege castles 56, 57, 60,
    76n78, 191, 192
  slighting 111–15, 257
  towers and superstructures 88,
    90, 100–4, 110–11, 235
Mountsorrel (Leics.) 112, **113**, 230–1,
  231, 288, 293
Mowbray family 231

naval warfare 39, 255
New Buckenham (Norfolk) 202,
  229
Newark (Notts.) 209, 226
Newbury (Berks.) **54**, 60, 61
Newcastle (Northumb.) 143, **144**,
  214
Nigel, Bishop of Ely 6, 25, 85, 187,
  207, 256, 257, 258, 259, 260
Norham (Northumb.) 39, 294
Norman Conquest 2, 8, 13–19, 32,
  98, 103, 286, 289
  archaeology of 8, 13–19, 119–20,
    123, 127, 137, 139, 149, 188, 233,
    284
  impact on the landscape 13–19,
    188, 233, 245

Normandy 2, 6, 7, 20, 21, 23, 24,
  27–32, 42, 48, 49, 52, 53, 56, 83,
  129, 134, 156, 189, 203, 220, 225
Northallerton (N Yorks.)
  Battle of the Standard/
    Northallerton 24, 30, 34, 40,
    43–7, 155, 162, 163, 167, 168, 173,
    175, 181, 283, 293
Northampton 15, 19, 26, 139, **140**,
  142, **144**
Northumbria 38–9, 241, 284
Norwich (Norfolk) 15, 16, 18, 130,
  140, **144**, 214, 215, 223, 224, 229,
  249n46, 264, 289
Nottingham 16, 25, **140**, **144**, 148,
  192
nuns and nunneries 108 198, 199,
  208, 285

oaths 20, 112
Old Buckenham (Norfolk) 202
Old Sarum (Wilts.) **5**, 18, 130, **140**,
  144, 145, 208, 209, 289, 291
Ongar (Essex) **237**, 238
Orford (Suffolk) 39
ornamental landscapes *see* designed
  landscapes
Oxford 15, 25, 26, 111, 187, 228
  Angevin base, as a 26, 27, 68
  Beaumont Palace 60
  castle 48, 116n17, 293
  mint **144**, 145
  siege castles at **54**, 60, 225
  sieges 48, 60, 224

paints and painting 132, 159, 160,
  165
palaces 8, 15, 18, 48, 60, 85, 104, 123,
  126, 185, 208–13, 221, 224, 257,
  280, 289, 290, 291
parks 60, 85, 98, 108, 176, 208, 209,
  228, 229, 235, 257, 285, 287
peace, peace treaties and peacemaking 24, 29–30, 34, 42, 73, 83,
  87, 111–2, 114, 115, 137, 141, 149,
  186, 202, 208, 230, 283, 291, 293

peasants 17, 48, 81, 124, 155, 189, 236
Pembroke (Dyfed) **140**, 141
pendants *see* harness pendants
Peterborough (Northants.) 251, 252
Pevensey (Sussex) **5**, 27, 56, 140, **144**
Pickering (N Yorks.) 47, **54**, 56, 77n89, 293
pipe rolls 6, 49, 104, 156, 168, 244–6
Plympton (Devon) **5**, 31, **41**, **54**, 91
pommels *see* swords
Pont Audemer, Normandy, France 48, 49
Pontefract (W Yorks.) 124, 163, 207
population 14–15, 16, 247, 283
Portable Antiquities Scheme vii, 121, 160, 183n99, 184n139
Portchester (Hants.) 19
Portland, Isle of (Dorset) 85
pottery 11, 13, 15, 57, 58, 90, 92, 94, 119, 121–5, 150, 227, 234, 280–1, 284
Prestwich (Lancs.) 148
priories *see* monasteries and priories
prisoners 26, 47, 48, 67, 224
prospect mounds 92
Purton (Wilts.) 5
pyxes 45, 160, 175

Quenington (Glos.) 129
Quidenham, Norfolk **178–9**

rabbits 111
Radcot (Oxon.) **5**, 86, **103**
raids 8, 21, 35, 39, 40, 47, 53, 68, 69, 203, 204, 205, 261, 263
Rampton (Cambs.) 235, **270**, 272, 292
Ramsey (Hunts.) **5**, **186**, 205–6, **206**, 213, 261–4, 267, 269, 273, 274, 292
Ranulf, Earl of Chester 25, 27, 64, 68–9, 86, 95, 110, 112, 135, 157, 181, 200

ravaging *see* waste and wasting
Ravenstone (Leics.) 112
Reading (Berks.) 21, 65, 68, 69, 79n174, 130, 131, **186**, 206–7, **206**, 218n123
Reginald, illegitimate son of Henry I 25, 204
Reginald de Dunstanville 204
renaissance, twelfth-century 125–6
Repton (Derbys.) 94–5, 114–15, 174, 194, 202
Revesby (Lincs.) 200
Richard de Camville 102, 115, 234
Richard de Lucy 69, 135
Richard de Redvers 84
Richard fitzNigel, treasurer of Henry II and later Bishop of London 6
Richard I, King of England 168, 174, 177
Richard of Okehampton 201
Richmond (N Yorks.) 16, **140**
rings 127, 128
ringworks 9, 52, 56, 57–60, 71, 72, 91, 94, 98, 100, 105, 108, 114, 115, 131, 194, 235, 258, 264, 274, 290, 291
Ripon (N Yorks.) 155
rivers 39, 42–3, 73, 85, 163, 252, 259
Robert Bouet 225
Robert Curthose, Duke of Normandy 21, 131, 159
Robert de Beaumont, Earl of Leicester 31, 88
Robert de Ferrers, Earl of Derby 137, 146
Robert de Mowbray, Earl of Northumbria 53, 214
Robert de Stuteville 146
Robert de Waudari 90, 225
Robert Earl of Leicester 31, 88, 112, 177, 230, 236
Robert Marmion 194
Robert of Bampton 21, **41**
Robert of Torigni 6, 73, 79n174, 87, 94, 116n37, 218n123

Robert, Bishop of Lewes 228
Robert, Earl of Gloucester 20, 24,
    25–6, 157
  castles 27, 85
  coinage 145, 286
  death 28, 131
  military activities 25–6, 42, 43, 85,
    224
Rochester (Kent) 52, 83, 104, 134
Roger d'Oilly 102, 236
Roger de Mowbray 203, 204–5
Roger of Howden 146
Roger of Wendover 104
Roger, Bishop of Salisbury 21, 25,
    130, 139, 187, 194, 208–9, 213,
    228, 256, 291
Roman sites, reuse of 25, 52, 56, 57,
    84, 86, 92, 94–5, 122, 131, 209,
    221, 227, 266, 267, 272
Romanesque 18, 88, 90, 105, 121,
    125–33, 177, 179, 209, 289, 291,
    292, 293
Romsey (Hants.) 214
Rouen, Normandy, France 18, 27,
    28, 53
Royal Armouries 158, 182n45
rural settlement 16, 177, 219, 232–6
  see also villages; village
    fortifications
Rye (Sussex) 139, **140**

Saffron Walden (Essex) **5**, **103**, 110,
    201, 205, 226, 229, **230**, 249n57,
    259–60
St Albans (Herts.) **5**, 26, 259, 260
St-Omer, Pas-de-Calais, France
    158
Sainte Suzanne, Normandy, France
    52
Salisbury (Wilts.) *see* Old Sarum
Sandwich (Kent) **140**
Savigniacs 189, 196, 197, 199, 202–4
Savigny, Normandy, France 189, 197,
    203
Sawley (Lancs.) **198**, 201
Sawtry (Cambs.) 203, 274

scabbards 127, 163, 165–6, 181, 280,
    282
Scotland 2, 8, 32, 39, 87, 130, 188,
    197, 247
Scraptoft (Leics.) 92
sculpture 11, 13–14, 90, 119, 121,
    126–33, 150, 160, 161, 189, 212,
    214, 284, 289, 291, 292, 293
seals 11, 121, 126, 127, 133–6, 146,
    159, 174, 175, 176, 177, 286
Selby (W Yorks.) **186**, 205, 207,
    244
Selsey (Sussex) 18
sergeants 168
Shackerstone (Leics.) 92
Shaftesbury (Dorset) **140**
Sherborne (Dorset) **5**, **144**, 146, 208,
    289, 291
sheriffs 15, 31, 110, 115, 201, 215, 224,
    261
shields 135, 136, 157, 159, 160, 165,
    173, 174–5, 176, 178, 179, 181,
    182
shoes 128
Shrewsbury (Salop) **140**
sieges and siege warfare 6, 8–11,
    25, 34, 37, 47–74, 155, 157, 180,
    182, 190, 200, 204, 208, 219–23,
    224–7, 232, 241, 247, 275, 280,
    282, 283, 286
siege castles 9–10, 47, 51–62, 64–74,
    81, 85, 87, 114, 122, 155, 169,
    190, 264, 282, 290–1, 293
siege engines 48–51, 56, 61, 74, 172,
    192, 225, 291
sigillography *see* seals
Silchester (Hants.) 86, 94–5, **95**,
    131
Simon de Montfort, Fifth Earl of
    Leicester 172
Simon de Montfort, Sixth Earl of
    Leicester 42
slings and slingers 168
South Cerney *see* Cerney, South
South Mimms (Middx.) 100–1, **120**
Southampton (Hampshire) **5**, 144

Southwark (Surrey) **140**

Southwell (Notts.) **186**, 192–3, **193**, 293

spears and spearmen 155, 157, 159, 166, 171–2, 259

spurs 160, 163, 177, 179, 181, 282

Stafford **140**

Stamford (Lincs.) **5**, 56, 72, **140**, 142, **144**

Stamford ware/Stamford-type ware 120, 123, 124

Standard, Battle of the *see* Northallerton

Stephen, King of England
  accession 6, 21
  castle-building by 82, 191, 208, 263–73, 287, 292
  Church, and the 187, 199, 202–4, 256
  coinage 138–43
  death and burial 30, 131–3, 199, 220, 292
  family and early career 20
  historiography 2–3, 4, 7
  itinerary 19, 22
  Jews 223–4, 289
  military campaigns 20–30, 39, 40, 42, 46–7, 65–74, 83, 156, 157, 163, 181, 172, 194, 242, 256–75
  Normandy 23–4
  peace settlement with Henry of Anjou 29–30, 111–12
  religious patronage 30, 131–2, 188, 199, 203–4, 220, 292
  sieges 24, 30, 48, 49–74, 84, 85, 86, 97, 162, 168, 190, 191
  seals 134
  Wales and Scotland 21, 24, 39, 53

Steyning (Sussex) **140**

stirrups 160, 177, 184n131

Stoke Holy Cross, Norfolk **178–9**

strap-ends 128

Sudbury (Suffolk) **140**, **144**

Swannington, Norfolk **178–9**

Swansea (Glam.) 148

Swavesey (Cambs.) 235, **270**, 272, 273

swords 11, 27, 46, 133, 134, 135, 146, 154, 157–60, 163–8, 173, 177, 181, 191, 282

Tamworth (Staffs.) **140**

Taunton (Som.) **140**, **144**

tax and taxation 4, 15, 81, 156, 205, 235–6, 282

Templars *see* Knights Templar

tenserie 156

Tetbury (Glos.) **5**

thegns 145, 214, 235, 267, 271, 287

Therfield (Herts.) 114, **237**, 238, 292

Thetford (Norfolk) **140**, **144**, 194, 195, 199, 211, 213, 255

Thirsk (N Yorks.) 231–2

Thurstan de Beauchamp, Earl of Warwickshire 229

timber-framed buildings 234

Tinchebrai, Normandy, France 77n86, 169

Tiron, Eure-et-Loir, France 197

tombs 131–3, 158

tournaments 47, 76n66, 176, 180–1, 283, 286

town defences 25, 46, 190, 199, 221, 225–7, 290, 273

towns and urbanism 15–16, 18, 104, 209, 220–3, 228–32, 247, 255, 284, 288

Towton (N Yorks.) 161

trade 39, 122, 206, 221, 223

treaties and agreements 29–30, 83, 111–2, 114, 115, 137, 230, 293

trebuchets *see* siege engines

Trowbridge (Wilts.) **5**
  Anarchy-period castle 95–7, **96**, 98, 115, 116n17, 122, 136, 176, 271, 291
  church, cemetery and castle 195
  finds from castle **170**, 171, 176
  mint 145, **144**, 146
  settlement 97, 226
  siege 56
  slighting of castle and later occupation 115

truces 24, 29, 36, 38, 69, 73, 74
Tutbury (Staffs.) **5**, 56, 72, 137, **144**, 146
Tynemouth (Northumb.) 53, 214

unlicensed castles *see* adulterine castles
urbanism *see* towns and urbanism

Vadum Iacob, Israel 162, 171, 173
Vatteville, Normandy, France 53
Vegetius 49
Vikings 94–5, 164, 172, 194, 213
village fortifications 219, 236–40
villages 11, 14, 16–17, 48, 92, 93, 97–8, 108, 188, 219, 226, 230, 232–40, 242, 247, 256, 258, 262, 265, 266, 274, 287, 294
see also rural settlement
villas, Roman 56, 122
vineyards 214

Walden *see* Saffron Walden
Waleran de Meulan, Earl of Worcester 28, 31, 136, 197, 224
Wales/Welsh 2, 7, 14, 16, 26, 30, 32, 38–9, 40, 46, 53, 123, 130, 142, 148, 163, 175, 241
wall paintings 160
Wallingford (Oxon.) **5**, 11, 34, 38, **54**, 62–74, **63**, **66**, 70, 71, 284, **Plate 4**
bridge, fortification of **70**, **71**, 82
burh **63**, 63–4, 65, 227
castle 25, 62–74, **63**, 85, 116n17, 291
charter 232
charters issued at 69, 62
churches, fortification of 191
ecclesiastical sites 15, 67–8, 73–4
finds from the River Thames 166, 167–8
hospitals 73–4
mint 78n134, 143, **144**

peace negotiations at 29, 42, 73
siege castles at 58, 61, 67–74, 155, 168–9, 225, 291
sieges 27, 29, 47, 48, 62–74, **66**, 224, 248n4
tournaments 180
Wareham (Dorset) **5**, 26, 29, 39, 104, 114, **140**, 142, 145, 169, **170**
wargames 46–7, 180–1
warhorses *see* horses
Wark (Northumb.) 39, 49
Warwick **5**, **140**
waste and wasting 6, 24, 37, 40, 204, 223, 240–7, 258, 261, 281
Watchet (Som.) **140**, 142
water defences 50, 65, 92, 97, 112, 115, 209, 211, 258, 272–3, 292
Waterford, Ireland 56
Watford (Herts.) 140–1, 148, 149
weapons *see* arms and armour; archers and archery; axes; bows; crossbows and crossbowmen; daggers; lances; maces; slings and slingers; spears and spearmen; swords
Weardale 142
Wellow (Notts.) 238–40, **239**
Wells (Som.) 228
Westminster (London) **5**, 21, 39, 90, 199
Wexford, Ireland 56
Wherwell (Hants.) **5**, 26, **186**, 208
Wight, Isle of **5**, 84
William Adelin, son of Henry I 20
William Boterel 69
William Clito, son of Robert Curthose, Duke of Normandy 21, 158, 174
William d'Aubigny 25, 142, 200, 261
William de Chesney 111, 201
William de Say 262
William fitz Alan, 225
William fitz Herbert 204
William fitz Robert, Earl of Gloucester 145

William Giffard 102, 209

William I, King of England 18, 20,
    38, 50, 85, 131, 223, 252, 255, 256,
    257, 258, 259

William II, King of England 523,
    130, 134, 139, 214

William Marshal 61, 157

William Martel (King Stephen's
    steward) 26

William of Aumale, Earl of York
    146, 181, 207, 231

William of Dover 227

William of Malmesbury 4, 46, 67, 85,
    137, 143, 172, 200

William of Newburgh 6, 99, 111,
    137, 156, 187, 194, 244

William of Poitiers 65, 168

William of Roumare, Earl of
    Lincoln 25, 200

William of Ypres 39, 156, 202

William Paynel 192

William Peverel 233

William, son of King Stephen and
    Count of Boulogne 29

Wilton (Wilts.) 5, 26, 35, 40, 48, 140,
    186, 208, 227
    Battle of Wilton 26, 40

Winchcombe (Glos.) 5, 48, 116n17,
    186, 190

Winchester (Hants.) 5, 140, 222
    archaeological sites and
        assemblages 168, 170, 171, 172,
        280
    Bible 126, 159, 174
    Bishop of *see* Henry of Blois

defences and castle 48, 221–3, 222,
    224
ecclesiastical sites 18, 126, 222,
    249n46
legate held at 26, 187
mint/moneyers 139
royal government and 15, 21,
    220–3, 289
siege/rout of 26, 35, 40, 43, 46, 155,
    163, 181, 204, 209, 220, 221–3,
    222, 224, 241, 283
Treaty of 29, 111, 114, 115
Wolvesey Palace 123, 126, 209–11,
    210, 212, 213, 221, 280, 289, 291,
    Plate 17

Withersdale, Suffolk 178–9

Witney (Oxon.) 86, 210, 211–2, 212

Wiveliscombe (Som.) 144, 146

Wolvesey Palace *see* Winchester,
    Wolvesey Palace

women 2, 136, 157, 172

Wood Walton (Hunts.) 98, 262,
    273–4, Plate 19

Woodchester (Glos.) 86

Woodgarston (Hants.) 86

Woodstock (Oxon.) 5

Worcester 5, 19, 28, 38, 47, 54, 140,
    181, 215, 224

wounds 53, 67, 161–2, 214, 257, 264

Yarmouth (Norfolk) 140

York 5, 15, 24, 26, 28, 42, 69, 140,
    144, 146, 150, 155, 181, 205, 207

zooarchaeology 109, 176